Mastering
Sociology

Palgrave Master Series

Accounting
Accounting Skills
Advanced English Language
Advanced English Literature
Advanced Pure Mathematics
Arabic
Basic Management
Biology
British Politics
Business Communication
Business Environment
C Programming
C++ Programming
Chemistry
COBOL Programming
Communication
Computing
Counselling Skills
Customer Relations
Database Design
Delphi Programming
Desktop Publishing
Economic and Social History
Economics
Electrical Engineering
Electronic and Electrical
    Calculations
Electronics
English Grammar
English Language
English Literature
Fashion Buying and
    Merchandising Management
Fashion Styling
French

Geography
German
Global Information Systems
Human Resource Management
Information Technology
Internet
Italian
Java
Management Skills
Mathematics
Microsoft Office
Microsoft Windows, Novell
    NetWare and UNIX
Modern British History
Modern European History
Modern United States History
Modern World History
Networks
Organisational Behaviour
Pascal and Delphi
    Programming
Philosophy
Physics
Practical Criticism
Psychology
Shakespeare
Social Welfare
Sociology
Spanish
Strategic Management
Statistics
Systems Analysis and Design
Theology
Visual Basic
World Religions

www.palgravemasterseries.com

Palgrave Master Series
Series Standing Order ISBN 0–333–69343–4
(outside North America only)

You can receive future titles in this series as they are published by
placing a standing order. Please contact your bookseller or, in case of
difficulty, write to us at the address below with your name and address,
the title of the series and the ISBN quoted above.

Customer Services Department, Macmillan Distribution Ltd
Houndmills, Basingstoke, Hampshire RG21 6XS, England

Mastering
Sociology

Fourth Edition

Gerard O'Donnell

palgrave

First edition 1985
Second edition 1988
Third edition 1994
Fourth edition 2002

Published by
PALGRAVE
Houndmills, Basingstoke, Hampshire RG21 6XS and
175 Fifth Avenue, New York, N.Y. 10010
Companies and representatives throughout the world

PALGRAVE is the new global academic imprint of
St. Martin's Press LLC Scholarly and Reference Division and
Palgrave Publishers Ltd (formerly Macmillan Press Ltd).

ISBN 0-333-91956-4

This book is printed on paper suitable for recycling and made from fully managed and sustained forest sources.

A catalogue record for this book is available from the British Library.

10   9   8   7   6   5   4   3   2   1
11   10   09   08   07   06   05   04   03   02

Printed and bound in Great Britain by
Creative Print & Design (Wales), Ebbw Vale

To Sara, and to Fay – our first grandchild

■ ⌄ Contents

Part nine   The political system

▶ The exam and preparing for it

1   Although the questions and answers in this book have been prepared with the more able candidate in mind they will provide a useful preparation for a wide range of sociology and social science candidates.

2   In answering the sample examination questions set in the earlier sections of the book it must be borne in mind that while it is necessary to subdivide the book into syllabus headings in order to present the subject coherently, the areas of sociological study are interdependent. A particular question may require information drawn from a number of sections (e.g. family, class and education). When you have finished the book, try working through some of your earlier efforts, drawing this time on all the knowledge that you have acquired during the course.

3   All examinations seek to give you credit for what you do know and can do, the examiner is not trying to 'catch you out'. Different levels of achievement have to be rewarded; for example this 'differentiation' is achieved in written examination papers by:

   (a)   The use of a series of questions of increasing difficulty, those at the end showing most need for evaluation by the candidate. (These may be described as 'on an incline of difficulty' or 'stepped questions' or 'structured questions'.)

   (b)   Longer questions in which the depth of the candidate's response can be measured.

   (c)   Differentiation may also be achieved in Course Work Assessment or Projects in which skills in planning, research and weighing up the evidence can be tested. A great deal of freedom is usually permitted in this Course Work in order to ensure that candidates follow programmes which are of particular interest to them.

4   If the question is broken into sections, look for the number of marks awarded to each part. It is a waste of time to devote several lines to an answer that can gain only 1 mark; the examiner will expect only a few words. A common (and disastrous) error is to write almost all you know about a particular topic in answer to a section attracting few marks and then fail to repeat relevant information in the major section which is intended to attract that information.

5   In longer answers write in essay form – do not write notes as your answer, although you may wish to make a few notes on your paper before commencing your real answer. (Put a neat line through these and the examiner will ignore them.) Remember the examiner will have hundreds of

papers to mark in two or three weeks – he or she will not spend a lot of time trying to work out what you mean or in deciphering your handwriting; the repetition of points to try and make a scrappy answer look longer will not impress and flowery description is a waste of time.

6 A mere recital of the names of sociologists gains no marks at any level.

7 Do not try to learn a mass of statistics off by heart – the examiner is interested in your understanding of sociology rather than your ability to remember lists of facts. You should be able to make balanced judgements about the structure and institutions of society, but mere unsubstantiated opinion is worthless. You should know something of the various methods of research used by sociologists and be able to interpret and analyse evidence presented in a variety of ways – that is one reason why graphs, tables and extracts are included in the book.

8 Sheer length gains no marks. Time will limit your length in any case – aim to produce well-constructed answers with all the relevant points.

9 Work out how much time you can afford to spend on each question; when the time is up, move on to the next question – you can return to complete unfinished answers if you have time. Three good answers will almost certainly gain fewer marks than five average ones.

10 Spend some time reading through the paper carefully and choose those questions you known most about (not those that sound easy). Some people find it best to write up their second-best answer first, so that they become more confident as they progress.

11 Do not answer more questions than you need – some examination authorities exclude all surplus answers written after the required answers, others mark them all and take the best answers up to the required number, but you are always wasting valuable time.

12 Answer the question asked, not the one you hoped would be asked. If you have read 'model' or 'specimen' answers, do not be tempted to regurgitate them verbatim; extract from them the material relevant to the question asked.

13 The 1950s, 1960s and 1970s in Britain saw the first major invasion of Britain by Sociology. In these years many standard, popular sociology texts were introduced which gave (and still give) valuable insights into sociological concepts. N. Denis, F. Henriques and C. Slaughter (1956), *Coal is Our Life*; M. Young and P. Willmott (1957), *Family and Kinship in East London*; J. Tunstall (1962), *The Fishermen* remain useful books, particularly for comparative purposes, but students do need to be aware of how dated some of these studies now are and compare them critically with the realities of the twenty-first century.

■ Y Acknowledgements

The author and publishers would like to thank the following photographic sources: Steve Eason/Photofusion, pp. 5, 353; Gordon Roberts, pp. 33, 34, 188; Tina Gue/Photofusion, p. 97; Ute Klaphake/Photofusion, p. 148; Peter Marshall/Photofusion, pp. 76, 362.

The author and publishers would like to thank the following for permission to reproduce copyright material:

Atlantic Syndication Partners for a cartoon by Mac, 'To save you wasting any more time working out if you've passed . . .', *Daily Mail*, 18.8.00

David Austin for his cartoon, 'Would you like me to read them out to you?' *Guardian*, 18.8.00

Blackwell Publishers for abridged extracts from A. Cambell, *Girl Delinquents*, 1981; also for extracts from *Gender Contradictions in Families*, Bahira Sherif, *Anthropology Today*, 4.8.99

Cambridge University Press for data from Robin Gill, *Churchgoing and Christian Ethics*, 1999, Table 1, p. 70

The *Daily Telegraph* for material from Philip Johnston, 'The traditional family faces a minority role' 9.1.00; Anne Atkins, on parental responsibility 17.7.00; Philip Johnston, 'One in five children is living in poverty' 14.6.00; news items on class 16.7.99; Philip Johnston, 'Number's up for the prophets of doom' and associated population map 12.10.99; Matt Ridley,' For the good of the country, let's have more immigrants' 24.7.00; Christie Davies, 'Soft on crime, soft on the causes of crime' 28.4.00; obituary on Ezequiel Gamonal 24.7.00

The Guardian and Observer News Service for material from Dr John Collee, 'Stupid Cupid', *The Observer Life*, 10.10.93; editorial, 'The arithmetic of bias', *Guardian*, 5.6.00; David Brindle, 'The UK is healthier than US', *Guardian*, 5.6.00; and graphic, 'Access to top five universities', *Guardian*, 5.6.00

Her Majesty's Stationery Office for data from 'Mortality Statistics', The Black Report', National Statistics. Crown copyright ©

Andrew Mann Ltd on behalf of Alex for a cartoon first published in the *Daily Telegraph*

Oxford University Press for material from A.H. Halsey, *Change in British Society*, 1981. Copyright © A.H. Halsey 1978, 1981

Palgrave Publishers Ltd for material from David Butler and Dennis Kavanagh, *The British General Election of 1992*, 1993, and *The British General Election of 1997*, 1999

Penguin Books Ltd for Material from Paul Marrison, *Inside the Inner City: Life Under the Cutting Edge*, Penguin 1983. Copyright © Paul Marrison 1983; and Jean Blondel, *Voters, Parties and Leaders: The Social Fabric of British Politics*, Penguin 1963. Copyright © Jean Blondel 1963

Royal Society of Arts for material from Dr Kimberley Reynolds on images of gender, *Journal* 2.4.99; Reva Klein, 'Lost at School', *Education Futures 2000*; Cary Cooper, 'The psychological implications of the changing patterns of work', *Journal* 1.4.98; from a lecture on the future of work, *Journal* 2.4.00; Leon Kreitzman, 'The 24 hour society', *Journal* 2.4.99; Meta Zimmeck, 'Re-defining Work', *Journal* 3.4.98; Dr Kamal Aboulmagd, 'Islam and the West, *Journal* 4.4.98; Paddy Ashdown, 'Proportional representation and its consequences for British politics, *Journal* 2.4.99

Office for National Statistics: *Social Trends 29*, 1999: 'Percentage of women cohabiting: by age'; 'Births outside marriage'; 'Percentage of dependent children living in different family types'; 'Students in further and higher education'; 'Highest qualification held: by gender and ethnic group'; 'Population of working age: by gender and social class'; 'Infant mortality: by social class'; 'distribution of wealth'; 'Composition of the net wealth of the household sector'; 'Real gross weekly earnings'; 'Average gross weekly earnings'; 'Labour disputes, working days lost'; 'People in employment with a second job'; 'Unemployment, by gender'; 'Net international migration'; 'Offenders found guilty of, or cautioned for, indictable offences'; 'Offenders as a percentage of the population'; 'Sentenced male adult prisoners'; *Social Trends 27*, 1997: 'Holiday taking: by social grade'; 'Changes in employment'. *Social Trends 18*, 1988: 'Distribution of wealth'. All Crown copyright©

Trentham Books Ltd for material from R. Kelsall, *Population in Britain in the 1900s and Beyond*, Trentham Books, 1989

Every effort has been made to trace all the copyright-holders, but if any have been inadvertently overlooked the publishers will be pleased to make the necessary arrangement at the first opportunity.

Part One

What is sociology?

▮ ▾ ▮ Sociology terms and concepts

1.1 Culture and social order

The word 'sociology' was used first by a Frenchman, Auguste Comte, in 1838 to describe what he called 'the science of the associated life of humanity'. Many people before Comte had studied aspects of society in a systematic way but Comte sought to establish Sociology as a distinct discipline; in fact he regarded it as the most important science, at the top of a hierarchy of science of increasing complexity. On the other hand some people do not regard Sociology as a science at all, but as a way of wrapping up the obvious in complex terms. In Chapter 2 we shall have a look at Sociology as a 'science'; in this chapter the intention is to establish what it is that sociologists study – the 'associated life of humanity' referred to by Comte.

Most animals live in groups in order to protect themselves, raise their offspring and to improve their efficiency in providing themselves with food and shelter; because they have to co-operate, certain rules and expectations develop.

If a group of chickens fought constantly over their food they would often injure each other but this is avoided by the establishment of a pecking order or 'hierarchy' in which the right of the more aggressive chickens to eat first is established.

People live much more complex lives than chickens and it is more important for them to co-operate with others; certainly few people would wish to live in a society dominated by the most aggressive individuals. When co-operation takes place it is necessary for the people concerned to agree on certain ideas and share a similar pattern of behaviour. In Britain it is accepted that the first person to start a bus queue has a right to get on the bus first and people arriving later will usually be deterred from pushing in by the expectation that others in the queue will disapprove.

When a group of people establish a way of life in which there are generally accepted modes of conduct and beliefs their behaviour and morality is described as their **culture**.

A culture will include speech, dress, food and general behaviour; but, perhaps more importantly, it will include thought processes.

A country will generally share a cultural pattern and so we may refer to the British culture or French culture but there will usually be differences between the behaviour and beliefs of groups within any single country based on such facts as class, age or ethnic background. In Britain it has been usual to distinguish between 'working class' and 'middle class' cultures, although such a distinction is now becoming progressively blurred.

An American sociologist Oscar Lewis has suggested that a distinctive 'subculture' is found in the slums of large cities. This 'culture of poverty' has its own distinctive beliefs and behaviour including a mistrust of authority, hatred of the police, feelings of inferiority linked to an idea that it is impossible to influence events, and a belief in male superiority.

The term 'community' is sometimes used to describe all the people that share a similar culture, but it usually refers to a closer sense of identification between individuals in terms of co-operation and a sense of belonging. For most practical purposes it is better to think in terms of a community as sharing a territory well known to all its members whether this is a monastery or a set of city streets and to distinguish this social grouping from a 'culture'.

A community implies shared needs in terms of such factors as schools, safe roads, housing and protection; there is therefore a need for co-operation. A common culture is one way in which such co-operation is ensured, although different cultures within a society may bring variety and colour to our lives, provided that there are certain shared values to prevent disorder.

1.2 Socialisation

There are a number of ways in which social order can be maintained, including the use of force. However the most effective way of ensuring that the people within a society work together without disorder is for them to be brought up to expect to behave in a particular and broadly similar way.

From the moment that we are born we start to learn, first in the family then the neighbourhood and school. In this way we are 'socialised', brought up to accept certain forms of behaviour as appropriate for us and to expect other people to behave in a particular way.

We learn our **'gender' behaviour** – the way that little boys and little girls are expected to behave; our **'class' identity** – the way that we should behave if we are to be accepted into a certain social status group; our **'property values'** – which will ensure that our attitude to ownership will be appropriate to the society in which we live. If . . . during adolescence, the children who have been wearing trousers are urged to eat like growing boys, while the children in skirts are warned to watch their weight and not get fat; if the half in jeans runs around in sneakers or boots, while the half in skirts totters about on spike heels, then these two groups of people will be biologically as well as socially different,' (Hubbard, 'The Political Nature of "Human Nature" ', 1990).

What we learn during the first few years of life will usually prove critical in determining our future. Jesuits summed up this situation centuries ago – 'give me the boy at seven and I will have the man'. Most research, however, indicates that the most critical years for socialisation begin not at seven but at birth; one researcher, John Bowlby, has suggested that the most critical years for the formation of emotional stability were from birth to age three, although this is disputed.

Most animals live in groups

An interesting example of a deliberate attempt to influence the socialisation process was the replacement of houses and trees by guns and soldiers in books for little Japanese children before the Second World War.

1.3 Conformity and deviance

Most people within a society will behave as they are expected to behave – '**conform**'. If most people do not conform to the expected patterns of conduct, then either the society will break up in chaos, or a new pattern of conduct will emerge which will become the new 'conformity'. Most societies will also have some people who do not conform to the expected, they differ – '**deviate**' – from the normal. These '**deviants**' may be individuals who reject some or all of the beliefs of the society, and who may also behave in a way which is unacceptable to the majority within the society. The deviants may also, however, be part of a group, all of whose members accept different beliefs or practise different behaviour from that common in general society – in this case they are members of a 'deviant subculture'. The individual deviant may be a holy hermit or a child-molester; the member of the deviant 'subculture' may be part of a permanent community in a large city that makes its living from crime, or a transient member of a gang of Hell's Angels.

Deviance depends not upon a given action but upon the acceptability of a certain action in a certain circumstance. For example the injection of a drug by a nurse in a hospital may be socially approved, the injection of the same drug by a young person 'for kicks' may be condemned and punished.

As a society changes, its view of what is deviant will also change. It is now socially acceptable for young women unaccompanied by men to drink in public houses. In Britain some fifty years ago such behaviour would have labelled the girl concerned as a prostitute – a deviant from the accepted morality of British culture. But prostitution as an occupation has not been regarded as deviant in all cultures, for example there were sacred prostitutes in the temples of ancient Babylon.

What is deviance?

Girl delinquents

> An action that might be quite acceptable to one group of people may be severely sanctioned by another. A girl who shoplifts may be seen as deviant by her middle-class teacher but not by her peer group. How are we to decide whether her continued shoplifting implies the stronger influence of her peer group's values upon her or her failure to realize the negative view taken of it by her teacher?

Another problem relates to what is seen as constituting an adverse reaction from, or a sanction by, others in the group. Such a reaction does not generally take the form of expulsion from the group, for social psychological research has shown that deviant members are often a valuable part of group dynamics. Marsh's (1978) work on soccer fans shows that the 'nutter' of the group fulfils an important function in underlining normal conduct: his behaviour is not only tolerated but even encouraged by other members. The breaking of a social rule may provoke a number of immediate reactions. It has been suggested that anger, embarrassment and humour are three typical reactions to rule violation. However, they are also reactions to behaviour other than rule breakage. Humour may be a reaction to joke telling and anger to failing a driving test – neither of these is a breach of any rule. Another problem exists with respect to discovering what the social rules are . . . It is virtually impossible for someone to sit down and enumerate the rules of behaviour for, say, a dinner party. It is only when a breach occurs that we feel something has gone wrong – for example, when there is a long and embarrassing silence in the conversation, or when someone gets so drunk that he loses control over his behaviour . . . It seems that the search for an absolute and universal definition of delinquency has to be abandoned. Laws change; and the same action may have a multitude of descriptions applied to it.

(A. Campbell, *Girl Delinquents*, Oxford: Blackwell, 1981, abridged)

1.4 Roles and status

By definition, however, most people are not deviant, they behave in the way that people expect them to behave. Consciously or unconsciously they act as a part, they adopt a 'role'. In fact as people grow older they act many parts and so have to adapt to a variety of roles; they retain the basic role they have learnt in terms of personality but add to these new 'bit parts' as gang members or mothers or students. These '**multiple roles**' may conflict and cause tension and uncertainty; a man may be promoted at work and have to adopt the role of manager over his former workmates, although he still wants to be able to act his role as their mate. A woman may wish to start a job when her child is small but have difficulty in reconciling her role as a mother with her role as a worker. Society will expect her to be a good timekeeper as an employee but expect her to stay with her small child if it is sick.

Once learnt it is often difficult to unlearn our role and when people have to act a role which would not normally be expected of them it is called 'role reversal'; in some British communities today there may be jobs for women, but no jobs for men and the men who have grown up expecting to be the breadwinners find themselves unwilling house-husbands. They may seek other outlets to prove their masculinity; it has been suggested that this may be one of the many underlying factors contributing to violence in Northern Ireland.

All the roles we adopt in relating to other people are called our 'role set' and the people that we relate to in each situation are called our 'role others'.

Many of the roles we adopt are 'ascribed', that is they are determined in advance or without regard to our wishes – we have the status of a child or we become an Earl when our noble father dies. Other roles are 'achieved', that is we earn them in some way; we rob banks and earn the role of criminal or stand for Parliament and achieve the role of MP.

The roles we act will be important factors in determining our '**status**' in our society. Our status is our position in a hierarchy; it is the degree to which we command the respect of others in the community. We may have higher status than others within a society by virtue of the supposed worth attached to the job we do; or we may have higher status if we have won a Victoria Cross, thus demonstrating our bravery; or we may simply have higher status among our immediate friends because of some special skill we possess or trait of character that they admire.

Our status may relate to the degree that we behave in a manner approved of by our society. Or it may relate to a social position over which we have little control. Social class in Britain is still an example of this; if we are a member of the 'working class' (with a manual job) we will have less status than if we are 'middle class' (with a 'white collar' job). We may be able to achieve middle class status through education but if we are born into a middle class family our position will be protected by our family's ability to acquire greater opportunities for us in terms of education and contacts.

1.5 Norms and values

Although people will occupy different status positions within a society and act out differing roles there will be a certain behavioural pattern that will be regarded as 'normal' in any particular situation. This standard behaviour that we expect people to use is called a '**norm**' for short by sociologists, and it is the acceptance by most people of the norms of a society that allows the society to function reasonably smoothly.

If you went to see your doctor in their surgery and she or he was wearing nothing but underwear your confidence in her or him might be a bit shaken but the structure of your society would not be in danger of damage. However, if people came to expect to help themselves to anything they liked provided the owner was weaker than they were, then our society could not continue in the form we know.

Most people in our society would not consider engaging in such actions as indiscriminate stealing or killing because both would be against the 'moral values' of our culture. When a 'norm' reinforces one of the society's 'moral values' sociologists refer to it as a '**more**' and the moral value itself simply as a '**value**'. One such more in our society is the responsibility of parents to care for their children and treat them in a humane way.

Beating a child with a cane or stick now breaks a more of modern British society although violence against one's own children, short of permanent damage, would have been acceptable a hundred and fifty years ago. On the other hand, many British motorists drive at more than seventy miles an hour on motorways when they think it safe to do so, or a father buys his seventeen-year-old son half a pint in a pub. They are breaking the law but not one of our society's mores. Law and more are therefore not the same thing.

Some 'values' such as a respect for life are general to most cultures but there will be wide variations in many other respects such as property rights. Even the interpretation of respect for life will vary widely; in Britain there would be widespread support for a defensive war but in the forests of Paraguay the German-speaking Mennonites have established a flourishing community which has as a central 'more' a refusal to take up arms in any circumstance.

Less important norms are called 'folkways'; people who break them may be considered eccentric, as would a doctor holding surgery in his underwear, but they would not be regarded as doing anything morally wrong. Folkways may be transient – the fashionable length for females' skirts is an example of such a temporarily accepted mode of correct conduct – or they may be more permanent and are then referred to as 'customs'. A few years ago in Britain friends usually greeted each other by shaking hands or just saying 'hello', whereas in Italy they might well embrace and kiss each other on both cheeks. Now many people in Britain are adopting the 'continental' mode of greeting – our 'custom' is changing.

1.6 Conflict and consensus

Of course if everyone accepted all the values of a society and followed all its norms there would be no change in that society's culture; however societies do change, some more rapidly than others, despite social pressures to ensure uniformity of behaviour.

There are two major ways of looking at the process of social change; one way is that favoured by the '**Functionalists**'. Emile Durkheim – a Frenchman born in 1858 – did not invent the term 'functionalist' but it was he who emphasised that the most important aspect in integrating a society was a '**consensus**', or agreement, about the principles on which the society was based. Durkheim felt that there was a 'collective conscience' in a society reflected by the shared values and norms that it possesses. Functionalists believe that a society's culture reflects that society's needs, that each aspect of culture has a 'function' in ensuring the smooth operation of the society. The functionalist would therefore consider that a society adapts its norms to changing needs because once a norm or value ceases to be useful in assisting the society to operate it becomes 'dysfunctional' and is rejected by the society.

If change occurs too quickly the society cannot adapt quickly enough and people become confused by the lack of rules. They enter a state of 'normlessness' called 'anomie' and escape from their confusion by alcoholism and other forms of drug-taking, aggression and suicide. Durkheim's most famous study was one into the causes of suicide in which he related the suicide rates in various countries to the degree of integration of individuals within the culture of the country concerned.

While the 'functionalist' tends to emphasise the importance of change as a gradual process, others tend to regard change as a much more explosive process resulting from inherent conflict within societies. In his *Manifesto of the Communist Party* Marx stated 'the history of all hitherto existing society is the history of class struggles'. This '**conflict theory**' of social change has had a great deal of influence on sociologists.

Essentially what 'conflict theory' suggests is that the norms of a society must be meaningful to the individuals within the society or they will be 'alienated', or isolated, from them and rebel against them. As there is only a certain amount of wealth, power and other desired factors available within any society such conflict becomes almost inevitable.

Religion is a good example of an element within a society that may integrate and unite believers but also be a source of conflict, for example between Protestants and Catholics or Hindus and Muslims.

■ ⱱ **2** Sociological method

It would be tempting for sociologists to believe that because they study the past and present nature of society they will be able to provide the information which will control the future with some certainty.

Giddens (*The Consequences of Modernity*, 1990) warns against such a view, stating that although societies can use knowledge to learn to adapt, and will be able to show what possibilities and constraints an action may have, the future result cannot be foretold with any certainty because of the unintended consequences of human action and the unpredictability of social change. However he also made the case for the study of sociology – 'only societies reflexively capable of modifying their institutions in the face of accelerated social change will be able to confront the future with confidence. Sociology is the prime medium of such reflexivity.' Bauman (*Intimations of Postmodernity*, 1992) summarised the need for such sociological research 'as a minimum sociology studies society to analyse all the resources that are available to produce possible action – an inventory of ends and the pool of means'.

2.1 Major research methods

There are two main reasons for carrying out research into society. One is 'descriptive', to discover the facts: What is gypsy life really like? How many people are poor? The second reason is 'explanatory', to find the causes of particular forms of group behaviour: Why are people prejudiced against certain ethnic groups? Why are young people more likely than older people to be involved in crime? Often research will seek to discover answers to both types of question: How? and Why?

To explain an aspect of society we can start with a 'theory' – perhaps people are prejudiced against certain ethnic groups because they are frightened of them. We then have to test our theory by establishing some '**hypothesis**', some supposed relationship between cause and effect – perhaps people fear immigrants because they think they are likely to reduce their own chance of finding a home. Having established our hypothesis we then have to test it.

It is at the testing stage that arguments arise as to whether sociology is a science. Certainly a social science such as sociology is much less certain than a natural science such as chemistry or meteorology. One deals with a subject matter – human beings – with an almost indefinite number of variables; the others deal with inanimate objects with a much more limited range of possibilities. However chemists and weather-men are often wrong – there can be no certainty in any science; the essential aspect of a science is that a scientific **method** is used. The scientist must be 'objective', they need not be neutral in their views on the subject matter but they must ensure that their investigation is carried out in such a way that any personal views do not influence their research.

In testing the hypotheses the sociologist has to avoid personal bias that may influence the result; they must also try and avoid bias on the part of the group being studied. The group members may be eager to suggest reasons for their behaviour, because they hope for financial advantage or because they wish to please the researcher.

In all sociological research there is a need for 'data' – selected information on which tests may be conducted – and this data can be divided into two types. 'Quantitative' is anything that can be put into number form, the number of people in a particular age group or social class for example. 'Qualitative' has to do with matters not capable of being related to a statistical form, such as ideas that affect behaviour.

Although both forms of data may be used in the same research there are two main types of research technique appropriate to qualitative data research and two types appropriate to quantitative research. **Quantitative** research techniques can be divided into 'surveys' of various kinds and 'experiments'. **Qualitative** research techniques include 'participant observation' and 'in-depth interviewing'.

Sociological research can take place over a period of time so that trends can be observed and links established between cause and effect, the follow-up results being compared with information collected earlier. Such research over a long period is called a 'longitudinal study'. The problems of longitudinal studies include expense, contacting the original sample after a lapse of years and sorting out the degree to which effects relate to the original possible causation and to what degree they are the result of experiences meanwhile. A good example of a longitudinal study is *From Birth to Seven* by Davie, Butler and Goldstein published in 1972 which was the result of a survey carried out on 17,000 children born during one week of 1958, into the effect of social class position on the children's development. The children were subsequently investigated again at the ages of 11 and 15, and then in a television documentary up to the age of 35. A similar study started in 2000 using a new group of children and this should prove valuable in demonstrating how behaviour and cultural attitudes have changed over almost half a century.

2.2 Sources

You will have to choose appropriate methods with which to carry out your investigation, using the following investigative techniques (when you use these techniques yourself, the information you receive becomes your **primary sources**):

1 Participant observation
2 Direct observation

3 Experiments
4 Interviews
5 Questionnaires (open, closed and coded)
6 Surveys (comparative and longitudinal)
7 Sampling (representative and random)
8 Case studies
9 Hypothesis testing

Additionally, you may use **secondary sources**. These secondary sources may include:

1 Official statistics (for example, *Social Trends*, published annually by National Statistics – your library should have a copy). (Also much available on the Internet – see 7 below.)
2 Published studies (some examples of these are given in this book).
3 Other people's diaries/personal documents (for example, you may have a relative who has kept a diary, perhaps during the Second World War).
4 Public records (your parish church may give you access to birth, death and marriage records, which can provide fascinating facts relating to changing occupations locally, or the ages at which people married or died in the past).
5 Mass media reports (television, magazines, radio, films and newspapers – your local library should have a collection of newspapers, particularly local ones, often going far back into the past (usually on 'microfiche'). (Also on the Internet.)
6 Books, such as this one; but also novels, biographies and autobiographies.
7 Electronic media, such as the Internet. Most Government departments have good web sites.

Remember that although secondary sources:

• are cheap to use
• are quick to use
• allow you to go back in time
• compare one period with another

you may not be able to check

• how accurate they are
• how objective they are
• the purpose for which they were originally collected.

When you carry out your own primary research, the people from whom you seek your information are called the **respondents**. In general, the fewer respondents you have, the more time you will be able to spend with each one – your **level of involvement** will be high. This high level of involvement means that you will be able to examine each individual in much greater detail, perhaps acquire information which you had not even considered, and be more likely to find out the real truth. On the other hand, the more personal involvement you have, the greater the likelihood that you will influence the result – **interviewer bias**.

Participant observation

In participant observation the researcher becomes part of the group that is to be studied; this means that the researcher is very much involved with the day-to-day activities of the group and, ideally, may have the opportunity to observe the members of the group behaving as they usually do and thus acquire a deeper understanding than by other methods. However, this method is particularly susceptible to interviewer bias, as the researcher may become particularly friendly or antagonistic towards the members of the group and interpret and/or report their behaviour in a subconsciously biased way.

Advantages

1 Some groups may have a lifestyle which makes it difficult to study them in any other way. For example: delinquent gangs (might resent interviewers and refuse questionnaires); 'travellers' (move around frequently, might not be able to read questionnaires).
2 Researcher can fully understand relationships within the group being studied and therefore understand why people behave in a particular way (and appreciate their point of view).
. 3 It is possible to study everyday routines and spot factors which might not appear important to the group members and which it would not occur to them to mention in other circumstances.
4 Unexpected factors may emerge which the researcher might not have thought of.
5 The observer may not influence the group's behaviour if unrecognised as a researcher.
6 It is possible to record non-verbal communication.

Disadvantages

1 It may be difficult to control personal bias.
2 The presence of the observer may influence the behaviour of the group.
3 It may be difficult to gain acceptance by the group to be studied.
4 It may be difficult to record information as it occurs, and important details may be forgotten.
5 There may be legal or moral problems: for example, a delinquent gang may expect behaviour which is either illegal or contrary to the values of the observer.
6 There may be ethical implications: for example, 'undercover' operations tend to require the observer to lie in order to maintain 'cover'.
7 Participant observation is very time-consuming; it can create problems of cost and disrupt the 'normal' lifestyle of the researcher.

Examples

- James Ditton studied petty crimes of fiddling and pilferage in one Well-bread bakery. In his book, *Part Time Crime*, Ditton describes the research during which he worked as a baker for several months and then interviewed the roundsmen. Ditton found that roundsmen fiddle and steal from customers, but protect themselves by saying 'we all do it' or 'they [the customers] can afford it', and in the end they believe that fiddling is not really criminal.

- William Whyte spent three and a half years living with an Italian–American street-corner gang in Boston some sixty years ago, and wrote a classical research study, *Street Corner Society: The Social Structure of an Italian Slum*. Although he was aware of the danger of changing the behaviour of the group by his presence, he inevitably had some effect – one of the group members told him: 'Now, when I do something, I have to think what Bill Whyte would want to know about it . . . Before I used to do this by instinct.' Whyte claimed that during his research he changed from a 'participant observer' to a 'non-observing participant'.

- James Patrick joined a street gang in Glasgow under cover and in his book *A Glasgow Gang Observed* he described how he eventually had to end his study because he was expected to engage in violent and criminal behaviour. His dislike of the gang seems to have influenced his research.

- However, Patricia Moore did not appear to encounter research problems in a study which she described in 1999: 'Twenty years ago I spent four hours every day disguising myself as an old women and going out in character. On the first day I was hit by the fact that I had changed. Taxi drivers ignored me. An air stewardess spilt coffee in my lap and took a long time to bring me a cloth. Some children would take my hand and want to chat but others mocked me and threw pebbles at me. I was beaten by a gang of boys and left bleeding in the street' (from a lecture to the Royal Society of Arts 3 April 1999).

- Howard Parker's study, *View from the Boys*, in Liverpool was not under cover; and because the 'boys' knew he was not really a member of the gang they accepted that he had more to lose than they did and did not expect him to participate actively in crime. However, he accepted that he sometimes changed the way that the 'boys' behaved because he could not tolerate some criminal activity. This change in behaviour as the result of the presence of observers has become known as the **Hawthorne effect**, since Elton Mayo's study of the behaviour of production workers in Chicago in the 1920s and 1930s, when he noted that productivity tended to increase when he was present.

Direct observation (or non-participant observation)

In direct observation the researcher does not seek to become a member of the group to be studied, and such observation is often linked to other research methods such as interviews and questionnaires.

Often direct observation may be the only feasible method of study – for example, a study of young children's behaviour in a nursery. The observer cannot become a young child or pretend to be one successfully; questionnaires are obviously inappropriate; and interviews would be very brief and generally unilluminating.

Advantages and disadvantages

Some of the factors relating to participant observation are relevant to direct observation as well: Non-verbal communication can be noted; unexpected events witnessed; interaction between group members classified. Equally, personal bias may still be a factor: the observer is even more likely to influence the behaviour of some groups. This method is also expensive and time-consuming – although **time-sampling** (the allocation of specified periods, selected in advance either randomly or on a quota basis) can reduce the amount of time spent in observing the target group without reducing the effectiveness of the research.

Example

- M. Stanworth established that boys received more attention than girls in class in Cambridge schools. In *Gender and Schooling* (1983) she described how by tape-recording lessons she avoided influencing the behaviour of the group.

Questionnaires

Use of a questionnaire is one of the usual methods used to collect data for social surveys – research designed to collect standardised information representative of a particular group. Such a survey may be simply **descriptive** (for example, to find out how many unemployed people earn money 'on the side' in the black economy) or may be designed to test a **hypothesis**, a suggestion or 'guess' that there is a relationship between certain facts (for example, the hypothesis could be that people are not bothering to seek employment officially because they can earn more by combining social security benefit with unofficial employment). (*Note*: This is an example, not a fact.)

Answers in questionnaires can either be **closed** (e.g. asking respondents to tick the appropriate box) or **open**, asking respondents to write answers using their own words.

Questionnaires can either be sent by post or administered by a researcher – both methods have advantages and disadvantages. Both types need to be very clearly stated, postal questionnaires in particular.

Postal questionnaires

- Advantages
  1 Quick.
  2 Cheap.
  3 Easily tabulated and correlated.
  4 No interviewer bias.
  5 Gives people time to think before answering questions.
  6 People may be more likely to answer embarrassing questions.
  7 No geographical restriction: people anywhere in the world can be surveyed.
- Disadvantages
  1 Poor response rate (i.e. comparatively few questionnaires are likely to be returned).

2 Unrepresentative (as a result of the poor response rate); this failing is increased if the target respondents are self-selecting – e.g. returning questionnaires published in newspapers.
3 Questions may be misinterpreted (no one will be available to explain).
4 Little opportunity to elaborate answers.

Administered questionnaires

If a researcher asks questions based on a questionnaire or assists a respondent to complete one, it usually increases cost (because the researcher will probably have to be paid); it also takes longer and may introduce an element of **interviewer bias**, either because the interviewer asks the question in a way suggesting, for example, approval or disapproval, or because the age, sex, colour or dress of the interviewer may influence the respondent.

However, advantages over the postal method include a higher response rate, increased reliability and greater representativeness; additionally, there is more opportunity to ask open questions and thus achieve greater depth.

Interviews

Interviewing people may appear to be the obvious way to find out what we wish to know, but people are often reluctant to disclose their true behaviour or thoughts: they may seek to please the researcher by telling her or him what they think the researcher wants to hear, or they may deliberately mislead in order to appear more important, tougher or more sexually experienced than they really are.

The **structured** interview has a precise format, with definite questions in a clear sequence. It can be of use in providing factual information quickly – for example, on the use of local leisure or transport facilities. The unstructured interview allows the interviewer to ask questions out of sequence, rephrase questions and encourage the person being interviewed. This form of interview is potentially more useful in determining such qualitative aspects as depth of feeling but has certain disadvantages – it needs a more skilled interviewer who can put the person interviewed at ease without suggesting a particular kind of response. Tape recordings are now often used for unstructured interviews, allowing a greater free flow of information.

Some hints for you in conducting interviews are:

• Dress in a fairly neutral manner so as not to give a clear indication of your attitudes.
• Avoid badges or other clues.
• Be non-judgemental, i.e. do not express approval or disapproval.
• Be careful of non-verbal communication which might suggest a particular response.
• Introduce yourself to the interviewee and explain the purpose of your research – you need not tell the whole truth if you think this might suggest a particular response.

- Be sensitive in handling your interviewee, but remember that your purpose is to find out the facts – probe deeply when necessary.
- Keep your objective clearly in mind and do not deviate too far in an unstructured situation.
- Guarantee anonymity if appropriate.

Sampling

Most surveys are of groups too large for everyone to be questioned individually. It is necessary to select, or 'sample', some individuals for questioning rather than others, so that the numbers are large enough to fairly represent the group but also to be reasonably easy and economic to handle.

The normal way to carry out surveys is now based on **random sampling** techniques. This eliminates any possibility of bias, and is based on mathematical calculations that ensure that an appropriate number of people are selected on a random base from within the target group. The list of all the members of the group from which the random sample is to be drawn is known as the 'sampling frame'.

Some sampling frames

- Electoral register
- School roll
- College group register
- Youth club membership list
- Church membership register
- Magazine postal circulation list.

Depending on your resources, you may select perhaps every tenth or every twentieth name on the list – you cannot ignore a name or take a more convenient substitute, if you wish your research to be accurate.

In deciding upon a particular sampling frame you must decide how representative it is of the target population that you wish to study. For example:

- Ann Oakley used the patient lists of two doctors to select married women for her study *Housewife* – these were all in London and so might not represent women's attitude to housework elsewhere.
- The telephone directory will under-represent poorer people and not include those who are 'ex-directory' but who do have telephones.

Remember that **random sampling** is not haphazard sampling – you do not just stop anyone in the street.

Where the sample is based very accurately on representatives from each stratum, or layer, within the group, it is known as a **stratified sample**. This means that a sample is drawn in correct proportion from each identifiable section within the group being studied. For example, if 72 per cent of the group to be studied were men and 10 per cent were under eighteen, the same percentage figure for each stratum would apply in the sample group as well.

People are often reluctant to disclose their true behaviour

'If an election were held tomorrow, which party . . . ?'

Your purpose is to find out the facts – probe deeply when necessary

'No, he doesn't think his
parents are too strict'

Daily Telegraph, 3 June 1993.

A **quota sample** is a cheaper method of operating a stratified sample. A specified percentage, or 'quota', of each category in the target group is decided upon; but instead of particular individuals being selected by using a mathematical calculation, the interviewer can seek out anyone who fits the category being studied. The disadvantage is one of bias. For example, the interviewer may wish to interview fifty girls between the ages of fifteen and twenty. If home calls are made on a normal weekday between 10 a.m. and 4 p.m., most of those interviewed are likely to be unemployed or truanting. Both the simple random sample and the stratified random sample would have identified individuals and would thus have been more likely to produce a representative cross-section of the age group.

Multi-stage or **cluster sampling** is a process of breaking down a large area into smaller 'clusters'. The most frequent use of this method is in political opinion polls, where an area is broken down by random sampling first into constituencies, then into 'wards', then into polling districts, then into individuals within those polling districts – the individuals ultimately selected should be a fair representative sample of the whole of the original areas.

Stages in research

Whatever methods you use, your researcher should follow a logical sequence:

- **Planning stage**. Form your *hypothesis* (your 'guess' or 'hunch' that you wish to prove or disprove). Select appropriate methods for studying the problem you have identified.
- **Implementation stage**. Collect your data by using one of the primary methods of investigation and/or using appropriate secondary sources. You may decide to start off with a *pilot survey* to test whether the method/s you have chosen actually work, e.g. do your respondents understand your questionnaire?
- **Analysis stage**. *Tabulate*, or put in a logical order, the information you have collected. Then *correlate*, or compare, the variables – that is, those factors which it may be possible to alter by changing the situation causing it. (For example, if teachers give more attention to boys in mixed schools, do girls in single-sex schools perform better than girls in coeducational schools?)
- **Report stage**. *Write up your findings* in a clear and comprehensive way and state what conclusions you draw from your research.

Topics for 'enquiries'

Some suggested topic for 'enquiries' based on particular 'methodologies' include:

1 **Direct observation**: The candidate observes interaction in a classroom looking at the time the teacher spends with girls compared with boys. This study could be completed quantitatively by recording the number of times the teacher asks boys questions compared with girls or by making notes in diary form.

2 **Participant observation**: The candidate who has the chance of a work experience placement could study the workplace at first hand, choosing to concentrate upon the effect of gender, ethnic origin, or age in the workplace.

3 **Interviews**: A case study, using interviews, of the cultural style of a particular group of young people who may be defined by others as 'deviant' (e.g. football hooligans).

4 **Questionnaires**: Design and use a questionnaire which seeks to elicit people's attitudes to and views about the purpose of education.

5 **Survey**: A survey of attitudes to travellers or asylum seekers among the people of a locality where such groups are evident.

6 **Case study**: A case study of a local political campaign or incident (e.g. an attempt to stop a road from being built or to obtain a bypass).

7 **Official statistics**: An examination of the census results in the locality for 2001 and an earlier year. A comparison of the two surveys showing the changes, with suggestions for the differences noted.

8 **Mass media report**: A content analysis of one week's viewing of television; the comparison of one 'quality' and one tabloid newspaper, teenage magazines, romantic fiction; and an example of one other mass medium. The research could be concerned with the portrayal of women or men.

9 **Published studies**: The examination and assessment of an existing research study such as a published sociological study or newspaper article. This would include a description of the purposes, methods used and principal conclusions. A replication of the study using a different method. A conclusion as to the validity and reliability of the original study.

10 **Experiment**: (This is a difficult area for sociologists as people understandably object to being experimented upon. Milgram's study of 'Obedience to Authority' is one example – where the 'learner' was put in a kind of electric chair and the 'teacher' punished wrong answers with an electric shock. In reality there was no electric shock and the 'learner' was pretending – the reality was that the study was seeking to determine how far the teacher was prepared to go in administering punishment.) A possibility might be to examine the reaction of people of differing ages to a simulated aggressive argument – but care needs to be taken both to control the situation and to obtain any necessary permissions.

However, many projects, including those listed above, may benefit from the use of several differing methods; the governing factor may be the length of the project required by the examiner concerned.

2.3 The use of statistics

Official agencies need *facts* in order to be able to make decisions – these facts are expressed in the figures which we call **official statistics**.

In order to decide how many homes and hospitals will be required for old people in twenty years time, the government and local authorities need to know how many people there are between the ages of forty-five and sixty-five in the population now and also how many of these are likely to die during the twenty-year period.

Similar facts are needed to decide how many police, teachers and nurses will be needed – you will probably collect and use statistics in carrying out your sociology project or coursework assignments.

Without evidence in the form of statistics, it would be difficult to make many decisions, and you will be expected to be able to understand statistics presented in a variety of ways – as **tables**, **charts**, **graphs**, **pie charts**, or **histograms**.

Sometimes a table will give an immediate indication that some trite assumption may not be correct. For example, it may be presumed that the apparently rising crime rate is a direct result of rising unemployment; however, a glance at Figure 2.1 will show that the crime rate started to rise rapidly in the early 1960s, which was a time of full employment, so other factors are likely to be more important.

But is the crime rate rising? It probably is, but we cannot be certain merely by looking at statistics. Is the 'clear-up' rate for crime an indication of police effectiveness? Probably not. Crime figures, like most statistics, can be misleading, and may be misused by people wishing to present evidence for a particular point of view.

Some problems with crime statistics (Figure 2.1)

Many crimes are not reported – this is referred to as the 'dark figure' of crime. A rise in crime statistics may be related to a fall in this 'dark figure' and not an increase in social disorder (the *British Crime Survey* of 1982 found that four out of every five thefts are not reported to the police):

1 Some communities are *less likely to report crime* than others.
2 Some crimes are *less likely to be reported* than others: in America, surveys show that only 27 per cent of rape and 31 per cent of burglary cases get reported. All vehicle theft was reported, no doubt for insurance reasons. In 1997 the *British Crime Survey* found that 37 per cent of victims did not report a violent crime because they said it was a private matter, or they had dealt with the matter themselves, compared with just 5 per cent of those who experienced a theft from a vehicle.
3 Apparently statistical facts may be based on *subjective assumptions*. In 2000 new Home Office research claimed that there had been a huge underreporting of rapes and sexual assaults; it stated 'up to 295,000 women are raped or suffer other forms of sexual assault every year' – this figure was based on actual figures of 6600 rapes and 18,700 indecent assaults. But on the basis of various studies which had found that only between 10 per cent and 25 per cent of women who report rape in self-report studies actually reported the offences to the police the figures were magnified accordingly and could give rise to considerable and perhaps unnecessary alarm, particularly when linked to the 'fact' that the incidence of stranger rape – the attack most feared and almost always reported – had apparently declined from 30 per cent to 11 per cent of all rapes.
4 *Police activity varies*: particular forces wage campaigns against various forms of crime – in one area marijuana smoking may be tolerated, in another rigorously prosecuted. In 2000 the Home Secretary commented that because Kent and Lancashire had specifically targeted burglary the number of such offences had decreased in those counties more than elsewhere.

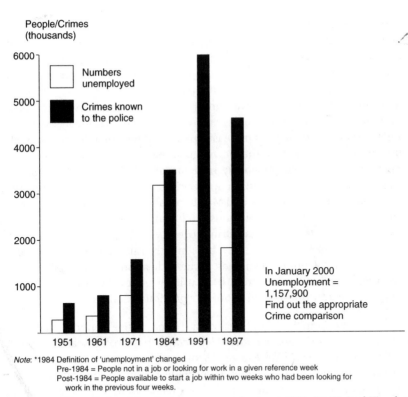

People/Crimes
(thousands)

Numbers unemployed

Crimes known to the police

In January 2000
Unemployment =
1,157,900
Find out the appropriate
Crime comparison

1951 1961 1971 1984* 1991 1997

Note: *1984 Definition of 'unemployment' changed
Pre-1984 = People not in a job or looking for work in a given reference week
Post-1984 = People available to start a job within two weeks who had been looking for
work in the previous four weeks.

Figure 2.1 The relationship of crime to unemployment 1951–97 (United Kingdom)

5 Police are *more highly trained* and *better equipped* than formerly: computer technology, motorised policing and radar and forensic advances are aids to increased detection; they do not increase criminality. Although the greater use of closed-current TV (CCTV) cameras in town centres was identified as one of the reasons for the apparent big increases in crimes of violence in 2000 (i.e. crimes were being recorded which would not otherwise have been reported).

6 Some crimes are *more likely to be discovered* than others: 'middle class' crime – tax evasion, embezzlement and fraud – is less likely to be revealed than 'working class' crime.

7 Some employers are *less likely to prosecute* than others: this is particularly so in the case of 'white collar' workers, such as bank employees, where public knowledge of criminal activity may lessen trust.

8 The *media* may create crime: 'copycat crime' may result from media publicity (e.g. the 'riots' in some British towns and cities in 1981, following the Brixton riot). Stanley Cohen, in *Folk Devils and Moral Panics* (1972) shows how the mass media created 'mods and rockers' in the 1960s – young people, police and the media converged on seaside resorts, anticipating trouble, causing a 'spiral of deviance amplification'.

9   The *size and nature of the police force* influences crime figures: more police may result in more crime detection. Between 1973 and 1982 the number of male police officers increased by 13 per cent and of female police officers by 145 per cent. It has been suggested that female officers pursue the law relating to prostitution more than do male officers.

10 *More laws create more crime:* the coming of the motor car has created offences (driving without tax or insurance, etc.) which did not previously exist.

11 *Public attitudes change* and increase apparent crime: people are less likely to tolerate child abuse or domestic violence than in the past and may report matters which would previously have stayed within the family. Domestic violence was not considered an appropriate political issue until the 1970s, when the Domestic Violence and Matrimonial Proceedings Act was passed in 1976. The Police remain notoriously reluctant to 'interfere' with domestic disputes and violence (Diana Gittins, *The Family in Question*, 1985).

12 *'Clear-up' figures* for crime may be similarly misleading: 'The ostensible clear-up rate for burglaries is not a true indication of police effectiveness. High clear-up rates often stem from a local policy ensuring that arrested burglars are fully questioned about any previous offences.'

These are the principal findings of a Home Office report, *Investigating Burglary: The Measurement of Police Performance*, based on research into police procedures in six areas (*Police Review*, 1986).

In 1986 a number of allegations were made by serving police officers that scores of fictitious crimes have been invented and then 'solved' with false confessions, to bolster the crime figures. 'One detective, with more than 20 years' experience, said: "It is all one big untruth, which is taken as an official white lie, and there is a knock-on effect. The police authority sit there telling us we are doing a wonderful job, when we're not. The real truth is that the figures are fixed to keep the local politicians off the chief constable's back. I think we should tell the truth"' (*Observer*, 1986).

But it is not only crime statistics that may be misleading.

Some examples of other statistics which may mislead

In the 1986 lead article in *Social Trends* the DHSS Economic Adviser's Office claimed that the incomes of the elderly have risen sharply in recently years (from an average of 41 per cent of the income of adults of working age in 1951 to 68 per cent). This was challenged later ('The Overpaid Elderly', by D. Thomson, *New Society*) on the grounds that the value of pensions was compared with the net earnings of male manual workers but that many other factors needed to be taken into account when comparing different periods – for example, the increase in the number of men in non-manual jobs, the number of their wives who hold paid employment, the size of their families, the income tax allowances available or the social security benefits received.

Similar criticisms have been made of the way in which the government calculates the rate of unemployment. Between 1979 and 1986 there were fifteen changes in the way in which the unemployment rate is calculated, fourteen of which had the effect of reducing the unemployment rate (e.g. the exclusion of men of more than sixty who are still seeking work).

Calculation of the 'long-term unemployed' is based on continuous unemployment – short retraining schemes remove individuals from those classified as 'long-term unemployed' even if they do not subsequently find work.

On 10 October 1993 the former Minister of Trade Alan Clarke referred on TV to the 'phoney schemes' during his time as Junior Minister in the Department of Employment as 'just a fiddle to reduce the unemployment figures'.

When referring to 'new jobs' created, it may not be clear whether this work is full or part-time (e.g. of the 1 million new jobs created since 1983, two-thirds are part-time).

Advantages and disadvantages of official statistics in research

Advantages

- They can help you establish a hypothesis.
- They can link variables in your research.
- They allow you to compare the present with the past.

Disadvantages

- They may hide distortions.
- They may be incomplete or inaccurate.
- They may be biased.
- They may be out of date.
- Some of these advantages and disadvantages apply to all secondary source data.
- Equally, the statistics you collect yourself as primary source data may be biased or incomplete, but you are in a position to know whether this is so and to take appropriate action.

SELF-TEST QUESTIONS: PART ONE

The answers to the questions in Self-test 1.1, etc. are on pp. 382–403.

Self-test 1.1

1 What is the name given to information which you have collected directly yourself? (*1 mark*)
2 What is the name of the suggestion or 'guess' which you intend to test later in a survey? (*1 mark*)
3 What kind of interview allows the interviewer to ask additional questions or change the order of questions? (*1 mark*)
4 Is a random sample one in which any number of people are taken in any order (i.e. in a haphazard manner)? (*1 mark*)

5　What are the two main features of a stratified sample? (2 marks)
6　State three secondary sources. (3 marks)
7　What are the four main stages of social investigation? (4 marks)
8　Explain what is meant by 'interviewer bias', and describe two ways in which it may occur. (4 marks)
9　Define the term 'sample', and give one reason why social scientists often take samples when conducting a survey. (4 marks)
10　What advantages may there be in using participant observation as a research technique? (4 marks)

(Total 25 marks)

Self-test 1.2

Participant observation

p

is for

PARTICIPANT OBSERVATION

when I do something I have to think what Bill Whyte would want to know about it. Before, I used to do things by instinct.'

The initial problem such researchers face is that of 'getting into' the group involved. Some managed this through previous contact with a member of the group, as Howard Parker did in his study of the 'Roundhouse' boys in Liverpool. Festinger *et al.* used fake stories to gain entry to a religious cult. A great deal depends on the sociologist's own personality and style. As Parker comments, 'If I hadn't been young, hairy, boozy, etc., the liaison would have

Simple observation of, say, a group of teenagers or strikers will tell sociologists what they are doing, but only by participating in people's activities will a real understanding be gained of why they are behaving as they are. Such participation can be fairly limited as, for example, in mingling with a football crowd. On the other hand, the observer might actually join the group under study – a religious cult, for instance.

Obviously such involvement raises the danger that researchers will become so immersed in the group's activities and values that their analysis will become biased and unobjective. Their presence may influence the group's activities to the extent that its members no longer behave 'naturally' – and become observers themselves.

The American sociologist W.F. Whyte, who made a famous study of a Chicago street-corner gang in the 1930s, found that the gang's leader, Doc, became a 'true collaborator in research'. This greatly helped Whyte's understanding, but led Doc to remark: 'You've slowed me up plenty. Now

failed'.

Once in, the researcher has to get into a position that will maximise his knowledge. Tom Lupton's jobs as a 'smearer' and a 'sweeper' in a factory allowed him to circulate freely; Roland Frankenberg actually became secretary of the football club of the village he was observing. But how involved should a sociologist become? Ned Polsky has argued for complete immersion even to the point of joining in a robbery, Howard Parker was prepared to receive 'knock-off', and in observing a Glasgow gang James Patrick was abused by others for not joining in a gang-fight but gained minimum acceptance by being picked up by the police.

Finally there is the problem of knowing what to observe and how to record it.

(Martin Slattery, *The ABC of Sociology*, Macmillan, 1985)

1　What is the name given to the situation where a research worker becomes a member of the group which he is studying? (*1 mark*)

2　According to the passage:

   (i)　What influence may the observer's presence have on the group being observed? (*1 mark*)

   (ii)　What initial problems do such researchers face? (*1 mark*)

SPECIMEN QUESTIONS AND ANSWERS

'Jobless fall a statistical fix?'

The fall in the jobless figures last month was a statistical fix, driven by the need for dole office managers to meet performance targets, secret internal figures for unemployment revealed yesterday.

Managers at most of Britain's 800 unemployment benefit offices reported a fall in the numbers claiming benefit, many of them showing near-identical percentage reductions.

According to the figures, some areas have been overwhelmed with green shoots – Shanklin in the Isle of Wight, for instance, recording a 46 per cent drop in unemployment with more than 2000 people suddenly no longer out of work.

Experts at the government-sponsored body Nomis – National On-line Manpower Information Service – at Durham University believe the sudden fall of 46,000 in claimants has little to do with people getting jobs, and more to do with civil servants striving to meet targets by the end of the financial year.

* * *

Sources said the thousands of people who were taken off the register last month included:

- Long-term unemployed moving to 'Restart' courses;
- Fraudulent claimants;
- Those 'not genuinely seeking work';
- Those 'unreasonably' refusing a job offer.

(*Observer*, 2 May 1993)

Sociologists use primary and secondary sources when conducting research.

1.　Explain the difference between primary and secondary sources, giving an example of each. (*6 marks*)

2.　Why do sociologists use secondary source data and what are the limitations of this material? (*14 marks*)

Answers

1   A primary source is information which the social scientist has collected directly for herself or himself (or which has been collected by researchers working under direction). This information might be collected by using the interview method, as did Sue Lees for her study, *Sugar and Spice*, about sexuality and adolescent girls in 1993. A secondary source is when the social scientist uses material which has been collected or produced by someone else, usually for a quite different purpose: one example is the *Annual Abstract of Statistics* produced by the Government Statistical Service and covering most areas of life in Britain – public health, education, transport, etc.

2   Secondary source data are usually readily available and are therefore quick to use and cheap to obtain: basically, all the work of collection has been done already. Diaries and novels can give an insight into thoughts and emotions as well as hard facts, while historical material for comparative purposes cannot be obtained in any way other than by using secondary sources. Some research can only be carried out by using secondary source data: for example, Durkheim's study of suicide in Europe required him to compare suicide rates in Catholic as compared with Protestant countries and it would have been impossible for him to collect this information personally.

Secondary source data, however, have many disadvantages: it is not usually possible to check whether they are accurate, whether they have been collected or collated in a biased way, in order to present a particular point of view, or whether apparently comparable figures really are comparable – for example, Durkheim's study of suicide in the nineteenth century has been criticised because different countries have different definitions of what constitutes a 'suicide'; in addition, the stigma attached to suicide will vary (in Catholic countries, preventing burial in consecrated ground) and thus suicide is more likely to be disguised as a natural death in some countries than in others.

Some statistics are particularly suspect. For example, crime figures do not include the 'dark figure' of crime, the high proportion of non-reported crime; they may also overrepresent certain social groups as criminal, in that 'white collar' crime is less likely than 'blue collar' to be reported or discovered. Additionally, raw figures do not show up changes in public attitude, which may lead to an apparent increase in crime as a result of more being reported or the greater effectiveness of the police in detecting crime.

Secondary sources cannot replace feelings and emotions expressed at first hand, and these may be vital ingredients in much social science research.

Part Two

The family

▣ 3 Development and characteristics of the modern family

3.1 What a family is

Defining 'a family' is not so simple as most people might immediately assume; there are many forms of family. In British society a basic family usually consists of a man and woman who have a steady relationship with each other and who also have children; children are essential to the idea of 'family', but they need not necessarily be 'consanguine' – that is, related by blood to the adults with whom they live – although they usually are. A simple group of this kind is called a '**nuclear**' family. Nearly all 'nuclear' families are related to one or more other nuclear families through parent–child relationships; mother will often have parents and brothers and sisters living and so will father. This family is called the '**extended family**' (Figure 3.1) and can include all known relations.

A good definition of a family was given by Burgess and Locke in their book *The Family* (1953) – 'The family is a group of persons united by the ties of marriage, blood, or adoption; constituting a single household, interacting and intercommunicating with each other in their respective social role of husband and wife, mother and father, brother and sister; creating a common culture'; however this definition is not sufficiently broad to cover all types of family

Our usual idea of a family is within a specific historical and geographical context. Talcott Parsons (*Sociological Theory and Modern Society*, 1967) argued that the nuclear family is particularly well adapted to the needs of our industrial society – the differentiation and diversification of occupations in such a society, with all the differing incomes, life styles and geographical mobility attached to these, would be difficult to operate within a wider kinship context. Within the context of such a nuclear family Parsons regarded the male function as 'instrumental' (providing resources for the family) and that of the female as 'expressive' the socialisation of the children and the managing of tensions within the family). 'The particular tasks assigned to the sexes are, in Parsons' opinion, due to the primacy of the relationship between a small child and its mother' (Cheal, *Family and the State of Theory*, 1991).

Such a view of a 'natural' division of labour is hardly compatible with the increasing expectation that women will have career opportunities equivalent to that enjoyed by men but 'recent surveys indicated that changes to the domestic division of labour have been slight. For example, the 'Women and Employment Survey" (WRES) findings on housework and childcare showed that women in the

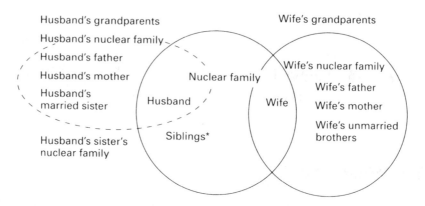

Husband's grandparents

Wife's grandparents

Husband's nuclear family

Husband's father

Husband's mother

Husband's married sister

Nuclear family

Husband

Wife's nuclear family

Wife's father

Wife's mother

Wife's unmarried brothers

Wife

Husband's sister's nuclear family

Siblings*

Note : children with the same parents

Figure 3.1 A typical 'extended' family

mid-1980s were still doing the bulk of the work' (H. Bradley, *Changing Social Divisions: Class, Gender and Race*, 1992).

It is unsurprising that the number of people marrying has declined, the age at which people get married has increased and the number of births has declined.

Marriage

In societies based on a subsistence economy all this is different. There is no wage-labour, and the production of food is the work of kin groups organized as teams. It is expected that everyone should marry as soon as possible . . . Women are expected, and expect, to bear as many children as they can. Marriage is a matter of the allocation of women to husbands, sometimes, but not always, taking individual choice into consideration. Personal compatibility is not a matter for much concern; spouses spend little time together in any case. Marriage is primarily of importance as a knot in the network of kinship links that bind such a society together. It is the formally recognized means of recruiting new members to a line of descent, and it creates alliances between such lines. The making of marriages depends in part on the claims that men are entitled to make on one another's daughters; in part on the kind of alliance that men, seeking wives for themselves or their sons, believe will be advantageous; and to a small degree, and more in some societies than in others, on the individual preferences of a man and a woman. Marriage is a matter of serious concern to a much larger number of people than the spouses themselves. Hence it is hedged about with rules and ceremonies to a much greater extent than it is in those societies, which Radcliffe-Brown long ago reminded us are exceptional, that make an ideal of 'marriage for love'.

(Lucy Mair, *Marriage*, Harmondsworth: Penguin, 1971)

The extended family

A clear father/husband figure is not present either in this picture of an extended family. In 1984 a survey carried out by the Harris Research Centre found that 79 per cent of people questioned thought that the typical 'household' in Britain consisted of a husband, a wife and two or three children; in fact only 14 per cent of 'households' fitted that description. Of course not all 'households' consist of families; a family need not 'constitute a single household' – most 'extended families' in Britain today do not.

3.2 Why families?

In nearly all cultures the family is the most important social group, although its functions will vary.

In a few societies one of the functions of the family is *political*, family networks are the major channels of power. In Britain today this function is virtually limited to the Royal Family, although economic power is still a factor, with a few families of major property owners and bankers exercising considerable influence.

In some societies *protection* is still a major function of the family; in some parts of Southern Europe, for example, the protection of the honour of its females may still be considered an important role of the male members of a family. Care of the sick, elderly, disabled or unemployed are all ways in which families have protected their members.

In many societies one of the family's functions is *economic*, as a unit both of production and consumption. In Britain the family is still a major unit of consumption, requiring items such as housing, holidays, television sets and cars, but industrialisation has removed joint working from most families, although it still does occur, for example, among farmers and Asian shopkeepers.

The family has a function in most societies of *regulating sexual contact*, but although important this is not an essential function of all family systems. In one study of 250 societies it was found that sixty-five allowed unmarried and unrelated people complete sexual freedom; so even if promiscuity is increasing in Britain it would not necessarily mean that the family was decreasing in importance. There are some societies, for example, where the connection between intercourse and birth is either not understood or disregarded, the husband simply regarding any child born to his wife as his own. This aspect of family life was summed up by Malinowski, an anthropologist. (Anthropology is the study of man and his development; particularly it is the study of primitive societies and of previous civilisations.) 'Marriage is the licensing not of sexual intercourse but of parenthood.'

In virtually all societies however the family is the main unit for *rearing children*, taking a major role in socialising them to play their part in society. Idealistic attempts have been made to abolish the family by various groups, for example by Russia in 1917, but the family has re-emerged as the basic social unit, handing on the norms and values of society from generation to generation.

In Israel communes called kibbutzim arrange for children to be looked after collectively so that men and women are free to work on equal terms. However, in recent years there has been an increase in the amount of time that parents and their children spend together.

The crucial role that the family plays in the socialisation of most people has been emphasised by many researchers (see section 1.2). Others such as Ariès (*Centuries of Childhood*, 1973) have on the other hand pointed out that this has not always been so and that rearing children has not always been seen as the

The nuclear family does seem to be the simplest structure for doing what it has to do

prerogative of the child's biological parents; in Europe, children have often been 'apprenticed' at about the age of seven and sent off to live elsewhere to learn a trade and proper behaviour.

In *A Sociology Portrait* (ed. Paul Barker, 1972) Geoffrey Hawthorne puts the case for the family very simply: 'The fact remains that the nuclear family does seem to be the simplest conceivable structure for doing what it has to do, and even if we do not know much about how it does it . . . that must be a very powerful restraint on change.' 'Perhaps the most solid evidence that family ties are important is that only 13 per cent of people said that they would rather spend time with their friends than with their family', and just seven per cent said that their friends were more important than members of their family' (*Social Trends*, 1999).

Child care

Mothering

The main reasons for regarding continuity as an essential requisite of mothering are the well-established associations between 'broken homes' and delinquency and the short-term disturbance which often follows a young child's separation from his parents. Both of these findings suggest that breaks in the parent–child relationship may have adverse effects, but as breaks are frequently associated with other adverse factors it remains to be established whether it is the separation as such which is the deleterious influence . . . That transient separations are not necessarily a bad thing is evident from the high rate of separations in normal individuals. A national sample of some five thousand children showed that by four and a half years of age, a third of children had been separated from their mother for at least one week. Furthermore, they showed that there was only a weak association between brief separations and delinquency (41 per cent separations in delinquents as against 32 per cent in controls). Of course, all children must separate from their parents sometime if they are to develop independent personalities, so the question is not whether children should separate from their mothers but rather when and how separations should occur. The finding that certain sorts of happy separation may actually protect young children from the adverse effects of later stressful separation also emphasizes the importance of considering the circumstances of a separation when deciding whether it is likely to be beneficial or harmful.

Perhaps an even more crucial point is the equation of 'separation' with 'discontinuity' in a relationship. Bowlby argued that the young pre-school child is unable to maintain a relationship with a person in their absence and that for this reason even brief separations disrupt a relationship. Experience with normal children suggests that this is not always so, at least in favourable circumstances. Of course, young children do find it more difficult, but it seems probable that environmental conditions as well as age influence a child's ability to maintain a bond during a person's absence . . .

Nevertheless his early dictum was widely accepted and led to a very marked reluctance by some Children's Officers to remove children from even appalling home circumstances. It also led to foster homes being preferred as a placement over children's homes in spite of the fact that discontinuity of mothering is often just as great in foster homes. Actually, there is no satisfactory evidence in support of the dictum 'better a bad family than a good institution'. Taken at its face value it seems to imply some mystical quality present in the family and suggests that the quality of mothering provided is irrelevant. This is such an obvious nonsense (and certainly not intended by Bowlby) that it scarcely warrants serious consideration.

Furthermore, the care in even the best institutions often falls well short of the average home although it is superior to the worst homes. As J. Bowlby, *Child Care and the Growth of Love* (1951), rightly noted, it does seem peculiarly difficult for an institution to provide parental care of the quality and quantity expected in a family setting.

Nevertheless, there is something in the dictum in that it is clear that the quality and amount of maternal care provided in the average institution is much worse than the average family.

(Michael Rutter, *Maternal Deprivation Reassessed*, Harmondsworth: Penguin, 1982, abridged)

3.3 Differing family patterns

Classifying family organisation

There are three basic ways in which a family may be constituted: **monogamy** (one man married to one woman); **polygyny** (one man married to several woman); **polyandry** (one woman married to several men). Polyandry is very rare and although about 25 per cent of the world's people live in societies where polygyny is accepted it is becoming less common as industrialisation and the modern wage economy, plus the extension of compulsory education, make the acquisition of additional wives and children more of an economic liability than an economic asset. Polygamy is the term used to cover both polyandry and polygyny.

There are usually good economic, sexual and social reasons for the existence of any particular family pattern, for example in societies where polygyny is practised there are usually more girls than boys.

In all societies whatever the family pattern there are two aspects of the family co-existing (see section 3.1). There are parents and their siblings (children with the same parents) – this group is called the 'nuclear' family. In a polygamous society there will be several nuclear families each having one parent in common.

Each nuclear family will usually be related to many other people including aunts, uncles, grandparents, nephews and nieces; all these people in '**kinship**' with each other are the '**extended family**'.

In some societies the extended family may all live together, share their property and operate as a unit, in which case they are known as a '**joint family**'.

In other societies the extended family may not operate as a unit but will still be very important to its members – assisting each other if unemployed or ill, helping to look after each others' young children, caring for its elderly members; this pattern of help is called a 'mutual support system'. In some cases the nuclear family may have little or no connection with the other members of its extended family.

There are also other ways of classifying family organisation:

- **Power**
  Patriarchal: wealth and prestige come from the father and he controls the family (e.g. Arabs).
  Matriarchal: the mother controls the family (e.g. Trobriand Islanders).
  Egalitarian: authority in the family is more or less equally divided (e.g. modern Britain?)

  (*Note*: A dominant woman may have control even in a society which is nominally patriarchal, and vice versa.)

  In Britain the family is said to be more egalitarian than formerly; however, it still can be patriarchal, as men tend to be the main wage earners and can, therefore, exercise more control.

- **Descent**
  Patrilineal: descent through the father – take father's surname; sons inherit.
  Matrilineal: Descent through the mother.
  Bilineal: Descent through both mother and father.

  In Britain children now have equal inheritance rights (except for aristocratic titles) but the father's surname is usually taken, although this is not a legal requirement.

or

  Patrilocal: families settle in or near the home of the husband's parents.
  Matrilocal: families settle in or near the home of the wife's parents.
  Neolocal: families live away from the locality of both the husband's and wife's parents.

or

  Exogamous: marriage normally to people outside the immediate circle of relatives or immediate community.
  Endogamous: marriage normally restricted to one's own kin or social group.

The norm of the modern British family can therefore be said to be monogamous, with a growing tendency towards being nuclear, egalitarian, neolocal and exogamous. Still patrilineal but becoming bilineal in some respects!

Gender differences within the family

What is a family?

As a consequence of industrialisation, the home means 'family' rather than 'work'. Our language contains the phrase 'a family man', but there is no corresponding phrase for women. It would be socially redundant: the family means women. Women bear children, women rear children, women are in the home as housewives: if the home means the family, then the family is women.

What kind of family is this?

Compared with other family systems throughout history and in different cultures, it is small, mobile and non-productive. On one level it is functionless: it has no broad economic or political or social significance. But on another level, its functions are crucial:

The family produces people. It does this in two ways – by socializing children, and by stabilizing adult personalities in the socially approved moulds of wife–mother–housewife and husband–father. The production of people is not a new function for 'the' family as such, but its significance in the case of the modern family is enlarged through the family's loss of its other, pre-industrial functions. Because women are the childbearers, the modern emphasis on people-production also affects women directly. This connection is clarified when the importance of gender – femininity and masculinity – in the structure of the modern family is understood.

Gender differentiation between the roles of female and male is the axis of the modern family's structure. 'Marriage is rooted in the family rather than the family in marriage.' Husband and wife are not the same sort of role, nor are father and mother, nor are housewife and non-housewife. The following are the conventional couplets: husband and wife, mother and father, man and wife. In each case a reversal sounds odd: wife and husband, father and mother, wife and man. The order of terms in the couplet 'husband and wife' indicates a patriarchal structure. (A. Oakley, *Housewife*, Harmondsworth: Penguin, 1974)

3.4 Family forms in Britain today

Before the Industrial Revolution (which started about 1750), most people lived fairly near relatives and did not travel much; the extended family was an important unit.

In rural areas, however, people might still live at a distance from their neighbours, and one sociologist – Laslett – has suggested that kin living in 'close geographical proximity may even be somewhat commoner in the contemporary industrial city than it was among the peasantry'.

Industrialisation started an exodus from the countryside into the town. Young people often set out independently to make their way in the world and many extended families split up. For a time many people lived as part of nuclear families isolated from their kin.

As children grew up and married they often settled near their parents and siblings and extended families once more became the norm; although it must be

Table 3.1 Percentage of dependent children living in different family types, 1972–98 (Great Britain, per cent)

	1972	1981	1998
Couple families			
1 child	16	18	17
2 children	35	41	37
3 or more children	41	29	25
Lone mother families			
1 child	2	3	6
2 children	2	4	7
3 or more children	2	3	6
Lone father families			
1 child	–	1	1
2 or more children	1	1	1
All dependent children	100	100	100

Source: *Social Trends*, 29, National Statistics © Crown Copyright, 1999.

remembered that immigration of young people from countries like Ireland, and a continued input from the countryside, always meant that there were numerous isolated nuclear families.

Today, however, the nuclear family is becoming the main operating unit in Britain particularly among the young middle class, and for most people the extended family is becoming less important. Although immigration from the Indian subcontinent has increased the importance of extended families in some areas, it seems unlikely that the extended family will re-emerge in importance as many of its functions have been taken over by the Welfare State (Table 3.1).

However the importance of the extended family should not be disregarded. In 1999 the Office for National Statistics conducted the first survey of Kinship Ties, and concluded, 'The results show that in contemporary Britain, the vast majority has close relatives in different generations with whom they are in regular contact.' The extended family is alive and well, is in frequent contact and in close proximity.

REVISION SUMMARY

Functions of the family

Political

Family networks may provide power, assistance in time of war or a mechanism for retaining economic power in a few hands. In Britain this is now not normally a function, except to a limited extent among the nobility, major property owners and some politicians.

Economic

The family is an important unit of production in non-industrialised societies (tasks being shared between husband, wife, children and other relatives). The need to keep children in education, more skilled industrial techniques and the division of labour have greatly diminished the importance of this function in modern Britain (although it can still be found, e.g. farmers, small shop-keepers). The family remains an important unit of consumption (e.g. housing, holidays).

Protection

The state has theoretically taken over this function; the family does, however, still often provide 'first line' defence (e.g. protecting young children from strangers; diverting the unwanted attention of men from younger daughters/sisters; ensuring safety against intruders). The family still often assists its sick, old, disabled or unemployed members.

Regularising sexual conduct

There is still strong religious and some social pressure persuading people that sexual relationships should be restricted to husband and wife. There is also a social taboo and legal sanctions prohibiting incest (sexual relationships between siblings, parents and their children, and other close relatives).

Socialisation of children

'Marriage is the licensing not of sexual intercourse, but of parenthood'. (Malinowski). Perhaps the most important function of the family, despite the growth of state socialisation (nurseries, schools) is that it is in the family that the child acquires its 'primary' socialisation – the norms and values of the home are likely to have a permanent influence on the kind of adult the child becomes; future physical health will depend largely on childhood environment and care; parental interest and encouragement will influence educational performance and career choice. Although the family is the first ('primary') instrument of socialisation and these early years are the most important part of the socialisation process, remember that this continues throughout life – other instruments may be peer group, education, religion, employment or even prison (which has been described as 'a finishing school for criminals').

Companionship

People live longer, and have more holidays and shorter working hours than in the past. Despite shift work and compulsory education, husband, wife and children are likely to spend much more time together – in the home (perhaps watching TV); in the family car (now owned by the majority); on holiday (75 per cent of manual workers now receive four weeks or more annually, compared with less than 1 per cent in 1970).

Social control

The family is one of the agencies in a society which controls the way people behave. Socially acceptable behaviour is enforced by sanctions: informal sanctions, such as public opinion, formal sanctions, such as imprisonment.

- A man may be imprisoned in Britain for failing to maintain his wife and children.
- A child will be encouraged to learn the gender roles regarded as appropriate to a little boy or girl by being dressed in a particular way and being given 'appropriate' toys – acceptable behaviour may be rewarded by a smile.

Differing family patterns

Polygamy: one man or one woman and more than one spouse.

(a) *Polygyny* = one man and more than one woman.

Surplus of women, sometimes artificially increased by early marriage for girls and late marriage for men – or by acceptance of homosexuality. Also, men more likely to be killed (e.g. war). (*Note*: Only the rich and/or powerful may have more than one wife)

Examples: Saudi Arabia, Turkana, Masai and Yoruba in East Africa (the Koran permits Moslem men to have up to four wives).

(b) *Polyandry* = one woman and more than one man.

Surplus of men – rare. May be enforced in order to limit children born and reduce pressure on scarce resources

Examples: Marquesas (Polynesia), Tibet, some Eskimos (Nunivak Eskimos had both polygyny and polyandry, depending on local circumstances).

(c) *Monogamy*: One man and one woman.

Roughly equal balance between sexes. Tends to occur as hygiene and medical care reduce imbalance between sexes (i.e. greater infant mortality among males) and/or modern wage economy makes additional wives/children economic liability rather than economic asset

Examples: Modern Europe, Turkey, United States.

▼ 4 The changing nature of the modern British family

4.1 The changing role of the family

Industrialisation reduced the economic role of the family; parents and children can now rarely work together. Increasing educational opportunities have limited this feature of family life still further; sons more rarely follow their Dad down the pit, or get fixed up at the shipyard through an uncle's influence. (The introduction of Labour Exchanges in 1909 had already reduced the need for such family patronage.)

Old Age Pensions, introduced in 1908, home helps and residential homes for the elderly reduce the need for the family to care for the retired. Compulsory insurance against illness from 1911 and the National Health Service have made it unnecessary for the family to act as a shield in times of disablement and illness. Unemployment benefit, supplementary benefits, council housing, free school meals, health visitors, home helps and social workers have all helped to reduce the social care role of the family. However such changes should not be over-estimated:

> The over-65 age group has practically doubled since 1951, and in 1987 was over 11 million. The care of the elderly involves an immense amount of work for women and for many, these additional demands on their labour prove impossible . . . If a growing number of women, for whatever reason, prove unable or unwilling to provide unwaged labour in the care of the elderly population, the economic consequences for State expenditure would be enormous. A[n] . . . Equal Opportunities Commission survey (1989) estimated that women's private care of vulnerable adults would cost approximately £24 billion per year if provided in the public sector and out of public funds.
>
> (Crowley, 'Women and the Domestic Sphere', 1992)

In 1870, the first Education Act began to eat away at the educative function of the family, and the raising of the school leaving age and an increase in nursery education has continued this process. The pre-school playgroup movement tries to retain family ties, however, and there has been a resurgence of interest throughout the education service in endeavouring to increase parental involvement.

The family has, however, maintained its primary role in the socialisation of the young child, but the decrease in family size has telescoped this function into a period of less than ten years for most families. However 'over the past twenty-five years, changes in the age profile of the population, in society's values and attitudes, and also in social legislation has led to something of a transformation in the structure and characteristics of households and families' (*Social Trends*, 1999). Rapoport, Fogarty and Rapoport (*Families in Britain*, 1982) have commented that 'Families in Britain today are in a transition from coping in a society in which there was a single overriding norm of what family life should be like to a society in which a plurality of norms are recognised as legitimate and, indeed, desirable'. Boh echoed this for Europe generally, stating that 'the only uniform trend in the overall development of family patterns is towards a recognition of diversity' (*Changing Patterns of European Family Life*, 1989).

4.2 Changing relationships within the family

Women and children are no longer completely dependent on their husbands and fathers and are therefore less subject to their control. In 1978, for the first time, the number of working wives exceeded 50 per cent of all married women, compared with 10 per cent in 1931, and by 1998 this had risen to 71 per cent among married/co-habiting women, while the Welfare State provides a safety net for those who leave home. The occupation of the husband is still however the major factor in determining the family's standard of living and class position. It has been suggested that it is the more upper class fathers that are now in a position of holding the greatest economic power over their children, as working class fathers now have little economic bargaining power. For example, middle and upper class children are more likely to remain in education after the statutory school leaving age and are therefore in a position of economic dependency. If children from poor homes do go to higher education their major award will make them relatively self-supporting. Children from richer homes will be dependent on their parents, usually their father, making up their grant.

Many children are now better educated than their parents and are less likely to hold them in awe or seek their advice, even although life experience might be a better source of wisdom than academic achievement.

The decline in the authoritarian role of parents and the growing equality between men and women has increased the degree of partnership within the home. In the 1950s Burgess and Locke were already saying that the family had moved from 'institution to companionship' and described this family form as the 'companionship family', and by 1973 Young and Willmott in *The Symmetrical Family* were describing the new family, with reservations, as 'egalitarian'.

However, a survey by the Economic and Social Research Council in 1993, which is tracking the lives of people born in Britain between 3 and 9 May 1958, found no evidence for the existence of 'New Men': two-thirds of the women surveyed still did most household chores.

4.3 Co-habitation

In 2001 a study by the Institute of Social and Economic Research based on a survey of 10,000 adults in 1998, was published and seemed to be another blow to those who champion traditional family values; despite a statement by the Prime Minister the previous week that marriage was the 'foundation of a strong and stable society'. Co-habitation was the first type of serious relationship that 70 per cent of the sample entered, and although three quarters planned to marry only three of the five co-habiting relationships do end in marriage. 22 per cent of children were born to co-habiting couples in 1997, compared with 2 per cent twenty years earlier. Despite high divorce rates 70 per cent of married couples do stay together until their children are over 16, compared with only a third of co-habiting couples.

The research further indicated that now one in five of the population would never get married.

Certainly major change in family life over the past ten years or so has been a fall in the proportion of people living as married couples and the increase in co-habitation. The General Household Survey shows that the proportion of all non-married women aged 18 to 49 who were co-habiting in Great Britain had doubled between 1981 and 1997, to 25 per cent. This increase and the trend towards couples co-habiting for longer has naturally led to a decline in the number of people marrying, with the number of first marriages in the United Kingdom decreasing substantially from its peak in 1970, although allowance must be made for the increase in the number of older people as a proportion of the population.

In 1996 a British Household Panel survey indicated that such co-habitation is increasingly seen as acceptable – less than 10 per cent of those aged under thirty thought that 'living together outside marriage is always wrong', compared with more than 30 per cent of those aged sixty and over. A significant indicator of the increasing acceptance of co-habitation as an alternative to marriage is that the proportion of never-married women who were co-habiting increased from 9 per cent in 1981 to 27 per cent in 1996–7. Although this trend might be seen as contributing towards the greater liberty of women the historical purpose of marriage was to create a contract which would ensure proper provision for women and their dependent children; such legal protection is substantially reduced outside wedlock.

By 1998 lone parents constituted 22 per cent of all families with dependent children and less than 40 per cent of such families were the result of divorce, compared with more than 50 per cent eight years earlier – an increasing proportion were the result of a co-habitation ending.

Although the stigma attaching to 'illegitimacy' has substantially reduced and as a result the term itself is falling into disuse, 'birth outside marriage' being the more usual and value free expression, the attitude of society to the mothers involved varies – from the 32 per cent who feel that 'unmarried mothers who find it hard to cope have only themselves to blame' to the 26 per cent who agreed that 'unmarried mothers get too little sympathy from society' (British Social Attitudes Survey, 1995).

Stupid cupid

In the last twenty years the number of never-married mothers has quadrupled [Figure 4.1]. A fifth of all families are now one-parent and more than a quarter of all babies are born outside marriage.

Is this such a great loss? It's true that the average marriage is far from perfect but the annoying thing is that, as a basic building block for society, monogamous partnerships seem to work better than almost anything else. Most free-love communes eventually come to resemble chimpanzee cages with the dominant male trying to inseminate all the females under some pretext or other.

Kibbutz-style communal living still appeals to me, but in practice those places tend towards the conventional norm. From what I hear of Israeli kibbutzim, the locals increasingly live normal suburban lives with their own kids in their own houses.

If you look to tribal societies for alternative models, you find that by far the most common social unit is one man, one woman and a bunch of their kids living in a detached bungalow. As an ageing hippy I really hate to say this but it seems unlikely we will ever find anything to beat that model.

The current trend towards single parenting is not a patch on conventional marriage, at least not from the children's perspective. To quote M. H. King and C. M. Elliott, in *The Oxford Textbook of Medicine* says: 'Individual children from single-parent families do worse than traditional families in every dimension in which they are measured – physically, emotionally, behaviourally, educationally [and] economically . . . [They] die earlier, do less well at school, are less well nourished, suffer more unemployment and are more prone to deviance and crime. They are

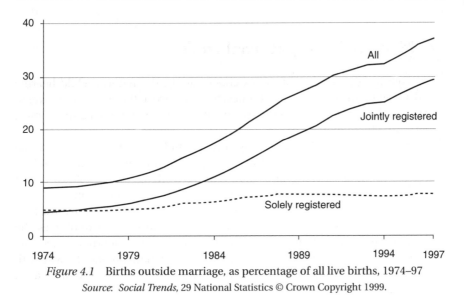

Figure 4.1 Births outside marriage, as percentage of all live births, 1974–97

Source: *Social Trends*, 29 National Statistics © Crown Copyright 1999.

between two and five times more susceptible to psychiatric illness. Even their bone age is delayed.'

Two parents are better than one?

This apparently remains true if you adjust for the relative economic deprivation of such children. It is a social effect which is visible in each stratum of society. Children with two parents do better than those with one. And children whose parents divorce are more likely to divorce themselves, so the malaise continues.

Until recently, my response to that depressing thought would have been this: surely a child growing up in a loveless marriage must be so negatively affected by the conflict at home that he or she is worse off than a child whose parents have separated? But apparently children under five have been shown to be fairly indifferent to how their parents get on. What they are most interested in is having access to mum and dad under the same roof. Indeed, up until their early teens the damage done by their parents splitting up is worse than if the parents stay together, even if the adult relationship is more of a death-grip than an embrace.

So the question is this: If we're interested in the welfare of our children, and there is truly no more healthy environment for them than a stable monogamous relationship, and if traditional marriage is going out of the window, then how can we make it more likely that couples will stay together?

(Dr John Collee, adapted from an article in *The Observer Life*,
10 October 1993)

4.4 Maternal and paternal roles

The decreasing importance of the extended family, the reduced child-bearing period, greater educational opportunities, the decrease in the economic power of fathers and the development of the Welfare State have altered the nature of most modern British families.

Traditionally, the mother would stay at home and care for the children while the father went to work. Men would not expect to do domestic tasks such as cleaning, shopping, cooking and child care; a working wife would also cast doubts about a man's masculinity and his ability to fend for his family.

In 1956, Dennis, Henriques and Slaughter produced their well-known work on the life of coal-miners, *Coal is Our Life*, and this very much reinforces the traditional stereotype of mother, 'maternal', and father 'paternal', roles, the husband spending most of his leisure time with his workmates and the wife with her mother and female friends. Such separate marriage roles are called 'segregated conjugal roles'.

However, at roughly the same time Young and Willmott produced their important work on family life in Bethnal Green and the suburb of 'Greenleigh', to which people from Bethnal Green were being moved as part of a slum-clearance programme. *Family and Kinship in East London* confirmed the traditional roles so far as older people were concerned but young fathers were spending more time with their children than had been the case. By 1963 John and Elizabeth Newson, in *Patterns of Infant Care*, had concluded that 'the modern father's place is in the home' and that both the mother and the father were becoming increasingly home-centred.

It is important to remember that although it is possible to state 'hard data' such as the average number of children in a family now compared with a hundred years ago exactly, it is not possible to measure changes in relationships and attitudes in the same way. However, it is clear that fathers generally are taking a much more active role in homemaking and family care than formerly. There is less formal punishment and more comradeship between parents and children than in the past with families spending more of their time together in the home, on holiday and on trips in the family car, and mothers are increasingly combining full-time or part-time work with their home-centred activities thus enhancing their status as contributors to the household budget. Maternal and paternal roles are starting to 'converge'.

Changing family patterns

The State has contributed indirectly towards the liberation of women, especially through the expansion of health services and education. But the loneliness of mothers with young children is still well attested and the absence of communal provision for such women remains an unsatisfied need. Meanwhile, more direct emancipating influences have come from developed methods of birth control and, most important, the gradual movement of women, including married women, into employment. In the first two decades of this century less than 10 per cent of married women in Britain went out to work: in 1951 the percentage was 21.74: by 1966 it had risen to 38.08, and by 1976 to 49. The slow spread of affluence has also played its part in combination with the invention of power appliances to relieve some of the drudgery of housework. Suburbanisation and geographical mobility have provided escape for some from the matrilocal matriarchies of the traditional urban working-class communities – a point which reminds us that women's liberation has discriminated so far in favour of younger as against older women. So we could go on through a catalogue of economic and technical changes, and their consequences, which have made possible the trend towards *The Symmetrical Family* of Young and Willmott.

Working men returning from the First World War had to accommodate, in many cases, to wives who had acquired a more independent outlook from having worked in the munitions factories, and from having run their homes unaided. Literacy and the wireless pushed back horizons between the Wars. Unlike previous wars, the Second World War did not tip the demographic balance in favour of men by killing more men than women: the number of men and women remained roughly in balance, the reserve army of women disappeared.

Still more important, seventy years ago, working men typically lived in local occupationally homogeneous communities. Such communities evolved essentially male public organizations – the pub, the betting shop, the football club; organizations which loosened marriage bonds and took resources away from women and children. But the newer patterns of inter-war industry around London and Birmingham, in the Home Counties and the Midlands, took their toll of the older male domination – reducing class solidarity perhaps and inviting more romantic love certainly. Particularly after Second World War, hours of work were reduced, holidays lengthened, home ownership became more common, children were less ever-present, and men were drawn into a more intimate and longer spousehood than their predecessors had ever known. Privatization was a key description of the affluent worker in Luton by the 1960s. It involved a closer, more co-operative, domesticity for millions of men.

(A. Halsey, *Change in British Society*, Oxford: Oxford University Press, 1981)

4.5 The nuclear family – its advantages and disadvantages

The nuclear family is sometimes called the '**conjugal family**' to emphasise the fact that the family type referred to is that of a man, his wife and their children ('conjugal' means 'to do with marriage'). However, the use of the term 'conjugal family' can be misleading. The man and woman may be living together unmarried; there may be only one parent whether by death, divorce, desertion or choice; the children may be adopted. Indeed by 2000 25 per cent of all dependent children lived with a lone mother.

The nuclear family has become increasingly important during the past forty years for a number of reasons:

1 *Increased educational opportunities* have led to young people becoming qualified for a wider variety of jobs and this has necessitated leaving their home neighbourhoods. They have often adopted a different lifestyle from their parents and have less in common with them.
2 The *run down of traditional industries* has resulted in a population movement, particularly of the young and mobile, from such areas as the North-west to the developing areas such as the South-east.
3 *Slum clearance and the building of replacement estates* elsewhere together with an increasing desire for home-ownership has led to young families being separated from their extended family to a greater degree than in the past.

4 The small modern family is *more easily cared for without external help* than was the family of a hundred years ago. However, this is not a recent phenomenon, as the average number of live births per married woman had already declined from about six in 1870 to about two in 1925.

5 The *services of the Welfare State* can be used to replace the functions previously provided by the extended family (but these same services often help to keep the nuclear family together in times of crisis).

6 *Greater physical mobility*, such as car ownership, communications such as television, and access to possible means of contact in an emergency (the telephone) make the removal from neighbourhood and extended family less daunting psychologically than formerly.

Goode, in *World Revolution and Family Patterns*, sees the emergence of the nuclear family as the main operating unit as a consequence of the needs of modern industrial society; certainly its mobility increases job opportunities and promotion prospects. The isolation of the nuclear family has tended to encourage its members to know each other as companions and to carry out activities together more, decreasing contact not only with the extended family but with other non-domestic acquaintances as well. This turning in of the nuclear family upon itself has been called 'privatisation'.

This privatisation can be an advantage in enhancing relationships within the family but it can lead to isolation, particularly of the young mother, graphically described by Hannah Gavron in *The Captive Wife* (1966). The social isolation of the privatised nuclear family may also strain relationships because of the lack of outlets in times of stress.

Although many old people are now more likely to feel useless and end their days in isolation, young married couples may be less likely to have access to a willing baby sitter, and infants may no longer have an opportunity to experience the early social contacts provided by granny and cousins: the 1999 Kinship Study by the Office for National Statistics (ONS) suggests that the supposed decline in the importance of the extended family may have been exaggerated and that with 75 per cent of the population belonging to a three-generational family, at least half of those with a living father or mother or eldest child saw them at least once a week. Daughters in their twenties and thirties had the greatest contact with their mothers, suggesting that help is still often at hand to look after grandchildren. One of the co-authors of the ONS report said that those who tended to form opinion on the state of the family – particularly journalists and academics – were likely to be more mobile than the rest.

But if the decline of the extended family has been exaggerated, the cultural change that has taken place within the nuclear group has been dramatic – especially the number of children being born in single parent households. One-fifth of all dependent children now live with a lone mother compared to only 7 per cent 30 years ago.

REVISION SUMMARY

Changing relationships in the family

Husbands and wives are becoming more equal (egalitarian) because:

- Wives are less likely to be economically dependent on their husbands (more than 70 per cent of all wives/co-habitees now work, compared with 10 per cent in 1931).
- Increased educational opportunities enhance the status of women.
- The welfare state provides a safety net for a woman and her children if she leaves her husband.
- There is no longer a surplus of girls of marriageable age in the population – males no longer have scarcity value.

Husbands and wives have less separate (segregated) roles because:

- The nuclear family is more important and so husbands and wives depend more on each other and less on relatives.
- Husbands and wives spend more leisure time together (companionate marriage).
- There is an increasing similarity between the kind of employment that men and women are likely to have – partially a result of equal education, partially because of legislation, partially because of the changing nature of industry and commerce.

Children have higher status in the home because:

- Fewer children in the family enhances the importance of individuals.
- Improved education means that many children are more knowledgeable than their parents. (It could, however, be argued that extended compulsory education makes children economically dependent longer, as does increased access to higher education.)

Changing family patterns

The nuclear family is becoming more important than the extended family as an operating unit in Britain today because:

- The reduced size of the family (from about six live births per woman in 1870 to about two in 1925) has made the direct help of an extended family less important to mothers, although the more recent growth in lone parent families has often increased the need for such assistance.
- The Welfare State has taken over responsibility for the ill, the aged and the unemployed, and for job finding and the formal education of the young – some of the 'welfare' functions previously the responsibility of relatives. (*Note*: The extended family does often still assist in these areas, particularly in times of crisis, e.g. death.)

- Increased educational opportunities have led to a wider variety of jobs being available, leading to geographical mobility. Differences in lifestyles develop among parents and their siblings themselves, weakening family bonds.
- Population movement has resulted from the decline of traditional industries (often from the North-west to the South-east).
- Slum clearance and an increasing desire for home ownership have led to the disruption of settled communities.
- Greater physical mobility (e.g. car ownership), increased mass communications (e.g. TV), improved personal communications (e.g. the telephone).

■ ⌄ **5** The stability of the family

5.1 Conflict within the family

Fifty years ago some sociologists, such as Parsons and Bales, concluded that the family was growing more important and stronger because of the increasing emphasis on children and partners as individuals; isolation increasing the partners' importance to each other. But this isolation had made the tasks of husband and wife more difficult and as difficulties increased more people could be expected to fail to overcome them.

Although one of the main changes in family life in Britain during the recent past has been the fall in the proportion of people living as married couples and the increase in co-habitation; such couples, as with spouses, must be friends as well as partners. Economic responsibility is still focused on the adult male while the children are young. The young wife may be isolated with young children all day at home often having been educated to expect that she herself would achieve success in the workplace rather than prepared for domesticity; or she will attempt to juggle the role of mother and wage earner. The scene is set for tension, frustration and despair.

In the past, husband and wife had established roles to play. Now both members of a partnership are much less certain of what is expected of them – there is a degree of 'anomie'. Both partners may have conflicting wishes. The woman may expect the man to be the strong authoritarian figure which she has been socialised to associate with masculinity, but at the same time want a comrade of equal status who will change the baby and do the shopping. The man may expect feminine domesticity, but also a partner with whom he can argue world events on equal terms or who can go to work to supplement the family income. Role conflict may be a major source of family conflict.

Children, too, have greater difficulty in knowing what to expect of parents, particularly when the value systems of home and school do not correspond in terms of discipline. Extended education brings continued dependence, at the same time as children are maturing physically earlier and being sub-jected to more commercial pressures. Television introduces other life-styles to young people and may increase the natural rebelliousness of youth to adult authority.

There are increasing examination pressures on the young and children may despise their less well educated parents (see section 4.2). The family may at times seem oppressive and restrictive of the freedom of expression that the modern emphasis on the importance of the individual has aroused as an aspiration. Sir

The differing views of young and old are often referred to as the 'generation gap'

'I know it's a bit late, but looking at our Nigel, I think I'm starting a post-natal depression.'

Edmund Leach in 1967 went so far as to say: 'The family with its narrow privacy and tawdry secrets is the source of all our discontents.'

The difference in views of young and old is often referred to as the '**generation gap**', however, this can be overestimated. Certainly parents today have more time to spend with their children, and argument has replaced physical punishment in many homes. In 1993 a Gallup Poll on teenage attitudes found that a majority felt they had more in common with their parents and older people in Britain than with young people elsewhere. The person they were most likely to take seriously was their father (equally with their doctor), closely followed by their mother. The survey commented: 'there are few signs in the survey of a real generation gap.'

5.2 The law and the family

Prior to 1870 the legal status of women was the same as for children and lunatics: they were in effect the property of their husbands. In 1882 the Married Woman's Property Act gave married women the right to keep their own earnings, to contract life insurance and to own personal property up to the value of £20. In 1882 women could sue in the law courts, and could be sued.

In 1918 the Suffrage Acts gave the women the vote and in 1923 the Matrimonial Causes Act awarded equal rights of divorce. The Matrimonial Proceedings and Property Act of 1970 made it possible for a divorced wife to be given a share in the home as of right. In 1970, too, the Equal Pay Act was introduced and by 1975 all women should have been receiving the same pay as men doing similar work. Women are now in law fully equal to their husbands.

While women have been gaining equality, the rights of children have also improved by acts insisting upon their education; controlling adoption; protecting them in employment and making arrangement for them to be taken away from their family and put in the care of local authorities if they are in physical or moral danger. The Childrens Act 1989 brought together most private and public law about children, stating that the 'children's welfare and development are paramount'; for example it states that those working with children should enable 'the children to develop positive attitudes to differences of race, culture and language and differences of gender.' (See <www.doh.gov.uk/busguide/childhtm>.)

The law has not only assisted in changing the status of women and children within the family, it has increasingly assisted in the dissolution of marriage. Until 1920 and the introduction of the 'Poor Person's Rules' divorce was really possible only for the more well-to-do; possibilities for divorce were further increased during the Second World War when a Legal Aid Scheme was introduced for the forces. This was extended to civilians in 1949. Until 1937 the only ground for divorce was adultery but a further Matrimonial Causes Act then extended the grounds to desertion, cruelty and incurable insanity.

More generous legal aid was made available from 1961, and in 1969 the Divorce Law Reform Act (operational from 1971 except in Scotland, where the law did not change until 1977) introduced a new and easier conception of divorce based on the 'irretrievable breakdown of marriage'. The Matrimonial and Family Proceedings Act of 1984 reduced the minimum period after marriage before a petition for divorce could be filed.

There is a variety of other ways in which the law may affect the family. In 1969 the Family Law Reform Act reduced to eighteen years the age at which a person could marry without parental consent. The Child Support Agency (CSA) was established in 1993 with the objective of ensuring that separated parents bore the financial responsibility for their children, rather than the tax payer. In 1999 the tax advantage for marriage, 'the married couples' allowance', was abolished. In general, changes in the law relating to the family – like most law changes – reflect the changing attitudes and values in society.

5.3 Divorce and remarriage

Changes in the law have certainly had an impact on the divorce rate, but other factors may be of greater importance in creating unhappy marriages, the law merely providing the machinery to end them:

1 The nuclear privatised family puts greater pressure on the marriage relationship (see section 4.5).
2 The breakdown of the established roles for women and men creates uncertainty and tension (see section 5.1).

Divorce and remarriage

'I have a feeling we've met before. Were we once married?'

3 Equality of job opportunity creates a greater likelihood of men and women forming alternative liaisons at work.

4 The younger the age of marriage, the greater the statistical likelihood of divorce. In the 1960s there was a trend towards earlier marriage. Although this is now reversed, there were more young people marrying in the late 1970s and early 1980s because there were more young people in the population. (In 1971, 2.6 per cent of males and 10.8 per cent of females between the ages of sixteen and nineteen were married, compared with 1.4 per cent of males and 6.5 per cent of females in 1980.) Between 1971 and 1996 the average age at first marriage in Britain rose from twenty-five years to twenty-nine years for men and from twenty-three years to twenty-seven years for women; and the fact that the majority of people are now getting married at a later age may be a factor in the levelling off, or even decrease, in the divorce rate now evident.

5 Marriages which are primarily the result of pregnancy are more likely to break down – such marriages have probably increased (co-habiting couples are more likely to marry when the woman becomes pregnant).

6 People are living longer and therefore have longer to get tired of each other! Although the biggest increase in divorce is now between the recently married (9 per cent in 1996, compared with 1 per cent in 1961) – 20 per cent of divorces are among those married for twenty years or more.

Where marriages have broken down, not only is it easier to terminate them legally but there are now fewer social penalties than in the past:

- There is a greater social acceptance of marriage breakdown and little social stigma attaches to the divorce, within the secular society.
- Welfare benefits and a more equable share-out of family possessions decreases the financial penalty of divorce for women, particularly for those with children.

Although divorce remains high and the number of marriages is decreasing, most people still marry and re-marry if divorced, so that divorce does not appear to be a symptom of the rejection of marriage as an institution. In 2000 70 per cent of young people in a national survey said they hoped to marry one day.

Family change – gain or loss?

'Divorce is difficult, but I'd like to make this hard time easier for you.' So reads a 'commiseration card' perched between the wedding bells and mourning plumes in our sub-post office. The Lord Chancellor has not to my knowledge sent one of these newly fashionable missives to any of the 160,000 couples who will get divorced in 2000, but his office is known to be looking very hard at ways and means of alleviating the misery of divorce – and of cutting its cost to the state.

Britain spent an estimated £1.4 billion on divorce in 1990: £120 million went on housing benefit, £191 million on other benefits, £72 million on legal aid, £805 million on income support and £27 million on children in care. There were additional hidden costs to the National Health Service. Don't panic. Divorce is still a minority activity, steadying up now at one in three marriages. A third of divorcing couples have no children, and another 14 per cent wait until their children are grown up before separating. But just over half of couples who divorce have at least one child under sixteen, and it is these broken families that will concern the Law Chancellor most.

The abolition of marriage?: 1

William J. Goode (1993) *World Changes in Divorce Patterns* lays our woolly visions of past golden ages of matrimony conclusively to rest. Even in Catholic Italy as many as 400,000 couples were already tacitly living apart before the 1970 legislation gave them an official way out.

Divorce, Goode reveals, is by no means a western disease, but endemic, even popular, right across the world. Nearly half of all Japanese marriages end in divorce, and in Indonesia a village spiritualist may well advise an older couple to separate because they are not suited to each other 'in a mystical sense'.

The Japanese divorce rate in the late nineteenth century outdid even that of the USA today. So many marriages failed early that the register was rarely signed for a year at least. But there was an important difference. There was no stigma attached to the bride returning home and having another shot at marriage later on. 'The key to successful coupledom,' Goode suggests, 'is a high divorce rate coupled with an equally high remarriage rate.'

A high remarriage rate is associated with a properly instituted system of divorce: no 'fault', and fair recompense for all affected parties. The evidence from right across the world is that the laws can do little to slow the trend to marriage break-up, but Goode argues that they do have a role in the pragmatic task of 'institutionalising' divorce, something which is now as necessary in the West as institutionalising marriage. It needs to be clearer – as it in fact was 50 years ago – that there are set penalties and costs when a marriage fails.

Goode sees Scandinavia as already on a road that we too need to travel. A broad distribution of welfare payments and support for lone mothers means that although there are still disadvantages to broken homes, a smaller percentage of families live in poverty, few children born out of wedlock are deprived of support, and ex-husbands are less likely to escape financial responsibilities.

Which way will Britain go? The establishment of the Child Support Agency to dun fathers for maintenance was a positive step to the Nordic pattern, and the shocked reaction of many ex-husbands to the demands only reflects how they have underestimated the awesome nature of parental responsibility. Awarding an ex-wife a share of a husband's pension is another option attracting attention: it is already part of divorce settlements in Germany and Italy . . .

'The problem has been the degree of importance given to sexual relationships in marriage since the war,' says Theodore Zeldin, the distinguished historian, who is just finishing a history of humanity.

He emphasises the fragility of relationships built primarily on feelings and dependencies, which bring exaggerated mutual expectations to both partners, and suggests that they are now giving way to more independent relationships, in which shared interests and conversations replace the older notion of 'eternal love'.

(*Daily Telegraph*, 27 September 1993, abridged)

The abolition of marriage?: 2

'The voices of despair argue that times have changed, that underlying forces ripping our marriages apart are too powerful to resist. A quick scan of international data, however, suggests that marriage and modernity are not nearly so incompatible as the divorce advocates would have us believe. Germany, for example, has an illegitimacy rate of 15 per cent, half of that of America's. In Italy the rate is 7 per cent. In today's Japan, just 1 per cent of babies are born outside of marriage, the same proportion as in 1970.

(*The Abolition of Marriage*, Maggie Gallagher, internet – <*www.divorcereform.org/ill.html* 2000>

Table 5.1   Divorce, Persons per 1000 married people in the
population, 1961–95

Year	1961	1971	1981	1991	1995
%	2.1	6.0	11.9	13.6	13.2

The number of petitions for divorce increased from about 400 in 1880 to 172,000 in 1980 but the population also increased substantially. A better guide to the increase in divorce is the number of persons divorcing per 1000 married people in the population (England and Wales) (Table 5.1).

5.4 Marriage breakdown – its social and personal cost

About 60 per cent of divorcees have children under the age of sixteen and divorce remains a major factor in the creation of one-parent families and the proportion of state benefit for families in the United Kingdom going to lone parents has increased dramatically from 22 per cent in 1981–2 to 53 per cent of all state spending on families in 1997–8 (reaching a total of £9.9 billion). These figures illustrate the two main factors that give most cause for concern in estimating the damage caused by marriage breakdown: the effect on children and the cost to public funds. However, in 1993 it was also calculated that each divorce cost industry £5000 as a result of absenteeism, lateness and a drop in productivity as a consequence of the loss of a partner's support.

The cost of marriage breakdown is incalculable in terms of human misery, whether or not it ends in divorce. The full financial cost would be difficult to estimate as one would have to add work-days lost, medication and court costs to the more obvious direct payments. The psychological cost cannot even be estimated. There is some evidence that the trauma associated with marriage break-up or marital disharmony may contribute to delinquency and education problems. The Welfare State may provide a cushion for the one-parent family, but it is often a very uncomfortable one. The average income of one-parent families is under half of that of two-parent families.

The abolition of marriage?: 3

The importance which government gives to marriage as a stabilizing factor in society is illustrated by the government green paper 'Supporting Families' published in 1998 which had as one of its aims producing policies to strengthen the institution of marriage and to reduce the risk of family breakdown.

The argument about exactly what has happened to the family through the last 200 years of industrial upheaval continues to rage. In *The Making of the Modern Family* (1976) Edward Shorter argued that there has been a dramatic change, despite some of the evidence to the contrary. A revolution in sexual behaviour, the nature of romance, the relationship of the family to the wider community, and in ideas about child-rearing have created the modern, conjugal family (as Shorter calls it) hidden away in the privacy of its own comfortable little house.

Shorter's view is that because modern family ties between husband and wife are essentially based on sexual attraction, rather than some pre-arranged property deal, the family is essentially unstable. And because children have little sense of their family past, their parents lack authority. Shorter is not entirely gloomy. This instability, he says, was the price we had to pay for freedom: freedom for people to choose who they wanted to marry, and from the interference of the community in 'private' affairs.

(*New Society*, 17 January 1980, adapted)

By 2011 most of the adult population will be unmarried and living alone
The traditional family faces a minority role

By Philip Johnston, Home Affairs Editor

FRESH evidence of the traditional family's decline in Britain came yesterday with figures showing that within 12 years a majority of the adult population will be unmarried.

It would be the first time since census records began in 1801 that those who are cohabiting, divorced, widowed or have never married had outnumbered married adults.

Forecasts from the Government Actuary, whose statistics are used to guide policy on housing and social security, suggest that by 2011 the proportion of the adult population that is married will fall from about 55 per cent today to 48 per cent. By 2020, the figure will be 45 per cent.

Although the number of people cohabiting is expected to rise, it is predicted that this will not make up for the decline in marriage. As a result, fewer people will live as couples in the first quarter of the next century.

Marriage rates among the under-thirties will continue the steep decline evident since the Seventies and the proportion of adults who have never married will rise from 32 per cent to 41 per cent for men and from 24 per cent to 33 per cent for women. Half of all men aged between 30 and 44 will have remained single by 2021. It is also estimated that the number of cohabiting couples – now about 1.5 million – will almost double over the next 25 years.

The figures are the latest in a succession of indicators that have confirmed the marked social changes that Britain has undergone in recent years. Divorce rates, births outside marriage and cohabitation have all shown marked increases to levels above anywhere else in Western Europe, although the same trends are apparent there.

Two in every five marriages now is expected to fail, the number of first marriages is at its lowest level for a century and has halved in fewer than 30 years. Since 1986, there has been a 12 per cent fall in married couple families.

Chris Shaw, of the Actuary Department, said: 'These are big changes. What we're projecting in terms of marriage in the future is largely a continuation of changes that have already occurred. We've seen such a big fall in marriage rates at young ages and this is the result.'

The figures have profound social and economic consequences. Forecasts of the number of people likely to be living alone in the next century are being revised upwards, which means more houses will be needed to accommodate them.

Three years ago, the Government projected a need for an extra 4.4 million homes; next month, this figure is expected to be revised closer to five million.

On present trends, fewer than one in five households will comprise married couples with dependent children, and, with the age of first marriage rising, a much larger number of single men and women will want their own home. Almost 80 per cent of the demand for extra homes will come from the never-married, divorced and separated.

The growing number of divorces also has implications for the welfare system, since single women with children are increasingly forced on to benefits. Another consequence is the increasing 'disengagement' of men from family life. More than half of men aged 30 to 34 will be living on their own by 2016.

Last year, the Government proposed a series of measures ostensibly to support family life but ministers were at paints to avoid preaching the benefits of a particular lifestyle. The Green Paper, however, did concede that 'marriage is a strong foundation for stability'.

Sociologists are divided over how, or if, ministers should respond to the trends. Some experts believe that politicians should not accept the trends away from marriage as inevitable and should frame policies – including the tax structure – to reverse them.

Others, however, maintain that fewer marriages and greater cohabitation are now facts of life and that the focus of policy should be on parenthood rather than marriage.

(*Daily Telegraph*, 9 January 2000)

REVISION SUMMARY

Reasons for the substantial increase of divorce in Britain

- Expectations of marriage have increased; disappointment is more likely.
- The nuclear privatised family makes the married couple more dependent on each other.
- Husband and wife are less certain as to their roles – tension and uncertainty result ('anomie').
- People are living longer and have longer to tire of each other.
- Women are more likely to work outside the home; both men and women are more likely to work with members of the opposite sex than formerly; alternative liaisons are more possible.
- There is less social stigma attached to divorce.
- Welfare benefits and more equal financial settlements on divorce decreased the financial penalty of divorce for women (about 70 per cent of all divorce petitions are now brought by women).
- It is legally easier to obtain a divorce (e.g. The Matrimonial and Family Proceedings Act 1984 which allowed couples to file for divorce after their first wedding anniversary).

Effects of divorce

- Large sums are paid out in benefit to families left unsupported after separation or divorce
- More than 50 per cent of fathers lose touch with their children completely after divorce. Grandparents will often lose all contact with their grandchildren.
- The strain on single parents is considerable – both psychological and financial.
- The trauma associated with marriage break-up may contribute to deliquency and educational problems.

Arguments that support the view that marriage is not in decline as an institution

- The number of single parents may not have increased as much as is often supposed when compared with one hundred years ago – although death was the major cause rather than divorce; co-habiting partnerships ceasing; or the increasing number of births to single mothers.
- It is impossible to estimate how many marriages in the past were 'empty shell' marriages, without warmth or depth in the relationship.
- It has been argued that the trauma associated with marital discord may be greater than that associated with divorce.

- Three-quarters of divorcees remarry. (The upward trend in the numbers of partners divorcing for the second or subsequent time continued in 1993: about 34 per cent of divorces in 1990 involved at least one partner who had been divorced before, compared with 9 per cent in 1961.)
- By 1997 15 per cent of women who had been co-habiting in 1991 had married their partner, for many women co-habitation seemed to be a preparation for marriage rather than an alternative to it.

Arguments that support the view that marriage is in decline as an institution

- Divorces doubled between 1971 and 1981 in the UK (but rate is fairly stable since then).
- Births outside marriage have risen from 6 per cent in 1961 to over a third of all live births by 1997.
  In 1991 32 per cent of UK births were illegitimate, compared with 9 per cent in Belgium, 2 per cent in Greece. But in Sweden 60 per cent of children were born out of wedlock.
- Only half of all conceptions end in a birth inside marriage.
- Premarital co-habitation is increasing. The General Household Survey shows that the proportion of all non-married women aged eighteen to forty-nine who were cohabiting in Great Britain has doubled since 1981, to 25 per cent in 1996–7.

SELF-TEST QUESTIONS: PART TWO

Self-test 2.1

1 Give the term which is used to denote one man legally married to more than one woman. *(1 mark)*
2 Give one example of a community within the United Kingdom where the 'extended family' may still be the norm. *(1 mark)*
3 Give two functions that the family performs. *(2 marks)*
4 Give two reasons why the nuclear family is becoming more common as the normal operating unit. *(2 marks)*
5 Give two reasons why parents and children may spend more time together today than in the past *(2 marks)*
6 Give three reasons why it has been accepted in some societies that it is desirable for one man to marry several women. *(3 marks)*
7 Why is divorce becoming more common? *(3 marks)*
8 What is the 'generation gap'? To what extent does it exist? *(3 marks)*
9 What changes have taken place in recent years in the 'role' of (a) mothers and (b) fathers in Great Britain? *(4 marks)*
10 What evidence is there for the continuing stability of marriage? *(4 marks)*
(Total 25 marks)

Self-test 2.2

Divorce, England and Wales, 1961–89

		1961	1971	1981	1989
Total petitions for divorce (in thousands)	By husband	14	44	47	50
	By wife:	18	67	123	135
	Total	32	111	170	185
People divorcing per 1000 married people		2.1	6.0	11.9	12.7
Remarriages as a percentage of all marriages		14	20	34	36

1 What percentage of people who married in 1981 had been married before? *(1 mark)*
2 Is the husband or the wife more likely to file a petition for divorce? *(1 mark)*
3 Explain what is meant by the term 'divorce rate'? *(3 marks)*
4 Why might the 'divorce rate' given for a country be unreliable as a guide to how successful marriages are in that country? *(4 marks)*
5 Why has the divorce rate increased so substantially during the last thirty years? *(5 marks)*
6 73 per cent of petitions for divorce in England and Wales are now filed by wives; consider some explanations for this situation. *(6 marks)*

Self-test 2.3

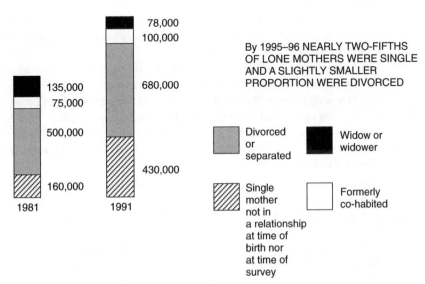

Lone-parent families (until recently usually referred to as single-parent families)

'During the present century there have been widespread changes in social conditions and attitudes affecting both men and women' (*Social Trends*)

1 In what ways have social conditions and attitudes changed, and how have these changes influenced the roles played by men and women in society? *(20 marks)*
2 What was the major reason for single-parent families in 1991? *(1 mark)*
3 Which group of single-parent families increased most between 1981 and 1991? *(1 mark)*

SPECIMEN QUESTIONS AND ANSWERS

1 Explain why the following measures have had an effect on the divorce rate:
   (i)   1949 Legal Aid Act *(2 marks)*
   (ii) 1970 Divorce Reform Act *(2 marks)*
2 Identify and explain three reasons, other than legal changes, for the increase in divorce over the last fifty years. *(6 marks)*
3 Why, despite the high divorce rate, is marriage still regarded as an important social institution? *(8 marks)*

Answers

1 (i) The 1949 Legal Aid Act has had an effect on divorce by widening the availability of legal aid, and the financial assistance thus given towards the legal costs has made it possible for more people to end their marriage legally.
   (ii) The 1970 Divorce Reform Act abolished the former limited grounds for divorce and by making the 'irretrievable breakdown of marriage' the only grounds for divorce effectively extended the reasons which could be used to justify divorce.
2 Three reasons for the increase in divorce over the last fifty years are: that women and their children do not suffer financially as badly as in the past if they divorce their husbands, because of the availability of Social Security and other benefits; that the stigma attached to divorce has reduced, thus making it possible for people to divorce without being shunned socially or losing job opportunities; and that the improved status of women makes it less likely that they will tolerate bad behaviour by their husbands.

   (*Note*: Do not give legal aid, the Divorce Law Reform Act, etc., because legal changes are excluded in the question. Only three reasons are asked for, but several alternatives, not given above, are equally acceptable – e.g. the decrease in the influence of the churches, longer life expectancy, the nuclear privatised family putting greater pressure on the marriage relationship, etc., see pp. 54–6. Note that the question asks for the reason to be both identified and explained in terms of how this affects the divorce rate; clearly the number of marks allocated anticipates only a very brief explanation.)

3   Although the divorce rate is high, this may be the result of increasing expectations from the marriage relationship and resulting dissatisfaction when high hopes are not realised; the fact that this may be the case is supported by the fact that the majority of divorcees remarry and although the marriage rate fell between 1981 and 1991 the United Kingdom had one of the highest rates in the European community during these years (exceeded only by Greece and Portugal).

Most people seem to desire the commitment and security which is supposed to exist in marriage and the public ritual confirming their right to live together.

A comparatively few people deliberately decide to have children out of wedlock although this number appears to have increased considerably in recent years. Most people seem to feel the need for children to be legitimised; even couples who live together without marriage often marry when a child is expected. Despite changing attitudes, there is still some social stigma attached to illegitimacy, and because the legal system is based on the presumption that most people will marry, there are many legal problems associated both with living as a couple out of wedlock and with being the child of unmarried parents – for example, inheritance laws favour the legitimate child.

The State regards marriage as important because it makes clear the joint responsibility of both parents for the child; and in recent years there has been concern in respect of the rising cost of social security payments to single-parent families. In 1993 the Government introduced the 'Child Support Agency' (CSA) in order to collect maintenance payments from fathers.

Although the influence of religion appears to have declined, this influence should not be regarded as negligible; religions in the United Kingdom had over 8,500,000 adult members in 1990. Moslems were the fastest-growing religious group and Moslems regard marriage as an important institution.

Many employers still seem to prefer employees to be married, regarding them as more stable and reliable (although this may not be the case) – this seems to be indicated by the fact that most application forms seek information on marital status. Leading political figures tend to emphasise their happily married status, and selection committees often require spouses to appear at selection meetings. These facts indicate that marriage is still regarded as an important social institution.

(*Note*: This question asks why marriage is still regarded as an important social institution. Do not write an essay explaining why the family is still so regarded – remember you can have marriage without a family and a family without marriage.)

Part Three

The sociology of education

■ ⊻ 6 Informal and formal education

6.1 The purpose of education

People start to learn from the moment they are born: initially most of this learning takes place in the home (Chapter 3) but later other agencies such as neighbourhood, religion, media and '**peer group**' – the term used for people of the same age – all join in this process of informal education.

Because family and friends can no longer teach most people all they need to know in order to earn a living in our increasingly technological and complex society, more formal institutions such as schools, colleges and universities have developed to prepare people for the world of work. Because relatives are no longer usually in a position to find young people jobs, careers advisers and teachers have replaced them.

Of course, educational establishments do not only prepare people for work – they are also concerned with passing on the norms and values of society. Sometimes the school or college's views of what norms and values are appropriate differ from the views of the home, and young people experience considerable difficulty in coming to terms with this conflict. Schools may well put an emphasis on discipline, team-work, theoretical learning and formal relationships, while the home is unstructured, less disciplined and individualistic. When such a divergence is marked the young people involved may well become alienated from either the school or the home.

There has been an increasing emphasis in recent years on 'social education' in the schools. This development of personal qualities may be seen as further intruding on the function of the family or as a necessary development to meet the needs of a society in which job-specific skills may be outdated very quickly. The privatised nuclear family may not provide a sufficiently wide range of relationships; and more leisure or unemployment may increase the need for people to develop the ability to make appropriate relationships with others.

In 1958, Cotgrove pointed out that although the extension of education to all had not proved the disaster that some expected, neither has it led to the equality anticipated by others. 'As certificates and diplomas are more and more the means of entry to the better paid, more secure, higher status jobs, education becomes increasingly important as a basis for occupational achievement and upward social mobility. The emphasis has shifted from socialisation to selection – an essentially aristocratic structure has been modified so that schools which once educated a social élite now educate an intellectual élite.'

6.2 Socialisation

Socialisation is the process of learning by which people of all ages acquire the culture of their society and of the various groups within the society to which they belong. Because we are constantly joining new groups through-out our lives, socialisation never stops. We have to learn the behaviour appropriate to a student, a husband or wife, and eventually of an old age pensioner.

If we were not socialised we would not behave like human beings at all, as is illustrated by the many stories of children found living with animals and behaving in a similar way to them. Some of these were no doubt abandoned in the first place because they had disabilities but some apparently did not.

A child is first taught to behave like a child and the 'expectations' of how a child should behave will vary from society to society; as the child grows older it will be expected not to be too babyish or too grown up. The child will learn its 'gender roles' (section 1.2) and the norms and values of its home. If these differ from those of the general society, the scene is set for future conflict. In *Sex, Gender and Society*, Ann Oakley took the view that sex was a biological concept based on biological factors, but that gender was an expectation of how men and women would behave starting at birth; she believed that there was little evidence of behaviour based on genetic factors. However, it is possible to take the argument that gender behaviour is all learned too far; for example, in 1986 Robinson and Morris found that the pre-school children they studied wanted gender stereotyped toys (domestic toys for girls and military toys for boys) despite being bought neutral toys (such as musical instruments) by their parents. This view that spontaneous gender wishes cannot be explained just by socialisation theory was put more succinctly to the author as a young lecturer some years ago when he was teaching a group of adults in Somerset and putting the view that our gender behaviour was learnt – to which a local farmer replied, 'I wish you would come and tell that to my bloody bull!'

Men as providers and their right to authority

From childhood onwards, men are socialized to be the economic providers and the authority figures within the household. This expectation is reinforced both by what many have seen at home and through the legal system. Most of the young men in my study came from households where the father was still the sole bread-winner. Often, their mothers had brought land and jewels into the marriage, but these had remained in their possession for their personal security, according to both custom and law. These older women tended not to contribute to the family income, and were in complete charge of the household. Within these families, men were socialized to define their manhood in terms of their economic and social authority over their wives. Yet, in the changed economic climate of modern Cairo, relatively well-to-do men have suddenly found themselves in the position of being dependent on their wives' incomes just to make ends meet and to keep up their position in society . . .

The distribution of earned income is also a serious source of dispute, particularly among young couples. Many young Egyptian women are brought up with unrealistic expectations about marriage and are pre-disposed toward being dependent on their husbands. Young unmarried women repeatedly told me that once they were married, their husbands would 'take care of everything'. After marriage, many of these same women suffered from disillusionment and subsequent disappointment in their marriages, because their husbands were unable to fulfil their wishes and expectations. The issues of money and work consistently emerged as major sources of tension in their marriages . . .

Traditional and often religiously based attitudes and role expectations are still strongly entrenched in the society, and both women and men are socialized in accordance with them, and not with the changed circumstances. In the case of most young, highly educated couples, the man expects his wife to work, at least before they have children. Nonetheless, he is unrealistic about his expectations when it comes to his control over his wife's activities, decisions regarding financial issues, the upkeep of their home and ultimately, the raising of their children. While this is a dilemma that is not unique just to Egyptian couples, it is, however, intensified through the social and legal tenets which indicate that women's work should be confined to the home.

(Barbara Sherif, 'Gender Contradictions in Families',
Anthropology Today, 4 August 1999, adapted)

Images of gender

Children are generally smaller, weaker and more vulnerable than adults – and as infants entirely dependent upon them. These differences have resulted in adults taking control of children, usually with the twofold agenda of trying to turn them into the kinds of individuals who, when they mature will be good for society (which usually means that they will not threaten the status quo) and who will behave in ways which are attractive and convenient to adults while they are young.

It is no accident that the myth of the beautiful child, epitomised by Frances Hodgson Burnett's *Little Lord Fauntleroy*, grew up in tandem with social and educational reforms which were largely designed to legislate children of the poor off the streets and into schools where they would be disciplined, cleaned and encouraged to internalise middle-class ideas about social behaviour. The impetus behind the decision to educate and so change the behaviour of large numbers of children from the lower classes was largely a reaction to the sense that they were neglected, causing some to run wild in street gangs while others were victims of overwork and various forms of abuse. However, underlying these philanthropic intentions is the power dynamic by which adults want to shape and mould children.

Images of gender

Well into the last century, infants and young children were effectively genderless. Boys and girls were both dressed in skirts and frocks. The boy's entry into breeches was a significant moment, signalling the process by which he began to achieve mastery over other groups – notably women and children. Although for practical purposes young children tended to be gender-neutral, images of children, especially those destined for a child audience, tended to conform to gender stereotypes, with boys engaging in activities out of doors while girls busied themselves at home.

(Dr Nimberley Reynolds, *RSA Journal*, 214, 1999)

6.3 Social control

In most cases the norms and values of the home are likely to reflect those of the society. The child will therefore be taught to accept the rules of that society by example, punishment and reward. These rules will receive more emphatic reinforcement in the formal education process.

British society is formed by layers of people in differing positions of power. This 'hierarchy' is reflected in nearly all schools with the Head at the top and layers of Deputy Heads, Senior Teachers, Heads of Department, teachers on various scales, caretakers, kitchen ladies and pupils. The pupil learns to behave appropriately within this rigid structure and to obey a myriad of rules and regulations, ranging from the very necessary to the (apparently) very silly. It has been suggested that schools have a 'hidden curriculum' preparing pupils for their roles in industry and bureaucracies; being prepared to accept subordination and alienation from decision-making. The structure of the school will be protected by a variety of formal and informal punishments and rewards 'sanctions' – exam passes, a smile, 'lines', detention, or exclusion. Schools reflect the values current in their society and there is an increasing amount of informality in many British schools.

As well as being one of the agencies of social control in the sense of trying to ensure that pupils and students operate within the guidelines established by the society, educational establishments are also 'custodial' institutions in which children and young people are placed to get them out of the way, both for their own safety and for the security and comfort of others. The increasing complexity and maturity required for many jobs today has resulted in the age of employment being postponed. Equally, taking large numbers of young people out of the job market is an effective means of rationing scarce employment. In this situation some formal education is seen as transparently artificial by some young people, to the extent of increasing the discipline problems that formal education is intended to assist in decreasing.

Young Asians in Bradford acquire part of the culture of their society

Discipline and the school

Patterns of discipline

There has been surprisingly little systematic research into the effects of different patterns of discipline. However, the few studies that have been undertaken both point to its importance and emphasise that discipline and punishment should not be seen as synonymous. As already mentioned, Reynolds [*Absenteeism in South Wales*, 1976] observed that the combination of good discipline (in terms of rule enforcement), the involvement of pupils in discipline (as shown by the use of a prefect system) and a low use of corporal punishment was most likely to be associated with good attendance. Heal [*Policy and Politics*] (1978) found that misbehaviour was worst in schools with formal punishment systems: and Clegg and Megson [*Children in Distress*] (1968) noted that delinquency rates tended to be highest in schools with a great deal of corporal punishment.* They also describe the improvement in one school where a new head reduced the number of rules . . . The use of some sanctions is clearly an essential element in any school organisation, but taking the findings on rewards and punishments together, the results do tend to suggest that the balance between punishments and rewards may be less than helpful in some schools. It may be difficult to design systems of rewards which will maintain their value and appeal to secondary school pupils, and especially to the oldest age groups.

* Corporal punishment is now illegal in British state schools and guidelines issued in 2000 make it increasingly unlikely in the private sector. (M. Rutter *et al.*, *Fifteen Thousand Hours: Secondary Schools and their Effects on Children*, London, Open Books, 1979)

Youth today

Is it within living memory that children did what their parents said? Is it only a generation since parents expected *obedience*? No rows, no tantrums, no Esther Rantzen?

Oh no, not another whinge about today's 'yoof'. No fear. (Socrates did it much better.) It's not the youth, but the parents who make interesting study. Modern children can't be blamed for being cocky, unbiddable, unable to sit still. They are only doing what is expected of them, as children always have and always will. It is we, the parents, who have changed. Here we are, in our fumbling, hectic way, trying to accommodate well-meaning notions about children's rights.

We scrupulously avoid laying down the law. We bend over backwards not to impose. We have taken in equal rights with our mother's milk: of course our children's opinions are as valid as ours. We listen, we guide, but never insist or enforce . . .

We have been cowed into thinking good parenting is a matter of compromise. So we dither uncertainly, like a nervous officer in battle – and what could be more terrifying for his men? We know the old chestnut: would you want your brain surgeon appointed on an equal opportunities basis? One could equally well ask: 'Would you want a surgeon who keeps deferring to your opinion?' Surely not. When we are vulnerable, we want to be in the hands of people who know what they are doing.

Childhood, supremely, is a time of such vulnerability. I could kick myself for the number of times I have said to our children, 'what do you want me to do?' They now tell me to pull myself together. 'You're the Mummy. You're supposed to *know* what to do.'

(Anne Atkins, *Daily Telegraph*, 17 July 2000)

6.4 The media and youth culture

'**Rites of passage**' exist in most societies to mark the different stages in a person's life. These rites are ceremonies such as baptism and circumcision or marriage which announce that a new person has been accepted into a society, or make it clear what sort of behaviour is expected of them, or towards them by others.

Many societies have an initiation ceremony near the time of puberty, announcing that the person concerned is no longer a child and that they are entitled to the prestige and privileges of an adult member of the society. At the same time the child accepts the responsibilities inherent in adulthood.

Although at about the age of puberty many young Christians are 'confirmed' in their faith and Jewish boys become full members of their religion at their Bar Mitzvah the increasing gap between puberty and work in modern industrial society has meant that there is a lengthening 'grey area' in which the adolescent is neither fully child nor fully adult. Lacking prestige and privileges, many young people become 'alienated' and set up their own status systems dependent on fashion, music, boy/girl friends and rebelliousness. Often responsibility is also rejected and authority derided – the peak age for crime is between fourteen and twenty years, and appears to be becoming extended as the age at first marriage increases.

Without the responsibilities of adults – rent or mortgage, rates, petrol, children's clothes – many young people have more surplus wealth than do adults to spend as they choose. It is not surprising that commercial organisations have sought to exploit this wealth by providing and advertising an appropriate consumer life-style in entertainment, fashion, cosmetics and 'durable' goods such as 'hi-fi' and motor bikes. This 'exploitation' (not necessarily a word implying wrongdoing) makes the adolescents more visually distinctive than they would otherwise be.

The media depend on sensationalism to sell, thus it is the young rebel rather than the more conventional young person who is newsworthy, setting up a copycat reaction. To an extent 'youth culture' is a creation of the media. However, the influence of the media on youthful behaviour should not be exaggerated. J. Klapper, in *The Effect of Mass Communications* (1960), found that 'media depictions of crime and violence are not prime movers to such conduct. The content seems to reinforce or implement existing and otherwise induced behavioural tendencies.' On the other hand a minority of teenagers might be influenced, as J. Halloran, in *The Effect of Mass Communications – With Special Reference to Television* (1964), found that frustrated children copied actions seen on television to release their aggression.

A special study *Broadcasting and Youth* (1979) by the Broadcasting Authorities and the Manpower Services Commission found little or no support for the 'one-step' theory of communication which suggests that all of those who receive a message will react to it in the same way, but that perhaps 'media messages shape out perception of the world in which we live'. For example the constant depiction of sexual relationships outside marriage and the acceptance of co-habitation as a normal, and even desirable, form of behaviour on television almost certainly results in that norm being accepted subconsciously by many.

In 1993 violent videos were regarded (both by the judges in each case and also by some psychologists) as contributory factors in two particularly horrific murder cases. (By 1997 over 82 per cent of households in Great Britain had a video recorder, which was more than double the proportion ten years earlier.)

It is the young rebel than the more conventional young person who is newsworthy

'Legalise Cannabis' marchers reaching Trafalgar Square, London, March 1998

Television and youth

It has become dangerously fashionable to blame television for the level of violence in society. Politicians from both right and left can hold forth on this subject without offending their leaders, sure of a sympathetic ear from a largely peaceable electorate. The most outspoken intellectual will not say a word in dissent. The issue is safe, the arguments supposedly incontrovertible. Scarcely a voice is raised to point out that they are all talking rubbish.

Statistics offer no support to media pacifists. Japan, for example, has one of the highest levels of screen violence, while street violence is exceptionally low. Television became generally accessible after the War, yet history has been riddled with murder and mayhem since the first caveman hit out with his first hand-axe.

Viking Berserkers did not psych themselves up by watching *The A-Team*; Genghis Khan's Assassins could hardly take *The Professionals* as role models: more recently, consider Adolf Hitler's taste for revolting saccharine Hollywood musicals. Since television invaded our lives there has been no major war, and visual contact with the remoter parts of the globe has heightened our understanding of and sympathy for other peoples. So much for political humbuggery.

With every mass murder, the tabloid press, hot on a popular scent, manages to discover that the unhappy psychopath worshipped such idols as Rambo or Clint Eastwood. These allegations are often disproved later, but that is irrelevant. A psychopath is always a psychopath: he will find his idols where he may. In the past, those murderously inclined have taken their bloodlust to the altars of Kali and Hecate, Ashtaroth and Baal – all without the help of the modern media.

If we wish to 'cure' violence, we might look for other causes of the problem, if only to prove the idiocy of such theorising. Soccer hooliganism, for instance, is basically gang warfare – and what is gang warfare but an extreme version of team games played in schools? The primitive concept of team spirit crushes individuality and teaches unquestioning obedience to the captain's orders.

Play up, play up, and play the game, says the poet: but what is the game? On the soccer pitch, teams kick balls. Off it they kick each other. Yet no one suggests banning soccer, rugger, basketball, hockey or even cricket from either schools or screens.

Violence is the product of energy – it is drive, conflict, competition, ambition. It can also be cruelty and brutality, if misdirected. But it is always there. It cannot be denied. It is no accident that Man is more given to needless violence than any other species. This same striving, thrusting, savage force brought us from naked ape to our relatively civilised state in a fraction of the lifetime of our planet.

Now, some of us are afraid it has outworn its usefulness. They are wrong. The energy of violence will urge us to combat pollution, to fight injustice, to campaign for democracy and human rights. It is in our nature, an essential ingredient of survival. Without it, we would degenerate into semi-vegetables, lotus-eating our way to extinction.

Violence must be accepted and challenged.

(Amanda Hemingway, *The Sunday Correspondent*, 4 February 1990)

'The slags hit back'

Though both are concerned with reputation, girls and boys talk about sex in quite different ways. For boys, sexual reputation is enhanced by bragging to other boys about how many girls they have 'made'. As one girl said: 'A boy can be called a stud and people like and respect him.' For a girl, reputation is something to be guarded. It is under threat not merely for having sex with anyone other than a steady boyfriend, but also for going out with different boys, or merely being seen with different boys, or perhaps talking to someone else's boyfriend.

In my interviews with 100 adolescent girls I found that, for a girl, the defence of her sexual reputation is crucial to her standing both with boys and girls. The importance of assumed sexual experience to a girl's reputation is shown by a whole battery of insults which are in everyday use among young people . . . A great deal of bullying and fighting among girls at school involves attacks on sexual reputation.

The term 'slag' implies that a girl sleeps around, but the insults might bear no relation at all to a girl's actual sexual behaviour. This does not make things any easier for the girl. An unjustified tag can stick as easily as a justified one. A girl can be referred to as a slag if her clothes are too tight, too short, too smart or in any way sexually provocative, if she hangs about with boys, if she talks to another girl's boyfriend, if she talks too loud or too much. It is an ever-present threat; a mechanism whereby boys can control girls' behaviour, whether sexual or otherwise, although no equivalent term exists for boys. Any girl is in danger from the 'slag' label at any time.

For boys, talking about sex whether bragging or putting down girls enhances camaraderie. Denigration of girls and women is a crucial ingredient in male circles. The masculine tradition of drinking and making coarse jokes usually focuses on the 'dumb sex object'.

The label 'slag' acts as a censure against being unattached. In other words any independent behaviour such as talking back to a boy or standing your ground in a dispute opens a girl up to verbal sexist abuse. It is therefore not surprising that all the girls agreed that there was only one way for a girl to redeem herself from the reputation of 'slag': 'To get a steady boyfriend. Then that way you seem to be more respectable like you're married or something.'

So how do girls respond to the double standards? It is too easy to conform and broadly accept the terms of abuse, even joining the boys in calling other girls 'slags'. Another response is avoidance which involves a girl in changing her behaviour to avoid abuse, by not going out with boys, not going out on her own and restricting her freedom.

(Sue Lees, 'The Slags Hit Back', author of *Sugar and Spice: Sexuality and Adolescent Girls*, *EVERYWOMAN*, September 1993, adapted)

'The trouble with boys'

'In shops they are watched suspiciously and in leisure centres they are always the first to get the blame'.

Looked at from a statistical point of view there is no reason why boys shouldn't get the blame. It is overwhelmingly boys who vandalise telephone boxes, crash cars, throw stones through windows, steal car radios and terrorise other citizens. One in three of them will commit a crime by the time they are 30 and they are five times as likely to get into trouble with the law as their female peers. Nevertheless, if we judge all boys and young men on the basis of this evidence, we are just as guilty of judgment by stereotype as all those people who used to (many still do) suggest that all women are naturally lousy at maths and intellectually inferior to the male.

We now know that it wasn't a hormone problem but there is no doubt that sex was a factor. When I was a teenager we were told that boys only wanted to go out with girls who were silly, giggly and in need of protection. Talent at maths was clear evidence of brains and, as such, must be ruthlessly suppressed. If you are 14 and life seems to offer a choice between sex and maths then sex will usually win (it is certainly more fun than maths). Fortunately for more and more girls the choice these days is a lot less stark. It is now possible to do maths and sex and so girls are doing better at maths.

The same kind of lessons need to be learnt about boys but we can only do that if we pay more attention to what is actually going on in their lives. Just as girls are not biologically innumerate, I doubt very much that boys are born to demolish telephone boxes. Most boys are not vandals even though most vandals are boys. Indeed, teenage boys are more likely to be victims of crime than perpetrators and they are a great deal more likely than any other group to be the victims of aggression. Nevertheless boys are under tremendous pressure to appear to be the kind of people who eat telephone boxes for breakfast.

> The difference here is that a boy who indulges in a kind of 'Me Tarzan' act at every opportunity is not trying to impress girls. On the whole that comes later. Mostly he is trying to impress his male peers. Boys learn masculinity from each other (fathers don't figure enough in most of their lives to pass on anything very useful). They judge their behaviour entirely by the level of acceptance from their peers and the lessons start the minute they enter the public life of school.
>
> (Angela Phillips, *The Trouble With Boys*, by Pandora Press, *EVERYWOMAN*, September 1993, adapted)

REVISION SUMMARY

Functions of formal education

Culture transmission

This passes on the norms and values of the society, but these will be the values of the dominant group. Culture clash may occur when home and school/peer group and school have different norms and values – this will often lead to the rejection of school and other means of gaining status being sought, sometimes leading to delinquent activities.

Training

Training for work prepares young people for work in a complex advanced society, but it has been suggested that this may entail preparing certain groups to accept unpleasant low-status jobs.

Social selection

This sorts out who has the ability to perform certain functions in society to ensure the best use of available talent. However, this might be (a) merely a legitimisation of the status quo, i.e. providing a justification for the best jobs to go to children of those already in high-status positions; (b) a way to simplify selection procedures, i.e. 5 GCSEs might be required for a job where they are unnecessary, to cut down the number of eligible applicants.

Social control

This teaches acceptable behaviour in order to ensure that the society runs smoothly and pleasantly for everyone, but one obvious function of schools and colleges is custodial – i.e. to keep young people out of the way because there is nothing that they can be employed to do in a complex advanced industrial society. It is suggested that another function is to ensure that they learn to accept their position in society through the hidden curriculum – this is what is taught in schools without being officially recognised:

- A *position in a hierarchy*. British society is formed by layers of people in differing positions of power. This 'hierarchy' is reflected in nearly all schools, with the Head at the top and layers of Deputy Heads, Senior Teachers, Heads of Department, teachers on various scales, caretakers, kitchen ladies and pupils. The pupil learns to behave appropriately within this rigid structure, and will then do so later in the world of work.
- A *competitive outlook* (in order to compete against each other rather than co-operate).
- An *acceptance of boredom* (to prepare for menial, repetitive jobs).
- An *acceptance of assessment* (to accept a subservient role).

Reasons for a youth culture

Increased dependency

Changes in the law have made children dependent on their parents for a longer period – often increased voluntarily because of increasing emphasis on qualifications.

Increasing spending power

In the 1950s and 1960s teenagers started to have more money to spend as they wished. Full employment meant that those in work earned comparatively high wages (with no adult constraints such as mortgages); more general affluence was passed on, reflected in pocket-money for those not working.

Consumerism

A market was spotted by commercial organisations, who moved in to 'exploit' it with fashion, entertainment and related consumer durables. The term 'teenagers' was invented by a nineteen-year-old student in Chicago in 1945 who set up Gil-Bert Teen Age Services to exploit the market he had identified.

Media

Watching particular television programmes becomes an important method of acceptance by the peer group and role models are instantly available (a role model is someone whose behaviour/style you can copy). On the other hand, teenagers spend roughly 9 per cent of their week watching television, less than other groups. (Belson, in *The Impact of Television*, 1967, reported that bringing television into the home seemed to push the teenagers out.)

Symbolic protest

Hall, in *Resistance through Rituals* (1976), concluded that style developed by working class youths is a symbolic protest against class in post-war Britain.

'Scapegoats'

Cohen, in *Folk Devils and Moral Panics* (1972), suggested that all the various youth subcultures, from beatniks to skinheads, have occupied a constant position as 'folk devils': visible reminders of what we should not be. Skinheads and similar groups are, therefore, modern witches, baddies. In the Middle Ages the witches were burned; in modern times they are pilloried in the press and television.

Urbanism

There is less 'intergenerational' authority. 'In the shifting populations of large cities, young people are less ready to accord respect to their elders. "Grandad" becomes a term of contempt' (A. Halsey, *Change in British Society*, 1981).

Education

An emphasis on qualifications leads those with less opportunity of acquiring them to adopt other mechanisms for acquiring status.

Earlier maturity

By the 1960s children were reaching sexual maturity three to five years earlier than in 1900; by 2000 it was confirmed that some girls were reaching puberty as young as eight (improved diet, etc.).

■ ☑ **7** Changes in British education

7.1 **Historical development**

The first schools in Britain were run by the Church and produced the clerics who doubled as priests and the civil service of the period. Later, the first 'public' and grammar schools appeared, to provide for the needs of the new merchant class.

In the nineteenth century the public schools grew in number as more administrators and officers were needed to serve the needs of the developing British Empire, while 'elementary' schools began to give basic instruction in reading, writing and arithmetic (as well as religion) in order to provide the skilled workers needed by the industrial revolution. By the middle of the nineteenth century Britain was lagging behind the United States and Germany in providing state education. In Germany one child in six went to school, in Britain only one in ten. Despite concern that the lack of an educated work force would hinder Britain's competing with other industrialised nations some politicians were warned that education would give people ideas above their station and encourage revolution. Others took the view that education would teach respect for superiors and the need for hard work. Towards the end of the nineteenth century the need to educate the masses if Britain was to continue to compete became inescapable.

Until this date working class children were unlikely to receive anything but a basic education; only about 10 per cent of children went to grammar school, and most of these paid fees. The kind of education received depended upon an ability to pay rather than ability to learn. Table 7.1 shows the main changes between 1870 and 1943.

7.2 **The bipartite and tripartite systems**

In 1944 a new Education Act (the 'Butler Act') was introduced by the wartime coalition government. Its main aim was to increase 'equality of opportunity' so that able children would not be prevented from contributing fully to their society because their parents could not afford an appropriate education. Pressure for reform had grown during the 1920s and 1930s, but it may be that it was hastened by those in authority who were surprised to meet so many people in the armed forces of high ability but little formal education and by middle class people coming into contact for the first time with ill-educated children from the slums.

Table 7.1   The growth of education, 1870–1943

Date	measure
1870	Forster's *Elementary Education Act* set up School Boards to build schools and to encourage attendance
1876	(Sandon's Act) Parents were given the responsibility of ensuring that children between the ages of five and thirteen went to school
1880	(Mundell's Act) Education became compulsory in theory; parents still had to pay a few pence a week in fees
1891	*Free Education Act*, most elementary education became free
1902	(Balfour's Act) Local Education Authorities (LEAs) set up to replace School Boards; new grammar schools were built and others received grants in return for providing a proportion of free places, in order to meet the needs of a better educated work force to occupy the increasing number of 'white collar' jobs in commerce and industry
1906	All secondary schools receiving public money had to offer at least 25 per cent of their places as free scholarships
1918	School-leaving age raised to fourteen (all elementary fees abolished)
1926	(Hadow Report) The Education of the Adolescent; planned a transfer at eleven and two types of secondary education: (a) *grammar* – an academic education with a school leaving age of 16+ (b) *secondary modern* – a practically based education with a leaving age of 14+
1938	Spens Report ⎫ Both these reports rejected the idea
1943	Norwood Report ⎭ of 'multilateral' (i.e. 'comprehensive') schools

The 'Butler Act' raised the school-leaving age to fifteen (with effect from 1947) and introduced reforms to raise educational and health standards in the schools. It retained religious instruction as the only compulsory subject. Most importantly it provided for a common education to the age of eleven followed by an education suited to the ability and potential of each child.

The type of educational system that developed from the 'Butler Act' was similar to that envisaged by the Hadow Report – practical education for the non-academic in secondary modern schools, academic education in grammar schools and secondary technical schools for those likely to become skilled craftsmen, although technical schools did not become widespread. When all three schools existed the scheme was known as '**tripartite**'; where there were only secondary modern and grammar, '**bipartite**'.

Although both kinds of school were supposed to be of equal status ('parity of esteem') it quickly became apparent that grammar school pupils had better opportunities when leaving school and selection at the age of eleven became a matter of 'passing' or 'failing'; thus the 80 per cent of the nation's children who did not attend grammar school started their secondary education regarding themselves as failures.

7.3 Comprehensive education

A much greater percentage of middle class children (section 8.3) 'passed' the 11-plus examination than did the children of working class parents and so the

The anonymity of larger institutions

bipartite system was seen to perpetuate and increase class divisions in society: it was 'socially divisive'.

It was argued that larger schools catering for pupils from all backgrounds and of all ability levels would encourage children from all social groups to mix together, thus increasing mutual understanding and in time reducing friction in industry. In these 'comprehensive' schools children would not pass or fail at eleven and thus all would have the opportunity to study to a high academic level if they had the necessary ability.

It was claimed that larger schools would increase opportunities by allowing subject specialists in minority interest subjects to be employed, perhaps a teacher of Russian or politics, and that economies of scale would provide a wider range of facilities.

Opponents of comprehensive education felt that academic children would be held back by the academically less able; that children of lesser ability would be unable to rise to positions of responsibility as they had in the secondary modern schools, and might suffer from the anonymity of larger institutions; and that those with greater ability would not be spotted and given special tuition to develop their latent potential.

It was also anticipated that comprehensive schools would accept lower standards of dress and objectives and thus create a norm which would reduce standards overall. It was also argued that the placing of pupils in general ability groups – 'streaming', or subject ability groups – 'setting', might heighten social distinctions if the higher sets or streams were mainly occupied by middle class children. In particular there is evidence that a low place in such streaming creates a 'self-fulfilling prophecy'; children come to regard themselves as of low ability and cease to try.

A further argument against comprehensive schools was that whereas bright working class children often travelled out of their environment to attend a grammar school they would now have to attend their neighbourhood comprehensive; if the neighbourhood was a poor one in which academic achievement was derided and most pupils were anti-authority then the academic child would suffer.

In 1950 there were ten comprehensive schools but the number of comprehensive schools increased rapidly during the 1960s and 1970s and in 1965 the Labour Government ordered local authorities to prepare plans for a completely comprehensive system of state education. This order was withdrawn by the Conservative Government in 1970 and renewed by the Labour Government of 1974.

In 1971 just over a third of children were being educated in comprehensive schools. By 2000 the proportion had risen to over 86 per cent, although there were several different types of comprehensive including 'all through'; 'eleven to sixteen'; and 'middle' and 'upper' schools.

With the growth of comprehensive education there has been a considerable increase in the number of co-educational schools, schools that have both male and female pupils. Many of the grammar and modern schools were single-sex, but most comprehensive schools outside London are mixed.

The supporters of co-education claim that boys and girls should grow up naturally to appreciate each other as people rather than sex objects and that facilities for all subjects should be available to both male and female. Opponents claim that boys may suffer from feelings of inferiority as girls mature earlier and that both are likely to be distracted from their study.

Comprehensive schools and achievement

Experts continue to disagree about comprehensive education.

Cox and his colleagues, in the 'Black Papers' on education, criticised the achievement of comprehensives. Ford, in *Class and the Comprehensive School*, studied a grammar, a modern and a comprehensive school in London but found that the comprehensive's aims were not being met (i.e. children's peer groups remained class-based). However, supporters of comprehensives do not think they can work well if grammar schools exist alongside and 'cream off' the most able.

National Children's Bureau research in 1974 indicated that the most able children did not suffer and the less able did rather better in comprehensive schools. Stephens (1980) found that the most able may have had their standard reduced slightly but that the less able had confidence boosted, with more examination entries in the Comprehensive system.

Lees, in *Losing Out* (1986), a study of sixteen-year-old girls at school, found that pupils in comprehensives remain very class-conscious. 'I think there's too much class. Everyone's sort of classed as "Oh we're snobs". They always think of us as snobs. Very much your accent I think . . . Then there're a lot of girls in our class who are East End and everything. They think of us as the brainy ones.' Lees found, as have earlier researchers, that girls in single-sex schools are more career-orientated – the fact that comprehensive schools are more likely than schools in the tripartite system to be co-educational (both sexes educated together) could mean reduced opportunities for girls (although there seems little evidence for this).

The 1984 British Social Attitudes Survey suggested continued support for the tripartite system. Half of those interviewed thought that the best all-round secondary education was provided by grammar and modern schools; two-fifths preferred comprehensive Schools.

In 1998 the Schools Standards Act set up a process whereby parents in those areas retaining grammar schools could vote on whether or not to retain selection. However by 2000 no such ballot had succeeded; for example in 1999 Kent campaigners to end selection dropped their attempt to force a ballot on the county's 33 selective schools after collecting only 7000 of the 45,959 signatures needed. In Ripon, North Yorkshire the activists collected sufficient signatures to force a vote, but parents voted by two to one to keep the town's grammar school.

Lost at school

The correlation between poverty and educational outcome has been well documented by post-war researchers. Of all the variables, it is family background – income, education and parents' occupational status – that is the greatest determinant of whether a child will succeed or fail at school.

This explains why there are still 220,000 young people who haven't obtained anything above a grade D despite the steady rise in GCSE results during the 1990s. Even where there is improvement, it has to be set in context. In the nine-year period ending in 1996, the number of children from professional families getting five A to C grades rose 18 per cent to 77 per cent. During the same period, the number of pupils from unskilled family backgrounds achieving at least five A to C grades rose by eight percentage to 19 per cent.

Why do poor children fare so poorly in school? The picture is complex and there are always exceptions to the rule. But the combined factors of low expectations, understimulation in the crucial early years and unrecognised special needs all contribute to persistent underachievement in low-income pupils. So, too, does the emotional and physical toll that deprivation takes on children. Attendance plays a big role in underachievement and the older a child gets, the more likely they are to be relied on for help from parents who can't cope on their own. And the more likely they are to simply bunk off.

Then there's the issue of how disadvantaged children relate to what goes on in school. Research by D J O'Keeffe, the author of two reports on truancy, has shown that half of the 66 per cent of secondary pupils who admit to truanting say they did so after registering in the mornings to avoid particular lessons that they disliked. Far from being blanket truants, the majority are selective in what they opt out of.

With the number of unmet academic, physical, social and emotional needs in our schools, there are a panoply of situations that children would be justified in wanting to avoid when they truant. When they are behind in their literacy or numeracy skills, what can be more humiliating and/or boring than sitting in English or Maths and not understanding or feeling left behind? When they are browbeaten at home or on the streets, what can be more insufferable than sitting in a class and being further hectored by a teacher under pressure to push 28 distracted, recalcitrant teenagers through a syllabus and get them to a position to pass exams? When their spirits are flattened by having to repress their own desires in order to care for others at home, what can be more galling than being bullied and teased at break time for wearing the wrong trainers or having a dirty neck?

Schools are microcosms of our society and our society is increasingly divided and unequal.

(Revanlern, 'Lost at School', *Education Futures*, RSA, 2000, adapted)

Naming and shaming

Nigel de Gruchy, general secretary of National Association of Schoolmasters Union of Women Teachers, said: 'I deplore the Government's determination to persist in promulgating its perverse view that school failure is entirely down to the head and teaching staff, regardless of the circumstances.

'I can only warn teachers who apply for jobs in "challenging" schools to do so with their eyes wide open. Their work will be constantly monitored and inspected and they will be blamed by the Government if they do not produce miracles.'

David Hart, general secretary of the NAHT, said: 'This will mean a sword of Damocles over the heads of a significant number of secondary schools for a lengthy period of time.'

Local government chiefs condemned the strategy and urged ministers to tackle the root causes of deprivation. Chris Waterman, general secretary of the Society of Education Officers, said: 'It is too easy to say there is no link between social factors and school performance. Naming and shaming will only discourage schools and demoralise teaching staff.'

(*Times Educational Supplement*, March 2000)

7.4 Public schools

Public Schools are private, fee-paying secondary schools, attendance at which may be thought to confer a privileged position in society. In fact, public schools are regarded by some as the linchpin of the British class system, and there is much evidence to indicate that a self-propagating élite (or power holders) still control top positions in British society.

The term is not used to include all private secondary schools, as some of these are specifically directed towards providing for the needs of young handicapped people, while others have no claim to academic excellence:

1 Sometimes the term 'public school' is used to describe only the 230 or so whose Heads belong to the Headmasters' Conference.
2 More usually the term is extended to include other major private schools associated with the Society of Headmasters and Headmistresses (about another 50). (Both (1) and (2) are mainly for boys, although an increasing number are co-educational.)
3 The 240 or so principal private schools catering for girls are also sometimes included in the category 'public school'.
4 There are also some 67 'public schools' overseas. These are private fee-paying schools with British connections (some are also members of the HMC).

In terms of examination results, many state schools achieve standards as high as, or higher than, those of many public schools. In 2000 some 5 per cent of secondary pupils might be described as attending 'public schools' as outlined in (1)–(3) areas, with some 7 per cent being educated privately overall.

'Wasting talent?'

> Oxford and Cambridge are among 13 top universities wasting state school talent, according to a report published today by the Sutton Trust.
>
> 'The field from which the country recruits its future elite turns out to be extraordinarily narrow,' the report by the education charity says.
>
> 'We are not advocating that leading universities take pupils in relation to school population but at a minimum in relation to achievement at A level,' the charity's report says.
>
> Oxbridge takes roughly half of its pupils from state school, when state schools provide about two-thirds of top A level grades.
>
> (*Guardian*, 5 June 2000)

...s to top five universities

	Actual		Benchmark*	
	No of young entrants	%	No of young entrants	%
From independent schools (7% of families**)	4580	48	3110	33
From less affluent social classes (50% of families)	980	10	1360	14
Total	9600		9600	
From low participation areas (33% of families)	450	5	730	8

*Benchmark is what the numbers should be, based on entry qualifications and subjects taught at the institution.

** Percentage of families in each category are the best estimates available.

(*Guardian*, 5 June 2000)

The arithmetic of bias

Too much still hangs on privilege

Though he might not enjoy the comparison, Gordon Brown in 2000 is Harold Wilson in 1963. That was the year when the new Labour leader made the speech at a Labour conference in Scarborough which became famous for its promise of a new Britain, forged in the white heat of a technological revolution. The main thrust of Wilson's argument, though, was his complaint that Britain was being held back by the flabby hand of the privileged, while people of talent born without such advantages were being repressed. 'For the commanding heights of British industry to be controlled today by men whose only claim is their aristocratic connection or the power of inherited wealth or speculative finance,' he said, 'is as irrelevant to the 20th century as would be the continued purchase of commissions in the armed forces by lordly amateurs.'

The term elite is variously defined, but in practice it usually means quite simply those who have got to the top. What Mr Brown is questioning is whether some who might have got to the top in a differently ordered society have in practice been stifled by the system. It is one of the oldest questions in politics and one which always evokes the same complacent response from the forces of conservatism. The equation of existing elites with the triumph of excellence is an old and shabby device. You can trace its lineage from the reactionary clamour when in the 1850s Northcote and Trevelyan dared to suggest that civil servants should be recruited not on the basis of patronage but through competitive examination; or when army reforms put an end to the practice of buying commissions. Of course society has everywhere lightened and loosened up since those days – and especially since Wilson's call for the liberation of talent back in the 1960s. William Hague, from Wath-upon-Dearne comprehensive, is not Wilson's much savoured target, the 14th Earl of Home; Greg Dyke (Hayes Grammar) is hardly John Reith. And surely no previous princess royal (see below) would have given an interview to The Grocer.

Yet the best statistics available show how urgent it is for this case to be made once more. Today we report telling new findings from the Sutton Trust, based on admissions to the top 13, and particularly the top five, universities. They confirm that the field from which this country recruits its future elite is 'extraordinarily narrow'. An assessment in yesterday's Sunday Times, largely hostile to Gordon Brown, estimated that private schools, to which 7% of our children go, account for 80% of the judiciary, 80% of the highest ranks in the army, 40% of the diplomatic service and even for a third of Tony Blair's own life peers.

This is not simply an issue of smug discrimination, though that is still a substantial part of it. It is also a mark of how badly Wilson's aspirations and the measures he hoped would liberate locked-up talent have fallen short of fulfilment over the past four decades. The end of the 11-plus and the general adoption of comprehensive schools, which he saw as one of the mighty engines of change failed to deliver.

(*Guardian*, editorial, 5 June 2000)

7.5 The future

The Educational Reform Act of 1988 seemed to make a return to more selective education likely as schools were then permitted to 'opt out' of local authority control; many of the 'opted out' schools were former grammar schools and seemed likely to wish to attract the most able academically. This trend was also likely to be assisted by the introduction of 'league tables' which list the educational achievements of pupils at various ages; this has led to increased demand for those schools that show the highest rating at GCSE and A Levels (which are likely to be those in the most middle class areas) and there was a possibility that the schools might seek to increase their competitiveness by restricting entry to those most likely to succeed.

However the return of a Labour Government in 1997 led to the effective stop to 'opting out' and an end to the assisted places scheme whereby some places for poorer students in private (including 'public' schools) were funded by the government. The government now put even more emphasis on seeking to improve state schools: 'naming and shaming' failing schools; closing down the worst performers and setting new 'National Learning Targets' in 1998, which state, for example, that by 2002 '95 per cent of 16 year olds will achieve at least one GCSE A*–G or equivalent'.

Despite the apparent support for selection in some areas the Education and Employment Secretary forecast in 2000 that by 2011 grammar schools will probably have disappeared – Mr Blunkett told the Sure Start conference in London 'I would like to place a little bet that selection is seen as a total anachronism because children have reached a point together where they can transfer to secondary schools in a way that makes separating them out look totally daft.'

The increased centralisation of the education system after 1979 culminated in the 1988 Education Reform Act. This included the introduction of the 'National Curriculum' prescribing what should be taught and setting targets and programmes of study. The Act had some unintended consequences, such as creating an unwillingness in some schools to allow students to continue after GCSE if they were not likely to obtain results which would enhance the school's position in the 'league tables'. Bowe, Ball and Gold (*Reforming Education and Changing Schools*, 1992) point out that various parts of the Education Reform Act were taken up differently by locals authorities, schools and their departments, tending to effects opposite to those intended by the Act.

In 2001 Mr Blair, the Prime Minister, introduced a Green Paper 'Schools – Building in Success', outlining a major shift in educational thinking and stating that the time had come to move to a 'post comprehensive' era. His spokesman, Alistair Campbell, bluntly stated, 'the day of the bog-standard comprehensive school is over'. The paper promised that secondary education would be transformed by developing a diversity of schools designed to meet the needs of pupils of differing abilities and aptitudes – the academically able would be placed in 'express sets' others would take a vocational route at the age of 13 or 14.

The earlier introduction of 'city technology' colleges, which are schools funded largely by the private sector, may increase opportunities in some of the poorer areas where they have been located.

Training Enterprise Councils (TECs) were established in 1991 with small groups of employers in each area of the country being given responsibility to ensure that appropriate education and training were available to meet the needs of industry; these were replaced in 2001 by Learning Skills Councils (LSCs) with a somewhat wider remit. The reason for these councils is because governments from both major parties were concerned that training in Britain was lagging behind its major competitors. This concern to enhance vocational education is similar to that which existed in the middle of the nineteenth century and which led to the provision of state education; it is further emphasised by the introduction of GNVQ (General National Vocational Qualification) courses equivalent to Advanced Level GCE but based upon vocational skills which the government introduced nationally in 1993 in an attempt to enhance the emphasis on vocational training in the United Kingdom.

As more routine jobs disappear they are being replaced by employment requiring higher levels of skills and education and there is an increased realisation of the need for extending education both for adults and for those young people who have previously left school early. This was recognised in 1993 by making all further education colleges in the country independent corporate bodies in an attempt to expand provision.

We must learn to teach old folks new tricks for the millennium

What will a child born this year need to know to be an informed citizen and an employable adult in 2020? It is an important question to ask, if impossible to answer with any precision. There are, however, some changes that we can see that are central to ensuring that every child has the life opportunity afforded by a good education.

Information and communication technologies are creating the capability that is driving globalisation of the economy, but without citizens confident and capable of living in a borderless world, we may well find that rather than creating a stable and prosperous world, that societal divides will create tensions between the haves and have nots.

It is my belief that no country in the world has an education system fit for the future. By and large, our conception of what it means to be educated is largely a product of an industrial society and economy. The emerging knowledge economy needs not only higher educational attainment, but also different sets of skills to those created by schools today.

This is not a tirade against poor teachers and schools, but a belief that we are living through a change in society and economy that is larger than the emergence of the industrial economy 200 years ago. In many ways, globalisation and the potential of the new digital media are creating a new Renaissance, where creativity, innovation and the emergence of new ideas of society, economy and work and the rejoining of arts, humanities, science and technology are becoming evident.

Our conception of reading, writing and arithmetic as the basic skills needed from education is only 150 years old. We ran an empire, and created many new ideas and inventions with a largely illiterate population.

My own feeling is that education in the new millennium will need to be more rounded rather than more specialised, that is to say, holistic.

More importantly, the rate of change that society is witnessing means that it is no longer possible to be taught all life skills by any age. Lifelong learning is not a new name for adult education, but rather an ethos that will determine whether the Britain of 2020 will have a prosperous economy and a cohesive society.

So, some predictions for 2020: first, children will leave full-time schooling at 12, but the minimum age for completion of education will be 21.

Second, schools will be smaller not larger and the boundaries between primary, secondary and colleges will be blurred. Learning in libraries will be part of the curriculum. All schools will be specialist and children will attend many schools, some physically and some virtually.

Third, teachers will work in teams, not individually. There will be fewer teachers employed in schools, but more educators overall in the economy.

Fourth, the emphasis on qualifications will shift from qualifying what has been learned to whether the individual is a competent learner.

Fifth, all children will be seen as having special educational needs. The technology needed to conquer disabilities will be widely available.

Sixth, education will be organised as a system of learning on demand for all ages. The national curriculum will be replaced by a national framework for personal curricula to international standards.

(Chris Yapp, *The Times*, 30 December 1998)

REVISION SUMMARY

Comprehensive education

Arguments for

- Will encourage children from all social groups to mix and increase mutual understanding; should lessen hostility in industry later on (not socially divisive).
- Children will not be labelled failures at eleven.
- Equal opportunity for all to proceed to A Level and to higher education.
- Larger size enables subject specialist teachers to be employed (e.g. Russian or Latin).
- Better facilities: larger size makes better facilities (e.g. computing laboratories, swimming pools, sports halls) viable.
- Will not distort primary education by making major objective passing the 11+ exam.

Arguments against

- Academically able children will be held back by less able.
- Reduced opportunity for non-academic to rise to positions of responsibility.
- Greater size brings more anonymity – perhaps ability might not be noted and encouraged.
- Lower standards of dress and objectives will create a norm, reducing standards overall.
- Streaming (placing students in classes by ability) or setting (subject ability groups) will heighten social distinctions if higher streams are mainly middle class.

- If neighbourhood is a 'poor' one, the ethics of the school is likely to be anti-authority and able children from that area will lose out by not leaving it to go to grammar school.
- Neighbourhood comprehensives draw their intake from immediate neighbourhoods and, therefore, do not decrease class distinctions.

•

■ ▼ 8 Ability and achievement

8.1 Heredity and environment

In the past it was assumed that some strata of society were superior to others because they inherited intelligence or artistic abilities along with their physical appearance, from their parents. This belief in 'genetic endowment' has been challenged during the last one hundred years and the 'nature v. nurture' debate continues.

Many definitions have been given to explain the nature of **intelligence**. A simple one is the ability to perceive and solve problems – the nature of the problems will, of course, depend on the society in which they exist. In our society intelligence tends to be thought of in terms of an ability to manipulate language and abstract concepts.

A great deal of research has aimed at establishing whether, and to what degree, intelligence is inherited. Conclusions have ranged from that of Watson (1931) who stated 'There is no such thing as an inheritance of capacity, talent, temperament, mental constitution and characteristics', and that of Floud, Halsey and Martin (1956), who argued 'it is well known that intelligence is largely an acquired characteristic', to that of Jensen (1969) and Eysenck (1973), who have maintained that genetic factors are much more important than environmental influences in producing differences in intelligence. Most research since has concluded that intelligence is in some measure inherited but that environmental factors can be conclusive in its development or otherwise.

In Britain the major argument with regard to heredity and environment revolves round its impact on differences in academic achievement between social classes. Although differences in measured intelligence have been noted, the impact of *environment* upon a child's educational chances seem of much greater significance.

Environment will include the kind of stimulus a child receives in terms of speech, books, encouragement and example. It will include facilities such as housing, computers, privacy and monetary resources; it will include the value system of the home, neighbourhood and local peer group. It will even include nutrition, for there is some evidence that severe malnutrition during the first two years of life affects the development of the brain.

Environment includes all the influences that may have an impact on the child

Regression to the mean

The term 'regression to the mean', in this context, refers to the tendency for children to be nearer to the population mean on a characteristic than are their parents. As a consequence, the children of very dull individuals are likely to be more intelligent than their parents whereas the offspring of highly intelligent persons are likely to be less intelligent than their procreators (M. Rutter and N. Madge, *Cycles of Disadvantage*, 1976). Environment includes all the influences that may make an impact on the child.

8.2 The culture of the school

The culture of the school tends to be a middle class one although schools vary in their education objectives. Some schools will emphasise their 'academic' role and be concerned mainly with achievement; some will concentrate on their 'pastoral' role of developing personal qualities and some will strive mainly to keep a maximum of good order and discipline, their 'custodial' role.

If the culture of the school is predominantly academic or custodial within a community which rejects concepts of betterment and authority then there is likely to be a development of anti-school and delinquent subcultures as illustrated by D. Hargreaves in *Deviance in Classrooms* (1975).

The school is an authoritarian institution (section 6.3) although the degree of authoritarianism will vary. Schoolteachers are middle class by definition. Although as a group they are likely to have a high proportion of first-generation middle class members, they have reached their position by accepting middle class values such as 'deferred gratification' (forfeiting immediate satisfaction for future gain) and completing their education at a late age with consequent loss of earnings in their youth.

In 1961 B. Bernstein, in *A Socio-linguistic Approach to Social Learning*, identifies the '**elaborated code**' (or 'formal language') of middle class speech patterns, with complex forms, and the '**restricted code**' (or 'public language') of many working class people, which is much simpler in form, using basic words. These language differences do reflect very different cultural backgrounds and present serious problems for youngsters from the lower working class, in particular, as they attempt to learn in school.

Self-fulfilling prophecy

Placing American kindergarten life under the magnifying glass, psychologist Dr R. C. Rist discovered just how far early judgements come to dominate the child's school career. In the kindergarten which he studied the head teacher sat children at one of three dinner tables according to her expectations for their future academic success. Her brightest hopes ate at one table, those she ranked as moderately intelligent at another while the ones she considered almost certain failures had their meals at a third. She picked children for each table on the basis of family background, the way they were dressed and how well they got on with staff. Despite the fact that IQ tests showed there was no real difference between the abilities of children at the three tables these groupings remained virtually unchanged during the next two years. The teacher saw little reason to promote any child from the 'failure' table or to demote any of those at the 'success' table.

As the years passed, however, changes in abilities between the groups became increasingly apparent. Children who had eaten with the success group did well while those who had dined with 'failures' did badly. Was she a highly perceptive teacher or could it be that those initial assessments set the course for the children's future progress through school? On the basis of other evidence the most likely explanation is that the attitudes of the kindergarten staff, conveyed to primary school teachers in the pupils' reports, which would then have gone with them to their secondary schools, established a pattern of prejudgement which played an important role in how each child was perceived. As Dr Rist commented, the head teacher's original predictions 'came to be justified not in terms of teacher expectations, but in apparently "objective" records of previous school working, including by the beginning of the second grade, reading test performance'.

In a study of the effect which a teacher's belief in the pupil's IQ has on attainment, Dr J. Michael Palardy of University of Georgia at Athens, Georgia, discovered that the brighter a child was assumed to be, the better the results the teacher obtained in class. Groups of boys, aged between six and seven, were matched in ability on the basis of intelligence tests. They were then taught reading in separate classes, by teachers with identical qualifications using exactly the same methods. The only difference was that some of the teachers were told their particular group consisted of boys with above-average ability who should prove faster and more able readers. There was, of course, not a grain of truth in this statement. But when the boys were tested at the end of the training period the teacher's false belief had been transformed into classroom reality. Those boys falsely credited with better reading ability could now read faster and more fluently than those in other groups . . .

The message from such studies is crystal clear. What teachers believe their students achieve. Classroom ability mirrors the attitudes of those who take the classes and run the schools.

(David Lewis, *You Can Teach Your Child Intelligence*, London, Souvenir Press, 1981)

8.3 The influence of family and class

In 1995 Teresa Smith and Michael Noble in *Education Divides* reported: 'Data from urban areas in 1993 shows that, in the poorest districts, comprehensive school pupils achieve on average approximately half the success rate in getting five-plus higher-grade GCSEs of comprehensive pupils in the most advantaged urban areas.' Reports from the Department for Education and Employment also point out that the bottom thirty local authorities at GCSE are in substantially deprived urban areas.

The current position reflects little change from other research over the past fifty years. Over forty years ago, Bernstein suggested that a major factor in explaining the success of the middle class child academically was that it used the same language as its teachers, not in terms of accent but in ability to grasp the more complicated ideas expressed by teachers in the elaborated code.

Newspeak: It's the real thing

By the dawn of 1984 the development of television, and other forms of electronic media, means that mass communication, both verbal and visual, is more pervasive and persuasive than ever before.

This technical potential for control must be set against ideas of how language works, notably those whose theories of the differences in linguistic practice between working class and middle class speakers of

English have emphasised how language can define and reinforce the social hierarchy. Bernstein is often interpreted to be talking about accent, especially the accent of the economically dominant South East, which is the accent spoken by those who attended certain educational institutions, and therefore the accent of national power, prestige and authority. This has also become the accent of broadcasting. In fact the core of Bernstein's theory is his distinction between a 'restricted code' spoken by some people and an 'elaborated code' spoken by others. 'Restricted code' was supposed to be the use of simple sentences, limited and inexplicit means of referring to things, lack of abstractions and lack of self-reference. Bernstein thought that working class children used this in schools, where 'elaborated code' was expected, and thus did poorly; he also concluded that 'restricted code' led to restricted ability to form concepts.

Orwell's Newspeak looks very like Bernstein's 'restricted code'. It has reduced complexity, few abstractions. But it is also a restricted code peculiar to the ruling class; the proles do not speak it. Its purpose is to provide a medium of expression for the ideology of the ruling elite, and also to make all other modes of thought impossible.

(C. Aubrey and P. Chilton (eds), *1984 – Autonomy, Control and Communication*, London, Comedia, 1983)

Working class children tend to be slower in learning to read and write than middle class children because of this language barrier and because intelligence tests are often based on words. This also gives the middle class child an advantage, which decreases when the intelligence test is based on arithmetic. Many other studies have highlighted the importance of family and class in determining a child's success at school.

In 1962, B. Jackson and D. Marsden published their study, *Education and the Working Class*, of eighty-eight working class children in Huddersfield who had been educated at grammar school, and found that how a child ultimately performs at school is influenced greatly by home background.

Jackson and Marsden showed that working class children start school disadvantaged and this disadvantage normally continues. The middle class advantages often include:

1 A greater concern with education on the part of parents.
2 The speech patterns at home and the availability of books improve the child's vocabulary.
3 The expected behaviour and speech used in school are of the middle class pattern.
4 The parents have greater expectations of the child.
5 Greater likelihood of travel and educational visits.
6 'Deferred gratification' – the expectation that work now will lead to better things later.
7 Facilities for quiet private study and perhaps private lessons.

8 More financial resources and therefore a greater likelihood of further and/or higher education.

Also in 1962 R. Fletcher, in *The Family and Marriage in Britain*, emphasised the importance of the 'educative' functions of the family and suggested that the upbringing of children is now undertaken in a far more considerate and careful fashion than in the past – with the child enjoying high status and increasingly treated as an end in him or herself. 'Throughout the entire period of the child's educational experience, the attitudes of the family, and the facilities offered by the family, are of vital importance.'

In 1964, J. Douglas in *The Home and The School* – a longitudinal study of over 5000 children begun in 1946 – investigated a variety of 'variables' and found that:

1 *Standards of 'care'* were highest in the upper middle class and lowest in the lower manual working class on all indices. (One must however beware the 'halo' effect of middle class researchers. For example, there was no investigation into 'the warmth of relationship'.) However these findings were also borne out by J. and E. Newson in *Patterns of Infant Care in an Urban Community*.

2 Middle class parents generally *take more interest* in their child's progress at school and become relatively more interested as the child grows up. This interest and encouragement resulted in improved scores in tests of school performance and mental ability (first tests at eight, second at eleven). These tests assess attainment and achievement in mainly verbal skills – not innate ability. These findings were born out by M. Young and P. McGeeney, in *Learning Begins at Home*. This stressed the importance of parents and teachers co-operating if children are to get the best out of their education.

3 Children's attitudes and behaviour were influenced by their *environment*. Teachers were asked to place children at the age of ten in categories from 'very hard working' to 'lazy'. This assessment related directly to class position: Hard Workers – 26 per cent upper middle; 17 per cent lower middle; 11 per cent upper manual and 7 per cent lower manual. This was a subjective test, so therefore teachers' own middle class norms, values and attitudes are likely to influence results, but the children will also be influenced by the high educational aspirations of their family, neighbourhood, friends and the local primary school that they attend. Those children not succeeding were more disorderly and restless in class.

4 *Position in the family* influenced ultimate educational attainment. Eldest boys, though not showing superiority in tests, ultimately did better than younger brothers and sisters or only children. (Not found in girls.)

5 *Linguistic development* was influenced by home background. The more children in the family when the child was learning to talk, the lower his score in the eight-year-old vocabulary test. This deficiency was not made up later.

6 Middle class teachers related better to middle class children because there was a common ground and mutual respect between teacher and pupils due to

similar manners, modes of address, and speech – similar values 'hard work', 'achievement' and 'deferred gratification'.

7 The *primary school* which the child had attended influenced the development of the child. Probably the 'neighbourhood' and the consequent degree of support, encouragement and co-operation from parents accounted for this result.

Douglas concludes that 'perceptive' and 'sympathetic' parents in the early years of a child's life give 'background' and 'meaning' to what is learned.

In 1976 S. Sharpe, in *Just Like a Girl*, emphasised the importance of the family in establishing sex roles particularly in the case of boys.

S. Cotgrove, in *Technical Education and Social Change*, which although published in 1958 is still relevant in Britain today, demonstrated that children from middle class homes benefit from parental encouragement in several ways but in particular from the guidance which their parents are able to give about careers, interesting courses, or educational alternatives. The cultural background of many children, however, deprives them of this guidance, as their parents have no experience of higher education, no friends with such experience, and often a suspicion that it is of 'no use' to them anyway.

Two Government reports emphasise the importance of home background and parental influence on the educational development of children.

Half Our Future, published in 1963, illustrated the connection between poor environment and poor school performance.

The Plowden Report, *Children and their Primary School*, published in 1967, traced the link between parents' attitudes and school performance:

1 Manual workers helped their children less with homework, either from lack of ability, tiredness of lack of interest;
2 Manual workers were less likely to buy children copies of schoolbooks for use at home;
3 Two-thirds of unskilled workers had five books or less at home (apart from magazines and children's books); this compared with only one in twenty of professional workers having so few books.

This report also reported on the disabilities suffered by children in overcrowded or shared homes and stressed the need to give early help to handicapped children and those with handicapped parents. It also urged 'positive discrimination' to make schools in deprived areas better then those elsewhere. A move was made in this direction in 1968 when 'social priority area' schools were introduced; teachers in these schools were given a special allowance and the schools some additional finance for equipment. The criteria used to determine which schools were 'social priority' varied but one typical Local Education Authority (LEA) decided levels of deprivation on the basis of how many children in any school were from large families, one-parent families, immigrant families or in receipt of free school meals, this last factor receiving a double weighting. However, doubts on the effectiveness of the scheme in attracting better staff to the most deprived schools led to the termination of the programme.

In 1972 R. Davie, N. Butler and H. Goldstein published From *Birth to Seven*, which was the result of a survey carried out for the National Children's Bureau of 13,000 children born during one week of 1958. This report showed consistently lower educational performances by children from working class homes (a direct correlation between oral ability and social class was found, except that marginally more children from Social Class 2 had below-average oral ability compared with Social Class 3; the biggest divide was between manual and non-manual workers' families).

Children from Social Class 5 were six times more likely to be poor readers at the age of seven compared with those from Social Class 1; and the same children fifteen times more likely to be non-readers.

Colin Lacey, in *Hightown Grammar* (1970), found that children split into two groups – one accepting the school culture and the other the 'alternative culture' (which might range from supporters of rock music in a public school to a delinquent 'subculture' in an urban comprehensive school).

Teachers first assist the groups to develop by ranking the students by a set of criteria based on an academically oriented value system and then repress the 'anti-group' which does not, or cannot, aspire to these norms.

N. Carter in *In to Work* (1966) described this process of separation. The groups taking exams have clear targets at which to aim and the work, even if it seems overburdening at times, can be seen to have a purpose. In other groups, however, problems tend to occur through boredom, frustration and, occasionally, aggression. Careers guidance is most difficult in these circumstances. Thus many youngsters, without advice from their parents, tend to drift into jobs knowing very little about the work and less about its prospects.

The middle class parents are able to show their children a range of careers, and research shows that they frequently advise their youngsters and discuss career prospects with them either directly or by calling on the assistance of family friends or professional associates. Similarly, the language skills which these youngsters have developed enable them to discuss with others the advantage of differing career structures and they also perform better in interviews with careers teachers, advisers and potential employers.

Various other studies also emphasise the close connection between home, socialisation and academic success:

1 In 1984 a middle class child was six times more likely than a working class child to go to University. This was the last date such figures were collected through UCCA (the Universities admission board), and appeared to show that 80 per cent of students admitted into Universities were middle class, while only 20 per cent were working class. M. Rudd (*Higher Education Review*, 1984), disputed the accuracy of these figures as they were based on the applicants' own statement of fathers' occupations; his view was that the true proportion of working class undergraduates was nearer one-third. What is certain is that there remains a huge class disparity in access to higher education, despite the growth of opportunities since 1984. In 1993 the Commission of Social Justice noted that 'only 1 per cent of women whose fathers are from Social Class V hold an undergraduate degree, compared with 41 per cent with fathers from Social Class 1. In 2000 a report by Peter Lampl for the Sutton Trust pointed out

that students are about twenty-five times more likely to get into a top thirteen university if they go to a public school than if they come from a lower social class. Pupils among the less affluent social classes account for 50 per cent of the population but only 13 per cent of entry to the top universities.

2 About half of what we learn is probably learned before the age of four.

3 The less formal 'discovery' method of teaching now popular in primary schools probably acts against the working class child who often has not had a home background which encourages the self-motivation required.

4 In the Summer 'A' Levels in 2000 girls outperformed boys for the first time in the exam's 49-year history. Girls passed more 'A' Levels than boys and passed them on average at a higher level (girls 51,600 Grade A's : boys 45,000 Grade A's) (Table 8.2).

5 The Robbins Report (Report of the Committee on Higher Education, 1963): 'The proportion of children reaching full-time higher education is 8 times higher among children whose father left education at 18 or over than among those whose father left school under 16.'

6 'The less bright in the upper streams tend to make most progress, the most bright in the lower streams will deteriorate most. Streaming is based on "ability" and the judgment of ability may be influenced by the types of homes the children come from' (Douglas, *The Unconscious Biases of Selection*).

7 M. Schofield, in discussing the reason for the ineffectiveness of sex education in *The Sexual Behaviour of Young People* (1964), comments: 'In fact there is some evidence to suggest that education of all kinds is not the powerful force for social or individual change that we think it is.'

8 G. Peaker studied some of the children seen for the Plowden Report (*Plowden Children Four Years Later*, 1971) and estimated that the influence of teaching is only about one-third that of home circumstances.

9 A. Little in 1971 ('A Sociological Portrait: Education', in *New Society*) commented that the difference between a good and a bad home is far greater than the difference between good and bad teaching.

It would appear that the problems inherent in the influence of the home environment can effectively nullify any attempt to increase opportunities by changes in school organisations.

The link between educational achievement remains strong, as illustrated in Table 8.1 – of the sample population aged between twenty-five and fifty-nine only 3 per cent of these with unskilled fathers possessed degrees and 60 per cent of this category had no qualifications at all.

By 2000 there was increasing concern in respect of the underachievement of boys. Dr Mary James of Cambridge University said that part of the blame lay with laddish magazines that encouraged boys to confirm to an anti-work culture.

8.4 Gender, peer and ethnic group

Just as parents' expectations and attitudes and, later, teachers' expectations and attitudes, can be crucial in deciding the educational achievement of those from

Table 8.1 Highest qualification held[1], by gender and ethnic group, 1997–8 (Great Britain, per cent)

	Degree or equivalent	Higher education qualification[2]	GCE A level or equivalent[4]	GCSE grades A* to C or equivalent	Other qualification	No qualification	All
Males							
Indian/Pakistani/Bangladeshi	18	5	16	14	25	22	100
Black	14	6	22	18	24	16	100
White	14	8	32	18	14	15	100
Other groups[3]	20	5	17	15	27	15	100
Females							
Indian/Pakistani/Bangladeshi	9	5	11	18	25	33	100
Black	9	12	14	27	22	16	100
White	11	9	16	29	15	20	100
Other groups[3]	12	8	15	17	33	15	100

Notes:
[1] Men aged 16 to 64, women aged 16 to 59.
[2] Below degree level.
[3] Includes those who did not state their ethnic group.
[4] In the Summer 'A' levels in 2000 girls outperformed boys for the first time in the exam's 49-year history. Girls passed more 'A' levels than boys and passed them on average at a higher level (girls 51,600 Grade As: boys 45,000 Grade As.)
Source: Social Trends, 29 National Statistics © Crown Copyright 1999.

differing class groups, so, too, can these expectations and attitudes influence differential achievement between boys and girls and between young people from different ethnic groups.

The academic performance of girls, as measured by public examination, has consistently improved since 1972, when the school-leaving age was increased to sixteen, when the number of boys leaving school with at least one 'O' Level increased by almost 50 per cent to 201,000, while the number of girls similarly qualified went up by 60 per cent to 212,000.

There is evidence that teachers expect girls to be more passive and compliant, and girls tend to accept this label and think it natural for boys to ask questions, challenge the teacher and demand explanations (Michelle Stanworth, *Gender and Schooling*, 1983).

Many of the disabilities of the native English working class relate also to the members of **ethnic minorities** (particularly West Indians), but their disadvantage is compounded by colour prejudice and – for some in the Asian community – language problems, although most young Asians have now been in Britain and do not have this problem (see table 8.1). In 1997–8 15 per cent of men from the white group in Great Britain held no qualification compared with 22 per cent of men from the Indian and Pakistani/Bangladeshi groups. The corresponding figures for women were 20 per cent and 33 per cent, repectively. However, Indian and Pakistani/Bangladeshi men were more likely than either white or black men to have a degree.

Among some black teenagers there may be some alienation from the educational system, not only because many fail to achieve within it, but also because they have seen those among them who do succeed fail to get jobs in line with their qualifications. The government-sponsored Rampton Report in 1981 showed that black children suffered at school from racism, inappropriate curricula, language difficulties and poor relations with teachers. Mirza (*Young, Female and Black*, 1992) has pointed out that grouping all 'ethnic minority' students together can paint a misleading picture; she argues that young black women have aspirations and achievements distinctive from young black men and young white women: this has often been ignored as research into race and education has focused almost exclusively on boys.

However, by 1992 the gap in achievement was narrowing. A study commissioned by the School Examinations and Assessment Council (SEAC), found that 10 per cent of black seven-year-olds gained the top grade in mathematics in the new classroom tests and 19 per cent did so in science; this compared with 6 per cent and 18 per cent, respectively, for whites. Similarly, girls performed better than boys in the same tests. A total of 84 per cent of girls reached or bettered the expected standard at writing compared with 73 per cent of boys, although they were only 3 per cent better in maths and 1 per cent better in science. Girls' performances at GCSE and A Level are now better than those of boys (see Table 8.2).

Boys' underachievement is usually seen as a working class and ethnic minority problem; but research funded by the Economic and Social Research Council and beginning in the early 1980s followed a group of 347 young men and women from private schools in a longitudinal study. All members of the group were identified as academically able at the age of eleven, but the study found that relative underachievement of males was as marked among these independent school products as elsewhere; 99 per cent of the women gained at least two A levels; 92 per cent gained degrees and 12 per cent higher degrees; the equivalent percentages for the men were 89, 73 and 9, respectively.

The researchers suggested that the boys' relative underachievement was a result of a complex mix of family, school and peer-group factors (Schoolboys and schoolwork: Gender Identification and Academic Achievement, Sally Power, University of Bristol, 1998).

Year 2000 – girls overtake boys at 'A' level for the first time: How the papers reported the news and proposed the possible reasons on Friday, 18 August 2000.

Table 8.2   Boys and girls at A Level, 2000

Paper	Reasons suggested (see below)	Coverage
Express	1, 2	Article on editorial page, 'keeping the issue in perspective'.
Guardian	2, 3, 6, 9, 10	Two-page feature, 'Boys in no-man's land', with cartoon
Independent	1, 7	Reference in general A Level results article
Mail	Nil*	Cartoon, several A Level stories but no gender references
Star	Nil	Nil
Sun	Nil	Mid-page article on A Levels but no gender reference
Telegraph	1, 2, 3, 4, 5, 6, 7, 8	Lead story, full-page feature 'Girl power leaves lads lagging behind', Editorial
Times	1, 7	Lead article, 'Are girls really in a class of their own' with cartoon warning not to overstate the position – girls 54% boys 46% of passes

Note:
* No references to A Level results.

1   'Lad' culture (Macho-anti-school culture), including 'laddish' magazines
2   Role model absence (particularly in primary school)
3   Peer pressure (fear of rilicule, bullying, fear of failure)
4   Girl power ('girls throwing their weight about')
5   Images of incompetent men (portrayed as idiots or lager louts on T.V. and in adverts)
6   Feminisation of society (caring, sharing and participatory)
7   Changing nature of examinations (sustained tasks such as coursework – boys prefer competitive 'sudden death' examinations)
8   Girls more attentive and willing to learn
9   Lack of macho manual jobs (changing nature of employment with resultant uncertainly)
10   Boys not prepared to compromise masculinity (by coming second to a girl)

Girls on top: 1

(*Guardian*, 18 August 2000)

Girls on top: 2

'To save you wasting any more time working out if you've passed – that's the gas bill'

(*Daily Mail*, 18 August 2000)

The influence of the peer group increases as the child becomes a young adult and seeks to find an identity and status away from the home, and naturally many of those of the same age who will influence the young person will be met at school. If the values and attitudes of the neighbourhood are antagonistic towards education, these are likely to be the values and attitudes of the peer group and an individual young person will find it hard to resist adopting the same approach.

Forget gender, class is still the real divide

Yet another simplistic, statistical interpretation of gender differences in examination results makes the national news: 'Boys are outperformed by girls in GCSEs.' As a result the Government wants all education authorities to take action in raising the academic performance of boys.

But beware: simplistic statistical analyses are dangerously misleading. We do not have a hierarchy in which girls are positioned in the top 50 per cent and boys in the bottom 50 per cent at GCSE. It is social class, not gender or race differences, which continues to have the single most important influence on educational attainment in Britain.

Fifteen years of Conservative education reforms and funding policies have demonstrated that, try though you might, social structure cannot be divorced from educational standards . . .

The majority of boys and girls from socially advantaged families do much better in all subjects at GCSE than the majority of girls from socially disadvantaged families. Similarly, girls' schools holding the top places in GCSE tables have proportionately few socially disadvantaged pupils . . .

While, overall, girls do out-perform boys at GCSE – working-class girls do marginally better than working-class boys in public examinations – the difference is not significant enough to reduce class inequalities within gender (or racial) groups. Analyses of external examinations at all ages show working-class underachievement is the real issue. The gap is particularly noticeable post-16.

The sharp increase in the number of young people staying on after 16 helps to disguise that it is those from poorer areas who are still much more likely to leave without qualifications – the staying-on rate can range from 35–78 per cent between local authorities.

Among the working classes higher education remains an exceptional experience.

Schools need to analyse the impact they have on pupils of different gender, race and class backgrounds and focus on those who need support.

(Dr Gillian Plummer, *Times Educational Supplement*, 22 January 1998, adapted)

REVISION SUMMARY

Advantages which middle class children have in education

- A greater concern with education on the part of parents.
- The speech patterns at home and the availability of books improve the child's vocabulary.
- The expected behaviour and speech used in school are of the middle class pattern.
- The parents have greater expectations of the child.
- There is a greater likelihood of travel and educational visits.
- 'Deferred gratification' – the expectation that work now will lead to better things latter.
- There are facilities for quiet private study and perhaps private lessons.

The influence of the school in education

Although the influence of the school is more limited than that of the home, the way that a school is organised and operates does have a considerable impact on educational achievement.

- Language and expectation. This is the language and expectation of teachers and the degree to which this relates to the home. Teachers may expect students with a particular accent or style of dress to behave in a particular way and treat them accordingly.
- Labelling. This can have a crucial influence on students. In 1968 Rosenthal and Jacobson, in *Pygmalion in the Classroom*, described a test given to students in a Californian school. The researchers told teachers that certain pupils had been identified who would improve dramatically academically; in fact, these pupils had been chosen at random and were no different from others. Without being aware of the fact, teachers started to treat the pupils identified in a different way; the pupils reacted to teachers' expectations by acting in the expected way. Within a few months the identified pupils had improved dramatically compared with others (a self-fulfilling prophecy).
- Streaming and setting. The theory is that children quickly learn what is expected of their stream and conform to the mould. In the top stream they are expected to be clever, and so become clever. In the bottom stream they are expected to be dunces, and so become dunces. The process may then be reinforced by what amounts to streaming the teachers: giving the best teachers and the best facilities to the top stream.

Functions of formal education

Culture transmission

This passes on the norms and values of the society, but these will be the values of the dominant group. Culture clash may occur when home and school/peer group and school have different norms and values – this will often lead to the rejection of school and other means of gaining status being sought, sometimes leading to delinquent activities.

Training

Training for work prepares young people for work in a complex advanced society, but it has been suggested that this may entail preparing certain groups to accept unpleasant low-status jobs.

Social selection

This sorts out who has the ability to perform certain functions in society to ensure the best use of available talent. However, this might be (a) merely a legitimisation of the status quo, i.e. providing a justification for the best jobs to go to children of those already in high-status positions; (b) a way to simplify selection procedures, i.e. 5 GCSEs might be required for a job where they are unnecessary, to cut down the number of eligible applicants.

Social control

This teaches acceptable behaviour in order to ensure that the society runs smoothly and pleasantly for everyone, but one obvious function of schools and colleges is custodial – i.e. to keep young people out of the way because there is nothing that they can be employed to do in a complex advanced industrial society. It is suggested that another function is to ensure that they learn to accept their position in society through the hidden curriculum – this is what is taught in schools without being officially recognised.

SELF-TEST QUESTIONS: PART THREE

Self-test 3.1

1 What term is used to describe the process by which the norms and values of our society are acquired? (*1 mark*)
2 What sociological term is used to describe something that becomes true because it is expected to become true? (*1 mark*)
3 What is meant by the tripartite system? (*2 marks*)
4 What terms are used to describe the placing of students in groups according to ability? (*2 marks*)

5   What major factors may be responsible for the development of a child's intelligence? *(2 marks)*
6   State three characteristics which may be part of a 'culture'. *(3 marks)*
7   What reasons might be given to explain the apparently increasing importance of youth culture in our society? *(3 marks)*
8   What functions does formal education, i.e. education in schools and colleges, perform? *(3 marks)*
9   Is the comprehensive system the most effective method of state secondary education organisation? *(4 marks)*
10   In what ways may the home influence the child's success within the education system? *(4 marks)*

(Total 25 marks)

Self-test 3.2

Losing out

Girls in the single-sex school are most career-oriented and the presence of boys as a disturbing factor does not apply. We have seen that class is also important. Middle-class girls are more likely to be career-oriented and working-class girls more likely to be already involved in domestic chores at the expense of school and homework. The girls are very conscious of class as manifested by accent and life style. A middle-class girl says: 'I think there's too much class. Everyone's sort of classed as "Oh we're snobs." They always think of us as snobs. Very much your accent I think.' Class divisions in behaviour and leisure time activities are reproduced in the school:

'When we arrived at this school the middle class were doing the same thing as the other middle class and the lower class as the other lower class. The middle class go out to classical concerts with their parents. You have to make friends from where your own interests are and when you're young your interests are what your parents' interests are so they sort of depend on class 'cos you sort of go along with your parents.'

In 1970 Ronald King researched the impact of class and gender on educational achievement in state schools and reported that middle-class boys were the most advantaged and working-class girls the most disadvantaged, the former having twenty-one times more chance of taking a full-time degree course than the latter. He discovered that the class gap (ratio of middle class to working class) rose as the educational level rose. At each educational level the sex gap increased (King, 1981).

But irrespective of class there is the overpowering pressure of gender stereotypes which acts on all girls.

Some of the girls in Mandy Llewellyn's study talked about girls who wanted a career very much in the same way as we have seen girls talk about one another as slags throughout this study:

Likewise the non-exam girls perceived the top-stream girls as 'clever', 'snotty', 'keenos', 'stuck up', but also: 'Exams won't get them nowhere, they'll be out with their prams next year – if anyone'll have 'em.' 'You see they way they dress? – wouldn't be seen dead like that.' 'Taint never seen them with a lad' (Llewellyn, 1980).

On one level these assumptions about adolescence are right – delinquency, drug addiction and violence are greater then than later. Yet what characterises the behaviour of most teenagers far more than their turbulence is their conformity, conformity to a patriarchal sexist society in which both sexes lose out. The boys, who are prepared like boxers for a fight to earn their living, find a wife to provide them with a family, yet retain their sexual and social freedom; the girls, even today, are prepared for a life centred on domesticity and motherhood, any career aspirations or personal ambition or freedom holding second place to the ideal of finding the man of their dreams.

I was interested in adolescence not as a period of turbulence – the girls I interviewed described few disagreements with their parents and particularly close relationships with their mothers – but as a process of conformity and transition into adult life. In particular I was interested in how girls become wives and mothers.

(Sue Lees, Losing Out, London, Hutchinson, 1986)

1 According to the passage, which group was identified as the most educationally disadvantaged in a research study? (*1 mark*)
2 According to the above information, why is class important in the education system? (*2 marks*)
3 Social class is a possible basis for school peer groups. Give three other bases for the formation of school peer groups. (*3 marks*)
4 Identify and explain three reasons, other than the influence of the peer group, why the working-class child may have more difficulty fitting into school than will the middle-class child. (*6 marks*)
5 Does a 'youth culture' exist in the UK? (*8 marks*)

Self-test 3.3

According to the information in Table 8.1 (p. 105)

1 Which of the groups listed was most likely to leave school with no qualification?
2 According to the above information, were girls or boys more successful in achieving:
   (i) GCSE grades A* to C or equivalent (*1 mark*)
   (ii) GCE A Level or equivalent (*1 mark*)

SPECIMEN QUESTIONS AND ANSWERS

Social stratification and inequality

(*Daily Telegraph*, 1997)

1 Identify three factors which might account for the fact that public school pupils are more likely than state school pupils to come to occupy high status positions in society. (*3 marks*)

2 Identify and explain three ways in which teachers may influence their pupils' educational achievement. (*6 marks*)

3 Examine why, in industrial societies, everyone has to go to school. (*8 marks*)

Answers

1 (Note that only three marks are awarded for this question – less than for the two following – so limit your responses to a few sentences; it would be possible to write an essay of considerable length on this question, obviously this is not expected or more marks would be awarded.)

1 mark for any three from the following:
- Self-perpetuating élite, i.e. those selecting from job applicants are likely to select those from similar backgrounds to themselves (consciously or unconsciously).
- Public school norms and values reflect those of the homes from whom pupils are drawn – which in turn reflect the norms and values expected among leaders in the general society (increasingly less likely) – including deferred gratification.
- Contacts made in school and family (the 'old school tie').
- Public school entrants are more likely to gain entry to the top universities from whom a majority of potential leaders are likely to be drawn.
- Any answer which deals with deference and/or snobbery or any perception that public school products are more likely to be acceptable to clients.
- Any answer which deals with the nature of public school teaching and/or the nature of boarding school education (e.g. smaller class size, better teaching, more discipline, supervised 'homework', greater self-reliance, etc. and the likely outcomes of these, in terms of improved examination performance, self-reliance, etc.

2 Teachers influence their pupils' educational achievement in several ways – they may expect a pupil to do badly because of the pupil's colour or because he or she speaks with a working class accent or does not conform to school rules on uniform. Once the teacher has 'labelled' a pupil as a failure or success (even subconsciously), the teacher is likely to treat the pupil in a way that will result in the pupil reacting appropriately and make the 'label' correct.

The teacher is middle class and will speak in a middle class way – what Bernstein called the 'elaborated' code. Working class children are likely to have used the 'restricted' code at home and are not as familiar with the formal language of the teacher as are middle class pupils. The working class pupil will not understand as fully as will the middle class pupil and will not do so well.

Pupils may also be 'labelled' by streaming or setting by teachers. Once a child is put in a high or low stream, he or she is likely to accept this estimation of academic ability and behave accordingly: a 'self-fulfilling prophecy' comes into operation.

(Note: As with Question 1, there are several other possibilities, including the kind of relationship which teachers establish with pupils, or the professional ability of the teacher. Make sure your answer relates to teachers as required by the question. Remember to identify how and explain the reason why teachers influence pupils.)

3 In industrial societies everyone has to go to school, because the increasing complexity of the technology and the sophistication of the communication system make it necessary for everyone to be able to read and write and preferably develop other skills, perhaps in computer technology, which will assist the economy of the society.

In fact, everyone does not have to go to school in the United Kingdom, but the law demands that they receive a satisfactory standard of education: in practice this usually means that everyone (except the rich, who might be able to afford private tutors) does go to school. It is inconvenient in a large bureaucratic system, such as a modern state, for people to behave in an unconventional way, and the law on school attendance is rigidly enforced (to opt out of the school system involves a lot of effort and argument, usually within the legal system).

School helps to ration the amount of available work by taking a group of the population out of the market. It also provides a safe and secure environment where young people are out of danger and not a nuisance to society generally. This is called the 'custodial function' of education.

As well as training for work and assisting in the selection of candidates for employment through the examination system, schools, it is argued by Marxists and others, prepare people for their place in society through the 'hidden curriculum': this is what is learnt in school without being overtly taught – respect for authority, obedience without question, toleration of boredom and the acceptance of a lowly place in an hierarchial structure.

(Note: With only 8 marks available, time is clearly limited. Do not overelaborate individual points but try to cover the demands of the question – ensure that you deal with apparently 'obvious' points, e.g. the legal position with regard to school attendance. You will gain some marks for these, but also look for the more sophisticated points you may have learnt on the topic, e.g. the Marxist 'conflict theory' of education, these are likely to be the points which score most marks. Incidentally, one sociologist, Syncler, has suggested that part of the 'hidden curriculum' is how to gain most credit with the least amount of effort!)

Part Four

Social differentiation

■ Ṁ **9** Stratification

9.1 Age stratification

Status may be based on sex

'In my day we *called* them ladies and *treated* them like women.'

In virtually all societies some people are regarded as more important than others; more worthy of respect or more useful than others either within the society as a whole or in certain situations. This position relative to that of other people in the group is called '**status**' and may be based on many factors such as wealth, heredity, possessions, sex, education, skin colour, job, 'social worth' or age. This 'prestige' may also depend on particular abilities regarded as of high worth within the group so that some young people will deliberately spend many hours becoming expert in pop-music so as to earn high status with their peers.

Status may not always be consistent. For example, a person may have high status by reason of occupation but a low status by reason of colour. Nor will everyone necessarily agree with the status ranking. For example, one study (M. Young and P. Willmott, *Family and Kinship in East London*, 1957) found that about a quarter of those interviewed put skilled manual jobs in a higher status position than routine non-manual.

Status may be '**ascribed**', that is, acquired with no effort on our part; we may have ascribed status as a nobleman or parent. We may also earn our status by acquiring a high-ranking job or by earning a reputation for caring for others, in which case our status is '**achieved**'.

Increasing educational opportunities and changes in the structure of employment has widened opportunities to enhance achieved status over the past fifty years. Ascribed status positions are also in the process of change, for example deference to those with titles is less likely. Sometimes we may have high status in one group and low status in another; we may have the 'achieved' status of a football hooligan and our violent behaviour may give us high status among other football hooligans but a very low status in the view of the majority of the population, which may in turn affect our employment prospects and other situations where it is important that people estimate us highly.

The most basic way of placing people in layers by their worth ('**stratification**') is by age. In most societies younger people are not regarded as worthy of as much respect as older people because their knowledge and skill is less. Young people have less responsibility and as a result less power; in some societies the oldest people have most power ('**gerontocracies**').

In our society the old, during the latter part of the twentieth century as non-producers and often poor, lacked power and as a result lost status; this loss of status appeared to increase in recent years as the extended family has lost many of its functions and the old became increasingly isolated.

The young, on the other hand, often had a greater surplus of income over expenditure on necessities compared with their parents (section 6.4); work skills were no longer usually learned at home; parents were often ignorant of subjects taught at school; the traditional scorn of the old for the ignorant young was often reversed.

However by 2000 the term 'grey power' had been coined because the increasing number of retired people in the ageing population made their vote increasingly important to politicians and because many had paid off mortgages, no longer had dependent children and with earnings related pensions they had surplus income which made them an increasingly attractive target market for suppliers and their advertisers – rather as the 'teenager' had become in the 1950s and 1960s (see p. 81).

Tribes

In every society, age is used as a basis for treating individuals differently. In western cultures, we limit certain activities, such as drinking alcohol, to those over a certain age. Becoming legally an adult depends on reaching a certain age.

In a large number of traditional societies, the moving from one age status to another is marked by various ceremonies, known as rites of passage. Moving from the status of a child to that of an adult is very important. It must be marked by traditional rites. These clearly announce the new status of individuals within the society. There are, of course, many examples of rites of passage to be found in modern industrial societies. We pass through various age-related status positions, such as youth, middle age and old age. At each point, we form bonds with others of a similar age. For example, teenagers form bonds with other teenagers and some young people join youth cultures.

In traditional societies, age is even more important. Among the **Nuer** people of East Africa, the status of any male depends entirely on the age set to which he belongs. Throughout his life, every **Nuer** man remains a member of the group of men with whom he was initiated into adulthood. He is always junior to those who became adult members of the society before him and senior to those who followed him.

The age set system is very important. It provides a way of sharing out authority and work. It gives both the young and old clearly defined roles, according to their age. The young men act together in defence of their tribe. Political decision-making is left to their elders, whose physical capabilities no longer allow them to take such an active part in society. It is also a way of providing status, because getting older is the main way of gaining status. In traditional societies, the elderly usually have a much higher status than do the elderly in modern industrial societies.

(D. Morris and P. Marsh, Tribes, 1988, adapted)

9.2 Feudalism

Apart from age most societies have some form of general stratification placing certain groups of people in superior and inferior positions, a 'hierarchy', of prestige and power. Most societies can be classified into one of three major types of stratification:

(a) feudal (or 'estate')
(b) caste
(c) social class.

The three 'estates' were nobility, church and townspeople, each with their own status systems; the peasants were sometimes regarded as a fourth estate.

The best known example of the feudal system was in mediaeval Europe where there was a pyramid of interlocking obligations between 'lord' and 'vassal' based upon the grant of a 'fief', which was usually land but could be an office or a means of collecting revenue such as the right to collect a 'toll'. In return for this fief and for protection the vassal accepted, there were certain obligations: to fight for his lord; accept the judgement of the lord's court; and pay his lord certain sums on particular occasions.

Essentially the idea of feudalism was one of 'tenancy'. Everyone was a tenant to a lord higher than themselves until one came to the King and he was tenant of God. As only God was the King's master only God had a right to overthrow him, thus we had the concept of 'the divine right of kings'.

Although feudalism did not always exactly follow the idea of a pyramid structure (Figure 9.1) – for example, a Knight might hold land directly from the

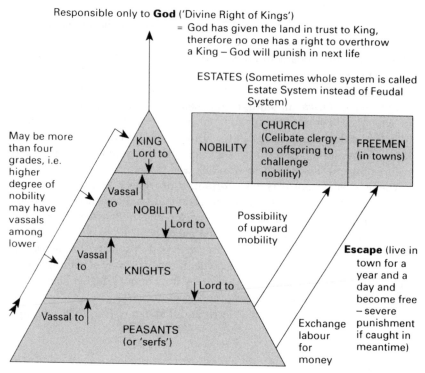

Responsible only to **God** ('Divine Right of Kings')
= God has given the land in trust to King,
therefore no one has a right to overthrow
a King – God will punish in next life

ESTATES (Sometimes whole system is called
Estate System instead of Feudal
System)

May be more
than four
grades, i.e.
higher
degree of
nobility
may have
vassals
among
lower

KING
Lord to

Vassal
to
NOBILITY
↓Lord to

Vassal
to
KNIGHTS
↓Lord to

Vassal to↑
PEASANTS
(or 'serfs')

NOBILITY

CHURCH
(Celibate clergy –
no offspring to
challenge
nobility)

FREEMEN
(in towns)

Possibility
of upward
mobility

Escape (live in
town for a
year and a
day and
become free
– severe
punishment
if caught in
meantime)

Exchange
labour
for
money

Figure 9.1   The feudal pyramid

King rather than from a Baron – it gave each individual a fixed place in a hierarchy which could be changed only by providing an outstanding service to one higher than oneself. Usually marriage took place to others from the same position in the social hierarchy as oneself. Escape from one's social situation was usually possible only by removing oneself from the service contract of rights and duties. Social mobility could however also take place by joining the church, which was open to people of any rank, and churchmen could reach high-status positions both in the church itself and as civil servants. However in Western Europe the clergy were celibate and so the social mobility of clerics was for one generation only and did not challenge the established order.

One of the few methods of escaping from the feudal situation was to move to a town, where work could be exchanged for money. It was the growth of towns, increasing circulation of money, political centralisation and professional courts that led to the ending of feudalism in Europe.

9.3 Caste

A **caste system** of stratification does not rest as a feudal system does on man-made laws, which can be modified. It is based on a system of religious belief that cannot be changed and it is therefore even more rigid than the feudal system.

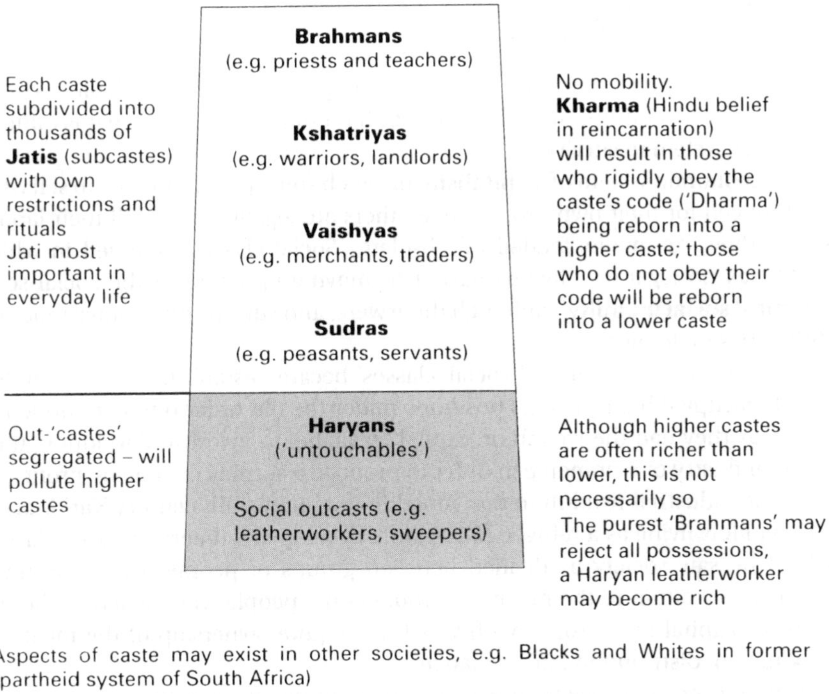

Brahmans
(e.g. priests and teachers)

Kshatriyas
(e.g. warriors, landlords)

Vaishyas
(e.g. merchants, traders)

Sudras
(e.g. peasants, servants)

Haryans
('untouchables')

Social outcasts (e.g. leatherworkers, sweepers)

Each caste subdivided into thousands of **Jatis** (subcastes) with own restrictions and rituals
Jati most important in everyday life

Out-'castes' segregated – will pollute higher castes

No mobility.
Kharma (Hindu belief in reincarnation) will result in those who rigidly obey the caste's code ('Dharma') being reborn into a higher caste; those who do not obey their code will be reborn into a lower caste

Although higher castes are often richer than lower, this is not necessarily so
The purest 'Brahmans' may reject all possessions, a Haryan leatherworker may become rich

(Aspects of caste may exist in other societies, e.g. Blacks and Whites in former Apartheid system of South Africa)

Figure 9.2 The Hindu caste system

The best example of caste is the Hindu caste system of India (Figure 9.2) which has existed for some 3000 years and was officially abolished only in 1947. The restrictions on social mobility imposed by the system are still very much in evidence. Hindus belong to one of four main groups, the Kshatriyas (warriors), Brahmans (priests), Vaishyas (traders and manufacturers), and the Sudras (servants) or they are 'outcasts' doing the most lowly work, or that associated with leather, from the sacred cow. Each group has a rigid status position, and within the main groups are many castes and subcastes each of which occupies a fixed position in the social structure. The 1901 Census identified 2378 main castes, and 1700 subcastes within just one of these main castes!

Status does not depend primarily upon wealth. Brahmans are of high caste though bound by poverty, leatherworkers may be rich. The caste system is based on the Hindu doctrine of reincarnation – good behaviour meriting re-birth into a higher caste – and this gives hope of a better future to those who work within the system (Figure 9.2).

There are strict food laws, and the breaking of these or other caste rules results in ritual pollution and a drop in status. Marriage is 'endogamous', i.e. it must take place within the caste, although within certain limits a woman may move up to her husband's caste on marriage, this being the only form of social mobility permitted.

(Aspects of caste may exist in other societies, e.g. Blacks and Whites in the former Apartheid system of South Africa.)

9.4 Social class

In both caste and feudal systems it is either impossible or very difficult to rise to a higher social stratum, status is 'ascribed'. If merit is to be rewarded it is difficult for either system to survive.

The economic system of '**capitalism**' in which some people are free to sell what is produced for their own profit, while others are legally free to sell their labour where they like, made 'feudalism' obsolete. 'Social classes' emerged in which there was no legal or religious barrier to moving up or down the social scale ('**vertical social mobility**') although there were, and still are, often grave practical difficulties in doing so.

As feudalism died out and social 'classes' became established those families which occupied high-prestige positions under the old order often continued to do so, as they had the wealth or 'capital' available to invest in developing their lands, industry or commerce in order to produce a surplus income or 'profit'.

As the industrial revolution developed in the nineteenth century Karl Marx, a German Jew living as a refugee in England, developed a theory of social class in which he saw society as divided between groups of people with a common identity in relation to the means of production – people who owned or did not own the capital to invest, or with which to acquire ownership of the means of production, distribution and exchange.

Marx did not see society merely as groups of people who were poor, rich or somewhere in the middle. A teacher, a shopkeeper, an owner of a small dress factory and a skilled mechanic might earn the same amount of money but would not belong to the same class.

Marx believed that as industry developed, and large numbers of workers were grouped together, they would realise that they had class interests in common. This '**proletariat**' would rise up against their exploiters and replace them in a society of equals. Class conflict and class-consciousness are essential parts of Marx's theory of class.

Capital and class

The value of every commodity is measured by the labour required for its production. Labour power exists in the form of the living worker who requires a definite amount of means of subsistence for his existence as well as for the maintenance of his family, which ensures the continuance of labour power also after his death. The labour time necessary for producing these means of subsistence represents, therefore, the value of labour power. The capitalist pays this value weekly and purchases for that the use of one week's labour of the worker.

The capitalist now sets his worker to work. In a certain period of time the worker will have performed as much labour as was represented by his weekly wages. Supposing that the weekly wage of a worker represents three workdays, then if the worker begins on Monday, he has by Wednesday evening *replaced* to the capitalist the *full value of the wage paid*. But does he then stop working? Not at all. The capitalist has bought his week's labour and the worker must go on working also during the last three week days. This *surplus labour* of the worker, over and above the time necessary to replace his wages, is the *source of surplus value*, of profit, of the steadily growing increase of capital . . . The day the capitalist extracts from the worker in the long run only as much labour as he paid him in wages, on that day he will shut down his workshop, since indeed his whole profit would come to nought.

Here we have the solution of all those contradictions. The origin of surplus value (of which the capitalists' profit forms an important part) is now quite clear and natural. The value of the labour power is paid for, but this value is far less than that which the capitalist manages to extract from the labour power, and it is just the difference, the *unpaid labour*, which constitutes the share of the capitalist, or, more accurately, of the capitalist class.

It would, however, be absurd to assume that unpaid labour arose only under present conditions where production is carried on by capitalists on the one hand and wage-workers on the other. On the contrary, the oppressed class at all times has had to perform unpaid labour. During the whole long period when slavery was the prevailing form of the organization of labour, the slaves had to perform much more labour than was returned to them in the form of means of subsistence. The same was the case under the rule of serfdom; here in fact the difference stands out palpably between the time during which the peasant works for his own maintenance and the surplus labour for the lord of the manor, precisely because the latter is carried out separately from the former. The form has now been changed, but the substance remains and as long as 'a part of society possesses the monopoly of the means of production, the labourer, free or not free, must add to the working-time necessary for his own maintenance an extra working-time in order to produce the means of subsistence for the owners of the means of production'.

(Karl Marx, Capital, 1, abridged and translated from 3rd edn, Moscow, 1958)

Marx died in 1883, and another German Max Weber developed a rather different theory of class in the early twentieth century. By this time it was clear that the class in the middle of the capitalists and proletariat had not disappeared as Marx had anticipated, but had grown in number and importance, while trade unions and Parliament had stopped some of the worst exploitation in industry.

Weber thought that the most important aspect of class was a person's ability to gain access to 'life chances' – that is, goods and services. Although he identified four main classes – manual workers, petty bourgeoisie, professionals and property owners – Weber did not think of a polarised society as did Marx, but one where there were many status rankings and power groupings. Usually a person with power also had status but it was not always so.

Today there is still support for Marx's theory, but more generally the word 'class' is used more in the way that Weber used it. The main access to life chances is through occupation, and this has become a major way of dividing people into class (or '**socio-economic**') groupings.

The scale used by the government in the census until 2001 is often called the Registrar-General's scale (Figure 9.3), as it grew out of the original Registrar-General's classification. It may be used for individuals in many contexts, but the 'census' has been based on the occupation of the 'head of the household' (usually a man where the household is that of a married couple). However a government review of social classifications was published in a report during November 1988 and this reflected the fact that the existing classification had become increasingly dated. As a result of this 'social class' and 'socio-economic group' are replaced by the new 'National Statistics Socio Economic Classification (NS-SEC)', which is based on occupation, employment status and size of the establishment:

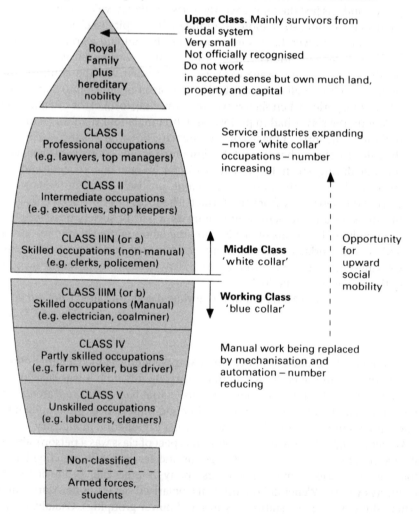

Figure 9.3 The Registrar-General's scale

NATIONAL STATISTICS SOCIO-ECONOMIC CLASSIFICATION
(as based on standard Occupational Classification, 2000)

This classification was used for the first time in the census of 2001; although the former 'Registrar General' scale will continue to be used for some other purposes for a number of years. (it is also necessary to know the Registrar-General's scale in order to understand official statistics collected prior to 2001, including comparisons with census data from the past.)

'The version of the classification, which will be used for most analyses (the analytic version), has eight classes, the first of which can be subdivided.
  The National Statistics Socio-economic Classification

1 Higher managerial and professional occupations
   1.1 Large employers and higher managerial occupations
   1.2 Higher professional occupations
2 Lower managerial and professional occupations
3 Intermediate occupations
4 Small employers and own account workers
5 Lower supervisory and technical occupations
6 Semi-routine occupations
7 Routine occupations
8 Never worked and long-term unemployed

For complete coverage, the three categories Students, Occupations not stated or inadequately described, and Not classifiable for other reasons are added as "Not classified".'

Examples of jobs in the NS-SEC Analytic Classes

1 Higher managerial and professional occupations
   Doctors
   Lawyers
   Dentists
   Professors
   Professional engineers
2 Lower managerial and professional occupations
   School teachers
   Nurses
   Journalists
   Actors
   Police sergeants
3 Intermediate occupations
   Airline cabin crew
   Secretaries
   Photographers
   Firemen
   Auxiliary nurses

4   Small employers and own account workers
    Non-professionals with fewer than 25 employees
        Self-employed builders
        Self-employed hairdressers
        Self-employed fishermen
        Self-employed car dealers
        Shopkeeper – owns own shop
5   Lower supervisory and technical occupations
    Train drivers
    Plumbers – employed
    Electricians – employed
    Foremen
    Supervisors
6   Semi-routine occupations
    Shop assistants
    Postmen
    Security guards
    Call centre workers
7   Routine occupations
    Bus drivers
    Waitresses
    Cleaners
    Car park attendants
    Refuse collectors

Note: This is a simplification – see 'Upwardly mobile Britain splits into 17 new classes' on pages 129 to 131 and/or visit website: <www.statistics.gov.UK/methods_quality/ns_sec>. Even before the Government introduced the new classification system, several attempts had been made to produce a more sophisticated scale. One often used is the Hall–Jones scale which splits Social Class III of the 'Registrar General's' scale into three separate classes. This is because more than half the population are in Social Class III and the division between 'working class' (IIIb and below) and 'middle class' (IIIa and above) is in that group:

Social Class 1 and 2	(The same as the Registrar-General's Scale)
Social Class 3	Inspectional, supervisory and other non-manual, higher grade
Social Class 4	Inspectional, supervisory and other non-manual, lower grade
Social Class 5	Skilled manual and routine grades of non-manual
Social Class 6	(As Registrar-General's IV)
Social Class 7	(As Registrar-General's V)

One criticism of the Hall–Jones scale is that it gives too high a status to white collar occupations.

Increasingly advertisers and pollsters use a 'social grade' classification. Social grade categories are based on the occupation of the chief income earner of his or her household as follows:

A: Higher managerial, administrative or professional
B: Intermediate managerial, administrative or professional
C1: Supervisory or clerical and junior managerial, administrative or professional
C2: Skilled manual workers
D: Semi and unskilled manual
E: State pensioners or widows (no other earners), casual or lowest grade workers or long-term unemployed

There has been a particular emphasis over recent years on the C2's, as this large group has become the most politically volatile and has been credited as the main factor in winning or losing General Elections as the allegiance of a substantial group within it change.

In Britain, the 'upper class' of landed gentry is too tiny a group to be recognised by most people as a distinct class and there is no special class of very small-scale farmers – 'peasants' – as there is in some other European countries.

Official assessment of a person's class position is not always accepted by the person concerned. Many people place themselves in a higher class position than would the Registrar-General; such placement is known as '**self-assigned class**'.

Upwardly mobile Britain splits into 17 new classes

WE are all middle class now. The government is to redefine Britain's class structure for the first time in nearly 80 years because so many people have joined the ranks of the upwardly mobile middle classes.

Since 1921, statisticians have divided Britain into six classes but the old rankings no longer reflect the social reality, according to research to be published by the government next month.

The rapid growth in the middle class – up from a third of the population in the 1970s to a half today – has forced the government to adopt a new system of classification.

Until now, people have been classified simply by their occupation. But the glut of workers in traditionally middle-class jobs, such as finance and management, has meant that social scientists have had to find an alternative means of dividing up the population. From next month, Britain will be officially segregated into 17 classes.

A modern citizen's social standing will be determined by a range of factors including how highly they are valued by their employer, how many perks they receive and how stable their job is.

'The uncertainty of work and the demise of a job for life have undermined the old classification system that determined status by occupational skill level alone,' said David Rose, Professor of Sociology at the University of Essex and author of the study.

'The new form of classification is based on occupation, size of organisation and the differences in the way employers treat employees.

It takes into account contract, pension rights and other perks such as healthcare and is better suited to the way the world is now.'

Teachers are among the winners in the new system, rising to class three, as are librarians, computer engineers and the police who also jump up the social scale. Nurses, too, have risen to the rank of associate professionals, class four.

Among the losers, however, are shop assistants, who have dropped out of the middle classes, from class three in the old system to class 10. 'People who have been regarded as non-manual workers such as shop assistants have been put in the working class because that is the nature of the job nowadays,' said Rose.

Some remain unchanged, notably those in the elite class one who include the Queen and owners of large companies. Many of those in the professional classes such as lawyers and doctors also retain their status – although they are now judged to be on a par with teachers and the police.

The reclassification also gives the lie to John Major's dream of a 'classless society'. With 17 categories, it is statistically more class-ridden, offering the prospect of creating new – as well as reinforcing traditional – class prejudices.

Emblems of class have changed, however. Where before they were largely to do with where you went to school and which family you were born into, today they are more to do with money, property and what you do.

Research on the difference in earnings between members of the new top and bottom classes who were employed showed that when comparing net weekly earnings, the top class earned over 200% more than the bottom class.

When pensions, health benefits and holidays were taken into account, a typical person in the top class was seven times more affluent than one in the lower class.

New levels have been added to cover the underclass: people who have never worked and the long-term unemployed. The self-employed, who represent 8% of the population, are classified separately for the first time, as are students.

All statistics collected by the government will adopt the new classification, which should be in place in time for the next population census in 2001.

The system is also likely to be adopted by the advertising and market research industries, which still use a six-class ABC1 system of social classification to identify and target consumers. For commercial application, Rose has devised a way of compressing the 17 class categories into a minimum of three groups.

'There has long been a recognition that the ABC1 system no longer accurately reflects society,' said Nick Sparrow, director of ICM, a market research company. 'The system is still used in some areas as it is well known, but its significance has been declining over the past 15 years and there have been many attempts to find alternatives. We await with interest the new government classifications.'

(Cherry Norton, *Sunday Times*, 13 September 1998)

REVISION SUMMARY

Status

Status is a person's social position as defined by others – the person with a high status is regarded as more worthy of respect, is accorded more esteem and has more prestige within the group:

- *Formal status* is prestige which arises automatically from having a certain position in society. A cabinet minister or lawyer has high status; a window cleaner or bus driver low status.
- *Informal status* is gained by individuals because of special talents or skills. A miner may have high status among his peers because he is a reliable and likeable workmate. A skinhead may have high status as a 'nutter' to be feared.
- *Ascribed status* is social position or roles into which you are born – you may have high status through being born into Social Class I or low status because you are black.
- *Achieved status* is status acquired by your own effort or actions. You may be born the illegitimate son of a servant girl (low status) and become Prime Minister (high status) as did Ramsay MacDonald; or you may start off as a peer of the realm and end up a penniless criminal. (It is usually easier to rise than to fall – because those in high-status positions have mechanisms which protect those positions.)

Percentage of population in each social class

(see Tables 9.1 and 9.2)

These 1998 figures are not directly comparable with the actual census figures in Table 9.1. However they do show the considerable differences in the 'social class' structure of men and women of working age when they are regarded individually – this is disguised in the census figures, which are based on the occupation of the 'head of the household'. They also suggest that the trends indicated in the census figures in Table 9.1 are continuing.

Table 9.1   Population and social class, 1931–91

Social class	1931	1971	1991
I	1.8	5.0	6.0
II	12.0	18.2	19.5
III	47.8	50.5	51.3
IV	25.5	18.0	16.9
V	12.9	8.4	5.7

Table 9.2   Population of working age[1]; by gender and social class, Spring 1998 (United Kingdom, per cent)

	Males	Females
Professional	7	2
Intermediate	27	24
Skilled non-manual	11	30
Skilled manual	28	7
Partly skilled	14	16
Unskilled manual	5	5
Other[2]	9	16
All (=100%)(millions)	18.7	17.1

Notes:
[1] Males aged 16 to 64, females aged 16 to 59.
[2] Includes members of the armed forces, those who did not state their current or last occupation, and those who had not worked in the last eight years.
Sources: *Labour Force Survey*, Office for National Statistics; *Social Trends*, 29 National Statistics © Crown Copyright 1999.

■ ⋎ **10** Wealth and income

10.1 Wealth and power

Usually a higher class position means that the person concerned is richer either through earnings or investment – this 'wealth' is the accumulation of money or property in its many forms. Wealth buys access to '**life's chances**': health care; education; housing; holidays. These life chances may thus influence such factors as expectation of life, infant mortality, height and weight of children, illness or school achievement.

Wealth also buys access to power – positions of authority where there can be a direct influence on the decision-making processes whether as company directors or Members of Parliament. Power is now however much more diffuse than formerly.

Earned income may reflect the fact that a person has reached a position of power, but education rather than personal wealth may have put them there. However, it is much easier for the children of middle class parents to achieve educationally than it is for children of the working class (section 8.3).

In considering wealth in Britain, it should be noted that the lower one goes on the social scale, the more the wealth that is owned comprises 'consumer durables' such as washing machines or cars, houses and insurance policies. None of these can normally be sold without replacement and therefore cannot be used to buy access to power. As one goes up the social scale the more the wealth that is owned comprises shareholding, bank deposits and cash which is readily available for use. Such ownership may also be psychologically beneficial to the owners in that they need not be fearful of losing their jobs and therefore feel a much greater freedom to express themselves as they wish.

Although wealth certainly does increase one's chances of access to power it must be remembered that trade unions in Britain are normally controlled today by those with little personal wealth, and yet the trade union movement still has power, despite its decline in the 1980s and 1990s.

Life chances are influenced by the nature of the job we do; our lifestyle (e.g. smoking or drinking); and the amount of wealth we have (e.g. to buy good living conditions or private health care).

The fact that 'life chances' can sometimes literally mean life has been consistently illustrated by reports over many years. In 1999 the British Heart Foundation reported a close link between social class, diet and health. Overall premature death rates for men, before the age of sixty-five, were 58 per cent higher for manual workers than for white collar workers. The rates for women manual workers were twice as high as for those working in offices. Men and women in the North, Scotland and Northern Ireland, where more people are in manual work, are at greater risk from premature death from heart disease than those in the South-east and in East Anglia. The rates for women in the North are nearly double those for women in East Anglia, while the risks for northern men are 50 per cent higher than in the South-east.

These figures echoed an earlier report in 1997 by the National Institute of Epidemiology at Surrey University, which showed that although people in all parts of Britain were living longer, those in affluent areas were extending their life expectancy much more rapidly than those in the inner cities. Men in Cambridge were living to an average of 76.6 years compared to 69.9 years in Manchester. The Cambridge men were living two years longer than a decade earlier but the Manchester men had increased their lifespan over the same period by only six months.

Women were living longest in Bromley with a life expectancy of 81.4 years, compared with those in Manchester who could expect to reach only 76.7 years. The Bromley women are also living for nearly two years longer than ten years previously, while the Manchester women were living for 1.3 years longer.

The study stated that: 'The prosperous, longest-lived populations have seen the greatest gains in life expectancy over the decade. In contrast, the most deprived areas – inner London, Manchester and Liverpool – experienced negligible improvements in longevity, despite having the lowests lifespans in the mid-1980s. The author of the study said that the trends, mirrored around the world, reflected the link between socio-economic circumstances and health. She said: 'Health inequalities are widening between both rich and poor countries and between the rich and poor within countries. It is important to recognise that poor health is not just a question of getting a disease . . . it is a cumulative lifetime of disadvantage. You take one step down the ladder and the whole process accelerates.'

'Where you live and how long you live'

Top five areas for long life	
Men	**Years**
Cambridge	76.6
Western Surrey	76.4
Eastern Surrey	76.2
Barnet	76
Solihull	76
Women	**Years**
Bromley	81.4
Dorset	81.4
Cambridge	81.1
Western Surrey	81.1
Exeter and north Devon	81

Bottom five areas

Men	Years
Manchester	69.9
Liverpool	71.2
East London and City	71.7
South East London	71.7
Camden and Islington	71.8

Women	Years
Manchester	76.7
Liverpool	77.3
Sunderland	77.4
St Helens and Knowsley	77.6
West Pennine	77.7

(Study by the National Institute of Epidemiology, Surrey University, 1997)

These reports are a continuation of many others that 'point to' the correlation between class and death; for example, *Inequalities in Health*, sponsored by the Department of Health and Social Security in 1980, under the chairmanship of Sir Douglas Black (the *Black Report*) found a direct correlation between class and life expectancy (Tables 10.1 and 10.2).

The report commented: 'The class *gradient* can be observed for most causes of death and is particularly steep for both sexes in the case of diseases of the respiratory system and infective and parasitic diseases (Table 10.3).'

The report concluded: 'The lack of improvement, and in some respects deterioration, of the health experience of the unskilled and semi-skilled manual classes (V and IV) relative to Class I, throughout the 1960s and early 1970s is striking.'

Inequalities in Health in the Northern Region (Northern Regional Health Authority/Bristol University, 1986) also found a direct link between the high death and illness rates in the region and poverty.

Table 10.1   Death rates by occupational class, 1951 and 1971

Class	1951	1971
I	103	79
II	108	83
III	116	103
IV	119	113
V	137	123

Note: A man from Social Class I can expect to survive seven years longer than a man from Social Class V.

Table 10.2 Infant mortality and occupational class, 1930–84

Class	1930–2	1949–53	1984
I	32	19	6
II	46	22	7
III	59	28	8
IV	63	35	10
V	80	42	13

Note: At birth and in the first month of life twice as many babies of unskilled manual parents as professional parents die.

Table 10.3 Mortality rate from bronchitis in males

Social class	I	II	III	IV	V
	34	53	98	101	171

Note: The lower a person's social class the more likely they are to suffer an illness that they have had for a considerable period of time.

A major survey in one local health practice in Stockton on Tees in 1986 suggested that the deprived group had three times more mental illness, 60 per cent more hospital admissions and 75 per cent more casualties than the control group.

In 1986 evidence suggested that people in Social Class V had a 150 per cent greater chance of dying at every age than people in Social Class I (compared with the *Black Report* figure of 23 per cent in 1930 and 61 per cent in 1970).

A Health Education Council report entitled *The Health Divide* (1987) and Richard Wilkinson, in *Class and Health* (1986), claimed that class differences in health had continually widened since the *Black Report* (see also Table 10.4).

However, these figures are disputed by those who say that the widening gap is artificial, caused by changes in the social classes rather than changes in people's health. There were, for instance, far fewer people in Social Class V (doing unskilled manual jobs) in 1971 than there were in 1931. Over the period, membership of Class I has grown by 178 per cent and membership of Class V has fallen by 35 per cent. So the low death rates in Class I now apply to a larger section of the population and the high death rates in Class V to a smaller section.

10.2 Distribution of wealth in Britain

In 1966, in *Relative Deprivation and Social Justice*, Runciman stated that 'it can safely be said that only among the non-manual class is there any significant

Table 10.4 Infant mortality[1], by social class[2], 1981–96
(United Kingdom, Rates per 1000 live births)

	1981	1991	1996
Inside marriage			
Professional	7.8	5.0	3.6
Managerial and technical	8.2	5.3	4.4
Skilled non-manual	9.0	6.2	5.4
Skilled manual	10.5	6.3	5.8
Semi-skilled	12.7	7.2	5.9
Unskilled	15.7	8.4	7.8
Other	15.6	11.8	8.3
All inside marriage	10.4	6.3	5.4
Outside marriage			
Joint registration	14.1	8.7	6.9
Sole registration	16.2	10.8	7.2
All outside marriage	15.0	9.3	7.0

Notes:
[1] Deaths within one year of birth.
[2] Based on occupation of father.
Sources: Office for National Statistics; General Register Office for Scotland; Northern Ireland Statistics and Research Agency; *Social Trends*, 29 National Statistics © Crown Copyright, 1999.

Table 10.5 Composition of the net wealth of the household sector, 1987–97
(United Kingdom, per cent)

	1987	1991	1997
Life assurance and pension funds	24	26	36
Residential buildings net of loans	35	32	23
Securities and shares	10	11	17
Notes, coins and deposits	16	17	15
Non-marketable tenancy rights	9	8	5
Other fixed assets	6	5	4
Other financial assets net of liabilities	1	1	1
Total (= 100%) (£ billion at 1997 prices)	2515	2800	3582

Source: Social Trends, 29 National Statistics. © Crown Copyright, 1999.

accumulation of wealth' and quoted a 1954 estimate that the top 1 per cent of British adults owned 43 per cent of total net capital and the top 10 per cent owned 79 per cent (Table 10.5). An even higher estimate for inequality of wealth ownership was given in 'The Meaning of Class' (*New Society*, 1964), '5 per cent of the population owned 75 per cent of all personal wealth'.

The major reason for differences in estimations of wealth distribution (Table 10.6) in Britain is that different surveys take different factors into account; some include insurance policies, housing and consumer goods, some do not.

Table 10.6   Distribution of wealth in the United Kingdom, 1991–95
(United Kingdom, per cent)

	1971	1981	1991	1995
Marketable wealth				
Percentage of wealth owned by:				
Most wealthy 1%	31	18 (26)	17 (29)	19 (27)
Most wealthy 5%	52	36 (45)	35 (51)	38 (51)
Most wealthy 10%	65	50 (56)	47 (64)	50 (64)
Most wealthy 25%	86	73 (74)	71 (80)	73 (81)
Most wealthy 50%	97	92 (87)	92 (93)	92 (93)
Total marketable wealth (£ billion)		565	1711	2033

Note: Figure in brackets is marketable wealth *less* value of dwellings.
Sources: Social Trends, 18 (London: HMSO, 1988); *Social Trends*, No 29 National Statistics © Crown Copyright, 1999.

Another problem is that wealth is deliberately concealed to avoid the payment of tax.

However the official figures published by the Inland Revenue show little change over the past thirty years, indeed when the value of home ownership is deducted (shown in brackets) the percentage of wealth owned by the most wealthy 50 per cent has actually increased since 1981, and this increase is most marked for the top 10 per cent.

The government publication *Social Trends* lists the distribution of 'marketable wealth', that is, those items that can be readily changed into cash if required (Table 10.5). In 1995 the most wealthy 1 per cent of the population were credited with 19 per cent of the wealth (a drop of 12 per cent from 1971). This decline in wealth ownership during the period by the top 1 per cent is counterbalanced by the almost static position of the bottom 50 per cent of the population, who shared 8 per cent of the national wealth in 1995, an increase of only 5 per cent during the period. It is apparent that there is an even greater disparity within the society when one considers what kinds of wealth. The less wealth you have the more likely it is to be in the form of house ownership, consumer durables and insurance policies. The more wealth you have the more likely it is to be in the form of shareholding and bank deposits (in other words, money that can be used to achieve power).

Income is less unequally shared than wealth. In 1996–7 households in the bottom 20 per cent of those in the United Kingdom had an average original income of £2310. After redistribution through taxes and cash benefits (for example, retirement pension and income support) these households had a post-tax income of £4430. Once the values of benefits in kind such as health and education are included, households in the bottom 20 per cent had a final income of £8310. In comparison, the top 20 per cent had an original income of £44,780 in 1996–7, reduced by redistribution to a final income of £31,780 per household.

10.3 Poverty

In the 1870s a rich Liverpool merchant, Charles Booth, objected to a statement made by the Social Democratic Federation that a quarter of the population were living in poverty. He carried out surveys himself to prove the point and was shocked to find that his estimation was even higher.

Later, Booth expressed his own concern at the lack of any systematic study of poverty: 'More minute, patient intelligent observation has been devoted to the study of earthworms than to the evolution, or rather degradation, of the sunken section of our people. Here and there in the immense field individual workers make notes, and occasionally emit a wail of despair.'

Booth drew up a statistical definition of poverty and as a base defined a '**poverty line**' under which it was impossible to live a healthy life; this concept of poverty is known as **absolute** (or subsistence) poverty. Booth published his findings in *Life and Labour of the People* (1889–91) and *Life and Labour of the People in London* (1891–1903). He went on to assist in the passing of the Old Age Pensions Act in 1908.

In 1899 Rowntree developed Booth's work in a survey of poverty in York in which he showed for example that '**infant mortality**' – the number of children who died in their first year of life out of every 1000 who had been born alive during that year – was 247 for families under his poverty line and 173 for those above it. Rowntree found that in a quarter of his 'poor' families the major wage-earner was dead, ill, disabled or unemployed. About half of the poor families had an employed head, but their earnings were insufficient to keep the family above the poverty line.

In modern times many money allowances and grants in kind have been introduced to reduce poverty, but those in poverty still tend to be those in the

The old are often poor in modern Britain

categories listed by Rowntree: the old; the mentally and physically disabled; the ill; single-parent families; and those with large families but low incomes, or who are unemployed.

Social security benefits under a variety of names have sought to reduce poverty since 1906; state retirement pension ('old age pension'); housing and council tax benefits; income support; child benefit; jobseekers' allowance; and unemployment benefit have all helped to reduce poverty, and around three in five families in Great Britain received some kind of benefit in 1996–7. However, benefits still guarantee only a fairly low level of subsistence and because those who are poor are also least able to care for themselves, or to manage money, their position is made worse. Also, many do not know the benefits to which they are entitled or are too proud to make a claim.

A 'culture of poverty' often exists among the poor which leads to a passive acceptance of their position allied to a hostility towards authority. Children growing up in a neighbourhood where such attitudes are the norm are likely to leave school early and enter unskilled and often low-paid, uncertain employment; marry early, and have larger families than people elsewhere in Britain. In turn, their children are likely to grow up equally deprived so that poverty becomes 'cyclical' – it is likely to be unbroken like a circle from generation to generation.

The cycle of deprivation ('vicious circle of poverty',
see Figure 10.1)

'in 1964 the US Council of Economic Advisors stated: 'The vicious cycle, in which poverty breeds poverty, occurs through time, and transmits its effects from one generation to another. There is no beginning to the cycle, no end.' This cycle is still evident in the United States and in Britain today.

In 1970 Coates and Silburn, in *Poverty: The Forgotten Englishmen*, described a series of problems which the poor suffer, which reinforce one another and which are likely to continue from generation to generation.

Rutter and Madge, in *Cycle of Disadvantage* (1976), found the cycle occurring when three factors were present (including a large family, inadequate home, poor education, family instability, educational subnormality).

The cycle of poverty was given wide publicity by Sir Keith Joseph when he was Secretary of State for Social Services in the 1970s (he is sometimes credited with inventing the term). The *Black Report* of 1980 asked for research into 'the routes by which some children escape what is for most born into similar conditions an unenviable fate'.

The existence of such a cycle has been disputed on the grounds that the factors quoted are symptoms, not causes, of poverty.

Culture of poverty

Oscar Lewis, in *The Children of Sanchez* (1962), suggested that the poor Mexicans he studied developed a culture which allowed them to cope with poverty, but which, in turn, perpetuated that poverty. This subculture was:

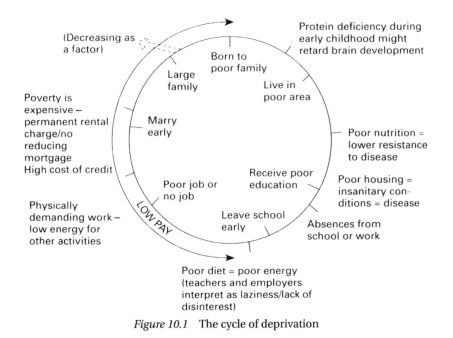

Figure 10.1 The cycle of deprivation

- **Fatalistic.** What will be will be, nothing we can do about it.
- **Anti-authority.** They will do nothing to help us (therefore suspicious of all officials, including teachers, social services, etc.).
- **Present-oriented.** Enjoy yourself now, you may not have the chance later (this is the opposite of deferred gratification, believed to be a feature of the middle class). The logic of this is apparent in the British Social Security system: benefits are often not payable if you have savings of more than a small amount so if you are likely to have to claim benefits in the future, why save now?

The existence of a 'culture of poverty' is disputed by several researchers, who have found evidence of active participation in politics and promotion of community action as well as apathetic resignation among the poor.

Structural poverty

Some studies have taken the view that the structure of society keeps people poor. J. Westergaard and H. Resley, in *Class in a Capitalist Society*, (1976), argued that government measures to deal with poverty cannot succeed, because 'they are not designed to produce wholesale change in the general structure of inequality' – the privileged position of the wealthy must be protected, and achieving this depends on working class poverty. This function of the poor view of poverty was also described by H. Gans in *More Equality* (1973): poverty ensures that dirty, dangerous, menial jobs are done and creates jobs and opportunities for people who 'serve the poor, or shield the rest of the population from them'.

One in five UK children 'is living in poverty'

By Philip Johnston, Home Affairs Editor

MORE children are living in poverty in Britain than in any other European Union country, with numbers having trebled in 20 years, according to Unicef, the United Nations children's agency.

A report published yesterday placed Britain 20th out of 23 countries in a league table of relative poverty.

Unicef said one British child in five lived in poverty – a worse figure than in all but one of the other 14 EU countries. It was also worse than Turkey and nations of the former communist bloc, such as Poland or Hungary.

In the world's most developed nations, there were 47 million children – one in six – living in poverty, it said.

The United States was second from bottom of the table, despite being among the wealthiest nations.

Mexico was rated poorest, with 26.2 per cent of children in poverty. The US was next, with 24.4 per cent, followed by Italy (20.5), Britain (19.8), Turkey (19.7) and Ireland (16.8). Those rated highest were Sweden (2.6), Norway (3.9) and Finland (4.3).

Critics of the findings questioned Unicef's measure of poverty. It defined as poor those on incomes less than half their national average.

In Britain that is about £10,000, but such an income – adjusted for currency fluctuations and other factors – would be beyond the wildest dreams of the poorest people in Turkey, they said.

Unicef said that in Britain child poverty had tripled over the past 20 years. However, it expected new welfare measures and the minimum wage introduced by the Labour Party to cut the rate to 17 per cent by 2002, still well short of Tony Blair's pledge to eradicate child poverty.

Unicef said the youngsters growing up in poverty were more likely to have learning difficulties, drop out of school, use drugs, commit crimes, be unemployed and become pregnant early.

'The persistence of child poverty in rich countries confronts the industrialised world with a test both of its ideals and of its capacity to resolve many of its most intractable social problems,' the report concluded.

Unicef could not identify a single explanation for child poverty, though in Britain it pointed to the high number of children in single parent families.

But it also questioned the assumption that large numbers of single-parent families meant more child poverty.

It noted that Sweden had the highest share of children living with one parent – more than 20 per cent – but the lowest relative child poverty rate. Countries with the lowest levels of child poverty allocated the most money to social expenditure.

(*Daily Telegraph*, 14 June 2000)

The poverty trap

An increase in gross income does not always lead to an improvement in net income (after tax and benefits). This is because any increase in earnings results in the loss of some means-tested benefit (e.g. housing benefit, free school meals, or Income Support). Attempts to reduce this trap in recent years has had some success in ensuring that people are better off working than remaining on benefit.

10.4 Relative poverty

The welfare state will normally act as a safety net for the worst cases of poverty so that people are unlikely to die of malnutrition or lack of heat if the welfare authorities are aware of their situation.

Rising living standards generally in society have, however, led to rising expectations so that when people compare themselves with others in modern Britain they may feel that they are badly off even although their standard of living might have been regarded as acceptable in Charles Booth's day. This 'poverty by comparison' has been termed '**relative deprivation**', a theory detailed by Merton in *Social Theory and Social Structure* (1968). Essentially, people tend to compare themselves with others in their 'reference group' to which they think they may fairly be compared because of broadly similar characteristics.

In *Poverty, Inequality and Class Structure*, Peter Townsend described those in relative poverty as having 'resources so seriously below those commanded by the average individual or family that they are, in effect, excluded from ordinary living patterns, customs and activities'. In the first study of relative poverty in the United Kingdom undertaken in 1960 by Townsend and Abel-Smith (*The Poor and the Poorest*) it was claimed that 7.5 million people (14.2 per cent) lived in relative poverty.

In the past, opportunities for comparison were normally limited to the neighbourhood – now they have been opened up by the media. Living standards of small families with both parents in regular skilled work have tended to increase quite sharply in recent years. 'Relative poverty' may therefore have increased. It may be true to say that the number of people in need is decreasing but the number of people in want may inevitably increase.

Some areas of the United Kingdom have considerably more poverty and other disadvantages than other areas. In 1999 the Joseph Rowntree Foundation published a report 'Monitoring Poverty and Social Exclusion' and found that the number of families and individuals living on low incomes remained close to the record level reached in the early 1990s although the report indicated that some of the measures which had recently been taken 'including the introduction of the minimum wage' might have some effect in avoiding an increasing gap between the rich and the poor.

One of the Labour Government's pledges on coming to power was to tackle what it called 'social exclusion'. Using fifty different indicators, the foundation

Relative poverty

"That's our problem, Charlie—the more we get, the more we want."

discovered that the number of people living on less than the average national income in 1997–8 was little changed from that of the previous year. This meant that, after housing costs had been deducted, 14 million people were living below a government recognised poverty line, including 4.4 million children.

The number of individuals on very low incomes had risen by more than a million since 1995–6, reaching 8 million in 1997–8. The figures also showed that the North–South divide remained; with twice as many people receiving government benefits in the North-east as in the South-east; as did the gulf between those living in council housing and those in privately rented accommodation or their own homes. There was little change in 'financial exclusion' with one-fifth of the poorest households still without a bank or building society account.

There was no general pattern of improvement. Inequalities in health and education seemed to be getting worse.

REVISION SUMMARY

Relative deprivation

Relative deprivation is a feeling of being deprived in comparison with other people with whom you feel you should be compared.

Wealth and power

- Wealth usually increases power. You are in a better position to make your own decisions (for example, which school your child attends or in getting an operation when you need one); you may also have personal contacts which puts you in a better position to influence the decisions of others.
- The most wealthy 50 per cent of the population own 92 per cent of all wealth.

Life chances

Life chances increase with wealth: These include
- Health
- Education
- Housing
- Employment opportunities.

The cycle of deprivation

The cycle of deprivation still exists and usually ensures that those born poor usually remain poor.

The culture of poverty

This is a coping strategy that enables people to deal with their situation but is also likely to perpetuate poverty.

The poverty trap

This is the mechanism which tends to result in those on low incomes losing benefit if their income increases even marginally and militates against those seeking to improve their situation.

▪ ᴍ **11** Social mobility

11.1 The extent of social mobility in Britain

There has been a significant change in the proportion of privately owned wealth in the hands of the top 1 per cent of the population, but the proportionate change diminishes as one climbs down the ladder of wealth ownership (section 10.2 and Table 11.1).

If one compares the 1995 position given with 1961 the situation is even more striking – although the top 1 per cent saw its share decrease from 28 per cent to 19 per cent of all marketable wealth, there has been no change at all in the share of the top 50 per cent of the population (92 per cent in both 1961 and 1995).

Attempts to redistribute wealth more evenly have been only partially successful because the very rich are able to protect their positions by employing skilled accountants and lawyers. For example, the Vestey family, whose interests include the Dewhurst butchery firm, have their wealth in the form of a family trust which provides the incomes and housing expenses of its members.

The British aristocracy continues to own 40 per cent of British land; although the 'privatisation' of the former nationalised industries, such as telephones, gas, electricity and railways in the 1980s substantially increased the number of shareholders in Britain from 6 per cent of the population in 1981 to 20 per cent in 1989. The number of shareholders again increased with the 'flotation' of several 'mutuals', such as Scottish Amicable Assurance and the Halifax Building Society in the 1990s, where ownership passed from the 'members' (i.e. borrowers, savers and policy holders) to shareholders, with members being given some shares ('windfalls') to persuade them to vote for demutualisation. About 25 per cent of the population now own shares, but these holdings are usually small and have not had a huge impact on the concentration of wealth, although it may be that attitudes have been substantially changed with more people thinking of themselves as 'capitalists' or as sharing in the ownership of British industry and commerce. The value of shareholding as a means of retaining and enhancing wealth might be indicated by the fact that Railtrack's flotation price of £3.80 per share had risen to over £10 a share by 2000.

But social class is not just a matter of wealth. Although this is a key factor, it also has to do with access to high-status occupations, educational opportunities and social acceptance generally, particularly with regard to 'life styles'. Some growing similarity in dress, access to foreign holidays, car ownership and the like has resulted in claims that class differences are declining.

Table 11.1 Decline in the proportion of marketable wealth 1971–95

The most wealthy 5% of the population had a 14% decline in wealth
The most wealthy 10% of the population had a 15% decline in wealth
The most wealthy 25% of the population had a 13% decline in wealth
The most wealthy 50% of the population had a 5% decline in wealth

There are still great variations in housing – dependent upon income and wealth; access to schools of variable quality; dress, which has all sorts of little nuances that can determine a person's class, and therefore their acceptability to others. The middle class person endeavouring to 'join in' in a working men's club would have problems, just as would the manual worker at one of the London 'Clubs' like the Athenaeum.

Among the young there appeared to be a brief flirtation with 'classless' life styles in the 1960s ('flower power'). Now there appears to be a move back across the class divide in youth culture.

By 1972 Professor MacRae, in an article called 'Classlessness' in *New Society*, doubted whether the British class system was even a system. He claimed that equal opportunities in education and the consequent 'rise of the meritocracy' had led to the discarding of class labels. In other words, he was saying that Britain was becoming a 'classless society'.

Although few would accept that Britain is a classless society, there are some trends that indicate a slow movement in that direction:

1 Patterns of behaviour do appear to be more uniform generally as a result of exposure to the media, greater mobility and increased earnings by many manual workers.
2 There has been some limited convergence of earnings rates for manual and white collar workers.
3 There is apparently no barrier to the children of manual workers moving to non-manual occupations, and the changing nature of the British economy has resulted in an increase in the proportion of middle class jobs available.
4 There is a greater degree of home ownership among manual and routine clerical workers than in the past.

However, accent and differing behaviour patterns do exist, educational opportunities vary by area of residence, and status judgements are still made on overt signs of class difference. For example schoolchildren listed BBC English and 'affected English' as of high status, and cockney and Birmingham accents as of low status in a 1973 study; the student may wish to carry out a simple survey to see whether this attitude still exists.

There is evidence that access to high-status positions is still considerably easier for those whose parents are themselves in similar occupations. Such judgements are usually based on whether children have been educated in 'public' schools (see Chapter 7). Less than 7 per cent of the population were being educated in public schools in 2000 (a similar figure to that of twenty years previously).

There still remains a remarkable educational élite

A high proportion of top jobs go to 'Oxbridge' graduates and by 2000 approximately 50 per cent of undergraduates at both Oxford and Cambridge had still been educated at public schools. This is a higher percentage of state education students than twenty years previously, but may be largely accounted for by the opening up of 'Oxbridge' colleges to girls who are less likely than boys to be educated at a public school.

According to the magazine *Commercial Lawyer* in July 2000, 42 per cent of new partners in law firms had been educated at public school (rising to 54 per cent in the prestigious City firms) and 24 per cent had attended Oxbridge (again increasing to 54 per cent in the City of London).

Ultimate power in any modern state resides with the armed forces, as it is they who must ensure that the law is enforced, should the police prove inadequate. It is not known what would happen in Britain should the interests of the ruling elite be seriously threatened by an elected government, but in many countries such a situation has provoked a military 'coup' (the nearest modern Britain has approached such a situation was the so called 'Mutiny at the Curragh', when Army officers threatened to resign their commissions just before the First World War, see section 25.4). British Army Officers are usually trained at the Royal Military Academy, Sandhurst, and although the intake of state-educated pupils has increased in the last twenty years it was still only about half the total of officer cadets in 2000.

By 2000 some 80 per cent of top army officers had had a public school education, as had 80 per cent of judges and 40 per cent of the Diplomatic Service. Butler and Kavanagh (*The British General Election of 1997*) found that about two-thirds of Conservative MPs and about one-sixth of Labour MPs had been to public schools; almost exactly the same percentages as in the previous three General Elections. Of the 418 Labour MPs elected in 1997 only 13 per cent had a background in manual work, the Labour Prime Minister had been educated at the leading Scottish public school (although the Conservative leader, by contrast, had been educated at Wath upon Dearne Comprehensive School in a tough former coal mining area, although both had been to Oxford.)

The ruling tribes

Lord-Lieutenants and High Sheriffs

ONCE THEY were a force to be reckoned with. Sent by Henry VIII to every county in the land to keep control of the population, the lord-lieutenants acted as the king's eyes and ears, sending back information to a monarch keen to make war and quell the monasteries.

But now dwindling powers and a falling budget mean that their position is under threat and things aren't what they were for the modern-day holders of an historically exalted office.

By the 19th century, the lord-lieutenants' traditional role as heads of local militia had been wiped out by the Victorians. Even the residual duty to "call on men of the county to fight" had been abolished by 1921.

Now that the Queen is rarely in need of a platoon of local mercenaries to protect her when she ventures outside her palace, the time may finally be up for Her Majesty's remaining 102 lord-lieutenants.

The Home Office is reviewing their £686,000 annual budget – described as "an extravagance" by the Liberal Democrat MP Norman Backer.

Mr Baker, MP for Lewes, has produced research on the lord-lieutenants showing that four out of 10 are old Etonians while a further three out of 10 went to other independent schools.

Of the 47 in England, 20 are members of either Brook's, White's, the Army and Navy or Boodle's gentlemen's clubs. In Northern Ireland, five out of eight are members of similar establishments, and in Scotland, 20 out of 31 belong to private clubs. There are 11 women among the group, and no members of ethnic minorities, according to parliamentary answers obtained by Mr Baker. Forty-five are former military officers.

Immortalised as heartless tax collectors by the Sheriff of Nottingham, High Sheriffs are appointed for a year to act as the unpaid enforcer of the Queen's writ in each county. They were formerly responsible for the safety of judges within their county and were liable for the safe custody of prisoners. Today they perform mainly ceremonial duties, but they retain a statutory duty to collect debts and enforce writs on behalf of the courts.

Anyone is eligible as long as they hold land in the county. Peers, clergy, officers in active service, barristers and solicitors cannot hold the office.

Outside Parliament, too, there is now less aristocratic influence; the Governor
and the Deputy Governor of the Bank of England both come from outside the
'charmed circle'; the chairman and director-general of the Independent
Broadcasting Association (IBA) are both outsiders; nearly all chairmen of big
corporations, scientists and vice-chancellors come from grammar schools; and
none of the leading entrepreneurs have been to university at all.

Yet alongside this new meritocracy there still remains a remarkable
educational élite which has maintained its continuity and influence through all
the political upheavals. Few people in the early Wilson years would have
predicted that in 1982 the chairman of the BBC, the editor of *The Times*, the
Foreign Secretary, the heads of both foreign and civil services and half the
chairmen of the big four banks would all be Old Etonians, while the Home
Secretary, the Chancellor, the Director-General of the BBC, a bevy of judges and
the other two bank chairmen would come from the rival foundation, Winchester.
Such a lasting duopoly must surely have some significance in Britain's anatomy.

Of course, it was never likely that two medieaval institutions which had
survived King Henry VIII, Cromwell, Victorian reformers and two world wars
would lightly surrender their influence to Harold Wilson or Anthony Crosland.
But far from retreating, they have advanced into new areas of influence; and their
success is more marked than in Macmillan's time or (as far as I can trace) than
in any earlier time. The Victorian professions were full of self-made men who
worked their way up to the top, and several schools prepared the way to power.
Macmillan's Britain included outsiders such as William Haley editing *The Times*
or Sir Norman Brook running the civil service.

But since then the products of these two ancient schools have reasserted all
their old ability to climb the ladders of power, with a continuity which has no
parallel in other industrial countries . . . The traditional élites have also retained
their own communication system which still gives them a special tribal role in
the midst of contemporary Britain (Anthony Sampson, *The Changing Anatomy of
Britain*, 1982).

11.2 Barriers to mobility

The most obvious barriers to social mobility are 'lack of opportunity', for
example, regional differences in employment and 'motivation', for example a lack
of desire to study in order to gain higher qualifications; however, these may not
be the most important factors.

Many occupations require a particular standard of education for entry and this
effectively means that social mobility can take place only between generations. It

also means that education is a major avenue of mobility and a major barrier for those who do not have access to an appropriate education, or who have not been socialised in a way that makes it possible for them to fully benefit from the educational process (section 8.3). Even when all manual workers' children are taken together – those from skilled families as well as those from poorer homes – these were still, by 2000, much less likely to enter a university than children of 'professional' fathers.

Major inequality in the distribution of inherited wealth is the first barrier to mobility in that it gives rise to the direct inheritances of particular positions, for example company directorships; or particular advantages to the children of those who know how the system works and can afford to educate their children appropriately – for example, many doctors are themselves children of doctors. Patronage by relatives is known as 'nepotism', the term originating from the placing by a fifteenth-century Pope of his illegitimate sons, called 'nephews', in positions of power.

Colour or ethnic origin is also likely to be a major barrier to social mobility for those concerned – 'Black people represent around 4 per cent of the total population. Can any profession boast that anything like that proportion of their colleagues are black?' (David Lane, Chairman, Commission for Racial Equality, 1982).

In England, Wales and Scotland there is no evidence that religion is a barrier to mobility but there is some evidence that Catholics have been less likely than Protestants to be socially mobile in Northern Ireland.

Perhaps the greatest barrier to mobility is that of attitude, which in turn influences the way the socialisation process prepares children for adult life. University admissions statistics show that, despite a growth of nearly 100,000 in the number of entrants to universities between 1970 and 1977, the percentage from Social Class I rose from 30 per cent to 36 per cent, while that from Class IV (all manual occupations) dropped from 28 per cent to 24 per cent.

Public school pupils also kept a virtual monopoly of top jobs. They comprise 80 per cent of High Court and Appeal Judges, 83 per cent of the directors of major insurance companies, 80 per cent of the directors of the clearing banks, 69 per cent of the directors of major industrial firms and 67 per cent of Conservative MPs (Ivan Reid, *Social Class Differences in Britain*, 1981).

11.3 Avenues of mobility

Education

The major avenue to social mobility in Britain is education, leading to an occupation higher up the social scale than that of one's father ('**inter-generational mobility**').

Provided the ratio of non-manual to manual jobs remained the same some upward mobility was inevitable in that for at least the last hundred years manual workers have had larger families than non-manual. In fact non-manual work has increased as a percentage of all work, thus opening up more opportunities for working class talent, usually selected by the educational process. For example, between 1911 and 1966 the proportion of employers and proprietors in the population halved. The proportion of white collar workers doubled. There was a slight increase in salesmen, but three times as many clerical (the biggest single group) and four times as many foremen and inspectors. By 1979 only 35 per cent of the population was middle class in occupation but by 2000 it had reached 50 per cent as heavy industry continued to decline and computer-driven technology created more opportunity for 'white collar' work (see section 14.2).

'Intra-generational' mobility – starting off one's working life in one social class and then moving to another – is less common. Opportunities for mobility within the work situation itself have declined because the expansion of higher education has resulted in many organisations recruiting graduate trainee managers rather than depending upon recruiting on merit from those joining the firm at an earlier age.

Fairly rigid pre-entry conditions have existed for the various grades in the civil service and armed forces since the ending of 'nepotism' in the twentieth century. This emphasis on formal entry qualifications is now also operating to an extent in the police service with graduate entry, as well as in industry and commerce.

Marriage

Generally, people marry within their social class but there is some upward social mobility through marriage, particularly in the case of women. In general, this tends to be a movement up just one rung of the social ladder but clearly there are notable exceptions.

Inheritance

Windfall gains in terms of inheritance, gambling and the like may result in upward mobility. Such mobility is rare, particularly bearing in mind that most inheritance is within the same social group. Sudden wealth may transfer a person nominally into another social class but attitude and life style may leave them culturally isolated. 'Class' does carry with it an implicit assumption of acceptance by a social group of the individuals assigned to it.

11.4 Social change

The degree to which the social structure of Britain is changing is a matter of dispute. In 1961 Zweig (*The Worker in an Affluent Society*) found that the better-paid manual worker was adopting middle class values and behaviour. This process has been called '**embourgeoisement**'. Goldthorpe, Lockwood, Bechhofer and Platt (*The Affluent Worker*, 1969–71) criticised this view and found that although there was some adoption of middle class life styles, attitudes and values had not altered.

In 1985 Anthea Holme ('Family and Home in East London') compared the life styles in Bethnal Green with those portrayed some thirty years previously in

Family and Kinship in East London – she found that families had become much more home centred, 'Do-it-Yourself, even in rented property, and television – not to mention the baby – were clearly strong competitors of the pub and the football ground.'

The view that the classes are drawing together – 'convergence' – because of the growth of white collar jobs and similarities of earnings, rather than one being absorbed into the other, is also open to question. In 1966, W. Runciman (*Relative Deprivation and Social Justice*) pointed to the greater security of employment in 'white collar' jobs and the better working conditions enjoyed by such workers compared with those in blue collar occupations, together with the fact that manual workers have to work longer hours for the same pay. While overall wage differentials narrow, 'fringe benefits' for white collar workers have increased – private pension schemes, greater holiday entitlement, private health schemes and company cars among them; and despite government attempts to tax these benefits they have continued to grow among white collar workers.

In terms of wealth ownership even the lower grades of non-manual workers are likely to be better off in the ownership of capital compared with the skilled manual. However, white collar jobs became increasingly unionised in the 1970s and 1980s and such workers increasingly identified with manual workers rather than management. This may be in part a consequence of the blocking off of their access to promotion (section 11.3), a consequent reduction in managerial aspirations and hence a loss of identification with management.

Equally the overall drop in trade union membership might imply that many workers no longer see a conflict between their own self-interest and the prosperity of the organisation with which they work.

It could be said that the growth in the number of working class children staying on at school implies an acceptance of the middle class value of 'deferred' gratification' (section 8.2). Equally, the growth of credit – particularly credit cards – among the middle class might point to a reduction among them of this middle class value. Westergaard and Resley (*Class in a Capitalist Society*, 1976) have suggested that some white collar workers are becoming more 'proletarian' (working class) and that 'proletarianisation' is taking place. Others see a degree of 'convergence' – the social classes becoming similar to each other.

So far as the future is concerned there are some who take the view that enhanced educational opportunities, more home ownership, a growth in self-employment, wider involvement in the stock market, general use of technology and a continued decline in manual work will through a process of 'stratified diffusion' filter down through the social classes so that ultimately there will be a commonality of interest – we will all be middle class. The pessimists see 'social exclusion' increasing and with it crime and criminality; those in sink estates becoming increasingly unemployed and unemployable; middle class morality becoming increasingly rejected (for example, some 10 per cent of social class 1 children are born outside marriage, compared with almost 50 per cent of those of social class V). They see a substantial portion of the former working class developing as an underclass along the lines of ghetto America – what the *Sunday Times* described as the 'New Rabble'.

Defining the middle class: 1

Mr Prescott once said: "My house and my Jaguar are symbols to me of where I've got to".

But he can also be apologetic about them, reflecting the schizophrenic nature of the modern Labour Party as it tries to cling on to its roots while reaching out to a middle-class electorate.

In his biography of Prescott, *Fighting Talk*, Colin Brown, says: "The angst clearly felt by Prescott has mirrored the struggle within Labour as it was turned into a centre party by Tony Blair."

Mr Prescott said: "My roots, my background and the way I act is working class. But it would be hypocritical to say I am anything else than middle class now.

"With me, what you see is what you get – unlike some middle-class people who try to hide things. I have made no attempt to hide my accent or my origins. A population census defines class by income – and mine is middle class."

His father, however, thinks he has softened his accent and "polished his way of speaking" – a reverse of Harold Wilson who, for political reasons, rediscovered his Yorkshire accent after tempering it at Oxford.

Yet, in the past he was happy to joke about his humble origins. He tells the story of a gathering where Lord Caradon was reminiscing about a ship-board conference over which he presided when Governor of Cyprus.

When Mr Prescott mentioned that he, too, had been present, Caradon asked him in what capacity he had attended. "I was the waiter," said the future Deputy Prime Minister.

(*Daily Telegraph*, 16 July 1999)

Defining the middle class: 2

The new system of social classification which will be used for the next government census has already split us into seven groups, in which teachers and social workers are now, effectively, upper class (1b).

Policemen and firemen are now in class 2, while Britain's new equivalent of the untouchables – car park attendants, cleaners, refuse collectors, labourers and road sweepers – remain at the bottom, in Class 7, until Mr Blair can devise a suitable ladder on which to deliver them into his new social order.

Will it really work? Can we be welded into a mega-middle unity, all wearing trainers and speaking Estuarial into mobiles? Or was John Betjeman right to prophesy that one topic will be "all-absorbing, as it was, is now and ever shall be, to us – class".

(*Daily Telegraph*, 16 July 1999)

REVISION SUMMARY

Factors indicating a reduction of the importance of class

- Patterns of behaviour do appear to be more uniform generally as a result of exposure to the media, greater mobility and increased earnings by many workers.
- There has been some limited convergence of earning rates for manual and white collar workers.
- There is apparently no barrier to the children of manual workers moving to non-manual occupations. Vance Packard, in *The Status Seekers* (1959), reported that one in three of the sons of manual workers proceeded to non-manual work, but usually to routine non-manual. The proportion is now almost certainly considerably higher.
- There is a greater degree of home ownership among manual and routine clerical workers than in the past.
- Over half the working population are now in white collar occupations (one-third in 1945) as a result of structural changes in the nature of work in Britain.

Factors which indicate that class continues to be important

Attendance at a public school is often regarded as an important indicator of social class (about 5 per cent of the secondary school population attend public schools).

- In 2000 both Oxford and Cambridge (regarded as the most prestigious of English universities) still accepted about half their intake from public schools.
- About 60 per cent of top executives attended a public school.
- About 60 per cent of leading company chairmen attended a public school.
- Eton has produced about 30 per cent of all Conservative cabinet ministers.
- About 60 per cent of army officers have attended a public school.
- About 80 per cent of High Court judges attended a public school.
- About 70 per cent of Conservative MPs have attended a public school.
- About 80 per cent of the directors of the major banks attended a public school.

Barriers to mobility

- Lack of opportunity (e.g. regional differences in availability of employment).
- Motivation (e.g. class attitudes).
- Educational factors.
- Inherited wealth.
- Self-selection by elite groups (e.g. nepotism – patronage by relatives).

- Colour or ethnic origin
- Structural factors. Opportunities for mobility within the work situation itself have declined, because the expansion of higher education has resulted in many organisations recruiting graduate trainee managers rather than depending upon recruiting on merit from those joining the firm at an earlier age.
- Religion may be a factor affecting Catholics in Northern Ireland.

Avenues of mobility

- *Education* – the major factor. It is estimated that nearly half (47 per cent) of those aged 18 in Social Class II in 1981 had entered since birth. The proportion of the cohort in Social Class I had increased only slightly. There was a substantial net movement out of the manual classes, some 9.5 per cent of the cohort (DES *Report on Education*, July 1984).*
- *Promotion.*
- *Marriage.* Usually people marry within their social class, but there is some upward social mobility through marriage – particularly in the case of women. In general, this tends to be a movement up just one rung of the social ladder, but clearly there are notable exceptions.
- *Windfall* – e.g. inheritance, gambling wins. Such mobility is rare, particularly when it is borne in mind that most inheritance is within the same social group. Sudden wealth may transfer a person nominally into another social class, but attitude and lifestyle may leave him or her culturally isolated.
- *Structural change.* An increasingly technologically based society has increased the need for professional and other white collar workers and reduced the need for unskilled manual workers (but the status of routine clerical work may have declined). A third of all male employees were in manufacturing in 1981, by 1988 this had declined to a quarter. One in every ten male jobs were in financial and business services in 1981, this had increased to one in six by 1988.

SELF-TEST QUESTIONS: PART FOUR

Self-test 4.1

1 What is the process whereby a person changes his social class called? (*1 mark*)
2 What is the name of possessions which are intended to indicate your supposed importance? (*1 mark*)
3 The term 'blue collar' is used to indicate what social class? (*1 mark*)

---

* *Inter-generational mobility* = moving from one class to another between two generations (i.e. entering employment in a class above or below that of your father).

  Intra-generational mobility = moving from one class to another within one generation (i.e. starting off one's working life in one social class and then moving to another). It is possible that this may be of waning importance (see above).

4   Roughly what proportion of wealth is owned by the bottom 50 per cent of the population? (*1 mark*)
5   Which Social Class categories which have been used by the Registrar-General compose the 'middle class'? (*2 marks*)
6   Name the two major categories into which poverty is usually divided. (*2 marks*)
7   What barriers to social mobility continue to exist within the United Kingdom? (*4 marks*)
8   What reasons are there for supposing that class is becoming less important in Britain? (*4 marks*)
9   Describe two differences between feudalism and class. (*4 marks*)
10 Define, and explain, what is meant by embourgeoisement. (*5 marks*)
(*Total 25 marks*)

Self-test 4.2

Old school ties rule in legal city

EITHER public schools and Oxbridge give a better education or legal firms maintain their old snobberies. According to a study of new partners, 42pc went to public schools, rising to 54pc in the magic circle of City firms, and 24pc went to Oxbridge, increasing to 54pc in the magic circle, according to the magazine Commercial Lawyer.

Over 74pc of the new partners were men and more than 92pc were white.
(*Sunday Telegraph*, 23 July 2000)

The ruling tribes

Behind all the swings and changes of the last decades was there any meaning left in the old idea of the Establishment, which had cast such a spell over the Macmillan years? Certainly the political leadership now shows little connection with that many-branched family tree of the Devonshires and the Salisburys which spread out to many of the key emplacement of power in the early sixties. Certainly school and university backgrounds have lost some of their significance in parliament . . .

Yet alongside this new meritocracy there still remains a remarkable educational élite which has maintained its continuity and influence through all the political upheavals. Few people in the early Wilson years would have predicted that in 1982 the chairman of the BBC, the editor of The Times, the Foreign Secretary, the heads of both foreign and civil services and half the chairmen of the big four banks would all be Old Etonians, while the Home Secretary, the Chancellor, the director-general of the BBC, a bevy of judges and the other two bank chairmen would come from the rival foundation, Winchester. Such a lasting duopoly must surely have some significance in Britain's anatomy... Two ancient schools have reasserted all their old ability to climb the ladders of power, with a continuity which has no parallel in other industrial countries... The traditional élites have also retained their own communication system which still gives them a special tribal role in the midst of contemporary Britain.

(Anthony Sampson, *The Changing Anatomy of Britain*, London, Hodder & Stoughton 1982)

1 According to the passage, what have lost some of their significance in Parliament? *(1 mark)*
2 Which two schools are described as a 'duopoly' in the passage? *(1 mark)*
3 Define and explain what is meant by a 'meritocracy'. *(4 marks)*
4 In what two ways might traditional élites maintain their position in British society? *(4 marks)*
5 Is Britain a classless society? *(10 marks)*

SPECIMEN QUESTIONS AND ANSWERS

Look at Table 10.6 (p. 138) on the distribution of wealth in the United Kingdom.

1 According to the information in the chart what proportion of wealth was owned by the most wealthy 10 per cent of the population in 1995? *(1 mark)*
2 According to the information in the chart, what percentage change occurred between 1981 and 1991 in the proportion of wealth held by the least wealthy 50 per cent of the population? *(1 mark)*
3 Efforts to redistribute wealth from the wealthy to the less wealthy have led to only comparatively small changes. Examine two reasons for the lack of success of these efforts. *(4 marks)*
4 Define and discuss the following terms:
   (i) cycle of poverty;
   (ii) cultural deprivation. *(6 marks)*
5 What is the relationship between wealth and social class? *(8 marks)*

Answers

1 50 per cent of wealth was owned by the most wealthy 10 per cent in 1995. (*Note:* Do not forget to put 'per cent'.)
2 The proportion of wealth held by the least wealthy 50 per cent of the population remained static between 1981 and 1991. (or 'no change' or '0' per cent.)
3 Efforts to redistribute wealth had been ineffective, because those at the top are in a position to protect their interests by employing skilled accountants and

lawyers to adjust their financial affairs – for example, by using mechanisms such as family trusts – to avoid the relevant taxation. A second factor, suggested by Westergaard and Resler in *Class in a Capitalistic Society*, is that the structure of society is based upon inequality and that mechanisms cannot be created to reduce inequality without destroying the system.

4   (i) 'Cycle of poverty' is the name given to the series of problems which the poor suffer, so that one factor such as poor housing and the resulting insanitary conditions lead to absence from school, which leads to a poor job (or no job at all), which leads to low pay, which leads to an inability to buy a house on mortgage, which means payment of a permanently high rent (rather than mortgage payments reducing in real terms), and so on: until children are born to the poor people concerned and the cycle continues into a new generation.

Jordan, in *Poor Parents*, argues that the factors mentioned are problems associated with poverty rather than causes of it, and there is an argument that all the problems are basically associated with low income rather than a separate culture and that people do, in fact, break out of the cycle. However, those escaping the cycle are a small minority and the cultural factors involved may keep many people in poverty.

(ii) 'Cultural deprivation' is the term used to denote a situation in which an individual or a group is seen as suffering disadvantage because they do not possess or develop the cultural attributes, such as dress, speech or thought processes, which might make higher-status positions within the society available to them. In Britain the working class, particularly Class V and members of ethnic minorities, may be seen as suffering cultural deprivation.

The measure of cultural deprivation is likely to be the degree to which a subculture within a society deviates from the accepted patterns of the dominant culture; the subculture itself may be a rich and varied one.

Conflict theorists see modern mass society as a wide variety of conflicting cultures, held together by agencies such as the mass media and education which impose the culture of the élite and devalue that of other groups, 'cultural deprivation' being a manifestation of this. An extreme extension of this is that 'high art' (opera, classical music, etc.) is a mechanism for keeping the lower orders in their place by demonstrating the superiority of the more highly educated élite.

Note: You are being asked to both define and discuss – it is easy to make the mistake of merely describing the terms. Adequate discussion is very difficult within the time limitation indicated by the marks allocated. A discussion implies differing points of view, so try to look at differing aspects of the topics, e.g. whether all sociologists agree with the concepts.

5   The Marxist concept of class is one which entails a common identity in relation to the means of production – ownership or non-ownership. Ownership implies capital, and capital is wealth. Marxists therefore believe that there is a direct relationship between wealth and social class and that the abolition of ownership is essential if a more equal society if to be established.

The Weberian concept of class is that of access to 'life chances', the ability to acquire better living conditions and power, and in modern Britain this is seen as mainly being through occupation. This is the basis of the Registrar-General's classification of Social Class and refinements to it, such as the Hall–Jones scale.

Class, however, does involve a sense of belonging to a particular social group and acceptance by it. Wealth alone may not give entry to high-status groups in society: accent, mannerisms and dress may identify a person as belonging to a particular status ranking regardless of earnings or accumulated wealth.

However, in the main the higher the social class the greater the likelihood of wealth possession. The bottom half of the population now share only 7 per cent of personal national wealth between them, while the most wealthy 1 per cent of the population own over one-quarter of this wealth (if the value their homes are excluded, 8 per cent and almost one-fifth if homes are included). Top wealth owners are mainly hereditary and have the attributes associated with the ruling élite, protecting their position by manipulating the economic and tax structures; within the group there remains a very clear link between wealth and social class.

Although the link becomes more diffuse as one descends the social scale (for example, many professionals may have been upwardly mobile and own little apart from their salary and savings), there is no doubt that the connection between wealth ownership and class remains.

Part Five

Work and leisure

░ ░ **12** The meaning of work

12.1 The effect of work on behaviour

Work is more than a job. It may be a place where we meet other people, make friends, perhaps marry. For many people it is a place where they acquire the status that they carry outside into the general society – a BMW on the drive rather than a Ford. Others will establish a status recognised by their workmates, as a person of skill or the man who is not afraid of the boss.

The kind of work we do is likely to influence our political views. For example until the 1997 General Election it was suggested that women were less likely to vote Labour than are men, partially, at least, because they are more likely to work in the middle class ambience of an office, with more direct contact with management. In 1992 Gallup's post-election survey found that 44 per cent of women voted Conservative compared with 38 per cent of men; but gender difference had little impact in 1997, perhaps because Labour was no longer perceived as a threat to commercial interests and many managers supported 'New Labour' as well.

Roles at work

People adopt a role when they take a job; there is a socially shared expectation of how they should behave. 'A judge is supposed to be deliberate and sober, a pilot in a cockpit cool, a book-keeper to be accurate and neat' was true when Goffman wrote it in 'Encounters' in 1972, and it is still true today – although the 'bookkeeper' might be working at a computer. People adopt their work roles as part of their self-identity and carry them forward into their life outside work. Work is part of the process of socialisation.

The type of work we do is likely to affect our family relationship; perhaps because long absences make our family more strangers than are our workmates or because the nature of our work makes us almost totally uninterested in it, so that we focus our attention on our relationships elsewhere.

Motives for work

In 1974, in *The Social Psychology of Work*, Argyle listed the main motives for work, which still apply today:

1 **Economic** – to obtain money and fringe benefits
2 **Satisfaction** – an avenue of achievement and source of personal pride and interest
3 **Social** – to achieve status, companionship and security.

Alternatively it may be said that the function of work is to provide status, identity and income. Of these three, income may not be the most important, although most people may claim that it is. A survey, *Teenage Attitudes*, of 3925 young people between the ages of 15 and 19 in Ipswich, in 1984, showed that 60 per cent would have preferred to be paid the same as the 'dole' and have a job, than to have no job at all. As a mnemonic, or aide-memoire, it could be said that people work for CISSES:

- Contribution
- Integration
- Status
- Satisfaction
- Economic reward
- Social contact.

Most people object to what they would call 'charity' – they need to feel that they are making a contribution to their community. Work integrates the young into the adult community and assists them to move from the dependence of childhood. Work provides our status and many people obtain their major feelings of satisfaction and fulfilment from work. Economic motives are the most self-evident reason for work, and without work most people's social contacts – their opportunities to meet people beyond their immediate family and neighbourhood – would be severely limited. If the opportunity to work disappears it is not sufficient to replace it with financial benefits alone.

Patterns of work

Although S. Parker wrote *The Sociology of Industry* in 1967, it still has validity. He divided work into three patterns; 'extension', 'neutrality' and 'opposition'. A person with an interesting job may be absorbed in it and not distinguish readily between 'work' and 'non-work'. A doctor may attend patients at irregular hours and be assisted by a spouse; a child care officer may devote much free time to matters connected with work – their work is 'extended' into their other activities.

Some, such as bank employees, work regular hours and there is little relationship between work, family and leisure other than income – the position is 'neutral'. Others, such as miners, whose work is physically or psychologically exacting, seek to escape from it as much as possible in their non-work activities – theirs is a position of 'opposition'.

Many of the examples given by Parker are still relevant, but the increase in technology based work, self-employment, and smaller rather than larger units of employment will make it necessary to make some alteration to where a job might be classified – the routine repetition of the call centre with little personal autonomy may result in 'opposition', or at least 'neutrality'. The growing number of the self-employed in the official category that covers 'artistic and literary creation and interpretation and hairdressing and other beauty treatments' which increased by 62 per cent between 1992 and 1998 may well be increasing those in the 'extension category'.

From 1984 to 1994 the number of men working part-time doubled, and the number of people employed by firms of more than 500 slumped to just over a third of the employed population, with over one in eight of British workers now self-employed – this gives greater freedom of action to many people, but the price is lack of job security.

The reason for work

The work ethic

> This is an interesting example of culture lag – people have been socialised for a world which no longer exists. This is always a danger at times of rapid technological and social change. A puritanical work ethic was functional in a society which needed large numbers of manual workers, but in a society where this kind of work has been taken over by automation and computer control, then such attitudes are dysfunctional.
>
> In future, it may even become necessary to 'ration' work, whereas, in the past, holidays or free time were rationed. The major difficulty will be to persuade people to re-adjust to a new and very different situation. This will need a change of attitude not only on the part of the unemployed, but also a change of attitude by some politicians who continue to associate the unemployed with scrounging and immorality.
>
> But meanwhile it is quite wrong to equate 'unemployment' with 'leisure'. Leisure implies not only time, but sufficient money and opportunity for enjoyment. Most of the long-term unemployed are both poor and miserable.
>
> (*New Society*, 11 February 1982)

It is interesting to note that the leisure boom envisaged in this extract has not materialised. By 2000 unemployment had fallen rapidly and with the considerable increase in women in employment the number of people actually in work was greater than had ever previously been the case. Hours of work actually increased and a growing number of people had two jobs. However, there continued to be a core of long-term unemployed, particularly in areas where traditional industries had declined or disappeared.

The psychological implications of the changing patterns of work

More organisations are downsizing, market testing and outsourcing, which means more of us in the future will be selling our services to organisations on short-term contract or freelance bases. What are the implications for the wealth of the individual, his/her family and future organisations? Can individuals commit to organisations that don't commit to them? Can families survive the conflicts surrounding the changing role of men and women? Will women become the main breadwinners, given their flexible approach to work? Will these developments create 'virtual organisations' with more teleworkers?

The last half century has seen an enormous change in the nature of society and the workplace. The '60s epitomised the limitless possibilities of change, as society confronted the horrors of the Vietnam War and the traditional and established lifestyles of the post war period. It was an era that embraced new technology, with Harold Wilson proclaiming that the 'white heat of technology' was about to transform our lives, producing a leisure age of 20-hour weeks. This was followed by the '70s, a period of industrial strife, conflict and retrenchment. The workplace became the battleground between employers and workers, between the middle classes and the working classes, between liberal- and conservative-thinking. This industrial confrontation was highlighted by Studs Terkel in his acclaimed book of the period *Working*:

'Work is by its very nature about violence – to the spirit as well as to the body. It is about ulcers as well as accidents, about shouting matches as well as fist-fights, about nervous breadowns as well as kicking the dog around. It is, above all, about daily humiliations. To survive the day is triumph enough for the walking wounded among the great many of us.'

Out of the turmoil of the '70s came the 'enterprise culture' of the '80s, a decade of privatisations, statutory constraints on industrial relations, mergers and acquisitions, strategic alliances, joint ventures, process re-engineering and the like, transforming workplaces into free market, hot-house cultures. Although this entrepreneurial period improved our economic competitiveness at home and in international markets, there were also the first signs of strain, as 'stress' and 'burn-out' became concepts in the everyday vocabulary of working people.

By the end of the '80s and into the early '90s, the sustained recession, together with the privatising mentality with regard to the public sector, laid the groundwork for potentially the most profound changes in the workplace since the Industrial Revolution. The early years of the '90s were dominated by the effects of recession and efforts to get out of it, as organisations 'downsized', 'delayed', 'flattened' or 'right-sized'. Whatever euphemism you care to use, the hard reality experienced by many was job loss and constant change. There were fewer people, doing more work, and feeling more insecure. The rapid expansion of information technology also meant the added burden of information overload and the accelerating pace of work, with people demanding more information, quicker and quicker. From the mid-'80s through the '90s, we also saw the massive expansion of women in the workplace, with a noticeable pushing (not shattering) of the glass ceiling further upwards. The changing role of men and women at work and at home added another dimension to the enormity of change taking place in the offices, factory floors and technocultures of UK plc . . .

Will this trend toward stable insecurity, freelance working and virtual organisations continue? More importantly, can organisations, virtual or otherwise, continue to demand commitment from employees they don't commit to? In comparative terms the UK economy is doing remarkably well but the levels of job insecurity and dissatisfaction are high. Developing and maintaining a 'feel good' factor at work and in our economy generally is not just about bottom line factors, such as higher salaries, a penny off income tax or increased profitability; in a civilised society it should be about quality of life issues as well, like hours of work, family time, manageable workloads, control over one's career and some sense of job security. The social anthropologist Studs Terkel suggested,

'[work] is about a search for daily meaning as well as daily bread, for recognition as well as cash, for astonishment rather than torpor, in short, for a sort of life rather than a Monday through Friday sort of dying.'

As we approach the millennium, I hope employers will reflect on where they are going and what that might mean for employees and society in the future, and try to action their often espoused but rarely implemented belief: 'Our most valuable resource is our human resource'. Let us all remember what John Ruskin wrote in 1871:

'In order that people may be happy in their work, these things are needed: they must be fit for it; they must not do too much of it; and they must have a sense of success in it.'

(From a lecture by Cary Cooper, Professor of Organisational Psychology, UMIST, *RSA Journal*, 1 April 1998)

12.2 Alienation and job satisfaction

Alienation

Marx thought that increasing mechanisation would assist in the final removal of class differences because the worker would become 'alienated from the means of production', realise his identification with others in a similar position himself, and 'expropriate the expropriators'.

Alienation of labour: 1

> In what does this alienation of labour consist? First that the work is external to the worker, that it is not a part of his nature, that consequently he does not fulfil himself in his work but denies himself, has a feeling of misery, not of well being, does not develop freely a physical and mental energy, but is physically exhausted and mentally debased. The worker therefore feels himself at home only during his leisure, whereas at work he feels homeless.
>
> (Karl Marx, *Economics*, 1844)

Although the concept of **alienation** has been challenged, most sociologists have seen it as an explanation of many problems in industry and of subsequent behaviour in non-work situations.

Alienation of labour: 2

> Typically the worker does not own the tools with which he works, or the capital which is employed in the production process. He is also separated from the product of his work . . . a sense of lack of wholeness, a sense of frustration or of loss of humanity. It seems that men's lives and work are controlled by things – by money; by 'market forces'; by technology. 'Alienation', therefore, is more than just a sense of boredom at work; it also refers to a lack of power on the part of the worker.
>
> (Peter Worsley, *Introducing Sociology*, 1970, 1992 edn)

Division of labour

It may be that not only boredom at work but also a feeling that he is unimportant, and without power, encourages the worker to engage in strikes and leads to absenteeism, accidents, lateness and frequent job changes.

Although it would be nonsense to claim that in some past golden age everyone enjoyed their work, it is probable that job dissatisfaction did increase with large-scale mechanisation, when machines took over jobs previously performed by hand and thereby reduced the need for individual skills. Equally important is the effect of 'the division of labour' which developed from it. The essential ideal of the **division of labour** is that people perform better if they have only one task to perform. The production process is broken down into a series of tasks and individuals concentrate their activity in only a few of these areas. This principle has led to assembly-line working and has had a number of advantages in addition to the main one of faster, more economical working. Training is simpler and quicker; a worker can be selected and put to do the task he does best all of the time; people with disabilities can sometimes do a job whereas they could not master more complicated operations; increasing productivity leads to cheaper goods and an improved standard of living. The disadvantages are mainly social:

loss of job satisfaction; boring work may reduce individuality and this may be carried forward into non-work activities as well; monotony may result in fatigue, increasing accidents; direct contact between management and worker decreases, with a consequent lack of communication and possible increase of industrial strife (see Figures 12.1–12.3).

The division of labour also lends itself to measurement and in the 1920s 'Speedy' Taylor introduced work study or 'time and motion', earning himself the title of 'the most hated man in America' despite the fact that, after finding the best man for the job and teaching him to do it with maximum efficiency, the intention was to use high wage rates as an incentive to a high rate of production.

However, in the 1920s Mayo's studies of Chicago car-workers already showed that men tended to work better when treated as individuals.

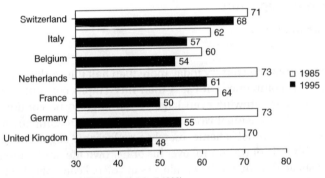

Source: ISR Survey (RSA Journal, 1 April 1998)

Figure 12.1   Employee satisfaction: employment security; 1995 and 1985 (per cent favourable re 1995 and 1985)

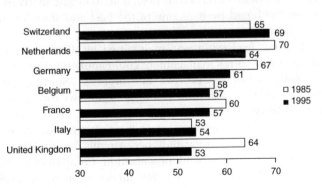

Source: ISR Survey (RSA Journal, 1 April 1998)

Figure 12.2   Employee satisfaction: country profile; 1995 and 1985

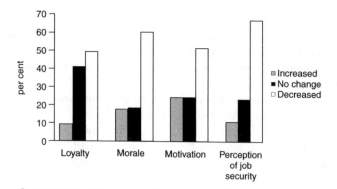

Source: Institute of Management (*RSA Journal*, April 1998)

Figure 12.3   Effects of recent organisational change on managers

Worker participation

The industrial illness

In any industrialized country today more than half the working population still works in companies with less than fifty employees. But some giant organizations are growing even larger – too large to be comfortable for employees. The individual working in a large modern company too often feels lost in the overall scheme, merely a replaceable cog in the industrial system, with little or no control over his or her own life until retirement . . . I cannot speak directly for the employees at Volvo. I can only observe how I see them behave in different situations. Since 1971, I have been able to see how union leaders conduct themselves as members of the company's board of directors. I have watched as they learned how the board functions and what kind of matters it handles. They now understand that the board is not engaged in activities that imply a conspiracy against the workers. These employee representatives have thus been able to negate many of the false myths about the board perhaps one of the best and soundest results of broadening the board representation.

In another era, leadership was maintained by disciplinary rules and punishment. A company's management could apply sanctions or even fire people, ruling labour by decrees and notices. 'Spitting prohibited', management could say. That time is long gone, and we can be thankful for the progress. Today we must grow closer to labor, no matter how busy management is . . . It sometimes scares me that what we do in Volvo is presented to others as an innovation, because this demonstrates, after all, how little has been done in work organization. Companies spend almost endless hours trying to provide change, incentive, interest, involvement, and motivation for top executives, yet almost no time is spent in looking at the rest of the work force in the same way. Until now, managers have not found it necessary. We are still in the era that Adam Smith described so many years ago, where 'a worker gives up his ease, his liberty and his happiness when he goes into industry'.

If we can give the worker back his ease, his liberty and his happiness, or at least provide conditions under which he can find them for himself, I believe we will come closer to a healthy, human, 'post-industrial' society.

(P. Gyllenhammar, *People at Work*, Reading, Mass., Addison-Wesley, 1977)

Note that this extract was written in 1977 but it provides an interesting comparison with today. Although organisations are now generally decreasing in size and many companies have introduced partnership schemes for their workers, increasing worker representation in decision-making forums and/or introducing an element of employee shareholding or profit sharing, there is nevertheless no evidence of a massive change in the attitudes outlined by Gyllenhammar.

12.3 Gender and work

The Mintel report (2000)

In 2000 Mintel published a report 'Family Lifestyles and the Effects of Work' based on a stratified random sample of 1774 Britons. The report found that traditional family roles were being reversed as fathers were increasingly prepared to substitute their career prospects and salary for the opportunity to stay at home and raise children.

- Men were willing to work fewer hours because they enjoyed their careers less than their wives or girlfriends enjoyed theirs, the women were more likely to enjoy the social activity and companionship of the workplace.

  However, mothers in full-time employment felt more guilty about working than anyone else and admitted buying presents for their children in an attempt to make up for not spending time with them.
- 53 per cent of the women questioned said that they enjoyed their job, compared with 47 per cent of men.
- While in the past the workplace was a key source of companionship and social activity for men, only one in four working fathers with children under sixteen said that this was still the case, compared with 40 per cent of working mothers.

  Work appeared to have more of an effect on the social and family lives of the men than it did on those of the women. Nearly 40 per cent of men complained that their social or family life suffered, against 30 per cent of full-time working women.

- Nearly one in four mothers who did not go out to work said that they would prefer to do so. The non-working mothers of children under five were the most dissatisfied, with 28 per cent of them wishing that they had jobs.

The report also indicated a decline in the traditional family unit of a couple with dependant children, which in 1979 had represented almost a third of all households in Britain.

By the late 1990s, less than a quarter of households were of this type, with one-parent families having almost doubled to nearly 7 per cent of all households.

This report gives some indication of the huge change in attitudes and behaviour since the standard studies of coal miners, fishermen, lorry drivers and textile workers in the 1950s and 1960s.

Coal is Our Life was a study of a coal mining community in Yorkshire by Dennis, Henriques and Slaughter published in 1956 and, as with the other studies, gave a graphic insight into how the work a person does has a dramatic effect on all the other aspects of that person's life, particularly relationships within the home and leisure activities and they remain valid as comparators with society today.

Mining

Mining has ceased to be a major industry in Britain but half a century ago a substantial proportion of the male population was engaged in this single-sex, dangerous, work carried out under often appalling conditions. It required a considerable amount of team work, and this social cohesion was carried forward into solidarity in political matters. The average miner expected his home to be the opposite of the pit – warm comfortable and tidy. The special-relationships established at work were also carried forward into leisure. Men tended to drink and gamble together, women were excluded, as they were in the pit. Relationships between husband and wife were often poorly established, the function of the family being restricted in the main to reproduction and the socialisation of children. The insecurity of mining decreased the incentive to save rather than increasing it. If money were saved it would decrease the miner's benefits in the quite likely event of an accident and so the miner sought to enjoy it while he had the opportunity ('short-term hedonism').

Fishing

A similar pattern emerged in the 1962 study by Tunstall of the trawlermen of Hull. They, too, engaged in a dangerous and physically demanding work often in foul conditions. *The Fishermen* illustrated how to most fishermen long-term absence from home, linked with shared dangers and discomfort, reduced the importance of the family while emphasising the importance of their mates. Brief shore excursions tended to be spent drinking and gambling with their shipmates rather than at home with their wife and family.

As with the miners' wives of 'Ashton', the wives of the trawlermen built up their own social relationships with women friends and relatives who would be available to help out when needed. Both groups had a generally low standard of living, the standards being set in early manhood on a low income. Any increase in money merely meant an increase in pleasure.

The close-knit Hull fishing community, like many of the mining communities, is now long gone but some of the attitudes of both males and females in these areas will be carried on, even if somewhat diluted, through the socialisation process. Today's boys look to their fathers and male relatives as role models for masculine behaviour, just as their fathers had done before them – the media may encourage change, the family tends to act as powerful counterbalance.

Lorry driving

In 1968 Hollowell divided lorry drivers into three categories and in *The Lorry Driver* showed how differences in their work situations influenced their non-work attitudes and activities.

Lorry driving as an occupation has increased considerably since the book was written, just as coal mining and fishing have declined, although the work has changed considerably with many more long-distance hauls across Europe and more sophisticated vehicles requiring less physical effort; there is no longer a nationalised sector and more truckers own their own trucks. Unlike mining and fishing, lorry drivers live in all parts of the country and so the reader may have the opportunity to compare the reality of today's lorry driver with that described by Hollowell.

Types of lorry driver

- **Shunter**. Local delivery driver, often takes the 'trunker's' lorry and may have to load and off-load (low status).
- **Trunker**. Long-distance with set route, often gets home every night or every second night. Does not usually load or off-load (high status).
- **Tramper** ('**rover/roamer**'). No fixed route. More loading and off-loading. More physically arduous, but more variety and less regularity (medium status).

Occupation and family life

The lorry driver's occupation meant that his presence in the home was more limited and irregular than in many other occupations. This was greatest at the time when children are growing up as it was at this time that economic necessity often resulted in a move to 'tramping' or 'trunking'; a desire for higher status also contributed to such a change. Particularly therefore in the case of the tramper the wife was likely to take on the role of organising the family, including house repairs.

Many drivers tried to compensate by intensive domestic activities when at home, and time off was likely to be spent in the home. Sexual relations were distorted by absence. Drivers themselves took the view that the tramper should be a single man. Wives, however, found adaptation to absence more difficult than did the drivers themselves and the opportunity which absence made for extra-marital relations made marriage breakdown more likely. Such breakdown is more probable in most 'mobile occupations' (e.g. Hull fishermen in

Tunstall's study accounted for 5 per cent of Hull divorces but only 2.5 per cent of the population).

Leisure

Long working hours and absence from home meant that lorry drivers' leisure activities in their own community were severely limited. A considerable minority were also absent at weekends. Unlike the fishermen and coal miners they did not have a geographical base in which their work norms could dominate and influence their non-work activities. Therefore approximately 50 per cent of leisure activities were home-centred and slightly less were 'family-centred' (e.g. out for runs in the car). There was not much participation in organised leisure – some 'club' membership, but all of those were in drinking clubs. 'I sleep, I've no hobbies', was one lorry driver's account of his leisure. 'Yes, it's a lonely job, but you are independent', said another. Trunkers had steadier friendships and more personalised conversation as they tended to meet up more.

Politics

Headlight, the drivers' paper, had a bias which was slightly right of centre in politics – which probably reflected their general mood and the emphasis was on individualism rather than the group solidarity of the miner.

The management of private firms was much more popular than the nationalised despite better comradeship, variety, pay and trade union representation in the nationalised sector. ('BRS won't let you use your initiative.') The tramper in both the private and nationalised firms had the most favourable view of management, perhaps because they were least in contact with their work superiors and felt themselves to be their own 'boss'.

Lorry driver compared with worker in textile factory

Hollowell also compared the attitude of lorry drivers to those of a group of textile workers. The lorry drivers expressed more satisfaction than did the textile workers in their jobs. Relations with fellow workers, familiarity with their job and wages were all more important to the textile workers than to the lorry drivers. The major dislike of the lorry drivers was the ordinary road-user. The major dislike of the textile workers was monotony and boredom, supervision and management. The main source of inter-personal relationships for lorry drivers was the people they met around the country rather than their fellow lorry drivers. Two-thirds of lorry drivers said they would not consider working in a factory even for more pay (this was particularly true of 'trampers'). A few lorry drivers did find the greater comfort, regularity and domestic routine of the factory worker attractive, but most disliked the idea of factory work for the same reasons as did the textile workers themselves. Particular mention was made by lorry drivers of the satisfaction they experienced from 'responsibility'.

Hollowell expressed his view that the lorry driver was 'alienated', however it may be felt that the lorry driver was not alienated in the generally recognised sense because he himself had a feeling of worth, status and responsibility.

12.4 The future of work

The future of work

A two-day week; a stimulating job involving decision-making technical skill and social worth; an income sufficient to indulge your wide recreational and educational interests? Sound exciting? But what would you do with all this free time?

It seems far-fetched in an age of rising unemployment, but with the advent of the micro-chip (the tiny circuit that controls your calculator or watch), most boring and repetitive tasks could be eliminated, and we could all have an interesting job and more leisure. The chip, some people argue, could bring work of a different kind, rather than simply fewer jobs.

If work is becoming less important, the corollary is that leisure is becoming more so. But are we really prepared for what could be a fundamental change in the human condition? Many writers think not, and the vision of future leisure as a great human problem has been summed up recently by one of the most famous science fiction writers. Arthur C. Clarke, author of 2001:

'In the world of the future, the sort of mindless labour that has occupied 99 per cent of mankind for much more than 99 per cent of its existence, will, of course, be largely taken over by machines. Yet most people are bored to death without work – even work that they don't like. In a workless world, therefore, only the highly educated will be able to flourish, or perhaps even to survive. The rest are likely to destroy themselves and their environment out of sheer frustration. This is no vision of the distant future; it is already happening, most of all in the decaying cities. So perhaps we should not despise TV soap operas if, during the turbulent transition period between our culture and real civilisation, they serve as yet another opium of the masses.'

One important factor in a person's choice of leisure activity is his occupation. In a study in 1963 by Stanley Parker, 200 people in ten occupations were interviewed. Several patterns were found. Bank employees were found to be least involved in their work, tending to see it merely as a means to earning a living. They were not so engrossed in their work that they wanted to take it over into their spare time, nor were they so damaged by it that they were hostile to it. Child care officers tended to enjoy their work, and often related it to their leisure. Work and leisure for them were often similar in content, and existed comfortably side by side.

Miners and deep-sea fishermen, on the other hand, had a pattern of opposition between work and leisure. Leisure functioned for them as something totally distinct and separate – something that compensated for dangerous and difficult work. There was what might be described as hostility between work and leisure . . .

Stanley Parker, who has done much modern research into leisure, has said that 'today vestiges of the Protestant work ethic remain, but it has been strongly challenged by a more leisure-based ethic: that work is a means to the end of enjoying oneself in leisure. Earlier, work gave a man his sense of identity. Today, it is claimed, his leisure is more likely to supply it.' The extent to which we in Britain are in such a leisure-centred culture is debatable.

(*New Society*, 1979)

By 2001 the reality was clearly somewhat different from that envisaged by Arthur C. Clark, certainly the expansion of leisure time had not materialised for most people. A more realistic vision may have been provided by Professor Peter Cochrane the Head of Research at BT in 1999.

'A leisure-centre culture?'

Getting the best from technology

Children tend to embrace technology. I bought my 11 year-old son a robotic arm for Christmas and he proceeded to eat his tea with it. He is going to be part of a new workforce that has never known a world without computers. So we have to think of how we are going to form a partnership with technology to get the best from both. I already think of my computer as the third lobe of my brain – without it I could do nothing.

My father had a working life of 100,000 hours. I could do everything he did in 10,000 hours and my son will be able to do it in 1000. This speed-up means that we have to think and behave in a different way. It took the UK 70 years to industrialise. Subsequently the US did it in 40 years, Japan in 27, China in 10. The US has created an information economy in 15 years whereas the Europeans persist in trying to create an information society. We have to focus on the wealth generation mechanisms first – and society second. If not, the competition will eat our lunch.

The future of work

Work is no longer a place, it is an activity. I work everywhere all the time and I go to my office to be disturbed, not to concentrate. My concentrated effort now takes place on trains and planes, in cars and hotel rooms, at home and not in my office.

Seven years ago my company had 242,000 people. Today it has fewer than 110,000 and the number will continue to fall. Much of the work previously undertaken by people is now done by machines. That is going to have a big effect everywhere. You might ask what is going to happen to the people who are put out of work. However this question is as relevant as the fate of unemployed monks and the destruction of the quill pen industry when the printing press was invented. People will be doing new things that we find difficult to imagine today. Only 500 years ago no one could imagine a computer let alone multi-media. In 50 years we will wonder what all the fuss was about.

Life is getting faster and not just in business. It is happening in healthcare and education and every other sector. Probably government is the only area that is totally immune because it has no competition. However, they should be aware that technology and society will render them irrelevant and by-pass them if they do not change and adopt new technology and organisational methods. I have travelled the planet, including the Third World, and the only place where I failed to get my computer to work was the House of Lords. The power sockets there are older than I am and the wiring is cotton-covered . . .

We are already creating a society of just two classes. The first and larger class will spend incredible amounts of time to save money. The second will spend incredible amounts of money to save time.

As we get more and more mobile devices we will see whole networks brought down by chaos. Imagine a large conference where 4000 are listening to a presentation and not making phone calls. At 10.15 coffee arrives and 200 mobile phones come out within two minutes and the system crashes. A motorway accident can give rise to 1000 calls within two minutes and again the system crashes. We have to think about how we organise our systems to cope with chaotic demand.

We now have Coke machines that ring up for more supplies when the sun comes out and chocolate-bar machines that ring up for more chocolate when the weather is cold. When you get married you buy your washing machine and tumble drier and so on and seven years later everything crashes and has to be replaced. The appliances have been designed to have a meantime between failure of about seven years . . .

More and more people are buying through virtual shops on the Internet. In this arena retail and wholesale have been wiped out by disintermediation. However they will soon reappear in a new form since the speed of the electronic world means that more and more intermediaries will be required . . .

Perils of continual reorganisation

For managers, the meantime between decisions is now greater than the meantime between surprises. More provocatively: the meantime between managers is greater than, equal to, or less than the meantime between reorganisations. Companies now have to reorganise continually in order to stay on top. Most are in one of three states: getting over a reorganisation, in the middle of one or thinking of having another. They are going to die of continual reorganisation strain. The problem is that they have not wrapped their arms round the combination of people, technology and behaviour change that they need in order to survive.

(*RSA Journal*, 2 April 2000)

REVISION SUMMARY

The effect of work on behaviour

S. Parker, in *The Sociology of Industry* (1967), divided work into three patterns:

1 **Extension**: A person with an interesting job may be absorbed in it and not distinguish easily between 'work' and 'non-work' (e.g. a businessman discussing business on the golf course; a teacher preparing a lesson at home; a doctor attending a patient out of hours; a policeman arresting a suspect off duty).
2 **Neutrality**: Applies to those with jobs that need not involve the whole personality, regular hours, a generally pleasant environment. There is little relationship between work, family and leisure other than income (e.g. bank employees; Civil Service clerical officers).
3 **Opposition**: Those with a dirty, dangerous, physically tiring or psychologically exacting job may seek complete escape from it in their non-work activities (e.g. deep-sea fishermen; refuse collectors).

It would be wrong to assume that every individual within each category regards his or her job in the same way – these are generalisations.

One British survey indicated that British managers, unlike the American ones studied by Parker, did not regard leisure as an extension to their work. Nor is it true that everyone with the same job 'label' does the same job and has the same attitude to it.

Alienation and job satisfaction

Peter Worsley (see p. 168) described this alienation as 'a sense of lack of wholeness, a sense of frustration or of a loss of humanity'. It seems that men's lives and work are controlled by things – by money; by 'market forces', by technology. 'Alienation' is more than just a sense of boredom at work; it also refers to a lack of power on the part of the worker.

Table 12.1

Dimension	Impact on worker if low	Example factors	Examples
The degree of control workers have over their work	**Powerlessness**	Tied to a machine/ closely supervised	Machine minder in textile factory;
The degree of meaning and sense of purpose they find in work	**Meaninglessness**	Division of labour into apparently unconnected repetitive tasks	assembly-line worker in car factory
The degree to which they are socially integrated in their work	**Isolation**	Cut off from other workers by noise; no freedom of movement	
The degree to which they are involved in their work	**Self-estrangement**	Undemanding tasks make no use of the workers' intelligence or personality	

Alienation may have an adverse effect upon employers as well as employees, because there is evidence to indicate that increased alienation leads to more strikes, lateness, frequent job changes, absenteeism, illness and industrial accidents, as well as to increasing damage to equipment and to a less satisfactory product.

■ M ■ 13 Rewards and conditions

13.1 Status

People work for 'CISSES' (section 12.1). The relevant importance that people attach to each is partially a matter of individual judgement and partially a matter of necessity. If people feel that they cannot aspire to a high-status position, they may dismiss such an objective and claim that they are only interested in money or job satisfaction.

Work objectives are clearly very mixed. Although financial considerations may appear to be paramount, the objective may be to buy a 'status symbol' – some visible item such as a large car – which will identify them in their neighbours' eyes as belonging to a higher social group.

Within the workplace, status rankings are still often reinforced by separate toilet, eating and storage facilities. In large bureaucracies, status may be officially recognised by the provision of status symbols such as larger offices and even pieces of carpet of varying sizes.

One motive for work is status

'I'm sorry, J.B., the Company feels that you have failed to live up to the desk.'

Some status is not connected with social class position. A shop steward may have high status among her workmates as someone who is not afraid to stand up to management; a headteacher may have high status among other headteachers as someone who can successfully run a difficult school.

13.2 Hours and conditions of work

Working hours

In 1938, as in 1918, the number of hours per week worked by men in manual occupations was 47; and by 1998, after a decline during part of the preceding thirty years it was back up to the 1918 level (indeed rather higher at 47.5 hours).

However, 'white' collar workers have traditionally worked shorter hours than 'blue', and full-time female employees have tended to work fewer hours than male, and it is the growth of the proportion of employees in these two categories that explains the fact that when the working hours of all employees are considered, both non-manual as well as manual and female as well as male, the average working hours per week reduces to 44 hours. However, even this represents a steady increase in the number of hours worked, from 43.7 hours in 1990 and 42.6 hours in 1984. It also refers only to 'main jobs' and does not take account of the growing number of people with two jobs (usually part-time).

Clearly the steady reduction in working hours forecast by many sociologists in the 1970 and 1980s has failed to materialise – there is no 'Leisure Society'. Indeed as people now tend to travel further between home and work the time spent in employment and travel to work is probably greater than in 1918. The 'Working Time Regulations' (an EC Directive) came into force on 1 October 1998. The Regulation requires employers to 'take all reasonable care' to ensure that employees do not work, against their will, more than an average of 48 hours a week. In addition, it gave employees an entitlement to four weeks annual leave from November 1999. (There are a small number of exclusions, including seamen and junior hospital doctors.)

Holiday time

It is in this area of holiday time that there has been a genuine increase in leisure. In 1961 less than 10 per cent of full-time manual employees received more than two weeks' holiday a year; by 1980 some 75 per cent received four weeks or more. By 1995 some 10 per cent of all full-time employees received more than six weeks (see Table 13.1).

During the last twenty-five years around 60 per cent of British adults have taken a holiday away from home each year; however, the proportion taking two or more holidays increased by more than half between 1971 and 1995. There is, however, a considerable amount of variation by social grade.

	Holidays in Britain	Holidays abroad	No holiday
AB	44	59	18
C1	37	47	31
C2	38	32	38
DE	28	20	57

Table 13.1   Holiday taking: by social grade, 1995 (Great Britain, per cent[1])

Note:
[1] Percentage of people in each social grade taking holidays in each location. Percentages do not sum to 100 because some people take holidays in both Britain and abroad.
Sources: British Tourist Authority; *Social Trends*, 27 National Statistics © Crown Copyright, 1997.

Overtime

White collar workers still have a shorter working week than blue collar employees, largely accounted for by an absence of overtime. The apparent 'convergence' of middle and working class earnings must be viewed in the light of these differing working hours (section 11.4).

Security of employment and saving

Traditionally, manual workers have had less security of employment than non-manual, being 'laid off' more readily in times of recession or when work was seasonal. This meant that it was more difficult for them to obtain extended credit – for house purchase, for example. It was also less sensible for them to save, as their savings would have to be used up before they could claim welfare benefits.

Changes to employment law and practice during the past twenty years changed the position to some extent, but the pattern of immediate spending has been established and there is still rather more chance of non-manual workers saving than there is of manual workers doing so. In the past, such differences were emphasised by the manual worker's weekly 'wage' and the non-manual employee's monthly 'salary', although computerised payrolls directly into bank accounts has substantially increased the number of manual workers paid monthly.

The ambience of the office or shop is more likely to encourage the employee to identify with management than is the atmosphere of the shop floor, even although the people in question may have the same earnings. Changes in the work situation for many white collar workers may result in an end to this situation.

Improving conditions of work

There have been a number of attempts to improve conditions of work:

- **Job rotation schemes** which endeavour to increase work satisfaction by training people for several jobs rather than one. Volvo, the Swedish car

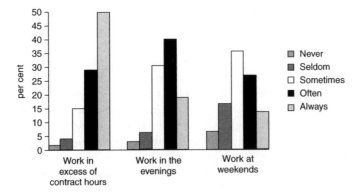

Figure 13.1   Working patterns, contract hours, evening and weekend work

manufacturer, replaced their assembly line with teams of workers who carried out all functions jointly. This is a form of the 'cell system' of organisation, also used by Philips' electrical appliance factories.

- **Four-day weeks** have been tried successfully as has 'flexitime', where people organise their own working times; some quarter of all women and one in six of all men now have some form of flexible working pattern.

More highly motivated workers do not necessarily work harder; but there is evidence of reductions in absenteeism, illness and accidents. Unsocial hours working has been increasing because of changes in the law and people's expectations. Although shift working declined in industry as a result of the reduction in employment in heavy industries such as coal mining and steelmaking, more people now expect services to be open longer, or even continuously (Figure 13.1).

The 24-hour society

In Britain society is governed by clock time. Other parts of the world use event time, when time periods are related to natural events. Torn between the attractiveness of event time and the efficiency of clock time, we have difficulty simply in finding enough time. Women who work full-time report that they now have 10% less time than they did in 1980, while men say they have 4% less. 70% of workers, particularly young people and women, want more flexible hours.

Balancing work and home

The stereotypical family was shattered long ago but the balance of responsibilities between the sexes has yet to reflect the new social order.

Domestic and work-sharing arrangements in Britain are none too enlightened. If a husband and wife are both working the same hours on average the woman does at least an extra nine hours a week of housework. Women not only work longer but they have a hard time adjusting between home and work. It is hardly surprising that working mothers are keenest on doctors and pharmacies opening early and closing late and would ideally like to see flexibility in the timing of the school day. Working women's demands for more flexible opening hours for services has resulted in 125 Italian cities adopting what they call 'city time'. A law enacted in 1990 gives mayors the ability 'to co-ordinate opening hours in a way that reflects the needs of users'. The female mayor of Modena led the way by providing one-stop centres for a range of council services so that citizens, particularly women, did not have to waste time dealing with different offices.

A 1996 Gallup poll found that more than 75% of working parents believed that people enjoyed less peace of mind than they used to. The UK economy doubles every 35 years and overall we have never been so wealthy. Yet we feel worse because we are finding it difficult to handle the combination of new family structures, lengthening working hours and the pressures of consumerism. The gap between our aspirations and reality is hard to handle in a society that judges people by what they own as well as what they are. More than 50% of the adult population agrees with the statement: 'I am often under time pressure in my everyday life.'

Our consumer culture

There are three ways to solve this problem. First, we could stop watching television, which would free three to four hours a day. Second, we could stop buying so many goods and services and so spend less time shopping. Third, if we bought less we could earn less and thus work fewer hours. We could do all those things, but we will not. To understand why we cannot reduce our consumption we have to understand human behaviour.

Consumption is more than ever before an experience which is located in the head. This century's triumph of marketing and advertising has been overcoming the law of thrift by translating wants into needs. A want is transferred into a purchase and is justified on the basis that it is now a need. Choice is overwhelming and it is intensifying. The Gap retail chain revamps its product line every six weeks. Nike introduces a new sports shoe every six weeks. Living in a consumer world requires money and time and most of us do not have both.

Extending the frontiers of time

We need to find more time but it is not a commodity that can be created. It seems to be a human characteristic that whenever we come up against scarcity in our environment we extend the frontiers. By colonising the night we can provide the means to use the available time more efficiently. The 24 hour society is more than simply extending shop opening hours. Eventually it will lead to a different construction of daily activities, freeing people from the restraints imposed by rigid adherence to the clock. It is about restructuring the temporal order in a way that makes sense in our age.

There is a strong link between work, shopping, services and transport, and they in turn affect patterns of land use. Government policies aiming to integrate transport or restrict land use need to include aspects of time. At present transport systems have to cope with peak capacity for four to six hours a day. They would operate more efficiently if there was equal loading throughout the day and night. The same applies to other utilities and services. If the working day was staggered over 16 hours, offices, shops and schools would have double the use they have now. We could get the same results as we do at present from half the buildings, which would have a substantial impact on land-use policy.

There are some who would go further than the 24 hour society and completely rethink the use of time. One suggestion is that we should switch to 28 hour days. Monday would be eliminated, on the basis that everyone hates Mondays. The work week would be four 10 hour shifts with a 56 hour weekend. Thursday might be a problem, being dark for most of the day, but as the originator of the idea suggested, Thursdays could be used for roadworks.

(From a lecture by Leon Kreitzman, *RSA Journal*, 2 April 1999)

How do you relate to the 24 hour society?

Michael Willmott of the Future Foundation is currently researching classification of how people relate to time. Here are some of his findings.

Fast laners −25%	Convenience driven −28%	Pressured conservatives −19%	Past timers −27%
• Under 30 without children	• 30–50 year olds	• Married with older children	• Mostly aged over 60
• Feel time-pressured	• Often married with dependent children	• Feel pace of life is too fast but are less pressured	• Majority are retired and children have left
• Enjoy the 24			

hour culture • Believe that their lives would be enhanced if services were available 24 hours a day	• Most time-pressured group • Believe 24 hour solution is a pragmatic answer to pace of life being too fast	than convenience driven group • Think 24 hour service is unnecessary and take moralistic line on it	home • Least time-pressured • Would like world to slow down to what it was in the past

(Leon Kreitzman, *The 24 Hour Society*, Profile Books, 1999)

13.3 Pay and 'fringe benefits'

Disposable income and income distribution

The amount of income remaining after all deductions is referred to as **household disposable income** and is a possible measure of living standards. Between 1971 and 1997 household disposable income per head rose by nearly 15 times, and when this is adjusted for inflation still results in a doubling of disposable income over the period, with the equivalent of an average growth rate of 2.6 per cent a year.

The extent to which people receive differing incomes is known as the **distribution of income**. These differences are then usually reduced by the redistribution of income through taxes and benefits.

Disposable income

Average real household disposable income rose by 55 per cent between 1971 and 1996. At the same time the gap between those with high incomes and those with low incomes grew. Between 1980 and 1990 the incomes of the top 10 per cent of income earners grew by 47 per cent compared with only 6 per cent for the bottom 10 per cent (Figures 13.2 and 13.3). Lone parents with children are the group which is much more likely than any other to be in the bottom 10 per cent.

'Fringe benefits'

Earnings from employment are the main source of income for most people; although 'fringe benefits' may include subsidised meals, company cars, share options, free transport, subsidised mortgages, non-contributory pension schemes and private medical care. In recent years governments have sought, with partial success, to tax fringe benefits in order to prevent their being used to provide untaxed salary increases – for example mobile phones were included in 1991. With the exception of subsidised meals and transport, fringe benefits

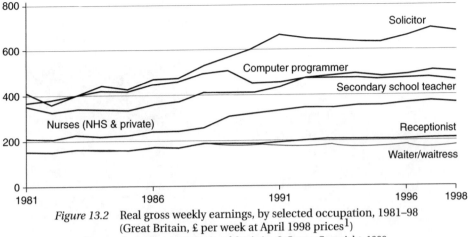

Figure 13.2   Real gross weekly earnings, by selected occupation, 1981–98
(Great Britain, £ per week at April 1998 prices[1])
Source: *Social Trends*, 29 National Statistics © Crown Copyright, 1999.

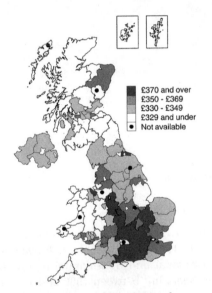

Figure 13.3   Average gross weekly earnings, by area, April 1998
Source: *Social Trends*, 29 National Statistics © Crown Copyright, 1999.

become increasingly prevalent the higher one climbs the class ladder. In 1996–7 3.2 million people in the United Kingdom received taxable fringe benefits, compared with 0.8 million in 1980–1.

The criteria used for deciding pay rates are partially a question of what the market will bear in terms of profit; partially a question of rewarding qualifications and scarce skills; partially sheer chance; and partially industrial muscle.

In 1999 the government introduced a National Minimum Wage as part of a plan to reduce poverty among those at work. This was set initially at 3.60 an hour for employees aged 22 and over and at £3 for those between 18 and 22. It is £4.10 from October 2001 and planned to be £4.20 in October 2002 for those 22 and over.

Status symbols such as company cars or houses bought with subsidised mortgages may be 'fringe benefits' – particularly higher up the class ladder

13.4 Trade unions

Decline in membership

By 1998 less than one in three workers in Britain were members of a trade union. In 1980 almost 13 million people belonged to 438 trade unions. Membership of both manual and non-manual unions had increased rapidly over the previous five years but between 1980 and 1985 trade union membership fell by 20 per cent, particularly in manufacturing. And the decline has continued every year since dropping a further 21 per cent between 1989 and 1999.

The decrease in highly unionised heavy industry as structural change took place in employment, self-employment, unemployment and legislation ending such practices as the 'closed shop' had reduced trade union membership to 10,700,000 by 1985, and by 1990 it had dropped to less than 10 million; it is now less than 8 million.

Future trends may be indicated by the fact that only 6 per cent of employees under the age of twenty are now trade union members, compared with about a third of those aged over thirty. Although the largest fall in membership occurred in 1992 during a time of substantial job losses, it has failed to recover the loss during the growth of employment since 1994.

History of unionism

Unions were originally set up in the middle of the nineteenth century to improve working conditions and pay; they still have these as their main objectives. Many employers are no longer hostile to trade unions, recognising that they may stop more 'unofficial' strikes than they start 'official' ones. In any case working days lost through strike action are now only a tiny fraction of those lost in the 1970s and 1980s.

The trade unions organised the skilled craftsmen first, restricting entry so that they could bargain from a position of scarcity. Unskilled workers were more difficult to organise and although many unskilled workers, particularly in the public sector (local government workers, for example) are now members of unions, a great many others such as those in hotels and catering remain unorganised.

There was a considerable growth in white collar unionism during the 1960s and 1970s, including those in the civil service, health service and teaching; and it has been suggested that this was because of an increasing identification with manual workers, open-plan offices like factories, limited promotion because of graduate recruitment, mechanisation and computerisation reducing some clerical skills to operative level, and larger organisations reducing the possibility of face-to-face contact with upper management. The larger and more impersonal an industrial or office unit is, the greater likelihood there is of it being unionised. Union membership rates are substantially higher in the public service than in the private sector and in larger workplaces compared with smaller ones.

Modern unions

Unions tend to fall into five main groups: those representing single industries; general craft unions dealing with several industries; skilled workers' unions; ex-craft unions now admitting semi-skilled workers; and white collar unions.

The number of unions and the overlapping of union membership within the work place often makes negotiation difficult and there have been successful attempts to negotiate 'single-union' agreements, although these are resented by the trade unions excluded from the plant. In 1978, the Bullock Report advocated that representatives of workers should sit on company boards of directors as they do in many countries including Germany. It was hoped that such worker participation might bring a new dimension to industrial negotiations which often appear to be based on conflict. However there has been comparatively little development along such lines in Britain. Despite justifiable concerns over preventing days being lost through industrial disputes it should be borne in mind that even in the worst years for industrial disputes the working days lost through strike action have only been about one-tenth of those lost because of sickness (Figure 13.4).

Trade unions and political power

The trade unions have traditionally had close links with the Labour Party and were instrumental in founding it. Most trade unionists, many of whom do not

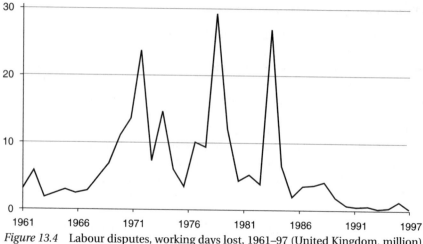

Figure 13.4 Labour disputes, working days lost, 1961–97 (United Kingdom, million)
Source: *Social Trends*, 29 National Statistics © Crown Copyright, 1999.

support the Labour Party, do not opt out of paying the 'political levy' from which much of the Labour Party finance comes.

There has been concern that such close links with one political party can be damaging to trade unionism during periods when the Labour Party is not in power. Equally, some believe that the Labour Party loses some public support because of its close connection with the trade unions. In 1993 mea-sures were taken to reduce the influence of the trade unions on the party, in particular the ending of the unions' block vote in the selection of parliamentary candidates. 'New Labour' elected in 1997 appears to have attempted to distance itself from its traditional ally as the party has sought greater support from 'Middle England', although it is still substantially dependent on trade union finance.

REVISION SUMMARY

Differences between manual and non-manual employees

Non-manual ('white collar'/'middle class') employees are:

- Less likely to have to 'clock on' at work.
- Less likely to have pay deducted for lateness.
- More likely to have time off with pay for personal reasons.
- More likely to have an employment pension scheme.
- More likely to have longer holidays.

Non-manual workers are more likely to have:

- Company cars.
- Subsidised mortgages.
- Non-contributory pension schemes.
- Private health care paid by company.

Manual workers are more likely to have:

- Subsidised meals.
- Free transport to work.

Trade unions

In the 1970 and 1980s there was an increase in trade union membership in some white collar sectors. This might have been the result of:

- Increasing identification with manual workers.
- Open-plan offices like factories.
- Limited promotion, because of graduate recruitment.
- Mechanisation and computerisation reducing some clerical skills to operative level.
- Larger organisations reducing the possibility of face-to-face contact with upper management.

However, there has been a substantial decline of trade union membership overall which can be accounted for by:

- A decline in the number of people employed in heavy industry (e.g. steel making), where 'working class solidarity' was the norm. The number of employees in manufacturing fell by over 40 per cent between 1971 and 1992.
- An overall change in employment from primary (e.g. farming) and secondary (e.g. manufacturing) sectors to the tertiary (or service) sectors.
- A reduction in number of public service employees (i.e. Civil Service and teaching, which were among the first 'white collar' employment areas to unionise).
- Changes in technology, which have particularly affected 'craft' areas, traditionally strongly unionised (e.g. the print industry).
- The new 'sunrise' industries (the new computer-based technologies) tend to be small units and small working units are less likely to unionise.
- Growth in self-employment. Partly as a result of government policies in the 1980s to encourage people to start up their own business, the number of self-employed people in Great Britain increased by 57 per cent between 1981 and 1990. By 1998 over 3,300,000 were self-employed (male 2.4 million, female 0.9 million – of these nearly one in five were working in the banking, finance, and insurance industries).
- Increased unemployment until 1994.

⊠ 14 The changing conditions of employment

14.1 Industrialisation, automation and mechanisation

Over a hundred years ago Marx saw that the methods used in production influenced all the other processes in society: social, political and intellectual.

Marx was writing at a time when revolutionary changes were taking place in the methods used in industry. People were flocking into the towns to work in factories and mines; machines were replacing many hand crafts; and the division of labour was permitting the development of conveyor-belt industrial processes (section 12.2).

Industrialisation with its concentration of manpower in large centres encouraged the organisation of labour into unions (section 13.4) and mechanisation, with its emphasis on the importance of matter rather than man, led to the alienation of many from their work. The methods of production had created an urban culture, and with it many additional problems of poverty, squalor and crime.

Automation is capable of taking over many industrial and commercial operations by replacing not just physical labour, as mechanisation did, but thought-processes as well. The computer must be programmed by people, but once the programme is in operation it can direct machines, alter schedules and correct itself. Automated machines have replaced many repetitive and undemanding work processes, but as computers have become more sophisticated, they have been used to replace the more skilled personnel as well. Ultimately the worker merely controls and supervises. Automation reduces the need for a division of labour, because a large workforce with each person doing a limited number of tasks is no longer needed.

Automation cannot be avoided any more than could **mechanisation**; international competition makes it inevitable that goods will be produced by the cheapest available means. The global market is with us and where goods (and increasingly services) can be produced more cheaply elsewhere, where labour costs are low, then production (or supply) migrates there.

14.2 Changing occupations and occupational structure

Automation is neither a good nor a bad thing in itself. It would be possible for the wealth produced by automated factories to be concentrated in a few hands; but this would be counterproductive. For if wealth is not distributed, consumers will not be able to buy the goods produced and the automated factories could not be kept in production.

Automation replaces both physical labour and thought processes

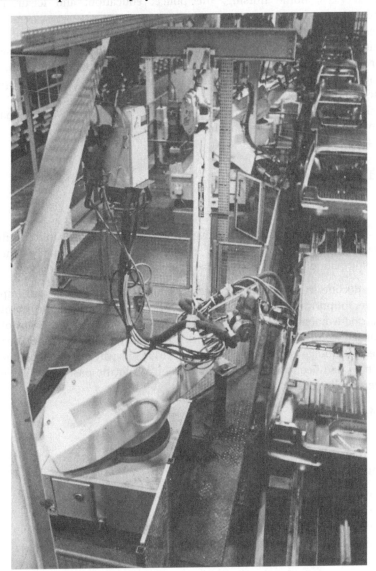

Alternatively, the process already started can continue with the number of jobs in manufacturing decreasing and the number of jobs in the '**tertiary**' sector – such service areas of work as distribution, health, information, and leisure – continuing to increase.

Traditional white collar jobs will not necessarily become more numerous as they have during the past half century, for many routine clerical functions can easily be automated. The word processor and the computer have already drastically reduced the number of 'typists'.

Essentially the greatest demand for labour in the future is likely to be in personal services of various kinds. The possibility of expansion in these areas is virtually limitless, given a determination that revenue should be spent on social services; home nursing; the police; education; and leisure-related activities.

The major possible advantage in the computer revolution is that it will reduce alienation by taking over the most tedious, repetitive and soulless processes. The major danger is that society will not respond quickly enough to the change, and produce a balance of work and leisure which permits people to live a purposeful and self-fulfilling life.

Behind the broad-brush official figures lies a complex web of changing employment patterns and opportunities (Figure 14.1).

14.3 Unemployment

Reasons for unemployment

In the late 1970s and 1980s unemployment started to increase rapidly in Britain, particularly among young people. This was partially a result of the new technology, but other factors were also involved.

- The decline in family size, increased educational provision and improved career opportunities resulted in a substantial increase in the number of married women working, passing the 50 per cent mark in 1980. Many of these married women 'returners' took work previously occupied by school leavers.
- The 'baby bulge' of the mid-1960s was working its way out of education. Even if there had been the same number of jobs as in the past there would have been insufficient.

Redefining work

The RSA *Redefining Work* report draws a clear picture of what the future world of work will be like:

- not enough paid work for all who want it
- rapidly evolving demands for skills and qualifications
- changes in the composition of the workforce (later entry, earlier exit, greater participation by women)

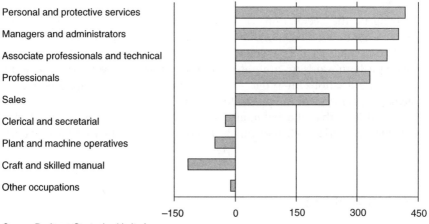

Figure 14.1 Changes in employment[1], by occupation, 1996–2006
(United Kingdom, thousands, 1996-based projections)
Source: Social Trends, 27 National Statistics © Crown Copyright 1997.

- expansion of non-traditional opportunities (part-time, temporary, fixed term work; self-employment; employment through intermediaries)
- new forms of careers
- greater personal responsibility for services hitherto provided by the state
- greater significance of unpaid work, particularly volunteering

In this new world of work few of us will have the stable, reasonably well-paid, 9-to-5 jobs now thought of as 'normal'. Instead most of us will have to cope with greater insecurity, greater demand for 'training up' and marketing ourselves, greater pressure for flexibility, and, probably, fewer net material rewards.

The altruism discount

The voluntary sector's workforce is not primarily motivated by material rewards. In accordance with the 'altruism discount' workers have shown a sophisticated ability to trade lower levels of material rewards – pay which is up to 30% less than in other sectors – for higher levels of non-material rewards such as work which is satisfying – varied, autonomous, egalitarian, meaningful – and work which is convenient – capable of being integrated with the rest of their lives.

The voluntary sector's workforce has developed an alternative form of career. This is not the 'linear' career which operates as the cultural norm –

moving up the occupational ladder with the same or similar employers in large and hierarchical organisations in order to acquire money, power and status. Rather it is a 'spiral' career – moving around, although not necessarily upwards, in a number of different lines of work in small and open organisations in order to create the optimum environment for achieving personal development fulfilment.

We believe that the voluntary sector's workforce – highly qualified, flexible, egalitarian, self-motivated – is a prototype for the workforce of the future.

Volunteering

Voluntary organisations are the chief venue of volunteering – in 1997, according to the most recent survey of the National Centre for Volunteering, on average 18.3 million volunteers donated 74 millions hours a week – and as such they are also the chief repositories of expertise in how to engage, motivate, and sustain people in unpaid work. In the new world of work, where employment is likely to be intermittent and we will need not only to fill our time productively and enjoyably but regularly to reposition ourselves in the labour market, this expertise will be of critical importance.

(From Meta Zimmeck, 'Re-defining Work', *RSA Journal*, 3 April 1998)

- A world-wide slump in trading, following the OPEC oil price increases early in the 1970s, was still out of control. A fear of hyperinflation prevented most countries reinflating their economies in order to boost trade.
- Some organisations took advantage of the excuse of the recession to rid themselves of the overmanning which had built up during the boom period, when trade unions could use their muscle to more effect to prevent labour shedding.
- Great Britain had fewer young people in full-time post-school education and apprenticeships than any other EC country; overall 44 per cent of sixteen to eighteen-year-olds were available for work or unemployment.

By 1986 more than 3 million people in Great Britain were unemployed, ranging from about 10 per cent of the working population in the South-east to about 20 per cent in Northern Ireland. The old industrialised areas were the worst affected.

However, between 1986 and 1990 unemployment almost halved as the number of sixteen to eighteen-year-olds in the population rapidly declined, numbers continuing into full-time education increased and the economy improved.

After 1990 the economy was hit by the effect of recent high interest rates and world recession and by 1993 unemployment was again approaching the 3 million mark; however, this time the greatest impact was in the booming service sector, particularly in the South-east which had been relatively unaffected previously.

After the 1993 peak, unemployment in the United Kingdom declined in each subsequent year, dropping to 1.8 million in 1998, and by 2000 it was at its lowest level for twenty years. Indeed by 2000 there were numerically more people in work than had ever previously been the case.

Reducing unemployment

Typically unemployment can be reduced by changing the **occupational structure** of our society (section 14.2): work sharing; abolition or reduction in overtime working; early retirement; extended education; longer holidays; a shorter working week; and new employment in industries yet unthought of that will be created by the micro-chip revolution – just as cars were unthought of before the industrial revolution, now mobile phones are commonplace (by 1998 three out of every ten households in the South-east had one). Computers are increasingly regarded as essential as the dot com revolution continues (in 1986, 16 per cent of all households had a computer, in 1996 26 per cent had); video recorders have been general for some years (by 1997 over 80 per cent of households possessed one, double the number ten years earlier).

Of the other measures, limited work sharing is occurring. Although overtime is not abolished the working week is legally limited to 48 hours, however in 2000 there was evidence of increasing overtime up to that level because firms were reluctant to take on additional employees as a result of employee protection legislation. Although many people are retiring earlier there are still over a quarter of a million people over state pension age in the workforce (indeed, it is now suggested that the ageing population will require people to work to a later age). Education is now much extended, now nearly two-thirds of sixteen- and seventeen-year-olds stay in full-time education; between 1990/1 and 1996/7 the number of students enrolled in full-time higher education increased by 55 per cent. In 1997 80 per cent more men were enrolled as undergraduates in British institutions than in 1970 and there was a 400 per cent increase in women over the same period – this trend is likely to continue as aspirations increase and the nature of work in Britain increasingly requires a better-educated workforce. Longer holidays are with us, but a shorter working week is not (section 13.2) (see also Figures 14.2–14.3 on pp. 210–11).

Effects of unemployment

All these solutions have problems of cost or political will and some people take a pessimistic view of the future – one in which there is little or no economic growth and the people of the United Kingdom are divided into those who number in their households at least one paid worker and those who, because they do not, are largely reliant on whatever unemployment compensation it is decided they should receive – what has come to be called '**the underclass**'.

One of the functions of work is the provision of status (section 12.1). It is probable that in a society of the permanently unemployed, status will be sought in other ways – some damaging to other members of that society.

Psychological shock

A major effect of unemployment is that it tends to be socially isolating. At the psychological level there is the shock, shame, loss of confidence and loss of occupational identity. This results in a tendency to withdraw from contact with others. There is also the direct loss of the work place as a source of conversation and social contact. The whole effect is exacerbated by the fact that the economic effects of unemployment enforce curtailing leisure pursuits and social life. Visits to the pub have to be cut down or given up entirely. The car may also have to be given up, so that visits to relatives become rarer, and so on.

For the family man, this means that the family itself becomes the main source of social contact and therefore the major social setting within which the stresses of unemployment are experienced and dealt with. However, when the father of a family ceases to be in full-time work, the balance of the family shifts. He feels he loses not only his occupational but also his sexual identity and comes under pressure to take on a more 'feminine' role: doing the housework, taking the children to school.

Sometimes the stresses of unemployment threaten the marriage itself. A 28-year-old man, married with two children, unemployed for 18 months, when asked what he did with his time replied 'Nothing'. He said he just sat in the house and argued all the time with his wife. His wife had actually been twice to a solicitor about a divorce. He said there was 'nothing to do at home but watch television, night and day'.

(John Hill, 'The Psychological Impact of Unemployment',
New Society, 17 March 1978)

Unemployment is not just differentiated geographically, it is also unevenly spread across the population; for example Jones (*Britain's Ethnic Minorities*, 1993) found that black unemployment rates are approximately double those of whites, and qualifications do not substantially alter this position.

The majority of people who become unemployed do find alternative work and such temporary unemployment is likely to become an increasingly common part of most people's life experience as the concept of 'a job for life' fades, and security of employment continues to reduce with increasing casualisation, rapid changes to skill requirements and more frequent re-structuring within organisations. However, there does appear to be a growing underclass of those who have never been employed and who do not expect employment; such groups are not restricted to sink estates in inner cities which have experienced a declining industrial base, but are more likely in such a situation (section 12.4) and dealing with this hard core of those who have become benefit-dependent is an increasing priority for government.

Fifteen years ago Frank Field addressed this issue: 'Some people have not had a job since leaving school. Children are being brought up in homes where paid work never features as part of everyday life. For other unemployment benefits are supplemented by crime and drug trafficking. This underclass now has a standard of living well beyond anything it could command by working, even if semi-skilled jobs were available . . . The most important action any government can take is to cut off the supply routes to this burgeoning underclass of young, unskilled unemployed men. This can only be done by implementing policies to achieve full employment.'

This theme was developed in the same year by Anthony Bevins:

'Social anthrax'

Frank Field calls it 'social anthrax', a killer mix of deep poverty and a breakdown of the conventional family. The chairman of the Commons Social Security Committee told *The Observer* that 'it is going to have a deadly effect for decades to come'.

Mr Field, the Labour MP for Birkenhead, is talking about mass unemployment, soaring numbers of one-parent families, and the high-speed spread of a drugs culture.

He has seen these things in his home town, but new figures for the rest of the country show that social deserts are being created in the most deprived areas of Britain.

The 1991 census, for example, shows that in some areas, more than half the children come from single-parent families. In Liverpool's Granby ward, part of the Toxteth district, about 2250 children were from single-parent families – nearly two-thirds of all children in the ward.

'In some areas, it's already socially desolate,' Mr Field said.

The picture the statistics revealed was condemned by the Anglican Bishop of Liverpool, Dr David Shepherd, who described growing poverty as 'the country's worst social evil and a national scandal'.

'It is shocking that so many people should be effectively excluded from normal life across the country. It should be our first priority,' he said.

Unemployment in Granby ward was more than 40 per cent in 1991, and in neighbouring parts of the city one in every eight people over the age of 16 classed themselves as permanently ill – another measure of Nineties' deprivation.

These unemployment figures will not reflect those put out by the Department of Employment, which restricts its count to those claiming unemployment benefit.

But the census figures give a unique insight into what is happening in the most deprived urban areas – enabling policy-makers to zoom in on hot-spots of social breakdown.

'You've got a breakdown of what's been a traditional family; you've got a breakdown of the traditional work support system . . . Donald Dewar,

> Labour's social security spokesman, said: . . . 'I think at the moment in this country, we've got a forgotten class. The danger is that we will drive it into what is called an underclass, and that people will become so distanced and so alienated that we will be left with a permanent divide, a major scar across the community, which becomes unbridgeable.'
>
> (*Observer*, 3 October 1993, adapted)

It would appear that this 'underclass' is now with us.

14.4 Women and work

The housebound wife

Before the Industrial Revolution the rural family worked as a unit, although the work roles were segregated with the women doing the less important jobs – particularly those in and close to the house, such as milking cows (P. Branca, *Women in Europe since 1750*, 1978). As she was likely to be more or less continuously pregnant or caring for babies this might seem reasonable enough. Children were necessary as a labour force and as an insurance policy for the parents' old age. High infant mortality rates required the birth of many so that at least a few would survive.

Enclosures and population growth drove people into the towns. Men went into factories, shipyards or mines, leaving their wives at home so that work became segregated from family life. Women were still bound to the home by children and tradition, and married women were not expected to work outside the home – and less than 10 per cent did up to the First World War. Even in 1956 the coalminers of *Coal is Our Life* regarded a working wife as a loss of status, the implication being that her man was unable to keep her. Many women worked part-time at home for low wages, and 'outworkers' are still badly paid.

Single women worked in factories, such as linen mills, or went into service. Conditions and pay were poor, and marriage ended their employment. Childbearing would usually cease only a few years before the average age of death, so there was little point in preparing for a career. Because women appeared to be prepared to work for low pay, male unions enforced sanctions against their employment in skilled sectors of industry such as engineering.

New careers for women

Shorthand appeared in 1870, the typewriter was invented in 1873, and the first telephone exchange in Britain was opened in 1876. These inventions provided socially acceptable employment for middle class women and an avenue of social mobility for the working class; but like nursing – already established as a woman's job – they could be badly paid. Teaching and the civil service also opened up career prospects for women, but they had to remain unmarried.

The First World War dramatically changed outlooks. Women had to replace the men away at the front, and proved that they could work in munitions factories and drive buses. After the war the unions insisted that old agreements banning women from certain jobs came back into force, but women were given the vote.

The Second World War renewed the demand for women workers, and facilities such as nurseries and school meal services were provided. The post-war boom enabled women to continue in employment and by 1981 56.2 per cent of all women aged between sixteen and sixty were at work; the number of married women working rising from 48.8 per cent in 1971 to 56.8 per cent in 1981.

The working mother

Family limitation facilities and improved education have provided opportunities for many women to plan a career. There are however still inbuilt disadvantages to women in employment, particularly a reluctance to train a woman because of the likelihood that she will marry and leave. Most importantly, women are still socialised to regard only certain jobs as appropriate to them (section 8.4).

Working mothers often experience role-conflict and feel guilty that they are neglecting their children, but there is little evidence that children over three do suffer.

In spite of claims in the past that the children of working mothers are likely to become delinquent or show psychiatric disorder, there is abundant evidence from numerous studies that this is not so. Children do not suffer from having several mother-figures so long as stable relationships and good care are provided by each. Indeed some studies have shown that children of working mothers may even be less likely to become delinquent than children whose mothers stay at home. In these circumstances it seemed that the mother going out to work was a reflection of a generally high standard of family responsibility and care. Two provisos need to be made with respect to these studies. First, there has been little investigation of the effects of mothers starting work while their children are still infants, although such data as are available do not suggest any ill-effects. Second, a situation in which mother-figures keep changing so that the child does not have the opportunity of forming a relationship with any of them may well be harmful. Such unstable arrangements usually occur in association with poor-quality maternal care, so that it has not been possible to examine the effects of each independently. However, in 2001, a study by the Joseph Rowntree Foundation which had followed the progress of people born in the 1970's concluded that pre-school children whose mothers worked full-time were less likely to achieve A-Levels than others. This study measured differences between siblings whose mothers worked during the formative years of childhood of one but not of the other. This meant that the main variant in their upbringing was the amount of time their mother spent with them (unlike an earlier report in 1997 which came to the same conclusion but compared the performance of children from different families.) However, the Department of Education pointed out that the Rowntree report was based on children 30 years ago when there was little quality childcare available.

> Much the same can be said about the effects of day nurseries and
> creches (particular forms of care often used when mothers go out to work).
> Assertions in official reports (WHO Expert Committee on Mental Health,
> 1951) concerning their permanent ill-effects are quite unjustified. Day care
> need not necessarily interfere with the normal mother–child attachment
> (Caldwell, Wright, Honig and Tannenbaum, 1970) and the available
> evidence gives no reason to suppose that the use of day nurseries has any
> long-term psychological or physical ill-effects
>
> (Michael Rutter, *Maternal Deprivation Reassessed*, 1972)

Equal pay for women

Equal pay for equal work was supposedly guaranteed from 1975 (by the Equal
Pay Act 1970) but this is still often circumvented. The Equal Opportunities
Commission was established in December 1975 under Section 53 of the Sex
Discrimination Act 1975. The functions of the Commission are:

(i)   to work towards the elimination of discrimination, as defined by the Act
(ii) to promote equality between men and women generally
(iii) to keep under review the working of the Act and the Equal Pay Act 1970
(iv) the commissioning or support of research and educational activities
      related to equal opportunities for men and women.

In 1993 a survey by the Economic and Social Research Council of 11,000 people
born between 3 and 9 May 1958 found a 'wealth of evidence that the feminist
revolution had failed the vast majority of women, leaving them still caring for
the children, doing most of the housework and earning less than men'. This
longitudinal survey, which is believed to be the largest of its kind carried out
anywhere in the world, also concluded that women who split with their partner
are likely to have a bleak future; they 'become highly dependent on state benefits
or earning low wages', and with the lack of a work pension their old age was also
likely to be impoverished.

Mintel also published a survey of 1500 adults in 1993 entitled 'Women
200' and found that only 1 per cent of the couples interviewed divided their
tasks equally. It was found that most men did very little or nothing at all at
home. By 2000 men in full-time work still had higher average earnings than
women in every age band, with men earning as much as 30 per cent more
between the age of 40 and retirement.

The weekly pay gap is a further dimension. In April 1998 women earned 80 per
cent of the hourly rate of men but only 72 per cent of their weekly pay. This
indicates that not only do men earn higher hourly rates of pay but that they also
work longer hours.

The changing role of women

In the 1970s Ann Oakley and Sue Sharpe wrote definitive books on women's role
and it is interesting to compare Sue Sharpe's observations with the realities of the
situation some thirty years later.

Women's roles

In 1857, an income of £1000 a year would support a family and at least five servants: an income of £500, a family and three servants. The wages of a 'maid of all work' were then between £6.10s and £10 a year 'with allowances for tea, sugar and beer'. From the mid century on, a large proportion of the rising number of females in the population was taken into domestic employment, which in 1881 accounted for one in seven of the total working population.

Nevertheless, from the 1870s on, domestic servants became harder to get, both because of the growing number of middle-class housewives who wanted them, and because girls who were potential recruits for domestic service began to move into the expanding feminine occupations of sales work, clerical work, and teaching. By 1900, there was a 'servant problem', and the possibility of conflict between the housewife and mother roles for the middle-class woman was widely recognized. It was argued that: 'the middle-class mother must perforce be provided with domestic assistance, not that she might indulge in indolence, but that she might be free to devote all her energies to the proper upbringing of her children.'

The servant shortage made the domestic roles of middle-class and working-class women more and more alike. The combination of the maternal role with the housewife/houseworker role, until then a feature of working-class life only, became the norm. Where the middle-class wife had been idle she now worked, and in this transition lies perhaps one explanation of housework's modern status as non-work. The mid-nineteenth-century role of housewife–supervisor became the twentieth-century role of housewife–worker. The working-class woman had long been in this situation, but this fact was concealed beneath her role as productive worker. At the point in history when working-class women began to turn to housewifery as a full-time occupation in significant numbers, the middle-class woman began to take part in the actual work required by it.

Other changes in the roles of women in the family during the later part of this period followed the same trend towards casting both middle and working-class married women in the modern role of housewife. First and foremost, a revolution was occurring in the role and status of the child in society. General mortality declined from the middle of the nineteenth century, and infant mortality – deaths in the first year of life – fell significantly around the turn of the century. The increasing likelihood that a child would survive into adulthood altered the attitude to children: the individual child came to be seen as irreplaceable. Whilst, in the seventeenth century, childhood ceased at seven or eight, the evolution of the modern school system removed children from the adult world for a much longer time, thus lengthening their period of dependence on adults. In 1833 the first allocation of money for educational purposes was made by the central government; by 1856, the state's expenditure on education had become so large that a

Department of Education was set up; in 1870 an Education Act provided compulsory elementary education for all children. Thirty-two years later came an Act which established a state system of secondary education.

The growth of the state educational system proceeded directly from the needs of an industrialized society. The specialization of work roles called for a more literate and knowledgeable population.

(A. Oakley, *Housewife*, Harmondsworth: Penguin, 1974)

Girls' lives

Many girls' lives follow a similar pattern – boredom with school, early leaving into a local job that has marginal interest, finding a steady boyfriend, saving up to marry, settling down and having a family. Marriage and home-making appear as a meaningful distraction or welcome release for those with boring jobs or those who have no intention of making work a central part of their lives. Girls' needs and feelings about this form part of an evolving self-identity. This is still malleable and open to change, but the consequences of choices made at this stage are often irreversible. Once technical or academic courses have been rejected it is very hard to pick them up again. Women who have left education a long way behind them while pursuing family roles often realize the vacuum when their children have grown, but their lack of qualifications and training makes only mundane work available. The paucity and narrowness of re-training schemes for women still leaves most with the typical range of lower level employment.

(S. Sharpe, *Just Like a Girl*, Harmondsworth: Penguin, 1976, abridged)

REVISION SUMMARY

Automation

Advantages of automation are:

- Workers may no longer be tied to a machine.
- Simple repetitive tasks will be reduced.
- Problems may require teamwork to solve them.
- Dangerous and unpleasant jobs will be reduced.
- More autonomy – the worker does not have to 'keep up' with a machine.

Disadvantages are:

- 'De-skilling' of crafts – loss of pride.
- Fewer workers needed.

- Workers unlikely to fully understand technology – will alienation increase?
- More shift work, because expensive machines need continuous operation for profit.

Unemployment

Methods of calculation vary slightly, and figures are not exactly comparable. For example, in 1983 men over 60 no longer counted, a reduction of 162,000.

How accurate are unemployment figures?

Unemployment figures are 'seasonally adjusted' to take account of normal variations in employment during the year (e.g. less employment in building trades/hotel and catering during the winter). This is normal practice, but there are other factors which may result in overestimates or underestimates of the numbers unemployed (see Table 13.2).

Underestimate:

- Adults and young people on programmes for the unemployed are not included.
- Men between 60 and 65 are not included.
- Married women who wish to recommence work will not usually be eligible for benefits and will not register if it is known that Job Centres have no work available.

Overestimate:

- People not really seeking work will register in order to claim supplementary benefits.
- Some people are working in the '**black economy**' but claiming to be unemployed.

Table 14.1 Increase in unemployment in the UK, 1961–98 (thousand)

	Total	Rate*
1961	300	1.3
1971	750	3.3
1981	2500	10.4
1985	3300	13.5
1991	2400	8.7
1998	1800	6.0

Notes:
* Per cent of those available for work unemployed.

In 1986 a Public Attitudes survey on 'The Unemployed and the Black Economy', under the chairmanship of Lord Plowden, claimed that up to 350,000 people, 9 per cent of the jobless total, were involved in the black economy. It also said that only about 1,000,000 Britons were 'genuinely' unemployed.

Reasons for the increase in unemployment

- New technology required fewer workers.
- The working population increased (by about $2\frac{1}{2}$ million between 1961 and 1985).
- More married women are working.
- The world slump which followed OPEC oil price increases in the early 1970s.
- Existing overmanning was reduced under cover of the recession.
- More 'moonlighting' (i.e. people who have more than one paid job).

Effects of unemployment

Demoralisation

Shock, shame, loss of confidence, loss of occupational identity.

Family stress, including break-up. Confusion over roles (e.g. loss of sexual identity), financial stress, too much 'togetherness' – no emotional release outside the home.

Dependence

Degrading to depend on others (e.g. social services, free school meals for children).

Social isolation

Little money to spend on leisure (e.g. visits to pub); loss of companionship at work.

Antisocial behaviour

Some people may reject the norms of the society which has apparently rejected them and engage in antisocial behaviour (e.g. crime). However, it should be emphasised that such people represent only a tiny fraction of the unemployed.

Women and work

In 1921, fewer than one in ten married women were working or seeking work, compared with one in two in 1981.

Before the Industrial Revolution the rural family was a 'unit of production'. Children were necessary as a labour force and an insurance policy for their parents' old age. Infant mortality was high and the birth of many was necessary to ensure that some survived – wives were therefore likely to be continuously pregnant. As a result of the primacy of child-rearing, women were engaged in work domestically related or near the home (e.g. spinning wool, milking cows).

Reasons for disassociation of women with paid employment

Industrialisation and the resulting urbanisation segregated work from family life and most women became 'housebound'.

- Married women were still bound to the home by children and traditions. Child-bearing was usually fairly continuous.
- The average age of death was early, and for many women there was no substantial overlap between ending child-rearing and death.
- What work could be done at home was badly paid (and still is).
- Single working class women worked in factories (e.g. linen mills) or went into 'service' (as maids, cooks, etc.). A condition of employment was usually dismissal upon marriage.
- Non-working middle class women became a status symbol and working class men strove to copy those higher up the ladder ('Principle of stratified diffusion': Young and Willmott in *The Symmetrical Family*).
- Because female labour was regarded as low-status and therefore worthy of low pay, male unions enforced sanctions against female employment in skilled-labour sectors.
- The law aimed at the protection of women and children removed areas of possible employment (e.g. mines).

Reasons for the improvement of the position of women in paid employment

- Inventions which made acceptable work for middle class women available (shorthand, 1870; the typewriter, 1873).
- What became the norm for the middle class became the objective for the working class.
- Service sector development (e.g. nursing, teaching, civil services) opened up what were regarded as 'suitable' job opportunities for women (hence, they were low-paid).
- The First World War and the scarcity of men opened up a wide field of job opportunities for women (partially lost when the war ended).
- Widening educational opportunities.
- The Equal Pay Act 1970 guaranteed equal pay for equal work (often circumvented).
- The Equal Opportunities Commission was established in 1975 and under the Sex Discrimination Act of 1975 had a duty:
  - (i)   to work towards the elimination of discrimination, as defined by the Act
  - (ii) to promote equality between men and women generally
  - (iii) to keep under review the working of the sex discrimination Act and the Equal Pay Act 1970

    (iv)   to commission or support research and educational activities related to equal opportunities for men and women.
- The Employment Protection Act of 1975 gave women the right to paid maternity leave (after two years' work they can claim six weeks' paid leave); it also gives a right to return to work for the same employer within twenty-nine weeks of the child's birth.
- The decline in the average number of children per family.
- Motherhood seems to have lost status (perhaps because of a shorter child-bearing period) – there is pressure on women to return to work to fully participate in society.

Reasons why females are still underrepresented in high-status jobs and positions

- Primary socialisation changes slowly and cannot be legislated for.
- The education system.
- Motherhood effectively:
  - (i)   provides initially an alternative source of fulfilment/status and defuses motivation
  - (ii)   makes employers reluctant to invest in training/promotional opportunities because they assume females will leave in due course
  - (iii)   removes females from promotion contest at crucial period – although this is now short, it is at a time of life when major promotion opportunities tend to occur
  - (iv)   makes it difficult for women to re-enter promotion contest because their competitors have moved ahead and their skills are out of date in an age of technological information explosion.
- Some movements towards greater opportunities for women have been counterproductive. For example, the change from single-sex to co-educational schools and colleges has resulted in a greater proportion of men in senior positions in these establishments (and, hence, acting as role models) for the reasons outlined above.
- Male bias (conscious or unconscious) and male socialisation condition men to stereotype females. Most senior management positions are held by men and it is therefore men who tend to have the major say in whether to appoint/promote women.
- Some women are unwilling to accept unsocial hours, or absence from home, which may be a consequence of appointment to higher-status positions, because of primacy of home and family.

SELF-TEST QUESTIONS: PART FIVE

Self-test 5.1

   1   What is the term used to describe a work situation in which the worker finds his or her work meaningless and experiences a lack of power?   (1 mark)

2 Give one example of the kind of work situation in which the answer to Question 'I' above is likely to occur. *(I mark)*
3 Give two examples of work areas in which trade union membership is increasing. *(2 marks)*
4 State two motives for work, other than economic ones. *(2 marks)*
5 What did the Bullock Report recommend in 1978? *(2 marks)*
6 Name three advantages, other than pay, enjoyed by non-manual workers as compared with manual ones. *(3 marks)*
7 What three patterns can 'work' be divided into? *(3 marks)*
8 Give three reasons why married women have increasingly continued with or re-entered employment during the last fifty years. *(3 marks)*
9 In what ways are women still disadvantaged in the work situation? *(4 marks)*
10 What effect may unemployment have on the individual concerned? *(4 marks)*

(Total 25 marks)

Self-test 5.2

The *Punch* cartoon (1933) below spells out the problem. *Punch's* fears of mass unemployment did not in fact materialise, but will this be the case in the future?

The saving of labour

The Robot: '*Master, I can do the work of fifty men.*'
Employer: '*Yes, I know that, but* who is to support the fifty men.'

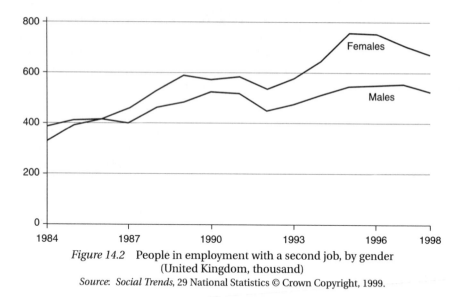

Figure 14.2   People in employment with a second job, by gender
(United Kingdom, thousand)
Source: Social Trends, 29 National Statistics © Crown Copyright, 1999.

1   According to Figure 14.2, how many females had second jobs (i.e. did more than one job*) in 1996? (1 mark)
2   Which group shown in the chart increased more substantially between 1984 and 1995? (2 marks)
3   Why did the fear of mass unemployment represented in the cartoon not materialise? (4 marks)
4   What criticisms might be made as to the accuracy of unemployment figures? (4 marks)
5   What effect may automation have on the workforce in the United Kingdom? (9 marks)

SPECIMEN QUESTIONS AND ANSWERS

1   Describe and explain changes in this century, shown in Figures 14.2 and 14.3 which have made of easier for women to take paid employment outside the home. (8 marks)
2   Despite the equal opportunities legislation, there are still comparatively few women in the higher-paid and high-status occupations. How do sociologists account for the low percentage of women in 'top' jobs? (12 marks)

Answers

1   A major reason why it is easier for married women to take paid employment outside the home is the reduction in family size, which had dropped to about

* This means a paid job; family responsibilities do not count.

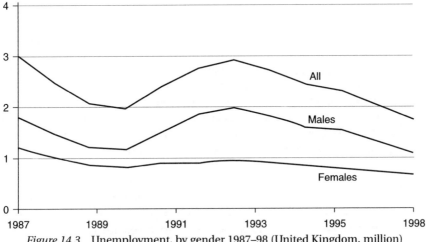

Figure 14.3 Unemployment, by gender 1987–98 (United Kingdom, million)
Source: Social Trends, 29 National Statistics © Crown Copyright, 1999.

two children per married couple by 1930, about the same size as today. There is therefore more time available for employment after, or during, child-rearing.

The First World War created a shortage of manpower and women were encouraged to take work from which they had previously been excluded. Women proved that they were able to do jobs previously regarded as suitable only for men; and, although there was some opposition from trade unions after the war, opportunities continued to increase. Employment of women was further boosted by the employment needs of the Second World War and the boom period for the economy afterwards, when there was a labour shortage.

Educational opportunities for women have widened considerably, in line with the enhanced status of women generally, and therefore married women are more likely to have appropriate qualifications, which enable them to return to work after family-building.

Increasing expectations has been one factor encouraging husbands to see the employment of wives as desirable – for example, increasing home ownership and the need to pay the resultant mortgages. The more married women who work, the more this becomes the 'norm', and now more than 50 per cent of married women do work – the non-working wife without young children is becoming the exception rather than the rule.

The growth of the service sector in industry has increased employment opportunities for female employment in a wide variety of jobs, regarded as appropriate to all social classes, while employment legislation such as the Employment Protection Act of 1975 made it easier to return to work after the birth of a child.

(*Note:* With only 8 marks available, you cannot devote much time to explaining each change – for example, why the family has reduced. As no specific number of changes is requested, concentrate on getting down as many relevant 'changes' as you can, with a brief explanation of how this change has made it easier for married women to work. Keep the wording of the question in mind throughout.)

2   Despite equal opportunities legislation, there are still comparatively few women in higher-paid and high-status occupations; this is partially the result of a time factor, as most of this legislation has been in force only since 1970, which is a comparatively short time-span in which to expect expectations and attitudes to change. However, there are major difficulties in women attaining high-paid, high-status jobs, regardless of legislation. Primary socialisation prepares girls for a domestic and subservient role, fixing employment expectations into traditional patterns – dolls, ironing-boards, nurses' uniforms, all reinforce the role models of their parents. This primary socialisation continues in the school, where early learning and peer-group pressure encourages girls into traditional female subjects even when teachers are eager to encourage equal opportunities, which is not always the case. There is evidence (for example, in Sue Lees' *Losing Out*) that teacher expectations still assist in girls taking a non-assertive role in class.

Motherhood removes women from the promotion race at a vital time in their life when major opportunities are likely to occur, and five or six years' child-rearing will mean that they return to work behind their male competitors and possibly with outdated skills. Women themselves will often see their family as their primary responsibility and would not apply for or accept positions which would interfere unduly with the needs of the 'home', e.g. unsocial hours, business conferences.

Employers are often reluctant to train women or to appoint them to key posts during their child-rearing years, because they fear that the women will leave to have a child; the fact that appointment elsewhere is more likely to cause departure than the birth of a child is disregarded.

Male expectations still remain a potent force in females being appointed to high-paid and high-status positions: historically it is males who are in the key positions, making appointments, and their prejudice, often unconscious, may inhibit female appointment and promotion.

■⩗ Part Six

Demographic and social
aspects of population

■ M ■ 15   Population change in Britain

15.1 Historical perspective

Demography

Demography is the study of human populations, particularly their size, structure and development. The study of demography in a scientific way probably started in 1662 when John Gaunt published *Natural Political Observations on the Bills of Mortality*, in which he showed a pattern between the proportions of deaths to various causes in London. He also tried to chart what happened to a group of children born at the same time up until their deaths. In the seventeenth and eighteenth century the development of life insurance encouraged the study of health, disease and death.

Malthus

The first major systematic study of population was Malthus' *Essay on Population* (1798), in which he claimed a 'law of population' – 'that the human species, when unchecked, goes on doubling itself every twenty-five years . . . while the means of subsistence, under circumstances the most favourable to human industry, could not possibly be made to increase faster than in an arithmetical ratio . . . man would increase as the numbers 1. 2. 4. 8. 16. 32. 64. 128. 256 and subsistence as 1. 2. 3. 4. 5. 6. 7. 8. 9.' Economic improvements could only be temporary, as the population would reduce itself by war, famine and disease once the optimum point was reached. Some used Malthus' theory to argue against improving the conditions of the poor, as this would only mean that more people would survive and bring the cataclysmic collapse of population nearer.

The census

In the nineteenth century the taking of a regular **census** encouraged interest in the study of population movements, mortality and fertility. The first census was taken in 1801, and there has been a similar survey, including every individual in the country, every ten years since (except the war year of 1941).

The questions asked in the census are not always the same. From 1851 to 1911 people were asked about infirmities, including deafness and blindness; in 1951 and 1961 adults were asked to state the age at which they ceased full-time education; in 1971 educational qualifications were asked for. However, in each census the size of the population has been established and since 1821 (except in 1831) details of people's ages have been obtained.

Births, marriages and deaths

Since 1837 there has been compulsory registration of births, marriages and deaths. Clearly, the government would not collect such information – at considerable expense – if it was not useful in predicting such matters as how many old people are likely to need care in the future, or how many school places are likely to be required in twelve years.

UK population

Demography is an inexact science. In 1972 the projected population of the United Kingdom for the year 2001 was 62.4 million, while the 1979 figures forecast 57.9 million; a difference of 4.5 million could clearly have considerable implications for the provision of services. No demography at all would result in chaos!

In the eleventh century there were probably not many more than 1 million people in England and Wales. This rose slowly to about 5 million in 1600, about 6 million in 1700, and 8,893,000 in 1801. There was then a 'population explosion' to 22,712,000 in 1871, because the birth rate remained about the same but the death rate generally declined (although not in some industrial centres) as a result of improving hygiene and medical knowledge. More children were surviving to have children themselves, an additional factor being migration from Ireland.

The population of the United Kingdom increased by 12 per cent between 1961 and 1997 to reach about 59 million. Individual countries have varied; Northern Ireland had the biggest percentage increase at 17 per cent, England increased by 13 per cent, Wales by 11 per cent, while Scotland decreased by 1 per cent.

The UK population is now expected to rise to about 61,000,000 by 2011 and to 62,000,000 by 2021.

Population growth over time in the United Kingdom and Ireland is shown on p. 225.

The population bomb

In his 1969 book, *The Population Bomb*, Paul Ehrlich predicted that by the following decade millions would starve to death as the weight of humanity bore down upon the earth.

Natural resources such as coal and oil would run out, agricultural production would fail to keep pace with the sheer number of people and the dark ages would descend once more.

Ehrlich's sensationalist gloom recalled the pessimism of an earlier era. Thomas Malthus, writing his *Essay on the Principle of Population* in 1798, predicted war, pestilence and starvation as a result of overcrowding.

Yet when Malthus was writing the population of the world was less than one billion. By the time Ehrlich joined the doom-mongers, it was 3.6 billion.

Today, according to UN predictions, the world's population will reach six billion.

It is tempting from a Western European vantage point to say that the Jeremiahs of the past have been proved wrong. The world's resources have not run out and the famines that have happened have been caused largely by war. Malnutrition has declined.

The number of people who starved to death in the final quarter of this century is less than the number who starved to death in the last 20 years of the 19th century.

In one sense the pessimists were right: the world's population has exploded. Over the past 30 years, it has increased by 62 per cent. But they grossly underestimated the capacity of the world to cope. As the population grew, so did food production.

Fiona Fox of the Roman Catholic aid agency Cafod said: 'The assumption that population growth will outstrip food production has bred grim predictions of widespread famine. But in fact, famines we see today, such as that in Sudan, are a product of war rather than ecological collapse.'

The rate of increase in the world's population peaked around 1970. Between 1980 and 1990, the world's population grew by 824 million. But between 1990 and 2000, the additional growth is expected to be 804 million.

The rate of growth and the total numbers being added to the world's population are predicted to continue to decline in the next century. Current forecasts suggest that by 2055, the world's population will stabilise at anything between 7.3 billion to 8.9 billion. Annual increases are expected to decline from 78 million this year to 64 million in 2020–2025 and then fall to 33 million in 2045–2050.

The main reason for this slowdown is that women are having fewer children, even in under-developed countries such as China. In many Western European countries the birth rate is below the 2.1 per mother needed to replace the indigenous population.

(From Philip Johnson, 'Number's up for the prophets of doom', *Daily Telegraph*, 12 October 1999)

Population facts

- In 1950, the population of Europe was 2.5 times larger than Africa's. Last year, Africa's population at 749 m overtook that of Europe (729 m)
- Fifty years ago, Britain was the ninth most populous country in the world. By 2050, it will be 30th on the list
- Asia accounts for 61 per cent of the world's population with 3,585 million
- The population of Latin America and the Caribbean is estimated at 504 m and that of North America at 305 m
- The rate of world population growth between 1995 and 1999 is 1.33 per cent compared to 2.04 per cent in 1965–1970

- Of more than 200 countries worldwide, the smallest population is on Pitcairn with 46 people. China, with 1.3 bn, has the largest
- Two out of every five people in the world lives in China or India
- One billion people are aged between 15 and 24. More than 60 m are aged 80 or over. About 135,000 are aged over 100. By 2020, the number of centenarians will top 2.2 million
- Italy has the oldest population, with 60 per cent more older persons than children
- Since 1950, the death rate has halved from 20 deaths per year per thousand people to 10. At the same time, global life expectancy has increased from 46 to 66 years.
- Fertility rates have halved from 5.9 to 2.6 in the last 50 years in Asia, Latin America and the Caribbean. Sub-Saharan Africa's rate has fallen more slowly from 6.5 to 5.5. Western Europe's rate has declined from 2.6 to 1.4, well below replacement level. Only North America has seen an increase in recent years to around 1.9, largely a result of Hispanic immigration

(*Daily Telegraph*, 12 October 1999)

UK is healthier than the US

David Brindle

The British weather might usually be grey and wet, and our diet might leave much to be desired, but life here is officially healthier than life in America.

According to the World Health Organisation, the US ranks a sickly 24th in a global table of healthy life expectancy. Compared with most other advanced countries, you die earlier and are more prone to disability in the land of the free.

The UK is placed an unremarkable 14th in the table, the first such rankings produced by the WHO, although that falls a long way short of the picture of life in Japan – the healthiest country on earth by some margin.

At the other end of the scale, the rankings reflect graphically the ravages of Aids in much of Africa. All 10 lowest rated countries are in sub-Saharan Africa and healthy life expectancy in strife-torn Sierra Leone, at the foot of the table, is put at less than 26 years.

Alan Lopez, co-ordinator of the WHO's epidemiology and burden of disease team, said: 'Healthy life expectancy in some African countries is dropping to levels we haven't seen in advanced countries since medieval times.'

Previous exercises of this kind have been based purely on death rates. These new rankings, published last night, aim to assess the number of years lived at 'full health', with periods of illness weighted by severity and subtracted from overall life expectancy.

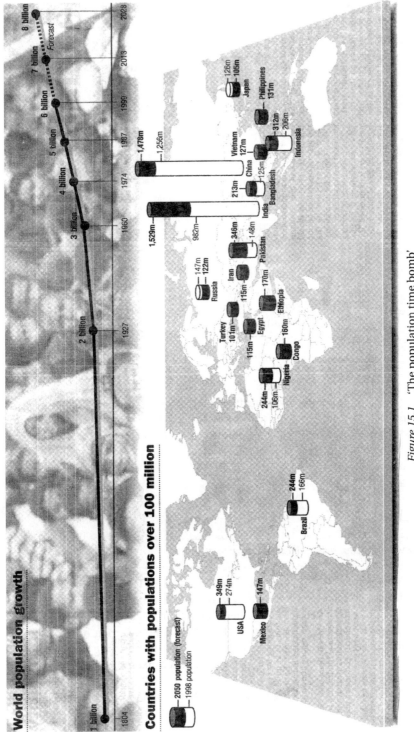

World population growth

1 billion — 1804
2 billion — 1927
3 billion — 1960
4 billion — 1974
5 billion — 1987
6 billion — 1999
7 billion — 2013
8 billion — 2028
Forecast

Countries with populations over 100 million

2050 population (forecast)
1998 population

USA 349m / 274m
Mexico 147m
Brazil 244m / 166m

Russia 147m / 122m
Turkey 101m
Egypt 115m
Nigeria 244m / 106m
Congo 160m
Ethiopia 170m
Iran 115m
Pakistan 346m / 148m
India 1,529m / 982m
Bangladesh 213m / 125m
China 1,478m / 1,256m
Vietnam 127m
Indonesia 312m / 206m
Philippines 131m
Japan 126m / 105m

Figure 15.1 'The population time bomb'

The top 20

Healthy life expectancy

	Years
Japan	74.5
Australia	73.2
France	73.1
Sweden	73.0
Spain	72.8
Italy	72.7
Greece	72.5
Switzerland	72.5
Monaco	72.4
Andorra	72.3
San Marino	72.3
Canada	72.0
Netherlands	72.0
United Kingdom	71.7
Norway	71.7
Belgium	71.6
Austria	71.6
Luxembourg	71.1
Iceland	70.8
Finland	70.5

On average, people in the healthiest regions lose some 9% of their lives to disability; in the worst-off countries, where disease often strikes young, people lose 14%. For the UK, babies born in 1999 can expect 71.7 years of healthy life. But there is a marked difference between females (73.7) and males (69.7).

Links

---

www.who.int/World Health Organisation

This gender gap is even more pronounced in France, which is placed third most healthy nation largely because of the striking healthy life expectancy of females (76.9) rather than that of males (69.3).

The WHO attributes this to the fact that French women have not been heavy smokers. But it says a recent upsurge in smoking among young women will inevitably cause a rise in tobacco-related disease and knock France down the table.

The US's bleak showing is linked partly to smoking and to high rates of heart disease and Aids, but also to violence and the plight of groups such as native Americans, rural blacks and the inner-city poor, whose health is said to be 'more characteristics of a poor developing country than a rich industrialised one'.

Average American healthy life expectancy is put at 70.0, below Israel and just above Cyprus and Dominica (both 69.8) and Ireland (69.6).

(*Guardian*, 5 June 2000)

15.2 Life expectancy

The **expectation of life** is the average number of years a person can expect to live at a given age, if the deaths at each age experienced that year occurred in all future years. A man born in 1901 could then have expected to live until 1949 if 1901 death rates remained unchanged between 1901 and 1949. If he survived this 'expectation of life at birth' beyond the average expectancy of 48 years he could at that stage expect to live until 1976, or longer if the death rates continued to decline. In 1991 a boy at birth could have expected to live until 73 and a girl could have expected to live until 79.

Because improving health standards have mainly improved the chances of young people to survive to an older age, the expectation of life for people who do survive into old age has not changed so much. In 1901, if a man had been fortunate enough to survive until the age of 80 he could expect to survive a further 4.9 years; in 1991 his chances of survival had increased by 1 year 2 months (female expectation of life increased by 2 years 8 months).

Overall life expectancy has been rising since 1971 by about 2 years for men and about $1\frac{1}{2}$ years for women. This increase is now expected to slow to about 1 year for everyone each decade.

The University of Kent research indicates that although life expectancy is increasing, the extra years of life gained bring with them a greater risk of disability and that healthy life expectancy remained virtually the same between 1976 and 1994, at about 59 years for men and about 62 years for women.

15.3 Post-1870 birth rate

The '**birth rate**' is the number of live births per 1000 of the population in a given year. This is sometimes also called the '**crude birth rate**' because it can give a misleading impression of fertility, if the number of women of child-bearing age in the population is greater at one point of comparison than at another. The '**fertility rate**' is the number of live births in any one year per 1000 fertile women in the population, between the ages of fifteen and forty-four. Although used less often, this is a more accurate reflection of the level of child-bearing than the 'birth rate'.

Fall in the birth rate

The birth rate started to go down steadily from about 1871. A number of factors were probably involved:

- Improving standards of health meant that people gradually realised that they did not have to have many children so that a few would survive to look after them in their old age.
- The introduction of full-time education made children an economic liability rather than an economic asset as they could not be put to work.
- The middle classes started to limit their children in the depression of 1870s when the cost of living rose but their incomes remained the same. The working class gradually followed this example, in order to maintain or improve their standard of living (J. A. Banks, *Prosperity and Parenthood*, 1954).
- Birth control became more general following the trial of Charles Bradlaugh and Annie Besant in 1875 for obscenity in circulating a birth-control manual written by an American doctor. The trial publicity boosted sales. Although sentenced to imprisonment, they were released on a technicality.

In 1871, the live births per 1000 fertile women (the fertility rate) was 151 (birth rate 37); in 1881 it had dropped to 146 and by 1891 it was 129 (birth rate 32). After 1891 the birth rate continued to drop until 1931 when it levelled out, with slight peaks in the late 1940s and early 1960s, followed by a further slight decline (Table 15.1). The continued trend after 1891 can be accounted for by:

- Old age pensions and other welfare benefits, making children less necessary to secure one's old age.
- Improvement in methods of birth control, particularly the introduction of the contraceptive pill.
- Changing attitudes – including a decline in the effectiveness of religious sanctions on birth control and fashion in family size, as smaller families became the norm.
- The legalisation of abortion in 1967.
- Improvements in educational opportunities and career prospects for girls and women has led to the postponement of families; decisions not to have a family at all and to concentrate on a career, or the earlier completion of family-building in order to return to work.
- Increasing expectations in terms of the standard of living; uncrowded homes,

Table 15.1 Births and birth rates. 1951–2011

	1951	1961	1971	1981	1991	2011 (est)
Births (live, thousand)	678	811	783	634	793	728
Birth rate (crude)[1]	15.5	17.6	15.9	12.8	13.8	12.1

Note:
[1] Total births per 1000 population of all ages.

foreign holidays and other material improvements; perhaps also a desi
give fewer children greater opportunities.
• The growth of the mobile nuclear family as the main operating unit with
the support of the extended family.

The slight increase in the late 1940s can be accounted for by large numbers of
men returning from war and delayed families being started, the bulge in the
1960s by the post-war babies growing up and starting families of their own. A
slight and temporary decline in the age of marriage and, possibly, upward
mobility for some encouraged them to adopt the rather larger family pattern
of the upper middle class. In addition there was a substantial increase in
immigration during this period from areas with a higher fertility rate than Britain
– perhaps a third of additional births were as a result of this factor.

15.4 Death rate and infant mortality

The '**death**' or '**mortality**' rate is the number of deaths per 1000 of the population
in a given year. The population rose dramatically in the nineteenth century
because the death rate declined, although it remained high, while the birth
rate remained the same. Although the death rate has continued to decline,
from 17.1 per 1000 of the population at the start of the century to 10.9 in 1995,
the population has not continued to explode because the birth rate has
fallen even more. In Britain the birth rate has fallen to below '**replacement
level**' only once this century – in 1976, that is, the death rate was higher-than
the birth rate and so the population was becoming smaller, if migration was
ignored. It is expected that the death rate will once more exceed the birth rate
from 2024.

Fall in the death rate

The death rate started to fall because of a combination of accident, medical
discoveries, legislation and invention. Among these are the success of the brown
rat in eliminating the black rat whose fleas caused plague (about 1750); the
improvements in farming at the beginning of the eighteenth century which
improved the diet of many people; the discovery of vaccination against smallpox
by Jenner (1796); the introduction of anaesthesia for operations in 1846; and the
Factory Acts laying down rules governing the conditions in which children were
permitted to work (1802, 1819, 1833, 1844). Public Health Acts (1872 and 1875)
established sanitary authorities responsible for sewerage, water supply and
refuse disposal and thus helped to eliminate cholera and typhoid, while the Sale
of Food and Drugs Act (1975) and other Acts to improve housing and medical care
also contributed to the decline in mortality, as did the drop in maternal mortality
resulting from excessive childbearing. The death rate was 22.5 between 1861 and
1870; but had dropped to 11.7 between 1961 and 1970. By 1995 it had reduced
further to 10.9.

Infant mortality

The major reason for the increase in life expectancy towards the end of the nineteenth century was the drop in the death rate among the young – those who survived into old age often lived as long as the elderly today.

Infant mortality is the number of live-born children who die before they are one year old out of every 1000 live births in the population, and is regarded as a good guide to the state of health and health services in a country. In 1990 Britain had a higher infant mortality rate than Sweden, Japan and France but lower than Italy, Greece or New Zealand.

In 1841, when death rates were first collected in England and Wales, a boy of fifteen could expect to live a further 43.6 years and a girl for 44.1 years; by 1960 he could have expected to live for 55.3 years and a girl for 60.9 years.

The decrease in infant mortality and the continued slight decline in the death rate generally during the twentieth century has largely been the result of continued legislation to improve health and hygiene, particularly the introduction of the National Health Service in 1946 and the improvements in ante-natal and post-natal care of the mother and child. The infant-killers of the past – diphtheria, whooping cough and measles – have either been eliminated or rendered non-fatal. An antitoxin for diphtheria was first produced in 1890 and greatly improved since, so that the 2400 deaths in 1940 had been reduced to nil by 1973. Penicillin brought a spectacular decrease in death from infections after its introduction during the Second World War.

Life expectancy

The major reason for the increase in life expectancy towards the end of the nineteenth century was the drop in the death rate among the young – those who survived into old age often lived as long as the elderly today

Infant mortality was about 150 throughout the second half of the nineteenth century; dropped to 53 by 1939, to 32 in the late 1940s and was down to 19 by 1965. There has, however, always been a considerable social class variation in the infant mortality rates. In 1972 the figure for Social Class 1 (Professional) was 11.6 and for Social Class 5 (Unskilled) 30.7; by 1980 these figures had reduced to 8.9 and 16.0, respectively, and since then the infant mortality rate has almost halved, from 11.2 overall deaths per 1000 live births to 5.9 deaths per 1000 life births. Despite this differences still exist between social classes, from 3.6 deaths per 1000 life births for those in the 'professional' category to 7.8 deaths per 1000 among the families of unskilled workers.

There were also differences in the rate for children born within marriage and those born to single parents (an average of 5.4 deaths per 1000 births within marriage, compared with an average of 7 deaths per 1000 outside.)

REVISION SUMMARY

Population growth (Table 15.2)

Table 15.2 UK population growth 1001–2011

England and Wales		
1001	1,000,000	estimated
1601	5,000,000	
1801	8,893,000	
1821	12,000,000	
1841	15,914,000	United Kingdom 1991
1861	20,066,000	Females 28,776,671
1881	25,974,000	Males 26,967,232
1901	32,528,000	census
1921	37,887,000	Projection for 2031
1941	no census (war)	Females 30,600,000
1961	46,196,000	Males 30,100,000
1981	49,634,000	
1991	49,193,915	
2001	51,065,000	projection by Office of Population Censuses
2011	51,488,000	and Surveys, 1986

Scotland		Northern Ireland	
1801	1,608,420	*	
1901	4,472,000	1,237,000	
1921	4,882,000	1,258,000	
1961	5,184,000	1,427,000	
1981	5,180,000	1,564,000	
1991	4,962,152	1,577,836	
2001	4,985,000	1,694,000	
2011	4,834,000	estimated	1,724,000	estimated

Note:
* No sepatate entity. Total Irish population 4,500,000 now; in 1871 was 5,398,179.

The birth rate

Reasons for declining birth rate after 1871

- Improving standards of health meant that people gradually realised that they did not have to have many children so that a few would survive to look after them in their old age.
- The introduction of full-time education made children an economic liability rather than an economic asset, as they could not be put to work.
- The middle classes started to limit their children in the depression of the 1870s when the cost of living rose but their incomes remained the same. The working class gradually followed this example, in order to maintain or improve their standard of living (J. A. Banks, *Prosperity and Parenthood*, 1954).
- Birth control was increasingly practised following the trial (and the resulting publicity) of Charles Bradlaugh and Annie Besant in 1875 for 'obscenity' in circulating a birth-control manual.

Reasons for continuing decline in birth rate

- In 1908 the introduction of old age pensions made children less necessary to secure one's old age.
- Improvement in methods of birth control, including the introduction of the contraceptive pill in the 1960s.
- Changing attitudes, including a decline in the effectiveness of religious sanctions on birth control and fashion in family size, as smaller families became the norm.
- The legalisation of abortion in 1967.
- Improvements in educational opportunities and career prospects for girls and women have led to the postponement of families; and to decisions not to have a family at all and to concentrate on a career, or the earlier completion of family-building in order to return to work.
- Increasing expectations in terms of the standard of living: uncrowded homes, foreign holidays and other material improvements; perhaps also a desire to give fewer children greater opportunities.
- The growth of the mobile nuclear family as the main operating unit without the support of the extended family.

Fluctuation in the birth rate

The increase in the late 1940s was due to the end of the Second World War and people having postponed child-bearing because of the uncertainty created by the war (e.g. being 'bombed out' or possible death of one's partner).

The increase in the 1960s was due to:

- The post-war baby 'bulge' growing up and having children of their own.
- A general mood of optimism, with full employment and rising living standards.
- A slight and temporary reduction in the age of marriage.

- A substantial increase in immigration from countries with a higher f[
rate.
- (Perhaps) upward social mobility encouraged some people to adopt the ......
larger families general in the upper middle class.

The death rate (or mortality rate)

Reasons for decline in death rate

- Improved hygiene and sanitation – e.g. water closets, mains sewers, clean piped water supply, official refuse disposal system. The Public Health Acts of 1872 and 1875 (these particularly helped to eliminate two big killers, cholera and typhoid).
- Medical advances – e.g. vaccination against smallpox (1796); anaesthesia for operations (1846); diphtheria antitoxin (1890); antibiotics, particularly penicillin (1929). Such discoveries may take some time to come into general use – penicillin did not do so until the 1940s. Improved health care generally (National Health Service, 1946).
- Higher living standards – improved diet (better farming techniques from the eighteenth century onwards made more food available); better housing (e.g. 'Council' housing from 1890).
- Change in lifestyles – reduction in 'maternal mortality' as family size declined and fewer women died as a result of childbirth; children ceased working (Factory Acts from 1802 onwards); industrial accidents and disease reduced as a result of legislation.
- Infant mortality reduced.

▾ 16 The effects of population change

16.1 An ageing population

The 'burden of dependency'

The fact that the birth rate has declined while more people are living longer means that more old people have to be supported by those of working age. This is sometimes called the '**burden of dependency**'.

In 1931 around 12 per cent of the population were aged over 65 and about 4 per cent over 75. By 1997 16 per cent of the population were over 65 and 7 per cent were over 75; by 2020 it is projected that over 19 per cent of the population will be over 65.

This ageing of the population is general throughout Europe and may create an economic advantage for those countries with younger populations. In Europe Italy has the greatest proportion of older people (22.7 per cent estimated for 2020), while the Irish Republic has the youngest population (with older people comprising 15.9 of the population by 2020).

When Lord Beveridge produced his report (*Social Insurance and Allied Services*, 1942) he suggested that old age pensions should be set at subsistence level in order to prevent the provision for the elderly becoming intolerable to those at work. Effective pressure from increasing numbers of old people, and a reasonable desire that old people should share in the affluence they helped to create, has resulted in substantially higher pensions than originally envisaged and many people share the view that they should be still higher.

Conventionally, a growing army of dependants should result in higher taxes for those at work, with a resultant pressure for higher wages leading to inflation, a lack of competitiveness, resulting in unemployment, with fewer people to pay the necessary taxes, therefore higher taxes for those at work, thus completing the vicious circle. This 'burden of dependency' has already led to a government decision to make the state retirement pension (the 'old age pension') payable to both men and women at 65, rather than to women at 60 and men at 65 as has been the case; the government has also introduced contributory 'stakeholders pensions' for those who do not have occupational pension schemes in order to reduce the number of future pensioners who would otherwise become dependent on state benefits.

Providing for the elderly

However, the computer revolution now makes it possible for more goods to be produced by fewer people, and so the question of provision for the aged becomes a matter of redistributing wealth at source rather than out of income. Changes in work processes may have come just in time (section 14.1).

Although financial provision need not now be a major problem, there are many social problems associated with an ageing population. The decline of the extended family as an operating unit has resulted in many old people living isolated lives, either independently or surrounded only by their peers in old people's homes. The problems of loneliness and a feeling of worthlessness, allied to relative poverty, reduces the quality of life for many of the elderly. Some attempts have been made to harness the knowledge and skills of the elderly for the good of the community – providing surrogate 'grannies' for the children of young housebound mothers, for example – but generally the old have been regarded as being of little importance in a society increasingly dominated by the young.

New economic power

However, a change may be detected from the 1990s as the economic power of the middle aged and elderly became more evident. Not only will this group constitute the bulk of the population, but, despite the fact that many remain dependent on state benefits, an increasing number with mortgages repaid and houses to be sold at sums many times greater than their original purchase price, and often with

More old people have to be supported by those of working age

substantial occupational pensions and other savings are becoming rather than the young, the main target of advertisers. The appearance of *The Oldie* magazine in the 1990s might have been the first evidence of this.

16.2 Population movement

Urbanisation

At the beginning of the nineteenth century only 25 per cent of the population of Great Britain lived in towns. Now the position is reversed, with 90 per cent living in towns, and many of the remainder working in towns, and almost all depending on towns for their shopping, education or entertainment. Just over half the population are now resident in the 66 largest urban areas, although these areas occupy only 6 per cent of the total land area of Great Britain. This process of living in and depending upon towns is called '**urbanisation**'.

Although the drift to the towns started in the Middle Ages, it was the industrialisation of the nineteenth century that attracted large numbers from the countryside to the towns and cities of Britain. Now one-third of the population live in seven huge 'conurbations' composed of adjacent towns that have grown and merged together – Greater London; West Midlands (around Birmingham); Merseyside (around Liverpool); West Yorkshire (around Leeds); and Strathclyde (around Glasgow); Greater Manchester; Tyne and Wear (around Newcastle). Britain has the fourth greatest 'population density' (the number of people per square kilometre) in Europe.

Social problems

The growth of conurbations brought problems of health related to pollution; road congestion and substandard housing. Also the less easily quantifiable problems associated with the anonymity of urban living, leading in its extreme form to suicide (P. Sainsbury, *Social Aspects of Suicide in London*, 1955) or more mildly to an increased emphasis on status symbols (section 13.1) which are not needed in the settled rural community where a person's worth is likely to be established by acquaintance.

It would be a mistake to presume that 'sociability' is always lacking in urban centres as there is evidence of 'urban villages' in most big towns where there is a settled community and a network of relationships between people well known to each other. Bethnal Green is 'a village in the middle of London' where 'most people were connected by kinship ties to a network of other families, and through them to a host of friends and acquaintances' (Willmott and Young, *Family and Class in a London Suburb*, 1960). Although Bethnal Green has changed greatly in the last forty years, as described by Anthea Holme in 'Families and Homes In East London' in 1985, such urban villages still do exist.

Crime is very much higher in urban areas. This is partially because there is more about to steal and damage, but it also has to do with a greater readiness to steal or vandalise the property of strangers. It has been demonstrated that the impersonality of the supermarket contributes to the higher rate of shoplifting there, as compared with the corner shop. The anonymity of towns also makes the chances of detection less likely.

'Suburbanisation', the Green Belt and New Towns

Between the wars 'suburbanisation' took place when residential estates grew up round the big towns. People moved to areas where there were fresh air and gardens but often regretted the lack of feeling of community and withdrew into their own 'privatised nuclear family' (section 4.5).

To combat the development of conurbations, 'green belts' were established. These are zones where no further development can take place. After the Second World War, a conscious attempt was made to disperse people from the old urban centres to 'New Towns' where living conditions were planned to be of a high standard, but where people – particularly the housebound mothers of small children – have often suffered psychologically from the impersonality.

Internal migration

Internal migration is mainly a result of economic pressures. There has been a reduction in the population of many of the old industrial centres, particularly in the North of England as traditional industries such as ship-building have declined, and from the rural areas of Scotland and Wales as the lure of the metropolitan areas have encouraged many young people to leave. Until the 1980s the main areas of population increase had been in the South-east and Norfolk, because of their proximity to London and continental markets, and the South-west, partially because of its popularity as a retirement area.

However by 1997 London was experiencing the greatest fall in population (55,000 in that year), while the South-west had the greatest rise (32,000).

16.3 The balance of the sexes

Why do women live longer?

Women live longer than men and the gap between the 'longevity' of men and that of women continues to widen.

- There may be biological reasons for this difference in life expectation, but the social ones are the more apparent and may in fact also be a factor in apparently biological causes. For example, more women are currently dying from heart disease and this could be a result of increasing tension as they adopt men's roles in positions of responsibility at work.
- Men are more likely to die in accidents, both because their jobs still tend to be dangerous and because they are more likely to be motorists or motorcyclists. Men used to smoke more than women and are therefore have been more likely to die of illnesses associated with smoking such as cancer

Table 16.1 Population of the United Kingdom, 1951–91
(thousand)

	1951	1961	1971	1981	1991
Males	24,118	25,481	26,952	27,050	26,967
Females	26,107	27,228	28,562	28,626	28,767
Total	50,225	52,709	55,515	55,676	55,734

and heart disease; although the number of adults smoking has been dropping since 1972 more men have stopped than women, so that there is now little difference between them (29 per cent of men now smoke compared with 28 per cent of women).

- Until now, men are more likely to have jobs in which tension-related disease is high. In the past men have been more likely to be killed in war but the surplus women resulting from the male slaughter of the First World War have now passed out of the population.

- In the past the balance between the life expectancy of men and women has been balanced to some extent by the risk attached to multiple child-birth. However, the great decline in the number of pregnancies the average woman is likely to experience, linked to the decline in the number of women dying as a result of childbirth ('maternal mortality') has resulted in a greater proportion of women in the older age categories than formerly. In 1840 the life expectancy of a man at birth was forty and a woman forty-two, by 1901 it was forty-six and forty-nine, respectively and by 2001 it is expected to be about seventy-five and eighty (Table 16.1).

- In most societies there are more women than men because although more boys are born than girls (in Britain about 106 boys for every 100 girls) this imbalance has been overcorrected in the past by the greater proportion of boys that died in infancy as a result of the greater delicacy of male infants (see Table 16.1). However, more boys are now surviving to adulthood. There are two results of this phenomenon: (a) the chances of a woman marrying or having a partner are now higher than they have ever been, which increases the fertility rate; (b) the prospect of large numbers of males who wish to find a partner but cannot is a phenomenon not previously faced in British society. Will polyandry be the solution? The prospect of parents' being able to decide what sex of child they have is another issue for the future.

16.4 Inner cities

Generally speaking the centre of a city is the original core from which it expanded. It therefore often contains the oldest housing stock, which is more likely than that elsewhere to be in a condition of decay. As the housing is undesirable because of its condition, and because of the other disadvantages

A 'twilight zone'

This term was first used to describe slum areas scheduled for re-development; as the property was scheduled for demolition it remained unrepaired and deteriorated further. Only those unable to move remained and low property costs attracted the very poorest, with consequent social problems, while deserted property and demolition sites encouraged vandalism. The term is now sometimes extended to cover areas which have similar problems even if the re-development is not taking place.

associated with the area such as noise, pollution and old-fashioned school buildings, those who can afford to do so have moved elsewhere.

Moving out

Recently there has been an outflow of population from some of the biggest cities. London lost 17.5 per cent of its people between the census of 1971 and that of 1981; metropolitan areas overall lost 360,000 people between 1981 and 1991 and this outflow has continued (section 16.2) while non-metropolitan Britain gained 1.6 million as people continued the move to the suburbs, or moved further out into dormitory villages, or businesses moved to smaller towns where rents and rates were lower. Twenty-eight new towns have been established, but development has now been stopped as there appears to be a danger that a continued outflow would destroy the infrastructure of the cities and leave an unmanageable proportion of deprived people needing help, as the most energetic and qualified moved elsewhere. Already the centres of many cities – 'inner city areas' – have deteriorated, with an abnormal proportion of problems in terms of deprivation and crime.

Staying put

Those most likely to live in the inner city areas are the old who cannot afford to move; people who are poor for reasons of unemployment, desertion or disability, sometimes with large families; immigrants who are often unskilled and without capital so that they have to live wherever is cheapest and where they will be accepted; and those who are unskilled, employed but on low wages.

The movement of businesses from city centres because of high rates and other factors has decreased still further the employment opportunities of those who must live in those areas. The deterioration of the inner city environment and rising crime rates make them still less desirable so that increasing numbers of those who are in a position to do so move; the inner city is in a spiral of decline. (For more information on the problems of inner cities see pp. 235–9 and the specimen answer at the end of this book.)

'Gentrification'

Over the past twenty years or so there has been a move in some areas – notably Notting Hill and Islington in London – towards 'gentrification'. The increasing costs and inconvenience of travelling to work in the city centre and returning to the suburbs to sleep – 'commuting' – has resulted in some middle class people seeking homes in the period houses of the inner city and renovating them. This movement has the beneficial effect of creating a vocal pressure group to improve local services and renovate the environment, but the damaging effect of increasing housing shortages for those who cannot afford prices in the improvement areas and perhaps creating a greater feeling of relative deprivation (section 10.4) for the poor neighbours of the middle class residents.

Deprivation in the cities

In August 2000 the Department of the Environment published the first 'Indices of Deprivation', 2000 contained more than 140 statistical entries which indicated where the worst and best social conditions were to be found in England – these entries included job opportunities, health, housing, education and access to basic services such as post offices and shops (Table 16.2).

Most of the most deprived were to the North and most of the least deprived to the South; but there were areas of deprivation, such as Hackney, in the South, and areas of affluence in the North.

Table 16.2   Deprivation in the cities, 2000

Ten most deprived areas	Ten least deprived areas
1 Middlesbrough	1 Hart (NE Hants)
2 Liverpool	2 Isles of Scilly
3 Knowsley	3 South Northamptonshire
4 Manchester	4 Wokingham
5 Great Yarmouth	5 Windsor and Maidenhead
6 Newcastle upon Tyne	6 Horsham
7 Redcar	7 Rutland
8 Easington (Co Durham)	8 Uttlesford
9 Wirral	9 Harborough
10 Hartlepool	10 Surrey Heath

Although the following extracts were written some twenty-five years ago it is remarkable how little has changed – there may now be fewer outside lavatories in central Liverpool but few will deny that most of the problems identified have actually got worse, as exemplified by the references to the new 'underclass' referred to elsewhere in this book (pp. 199–200).

Inner cities

While there are problems in defining terms such as 'urban', the definition of 'inner' and 'outer' urban areas is particularly difficult and there are many possible definitions.

During 1977 partnerships were established between local and central government to focus on selected parts of the inner areas of the largest cities, where the scale and concentration of problems was felt to be greatest. The inner areas defined by the partnerships provide an agreed definition for those cities. The seven areas concerned are parts of Birmingham, Lambeth, Liverpool, Manchester and Salford, and Newcastle and Gateshead, London's Docklands, and all of Hackney and Islington together.

Britain was the first country in the world to experience mass urbanisation, and by the end of the nineteenth century about three-quarters of the population of England and Wales lived in urban areas, a much higher proportion than in any other country. Not only did urbanisation occur early, it was also extremely rapid, and many of the problems of inner city areas today are related to the way in which cities developed in the nineteenth century . . . The space used for development in the cities in the early nineteenth century was extremely limited since almost everyone had to walk to work. Although the cities offered jobs, they could not provide sufficient houses or social facilities for the people who flooded to the towns from the poor rural areas. Most towns at the beginning of the nineteenth century had only very elementary arrangements, if any, for providing water, clearing refuse and sewage, or treating mass epidemics. These towns were completely overwhelmed by the influx of people, and conditions in large towns were abominable. Life expectancy in Liverpool and Manchester was almost half that in areas such as Surrey, partly because of very high infant mortality rates.

Appreciation of the appalling conditions, brought to a head by the cholera epidemics of the 1830s and 1840s, led in 1844 to the setting up of a Royal Commission on the State of Large Towns and Populous Districts and then to the introduction of the first housing and health reform acts. In the last part of the century the introduction of cheap public transport allowed people to live much further from work, and the boundaries of the cities expanded rapidly. Very high densities were no longer required, and those people who could afford to do so moved to the outskirts of the cities – a trend which has continued ever since. However, the casual nature of employment of many of the working class people, and the need for their wives and children to earn, forced them to remain in the centre.

The core areas of the largest English cities are now losing both population and employment in absolute terms and, in the absence of specific steps being taken to prevent it, may be expected to continue to do so. Some decline in population was necessary to reduce densities but this stage has been passed in most areas.

The average age of dwellings in inner cities is much higher than nationally. Just over a quarter of England's housing was built before 1919; but in the inner areas the proportion ranges between about 40 and 60 per cent, despite the large scale slum clearance programmes which have been implemented.

Not only are the houses old, many still lack basic amenities. Inner Liverpool and Manchester/Salford are particularly affected – over 16 per cent of households lacking at least one basic amenity, most commonly an inside toilet.

As the Inner Area Studies showed, progress with improvement can also be delayed because a significant proportion of inner city residents cannot afford their share of the improvement costs. Furthermore, some of the older residents do not feel improvements are necessary, while absentee landlords of rented properties may not wish to spend money on improvements.

The poor condition of much of the stock is not the only inner area housing problem. More households live in overcrowded conditions, and more share accommodation, than elsewhere. This is in part due to the fact that many of the old properties were built several storeys high, to achieve the necessary densities, and these are now multi-occupied, often rented privately, and often overcrowded.

Newer housing is not without problems too. Many of the estates built to rehouse people from slum clearance areas consist of tower blocks of flats or medium-rise deck access blocks, built so as to retain the densities of the earlier period. Many of these estates have become very unpopular, vandalism is often a major problem, the stigma attached to some of the estates may take many years to remove.

Although there are differences between the inner areas, a higher proportion of accommodation in inner areas is rented and less is owner-occupied than nationally . . . The population structures of the inner areas are therefore biased towards the manual working class. Although it is difficult to obtain details of those people who have moved out from the inner areas, all indications are that the trend – begun towards the end of the nineteenth century – for the better-off, more highly skilled, people to move out in greater numbers has continued. Not only are the better-off people able to afford the increased transport costs to work, but they are also able to afford to buy their own home and are therefore not restricted by the availability of rented housing or the operation of local authority residence requirements . . . the unemployment rate of each socio-economic group is higher for inner area residents than for those living elsewhere. Unemployment rates for young people and non-whites are also high in inner areas.

The areas in which the inner area residents can look for employment without incurring high commuting costs have been losing jobs for over a decade, and appear likely to continue to do so. The decline has been most pronounced in the older service industries and the traditional manufacturing industries which caused the major cities to develop so quickly, but which are now declining in the face of technological advance and reduced demand for their products. Just as the original housing all became in need of improvement at the same time, the traditional industries are declining together.

Some service industries have been growing, but not sufficiently to compensate for the decline in employment in the other sectors; and in general they do not provide many jobs for the low skilled manual worker, nor for those with the traditional skills.

The loss of jobs from the inner areas appears to be caused to a greater extent by closure or contraction of firms than by net emigration. This occurs in different ways in different areas; in some cases one major industry such as shipbuilding declines rapidly, in some there is a substantial net loss of small firms, and some are affected by the rationalisation of large multi-plant firms. Inner areas generally seem to have suffered from a lack of new firms.

Many factors have contributed to the low level of creation of new firms in the inner areas, and it is very difficult to determine the relative importance of each. Government planning policies have clearly played their part, but many firms in the newer more mobile industries find that the depressing and deteriorating environment, high land values, scarcity of large sites, lack of appropriately skilled local labour, and the problems of access, congestion, vandalism, and crime are deterrents.

There are considerable demands on the social and health services in inner areas. In any area it is the lowest skilled, low income people who require most assistance from social services, e.g. child care may be essential for single parent families and ones where the wife must earn to raise the family above the poverty line. Low social groups are most prone to ill-health. Low income elderly households often require special care. High proportions of immigrants can create various problems, e.g. for educational services because of language and cultural differences.

It should be remembered that the majority of people living in inner cities are not unemployed and do not live in overcrowded houses or lack the use of basic amenities. However they can be affected by dereliction, vandalism, and petty crime; and they may well have difficulty obtaining a mortgage, or find that their address makes it more difficult for them to get new jobs. Thus the concentration of poor housing, unskilled population, and high unemployment can have an indirect effect on even those residents who are not directly affected. (D. Allnutt and A. Geland, 'Inner Cities in England', *Social Trends*, 10, 1979, abridged)

(A number of reports are referred to in this article including: *Change or Decay: Final Report of the Liverpool Inner Area Study*, 1977; *Unequal City: Final Report of the Birmingham Inner Area Study*, 1977; *Inner London: Policies for Dispersal and Balance: Final Report of the Lambeth Inner Area Study*, 1977)

The 'dump' estates in the inner cities

Through its low rents, the inner city ingathers the disadvantaged from a wide area. Through various channels – slum clearance, homelessness, the points system – council housing in turn attracts a large proportion of the disadvantaged. The institution of the estate thus concentrates the social problems of the inner city in an even smaller and more intimate space, where they can interact more destructively. Within the council sector, the allocation game creates pockets of even greater deprivation: the dump estates.

These are the least attractive, worst sited, worst provided with amenities. Usually they are unmodernized estates of pre-war flats, but sometimes more modern estates, more deeply flawed than usual with architectural blunders. They are the inner city's inner city.

Disadvantaged people tend to get very much worse council housing than the norm: older rather than newer; flats rather than houses; higher floors rather than lower. Certain social groups fare badly: the homeless, the unemployed and blacks worst of all, with female single parents and unskilled workers not far behind. The public sector seems unable to allocate desirable and undesirable housing any more fairly than the private.

Allocators used to solve part of the hard-to-let problem by offering flats on the worst estates to those who got only a single offer and had no choice: the homeless. The homeless, inevitably, contain a higher proportion of disadvantaged and unstable families, evicted for rent arrears or split up by family disputes. Even among those with a supposedly free choice, there is a subtle self-selection process at work. Rent levels are one element here. . . . Then there is a factor one might call 'staying power': the determination to hold out on the waiting list, turning down the earlier offers until something better turns up, to avoid moving into a dump. Staying power is obviously less among those who are most anxious to escape their present accommodation, because of overcrowding, bad repair, shared amenities or family conflicts. Once again, these people tend to be among the poorest and most unstable families, for whom even a hard-to-let estate may seem preferable to what they have at the moment. Finally there are elements of a culture of silence among society's most unfortunate victims: a tendency to be unaware of rights, to have little confidence in their ability to control their own destiny, and – at the lowest levels – to be so demoralized or so habituated to a squalid environment as to be almost indifferent to their surroundings.

Once an estate acquires more than a certain proportion of disadvantaged tenants – perhaps, say, one-fifth or one-quarter – it can find itself trapped in a descending spiral which may continue until it is demolished or massively rehabilitated. The preponderance of single-parent families and families with conflicts caused by low income or unemployment weakens parental discipline, so vandalism and crime are more prevalent . . . The 'better' tenants, with higher incomes, savings or skills, or more persistence over getting a transfer, move out and are replaced by more disadvantaged people. The estate acquires a reputation, usually worse than the reality, which discourages those with any hopes for their own future from even viewing a flat there. It is exactly the same sifting process, in miniature, as that which creates and maintains the inner city as a whole.

(Paul Harrison, *Inside the Inner City*, Harmondsworth, Penguin, 1983, adapted)

REVISION SUMMARY

An ageing population

In 1991 there were 10.6 million people over the age of 65 in the United Kingdom (16 per cent). In 1901 there were 1.8 million over 65 (4.7 per cent).

Consequences of an ageing population

- More pensions and other benefits.
- More homes for the elderly.

- More hospital care.
- Increased home medical care.

Costs

- More family involvement (e.g. paid employment may have to be surrendered).
- More family stress (e.g. if the dependent relative is senile).
- Isolation and loneliness for more old people.
- Feeling of worthlessness by the old.
- An expanding market for the products of computer technology.

Possible benefits

- More employment in the caring professions.
- People with time and experience to assist others (e.g. 'surrogate grannies').

Population movement

The percentage of population living in towns and cities (urban areas): England and Wales is shown in Table 16.3.

Urbanisation

A conurbation is a densely populated urban area in which a number of different towns and/or cities have merged.

The process in which a population moves from mainly living in rural (country) areas to living in urban (town) districts is called urbanisation.

The reason why Britain became urbanised are:

- The decline in numbers required in agriculture as a result of mechanisation (by 1984 only 1.6 per cent of the working population were engaged in agriculture, forestry or fishing).

Table 16.3   Population in towns and cities, England and Wales, 1801–1981

Year	(%)
1801	17
1851	50
1911	78
1951	81
1971	78
1981	76

- Industrialisation (people moved to settle near factories, coal mines, shipyards, etc. from the mid-eighteenth century onwards; service industries, such as shops, developed to serve the new populations).

Advantages of urbanisation are:

- Access to more opportunities for more people – cultural, educational, professional.
- Wider choice – shops, clubs, theatres (later cinemas, etc.).
- Reduction in physical isolation.
- Easier communications.
- Merging of cultures (there are advantages and disadvantages in this).

Disadvantages of urbanisation are:

- Social isolation: loneliness among crowds. (In its extreme form this may lead to suicide.)
- More crime and violence because of a reduced common identity; fewer shared standards; more crowding; more opportunities; less certainty of detection.
- Greater competition for status symbols; more stress.
- More pollution, including more noise.
- Relationships tend to be superficial – a 'network of associations'. They also tend to be 'segmented' – that is, established for particular reasons and not developed.
- There is less 'intergenerational' authority. 'In the shifting populations of large cities, young people are less ready to accord respect to their elders. "Grandad becomes a term of contempt" ' (A. Halsey, *Change in British Society*, 1981).
- Less homogeneous – people tend to be different from each other; more potential for conflict (also greater potential for variety and stimulation, see 'advantages' above).

Tönnies (1887) used the term '*Gemeinschaft*', meaning community, to describe rural lifestyles, with their stress on family and community and greater mutual involvement and caring. The term '*Gesellschaft*', meaning association, he used to describe urban life, with associations formed for practical purposes and less of the informal 'nosey' contacts of the village.

Durkheim stressed the sense of normlessness – anomie – of urban lifestyles and suggested that many of the problems of urban dwelling could be traced to this lack of set standards by which conduct could be judged.

R. Frankenberg, in *Communities in Britain: Social Life in Town and Country* (1966), points to:

- The likelihood of friction between kin in rural areas and to fights between 'the lads' of neighbouring villages. (Rural lifestyles are not all peace and tranquillity as compared with those of towns.)
- The need to play several different 'integrated' roles (i.e. shopkeeper, church deacon, husband, employer) – all to the same audience.
- The greater likelihood of ascribed status (the status of your parents influences people in their treatment of you).

Suburbanisation/ruralisation

Since 1951 there has been a drop in the proportion of the population living in urban areas, particularly in the large conurbations
  Reasons for movement from urban areas are:

- Increased ease of transport – particularly private car ownership.
- House prices (higher in most urban centres).
- Higher council tax in most urban areas.
- Pollution, including noise, in urban areas.
- Shift of industry out of large towns and cities (e.g. clean computer-based industries are often small-scale).
- More affluence – desire to own a home.
- Crime in urban areas.
- Inflated urban house prices encourage the move to a cheaper/more pleasant area upon retirement (with a useful cash surplus).

Impact of change

The growing similarity of lifestyles in urban and rural areas is the result of:

- The merging of populations outlined above.
- Television projects the same messages to both types of area.
- Education is similar – e.g. syllabuses, textbooks. Often teachers in rural areas come from urban ones, and vice versa.
- Mechanisation and automation apply in both rural and urban areas – e.g. factory farming (battery hens, etc.).
- Increased holidays (urban dwellers to rural areas; rural people to urban areas).

The balance of the sexes

Most societies have more females than males, because although more males are born, they are also more likely to die earlier than females.
  Reasons why males have shorter life expectancy:

- Boys are 'weaker' at birth (UK infant mortality for boys 10.6; girls 8.3 in 1984 – but the decline since (see section 15.4) is now so low overall at 5.5 that in the future it will have little statistical significance in studying the relative life expectancies of those now being born.
- More likely to die in accidents: more dangerous jobs; more motorists/motorcyclists.
- Men smoke more – cancer/heart disease, etc.
- Men drink more – heart and kidney disease.
- More stress at work – jobs carrying more responsibility.
  But the situation may change:

- Women are taking on former male roles – e.g. jobs with risk of more 'tension-related' disease.
- Infant mortality has declined as a proportionate cause of death.
- Proportionately more women are now drinking, smoking and driving than previously.

In the past men have been more likely to be killed in war and women to die in childbirth – neither cause is now statistically significant.

■ Y 17 Migration

17.1 Emigration

History

Emigration from the British Isles started with the colonisation of the New World but became a major movement in the nineteenth century, particularly to America and to the countries now known as the 'Old' Commonwealth – Australia, Canada and New Zealand – and to South Africa. Emigration to these countries was actively encouraged in that it built up a white population of British stock who would maintain the dominance of the existing white settlers and who could be expected to be supportive to the mother country. Emigrants were often poor and sought a new life in countries with labour shortages or ones where whites were likely to be favoured in employment. Some also have seen emigration as providing a greater opportunity of advancement for their children in countries with fewer class barriers to mobility. Emigration to the 'New' Commonwealth countries, mainly in Africa and Asia, tended to be middle class and the emigrants went as administrators, traders or as owners of enterprises such as plantations or mines.

In the past emigration has usually exceeded immigration (see Figure 17.1) except for the period 1931–51 when there was a net import of some half a million people, many of them refugees from Europe; and from the mid-1950s to 1962, peaking at the end of that period as people sought entry before the first Immigration Act came into force. There was also a slight surplus inflow between 1972 and 1973 when Asians with British passports were expelled from Uganda; and a further inflow from the mid 1980's as refugees arrived from war-ravaged countries such as Somalia and from the Balkan conflicts. A peak period for emigration was between 1911 and 1921 when almost a million people left Britain, but emigration reduced during the mid-1970s as most destination countries experienced recession and unemployment and restricted migrants to those whose skills were required.

Balance of emigration and immigration

From the early 1980s more people have entered the United Kingdom (mainly England) than have left it and the Office of National Statistics has assumed a net inflow of 65,000 people a year from 1999, gradually declining to nil by 2018.

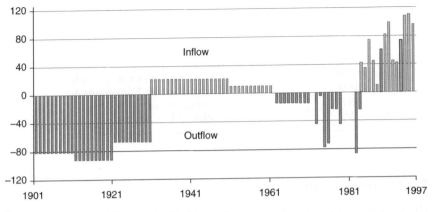

Notes:
1 Includes net civilian migration and other adjustments. Ten year averages are used before 1931 and between 1951 and 1970. A twenty-year average in used between 1931 and 1950. Data prior to 1971 are for calendar years, data for 1971 onwards are mid-year estimates.

Figure 17.1   Net international migration, 1901–97[1] (United Kingdom, thousand)
Source: Social Trends, 29 © Crown Copyright, 1999. National Statistics.

17.2 Immigration

History

Britain has a long history of absorbing immigrants: French Protestants in the seventeenth century; the Irish in the second half of the nineteenth century and the first half of the twentieth; Jews from Central Europe at the end of the nineteenth century and the 1930s; 'Iron Curtain' refugees in the 1940s and 1950s.

Since the mid-1970s there have been two major groups of immigrants: West Indians and Asians. West Indians were actively encouraged by London Transport and other undertakings to move to Britain during the 1950s to overcome the shortage of labour resulting from the post-war expansion of the economy. However, in the 1970s slightly more West Indians left Britain than entered it. By 1976 there were about 500,000 people of West Indian origin in Britain. West Indian immigration has now virtually ceased.

In the late 1950s a number of Asians were encouraged to enter Britain by former British Army officers who had been in Indian regiments. These saw the surplus population of India and Pakistan (part of which is now Bangladesh) as a source of labour for industries with recruitment problems such as textiles and foundry work. By 1976 there were 800,000 people from the Indian subcontinent in Britain, and by 1991 there were approximately twice as many Asians as West Indians in Britain. However, 'primary' immigration from the Asian subcontinent has now virtually ceased – the main source of immigrants being wives and children coming to join those already settled.

Table 17.1 Legislation on immigration, 1905–81	
Year	**Act**
1905	Aliens Act
1962	Commonwealth Immigrants Act
1968	Commonwealth Immigrants Act
1971	Immigrants Act
1981	British Nationality Act

Restrictions or immigration

The main legislation aimed at restricting immigration is shown in Table 17.1.

This legislation has effectively restricted immigration into Britain to those who have a special skill in short supply in Britain; to dependants of people already settled in Britain; and to those who have already acquired citizenship or have a parent or grandparent who was a British citizen; acceptances on the basis of marriage accounted for nearly 60 per cent of the total of those accepted for settlement by the mid-1990s. The higher levels after 1995 were owing to an increase in the number of asylum-related cases – that is people who had earlier been granted asylum or exceptional leave to remain, together with spouses or dependants who were then been given settlement.

The only exception to entry restrictions on non-British citizens has been those of the Irish Republic who have a right to unrestricted entry and full political and economic rights while living in Britain. The Irish have traditionally been the major source of immigration to Britain but in recent years there has been a net loss of Irish nationals (a net inflow of about 10,000 a year between 1961 and 1971 and a net outflow of about 1000 a year since). Since Britain joined the European Economic Community (EEC) there has been a right of unrestricted entry to community nationals but the immigration and emigration figures between Britain and the rest of the Community have remained roughly in balance, although migration between the European Community and the United Kingdom is increasing.

For the good of the country, let's have more immigrants

Barbara Roche, the immigration minister, has called for a debate on ending a 30-year ban on economic migration into Britain.

Between 1950 and 1971, Britain encouraged immigrants from the Caribbean to fill jobs here. When unemployment began to rise, the immigration was stopped. Since then the only people allowed to settle here have been asylum seekers and the spouses and dependants of those already here.

Now Ms Roche wants to 'be ready to think imaginatively about how migration can meet economic and social needs'. She is dipping a toe into shark-infested waters for there will be many prepared to play the demagogue against a new influx of foreigners. Yet the unpopularity of immigrants is partly the result of the present policy. By allowing in only desperate victims and smuggled illegals, many of whom go straight on to welfare, it gives immigrants a bad name. To open the door to the ambitious and skilled is the best way to change that – to receive people who are after private opportunities, rather than public welfare.

It is partly because economic migration is illegal that the whole immigration scene is such a disaster. As with the prohibition of drugs, the trade is driven underground where fat profits can be made, which attracts dealers such as the inhuman traders who killed 58 Chinese migrants in a lorry at Dover. A policy of prohibition deters the most desirable migrants and attracts the most desperate. By forcing an economic migrant to masquerade as a refugee, we base the whole system on a deceit.

Besides, history shows that immigration is generally a boon to a country, not just economically but culturally as well. Immigrants inject vitality, energy and novelty, as the United States has long demonstrated. To this day, immigrants and the children of immigrants are often among the most ambitious, successful and determined of citizens. Think of Colin Powell, George Soros or Arnold Schwarzenegger. Much of the can-do spirit of the United States stems from the way it kept refreshing itself with people who had the self-reliance and gumption to get up and go when things got rough at home.

For centuries, Britain, too, had a proud history of welcoming newcomers, many of whom were vital to our history. The contribution of the Ugandan Asians is a striking example, as were Huguenots and Jews before them. Indeed, we are all immigrants in some sense – be our blood Norman, Viking, Saxon, Roman or Celtic. The difference between us and, say, Australians is a matter of time, not kind. Our aborigines were just as surely displaced.

Besides, we were generous exporters of our people to other parts of the globe when our population was growing and theirs was not. Hence the vast diaspora of English-speaking people – and hence the fact that even today more British-born people live abroad than those of almost any other country.

Now the tables have turned and Britain (like the rest of Europe) is in demographic stagnation. According to the *Economist*, so fast is the birth-rate declining that just to keep its working-age population stable, the European Union would need to import 1.6 million people every year until 2050. To keep the ratio between workers and pensioners stable would require an even more rapid rate of immigration: nearly 14 million people into the EU every year.

The alternative, which is superficially attractive to nostalgic con-servatives, is that behind our walls we allow the working population to shrink and hope that machines can take over jobs like nanny, nurse and waiter so that the natives can continue to find employment as sociologist, aromatherapist or newspaper columnist. But that is a delusion. A shrinking and ageing population is a recipe for economic decline, and we would soon not be able to afford the luxury of cushy jobs at all.

Immigration, in other words, is not just good for the immigrants, who find new opportunities in the country they reach, but for the country, too.

(Matt Ridley, *Daily Telegraph*, 24 July 2000)

Assimilating the inflow

If the image of a 'brain drain' has given emigration a highly unfavourable connotation in the British public's mind, the rapidly growing immigration of the years up to mid-1962 created an equally unfortunate public impression. For despite the fact that those at least whose schooling had taken place in Britain had been taught what great benefits, material and other, had accrued to this country from earlier waves of immigrants, there seemed to be many features of the situation in the late 1950s and early 1960s that were different from previous occasions. For one thing, these were not to any marked degree refugees from political, racial or religious persecution. Nor were they from Europe. They came in larger numbers, from different areas and for different reasons from their predecessors. And though they provided a much-needed addition to the overstretched labour force (in nursing, in particular, the public gratitude for their help was both genuine and general), their coming came to be associated in the public mind with race riots in Nottingham and Notting Hill – a new and ugly feature of contemporary British life – and there were dark forebodings of what might happen when employment was no longer so full, when overcrowding and health problems became more acute as the flow continued. It was widely believed that assimilation was proving difficult if not impossible in many cases; and that the economic and other difficulties faced by the immigrants were leading them to settle in certain parts of the cities to which they went, with the consequent emergence for the first time of 'coloured quarters' with their attendant social evils and dangers.

As with the emigration case, there was a crying need for authoritative facts and figures, and amongst those who undertook special surveys to fill this need was Ruth Glass. In her study, *Newcomers*, she obtained information about a large sample of West Indians who had settled in London, between the beginning of 1954 and the end of 1958. Careful analysis of this material, together with published statistics from a wide variety of sources, enabled her to dispel a number of myths. She demonstrated, for example, that the widely held belief that almost all the newcomers were unskilled workers before they came here was unjustified. One in four of the men had, in fact, been non-manual workers, and only one in five had been semi-skilled or unskilled workers or farm labourers.

The migrants' job aspirations on arrival here had, of course, often not been fulfilled; downgrading, in status if not in economic terms, had been a common experience. The mistaken belief that almost all Commonwealth immigrants were completely unskilled gained some support even from official pronouncements of the time, despite the cautious wording used.

(R. Kelsall, *Population in Britain in the 1990s and Beyond*, 1989)

At the end of the twentieth century there was, as at the beginning, a flow of refugees/asylum seekers from Eastern Europe as a result of the collapse of communism and the resultant social upheaval, and a number of wars in the Balkans. There was also an increase in the number of 'economic migrants', usually entering illegally, which caused a considerable public debate, although the numbers involved were relatively small.

17.3 Ethnic groups

What is an 'ethnic group'?

An **ethnic group** is a group with a particular 'culture' (section 1.1): a way of behaving and thinking that makes it distinctive, perhaps including religious belief, language, dress and cuisine.

Ethnicity is sometimes confused with 'race'. Essentially race is a classification based on *physical differences* and usually divides mankind into three major groups: Mongoloid, Caucasoid and Negroid. There is considerable argument among biologists regarding methods of classification, and the concept has little practical value (Kohn, *The Race Gallery*, 1995); indeed in 2001 the first results of the 'human genome' project was published, this international study indicated that every person on earth shares 99.99 per cent of their genetic code with all other people. There is no separate Jewish race or Irish race. There is no evidence of racial differences in intelligence that could not equally be accounted for by environmental factors – intelligence tests given to army recruits in the United States resulted in negroes in each State scoring lower than whites, but the negroes from the Northern States had a higher average score than the whites from the Southern States (A. Barnett, *The Human Species*, 1957).

Group solidarity

Immigrants, in a new and often hostile environment, tend to congregate together in areas where housing and appropriate jobs are available; they mix mainly with each other, intermarry and try to maintain the traditions and customs with which they are familiar. Their group solidarity is often reinforced by a common religious belief.

The fact that the first wave of any group of immigrants tend to be young unattached males often leads to stereotyping – to a belief that all members of a group share the characteristics of a few that have been particularly noticed. Their behaviour in terms of drunkenness, fighting and 'chasing girls' is likely to be the same as a similar group of the indigenous population but they are likely to be more highly visible in terms of appearance or behaviour.

The immigrant is likely to be poor, and often unskilled, and will tend to settle in 'inner city' areas (section 16.4) where pressure on services is likely to be already high. The immigrant will be seen as a competitor for scarce resources, although it has been shown that immigrants on average receive less in terms of social service benefits than do native born residents.

'Second-generation' ethnic groups

Increasingly members of ethnic minority groups are not immigrants, but people born in Britain who see Britain as their permanent home; for example over 40 per cent of people of Pakistani/Bangladeshi origin are under the age of sixteen, and the vast majority of these were born in Britain.

17.4 Racism

What is racism?

Racism is an elusive concept, for example one study in 1993 (Back, 'Race Identity and Nation within an Adolescent Community in South London') found that while young white and black people on the estate shared a 'colour blind' world of inter-racial friendships, bound together by a strong sense of shared neighbourhood, the Vietnamese residents of the estate were perceived as outsiders and were frequently harassed and attacked.

Even the terminology used is often ambiguous (Modood 'Political Blackness and British Asians', 1994) points out that most 'West Indians' have actually been born in Britain. While the word 'black' is now acceptable although previously regarded as pejorative, while it is currently disputed as a suitable blanket term to include all non-white groups. Modood also points out that there are huge variations in the life experiences of differing ethnic groups within categories sometimes regarded as cohesive – for example many Hindus and Sikhs from India are entering the professions, operating successful businesses and achieving educational success in large numbers, while Sunni Muslims from Pakistan and Bangladesh often suffer acute disadvantage.

Because members of ethnic groups are often highly visible compared with the host group they can easily become the target for **prejudice** – a bias (usually hostility) without reasonable reason. Prejudice directed against members of a particular race or a particular ethnic group which results from such group membership is called 'racism'. Racism usually stems from fear – fear of competition for jobs, educational opportunities, housing or mates. Racism is more likely to occur among those who feel most directly threatened, and as many immigrants tend to be in competition most directly with those at the bottom of the social ladder it is usual to find the greatest degree of racial prejudice among the least skilled. Where vested interests are at stake higher up the social scale, as in South Africa, racism is likely to be prevalent among members of the middle class as well. It is increasingly recognised that racism cannot be studied in isolation from other forms of oppression and that although it is legitimate to look at race, class or gender separately it is necessary to see how all these intersect in order to fully understand the processes involved. 'Though all women are women no woman is only a woman', (Spelman, *Inessential Women*, 1990).

Racial scapegoats

In the nineteenth century the Irish were the major target for British racism, identifiable by accent and religion. As Jews, escaping pogroms in Central Europe, joined them at the end of the nineteenth century, they too became targets for abuse and discrimination. More recently, the even more visible West Indians and Asians have become targets; but gypsies, Chinese, Jews and other groups who can be readily identified as 'different' are also likely to be used as scapegoats and blamed for crime, unemployment, poor educational standards and other failings within society in general.

Legislation against race discrimination

In order to reduce open 'overt' discrimination, successive governments introduced legislation (see Table 17.2).

Growing tolerance?

Racism, however, cannot be abolished merely by legislation – it needs to be shown to be illogical and unfair. Fortunately, there is a considerable element of tolerance in British society; an Audience Selection Poll (1985) asked: 'Would Britain be a better place to live in if only white people lived here?' The overwhelming majority (80 per cent) said 'No'; only 15 per cent said 'Yes'. This is reinforced by the derisory vote received by political parties seeking to exploit prejudice.

Despite this racial harassment remains commonplace – the *Home Office Crime Survey* of 1992 recorded 140,000 episodes of racial harassment or attacks in that

Table 17.2 Race relations legislation, 1965–76

Act	Measures
Race Relations Act 1965	Banned discrimination on the ground of colour, race, ethnic or national origins in 'places of public resort'. Also made incitement to racial hatred illegal.
Race Relations Act 1968	Widened the concept of illegal discrimination to include goods, facilities and services; employment, housing, and advertising.
Race Relations Bill 1976	Tightened up the law.

year. Nevertheless the waves of immigrants over several centuries have integrated successfully within British society, mainly using education as the key to higher-status jobs and there is no doubt that this is now happening to the children and grandchildren of those who arrived in the second part of the twentieth century (see Figure 17.1.)

In 1992, a study commissioned by the School Examinations and Assessment Council found that 10 per cent of black seven-year-olds gained the top grade in mathematics and 19 per cent in science in the new national classroom tests; this compared with 6 per cent and 18 per cent, respectively, for whites.

REVISION SUMMARY

Reasons for migration

Most migrants are poor and move:

- To find work
- To improve the prospects for their children (e.g. fewer class barriers) } Applies to both emigrants and immigrants

Other reasons are:

- To escape persecution (e.g. Jews from Central Europe at the beginning of the century; Iron Curtain refugees in the 1940s and 1950s; Ugandan Asians in 1972 and 1973; Somalis and Kosovo Albanians in the 1990s).
- To enhance lifestyles and opportunities (e.g. middle class administrators, traders, etc. to Africa and Asia).
- To join relatives (now the majority group from the 'New' Commonwealth and Pakistan).

Racism

'Racism' is a term used to describe hostility felt for and practised by one 'racial' group to another. In fact 'race' classifications are confused and have little practical value – usually when people say 'race' they really mean ethnic group (*ethnos* is Greek for 'a tribe').

Reasons for racism (or racial prejudice)

- **Fear**. The immigrant is seen as a competitor for scarce resources: housing, education, jobs. ('The ordinary English worker hates the Irishman as a competitor who lowers his standard of life': Karl Marx.)
- **Stereotyping**. The fact that the first wave of any group of immigrants tends to be young, unattached males often leads to stereotyping – to a belief that all

members of a group share the characteristics of a few that have been particularly noticed.

- **Scapegoating**. The immigrants are usually easily identified by factors such as religion, colour, dress, etc. They are convenient targets to blame for general failings in society that would have existed anyway (e.g. poor housing, crime, unemployment).

SELF-TEST QUESTIONS: PART SIX

Self-test 6.1

1 What is the name given to the study of human populations?   *(1 mark)*
2 How often is the census taken?   *(1 mark)*
3 Name one conurbation in the United Kingdom.   *(1 mark)*
4 What was the 'birth rate' in Great Britain in 1991?
   What was the 'birth rate' in Great Britain in 1891?   *(2 marks)*
5 Name any two factors which you would expect to be shared by a member of an 'ethnic group'.   *(2 marks)*
6 Define the term 'birth rate'.   *(3 marks)*
7 Why is it necessary for a government to have details of the composition of its nation's population?   *(3 marks)*
8 What factors may give rise to racial prejudice?   *(4 marks)*
9 What disadvantages are there for the individual in urban living?   *(4 marks)*
10 Why may the lifestyles in urban and rural areas be becoming increasingly similar?   *(4 marks)*
          (Total 25 marks)

Self-test 6.2

1 Which of the areas shown in Table 17.3 had the most substantial increase in population numbers during the period shown?   *(1 mark)*
2 Which of the areas shown in the table had the smallest percentage growth in population during the period shown?   *(1 mark)*
3 Which area shown in the table had the highest population density in both 1911 and 1981?   *(2 marks)*
4 Why has the population increased in some areas more than in others?   *(6 marks)*
5 What differences would you expect to find living in a densely populated urban area compared with living in a rural area?   *(10 marks)*
          (Total 20 marks)

Self-test 6.3

Table 17.3   Population of the United Kingdom, by regions, 1911 and 1981

Regions/Counties	Area (km²)	Population (1000)		% growth
		1911	1981	
England:				
North	19,349	2,815	3,104	10
Yorkshire and				
Humberside	14,196	3,877	4,860	25
East Midlands	12,179	2,263	3,819	69
East Anglia	12,565	1,192	1,872	57
South East	27,408	11,744	16,796	43
South West	23,660	2,687	4,349	62
West Midlands	13,013	3,277	5,148	57
North West	7,993	5,796	6,414	11
Wales	20,763	2,421	2,792	15
Scotland	77,179	4,760	5,131	8
Northern Ireland	13,570	1,251	1,562	25

Source: Social Trends 1983 (London: HMSO, 1982).

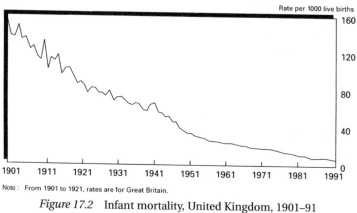

Note :   From 1901 to 1921, rates are for Great Britain.

Figure 17.2   Infant mortality, United Kingdom, 1901–91
Source: *Social Trends*, 23 (London: HMSO, 1993).

In 1987, the mortality rate among babies whose fathers had unskilled jobs was 70 per cent higher than among those whose fathers had a professional occupation (*Daily Mirror*, 5 December 1990). Looking at Figure 17.2:

1   What was the infant mortality rate for the United Kingdom in 1941?   (*1 mark*)
2   What geographical area is not included in the graph before 1921 but is subsequently?
(*1 mark*)
3   Define the term 'infant mortality rate'.   (*2 marks*)

SPECIMEN QUESTIONS AND ANSWERS

1 Identify and explain three reasons why the infant mortality rate in the UK has declined during this century. *(6 marks)*
2 Examine how and why the status of children and young people has changed over the past 100 years. *(10 marks)*

Answers

1 The infant mortality rate has declined because of improved medical facilities and knowledge. For example, 'scanning' equipment can detect abnormalities in mother or baby before birth, which it may be possible to rectify and thus improve the child's chance of survival; polio, measles and whooping cough vaccines have all reduced infant death by making these diseases less prevalent.

Improved diet and an awareness of its importance to the mother before birth have led to healthier, stronger babies being born, with better chances of survival. Better sanitation and hygiene have reduced the possibility of infection and thus reduced infant mortality.

(*Note*: Medical facilities and knowledge would probably count as two separate points, but it does not harm to give more points than required, although it is best not to do so too blatantly (giving the impression that you have not read the question). Remember not only to identify the factor, but also explain why this has led to a reduction in the death of infants under one year old.)

2 In most ways the status of children and young people has improved during the last 100 years. Families have become more 'child-centred' as the number of children in the family has decreased (from an average of about four children per family in the 1880s to less than two today). Having fewer children has meant that parents can spend more time with individuals, while the growth of the importance of the privatised nuclear family has emphasised the importance of the nuclear family members to one another.

Legislation has also enhanced the status of the child as an individual worthy of respect and protection. For example, the Children and Young Persons Act of 1933 made the causing of suffering or injury of health of a child punishable by a fine or imprisonment; incest is punishable under the Punishment of Incest Act of 1908; and in 1986 Parliament passed an Act prohibiting corporal punishment in state schools.

Compulsory and extended education has greatly improved the status of young people by making them more knowledgeable on many matters than their elders, although this may cause friction in the home if children 'look down' on their less-well-educated parents. The media tend to emphasise the importance of youth, as does the 'youth culture' industry – with youthful music, fashion and attitudes seen as more 'advanced' than those relating to older people.

However, although children are maturing physically earlier, they are also dependent on parents or guardians for longer, being unable to support themselves until the age of sixteen or even later, as a result of extended educational opportunities (whereas a child could work legally at the age of thirteen 100 years ago). The transition from childhood to adulthood is becoming increasingly blurred, with the absence of any 'rite of passage', as in many other societies, and for many a delay in obtaining their first job, which in the past has been a mechanism for integrating young people into the adult world.

(Note: The question asks how the status of children and young people has changed – you must describe both improvements and (perhaps more difficult) ways in which their status has got worse and/or become ambiguous.

This question is a good example of how information must often be drawn from a number of syllabus areas in order to answer a question – in this case your answer requires information on family, education, youth culture and work as well as 'population'.)

Part Seven

Social stability and control

■ ⋎ **18** The nature of social order

18.1 Conformity

Merton's five groups

There are many pressures urging the individual to accept particular patterns of conduct and thought, in order to meet the expectations of others (section 1.3).

Merton *(Social Structure and Anomie,* 1938) divided people into five main groups according to their adjustment to the norms of their society.

- The first group, the 'Conformists', are those who accept the goals of their society, and set about achieving these goals in a most generally acceptable way.
- The 'Innovators' are those who accept the goals of the society but not the accepted means of achieving them. For example, the desirability of wealth and all the status symbols that accompany it may be accepted but the means of acquisition may be fraud or robbery, or gambling which is now non-criminal but socially dubious.
- The 'Retreatists' avoid decisions on, or reject, society's goals or methods of achieving them and withdraw from society as much as possible, for example New Age travellers, alcoholics and some hermits.
- The 'Ritualists' do not believe in the goals, but go through the socially approved motions for fear of disapproval. For example, a couple may not accept the values of our society in relation to marriage, but still do marry even although they do not regard it as sinful to live together without marriage.
- Merton's fifth group – the 'Rebels' – overtly reject the values of the society, both goals and means of achievement. For example a young person may reject the whole notion of private property as an objective and join a revolutionary group to bring about the collapse of the existing order. The means he uses will decide his criminality or otherwise.

Conformity is much less interesting to most people than 'deviance', the breaking of the rules of the society, but it is much more important in that a society could not survive if most people did not conform to its norms and values. The ways that societies ensure this conformity is therefore of importance.

18.2 Deviance

What is 'deviance'?

In *Outsiders* H. Becker pointed out that 'we must recognise that we cannot know whether a given act will be categorised as deviant until the response of others has occurred. Deviance is not a quality that lies in behaviour itself, but in the interaction between the person who commits the act and those who respond to it.' A nurse injecting morphine into the vein of a patient to relieve pain is not acting in a deviant fashion; a drug addict injecting a friend with the same drug for 'kicks' is behaving in a deviant fashion.

Once a person has been 'labelled' a deviant they are likely to be regarded as having a number of characteristics in common with other people in the same category. For example, some people might still regard all homosexuals as a danger to small boys even although all the available evidence makes it clear that this is not the case.

Becker also comments that: 'labelling places the actor in circumstances which make it harder for him to continue the normal routines of everyday life and thus provokes him to "abnormal" actions (as when a prison record makes it harder to earn a living at a conventional occupation and so disposes its possessor to move into an illegal one).' This view has led prisons and Young Offenders Centres to be regarded as 'finishing schools' for criminals.

This labelling of a person so that the original deviance prevents them operating otherwise as a normal member of the society has been called '**stigmatisation**'. 'Most people drift into deviance by specific actions rather than by formed choices of social roles and statuses' (Lemert, *Humans*).

Teachers may have expectations of how a particular child or group of children may behave, the pupils may internalise these expectations and act them out (see section 8.2) This view that people are creative actors whose interaction with others results in particular conduct has been called 'symbolic interactionism'. For example, a person with a disability may be treated, or avoided, in such a way as to suggest that, for example, a lack of mobility implies a lack of intelligence. The person being labelled might accept that view and retreat into themselves, avoiding social contact, another might aggressively reject the implied label; in either case their manifest behaviour is a result of the behaviour of others.

Labelling – moral panic and deviance

A quarter of a century ago Peter Marsh and others published *The Rules of Disorder*, but it still seems as relevant today as when it first appeared – its reference to 'football hooligans' as the 'most recent' examples of 'folk devils' will strike a particular chord for those who remember the behaviour of British fans at the European Cup in 2000.

'Folk devils'

Mostly master and slave share a theory. And the reverberations of that shared theory may last for a very long time, long after the institution which was its natural concomitant in day-to-day social practices has gone. A striking example of this is the passive 'loser' social style of many American black people, the style that black militants have tried with some desperation and success to redress. It reflects a conception of themselves inherited from the theory of their nature and place in a slave society, a theory they shared with the slave owners, and from whom they learned it.

(P. Marsh, E. Russer and R. Harré, *The Rules of Disorder*, London, Routledge & Kegan Paul, 1978, adapted)

Moral panic

To explain the extravagant character of the attributions imposed upon disenchanted and rebellious schoolchildren and rumbustious football fans, we introduce Stan Cohen's concept of 'moral panic'.

Societies appear subject, every now and then, to periods of moral panic. A condition, episode, person or group of persons emerges to become defined as a threat to societal values and interests: its nature is presented in a stylised and stereotypical fashion by the media. Sometimes the object of the panic is quite novel and at other times it is something which has been in existence long enough, but suddenly appears in the limelight. Sometimes the panic passes over and is forgotten, except in folklore and collective memory: at other times it has more serious and long-lasting repercussions and might produce such changes as those in legal and social policy or even in the way that society conceives itself (S. Cohen, *Folk Devils and Moral Panics*, 1972).

Since the war, a succession of moral panics have spread through our society, each with its characteristic 'object'. These objects have ranged historically from Teddy Boys through to Mods and Rockers and Skinheads. The most recent are the football hooligans, who for many people, and not least the feature writers of our Sunday newspapers, have come to represent all that is most senseless and destructive in our society. Anyone doubting such a claim should simply scan, as we have done, headlines of the more popular newspapers from about 1968 onwards and note the frequency with which terms such as 'mindless', 'evil', 'thuggery', 'mad', 'violent', 'wanton destruction', etc., crop up in reports concerning football supporters. From reading such reports one might be forgiven for thinking that the football terraces ran deep with blood each Saturday.

From a sociological viewpoint, the function of Folk Devils is quite clear. In setting up certain members as visible examples of what is proscribed, by attributing forbidden characteristics to them, they serve as images of disorder and evil. Having created these images, our society is more able to ascribe to the majority of its members – the right-thinking corpus – a comforting sense of order and social propriety . . . Vandalism, for example, might be thought of as a collection of clearly identifiable acts requiring sanction for the simple reason that they offend against the property, both individual and collective, of members in society. But contrast the reaction to football fans who run through a town creating damage as they go with the reaction to university students during rag week creating similar damage. The former damage will be viewed as the result of 'destructive hooliganism' and dealt with accordingly, whilst the latter will be seen as arising from an excess of goodnatured high spirits and over-enthusiasm. Although the damaging acts are very similar, football fans are 'deviants' whilst students, for reasons not made explicit, are somewhat excused. We might also note that what constitutes an offence in legal terms also changes over time. Acts such as those involving homosexuality or abortion would, only a few years ago, have been held up as examples of 'hardcore' deviance. And yet those same acts today escape formal sanction.

(P. Marsh, E. Russer and R. Harré, The Rules of Disorder, London, Routledge & Kegan Paul, 1978, adapted)

A more recent example of moral panic and the 'folk devils' created by it or from which it stems was the belief in 2000 that 'refugees' were 'flooding' into the country and would become a major burden for taxpayers, even though numbers were not particularly large overall and were mainly concentrated in a few coastal towns. At about the same time 'football hooligans' made one of their periodic appearances as major objects of loathing – in particular those who were credited with having brought disgrace to Britain when they rampaged in a Belgium town during the European Cup; despite allegations of widespread violence and substantial damage only one person was convicted of an offence, and he was subsequently released on appeal.

Social control

The exclusion of a person who is deviant in one respect from participating as a full member of the society in other respects is one of the ways that social control is exercised. The earlier example of the homosexual might be used to illustrate how fear of being regarded as a perverted child-molester who would be excluded from employment opportunities and other social interaction might encourage someone with homosexual tendencies to sublimate them and either seek socially acceptable heterosexual outlets or enter an occupation where celibacy was the norm, although this has become much less likely today as homosexuality has become more socially acceptable.

Such informal social control is the main basis for social stability and operates in the main through approval and disapproval. The social institutions of enforcement 'codes, courts and constables' can be used in only a limited number of cases – the present overcrowding in British prisons is leading to an increasing number of non-custodial sentences, but there is clearly a limit to the capacity of courts, police and probation officers as well as of prisons.

Sanctions

A sanction is a method of enforcing obedience, and although most people will accept the officially 'sanctioned', or approved, behaviour as a result of social conditioning, punishments are also required in most societies to deter at least some of those who are tempted to disregard the accepted norms and values. Equally, rewards such as knighthoods or OBEs serve to emphasise the importance of the norms and values by publicly honouring those who have conspicuously assisted in maintaining them, whether by voluntary work in hospitals, reaching eminence in their professions or assisting a political party. Rewards may also be in the form of direct monetary payments which encourage members of the society to work hard in socially approved ways to attain both practical benefits and higher status.

Punishments are called '**negative sanctions**' and those that are the result of laws or laid down in regulations are called 'formal' negative sanctions. A formal negative sanction might include a girl in detention at school for smoking, or a murderer serving a life sentence in prison. An informal negative sanction might include such signs of disapproval as not saying 'good morning' to a neighbour who has offended us, or a man being 'sent to Coventry', so that no one is prepared to speak to him, as a punishment for not going on strike when the rest of his workmates had voted to do so.

Formal sanctions

Formal positive sanctions encourage socially approved activities

Rewards are called 'positive sanctions' and may include formal positive sanctions such as an MBE or a good exam pass. An informal positive sanction might include a child being given a sweet for doing a job for his Mum, or being sought after as a reliable friend. Positive sanctions tend to be more effective than negative ones in ensuring social control.

Labelling theory

Apprehension and labelling

The second stage in the process of becoming deviant, and one on which most labellists have concentrated, is that of **apprehension**. Becker (1963) says: 'One of the most crucial steps in the process of building a stable pattern of deviant behaviour is likely to be experience of being caught and publicly labelled as a deviant . . . being caught and branded as a deviant has important consequences for one's further social participation and self image.'

It should be made clear, however, that labellists do not consider the fact of being officially registered, or even the ritual ceremonies of status degradation that frequently accompany that official act, to be in themselves sufficient to convert normals into self-identifying deviants.

Degradation rituals

Degradation rituals such as drumming the coward out of the regiment, administering the pauper's oath, diagnosing the contagious illness and finding the accused guilty as charged may dramatize the facts of deviance, but their 'success' is gauged less by their manner of enactment than by their prevailing consequences . . . The ancient ceremonial . . . may strike [the accused] with awe and fear, but if nothing much happens as a consequence, the memory fades or is retrospectively rationalized . . . for stigmatization to establish a total deviant identity, *it must be disseminated throughout society.*

(Edwin Lemert, *Humans: Their Deviance, Social Problems and Social Control*, 1967)

The italics in this quote are deliberate for they prevent a simplistic rendition of labelling theory. Something other than a ritual ceremony has to happen. Being labelled deviant guarantees nothing. From the fact of apprehension and being formally registered as having committed a deviant act, most labelling theorists go on to discuss one serious consequence which might well contribute to further infractious behaviour – incarceration. Matza, however, takes a different route before arriving at incarceration. Most people who are caught are eventually released and not sent to prison. Can we assume that for this majority the process of building a deviant identity is necessarily concluded? 'No,' says Matza; apprehension has given them matters to consider. Not only have they experienced the simple fact of being registered, but during apprehension they have experienced derogation and representation – that is, they have suffered the abuse of people correlating the immorality of the act with their own immorality, and they have been treated in accordance with the status the State, in its bureaucratic routines, allots them – that of a criminal. It is when the State stops the relatively trivial activity of registration and gets down to the serious business of derogation and representation that the subject's conventional identity is shocked. As Matza puts it: 'To be signified a thief does not assure the continuation of such pursuits; but it does add to the meaning of theft in the life of the perpetrator, and it does add to the meaning of that person in the eyes of others ... To be signified a thief is to lose the blissful identity of one who among other things happens to have committed a theft. It is a movement, however gradual, toward being a thief ... to be cast a thief ... is to compound and hasten the process of becoming that very thing.' (S. Box, *Deviance, Reality and Society*, 1981).

REVISION SUMMARY

Conformity

Most people do what is expected of them: they *conform* to the *norms* of the society because they have been *socialised* to do so.

Merton, in *Social Structure and Anomie* (1938), divided people into five groups according to how they adjust to the expectations of others:

Some 'goals' of our society:
Secure job
Marry and have children
Own house
Obtain status symbols (e.g. car)
Avoid trouble with law (actual level of objective varies according to 'reference group')
For **some**: Climb class ladder

Conformists accept the goals (objectives) of their society; try to achieve these in most acceptable way (e.g. work hard, pass exams).

Innovators accept goals but not means ('deviant' means may be legal or illegal – e.g. gambling/fraud/theft)

Retreatists avoid (or reject) goals; withdraw from society (e.g. hippies, alcoholics, hermits)

Ritualists reject goals; appear to accept means for fear of disapproval (e.g. marry, even though do not regard marriage as necessary)

Rebels reject goals and means (e.g. reject the ownership of property as an objective in society or reject religious institutions; means to achieve their objective may be legal or illegal)

	Formal sanctions	Informal sanctions
Negative sanctions	Detention in school Imprisonment Unemployment	Not saying 'good morning' to a neighbour Sending a workmate 'to Coventry' Being refused entry to a nightclub
Positive sanctions	A GCSE pass A knighthood A large regular salary	A smile A pat on the back Being allowed to 'go home' early

Table 18.1 Sanctions

Deviance

Deviants may be:

- Individuals who reject some or all of the norms and values of society (e.g. hermit, paedophile).
- A group whose members accept different beliefs or practise different behaviour from that common in the general society – in this case they are members of a 'deviant subculture'. They may be part of a permanent community in a large city which makes its living from crime, or a transient member of a gang of Hell's Angels.

Labelling

Labelling is the process by which people are identified in a particular way and then receive special attention as a result of that label being attached to them, so that they come to be regarded by others and to see themselves in the way in which they are described by the label.

J. Young's 'The Role of the Police as Amplifiers of Deviancy' (in S. Cohen, *Images of Deviance*, 1971) suggested that the result of labelling marijuana (cannabis) users as deviant was to make their behaviour more deviant than it might otherwise have been. The process worked like this:

- Police raid drug users
- Drug users see themselves as 'outsiders'
- Isolate themselves because they accept the 'label' and reduce risk of informers
- Less contact with normal society ('insiders')
- Deviant behaviour increases.

Sanctions (Table 18.1)

A sanction is a method of enforcing obedience, and although most people will accept the officially 'sanctioned', or approved, behaviour as a result of social conditioning, punishments are also required in most societies to deter at least some of those who are tempted to disregard the accepted norms and values. Rewards also serve to emphasise the importance of the norms and values by approving those who have assisted in maintaining them.

■ ☑ 19 Agencies of social control

19.1 The family

The most important agency of social control is the family (section 1.2) for although the norms and values we learn in our family as a child can be modified later, all our later social learning will have to force its way through the 'mesh' of this early conditioning. That which is not in accord with our existing value system is likely to be rejected.

- The importance of the family as an agent of social control has been referred to by many sociologists. Anne Campbell (*Girl Delinquents*, 1981) found that delinquent children often 'reported a feeling of being rejected by either or both parents. Supervision over the child's activities and discipline was lax and erratic, and parent and child spent little time in recreational activities with one another.'
- The family may therefore fail to socialise the child in a socially acceptable way, by neglect, or by socialising the child as a member of a delinquent subculture. Usually however the family will begin the process of acceptable social learning.
- The family will be the agency in which gender roles are learned by providing toys and clothes appropriate to aggressive masculine or submissive feminine roles if those are the roles appropriate to the culture. Parents will provide role models so that sons and daughters will learn by observation what is appropriate behaviour for them as male or female, which may, of course, include drunkenness and violence.
- In the family, basic rules such as those relating to ownership of property will be learned as the child is allocated specific personal belongings. Children will learn of their parents' disapproval of certain other people in the community and certain kinds of behaviour; their own behaviour will be sanctioned by rewards and punishments.

19.2 Education

When children move into the school situation they have to learn to relate to a more formal, hierarchical structure than in the family (sections 6.3 and 8.2). They begin to learn to conform to a situation similar to that of their future world of work. Rules must often be obeyed without explanation; work is often apparently meaningless

We learn our future role in our family

and therefore alienating; individuals must be given signs of respect appropriate to their status. Sanctions tend to be more formal. Indiscipline or slackness is discouraged by detentions and the withholding of privileges; 'good' behaviour and hard work is rewarded by exam success and office, such as that of prefect.

However, while the education service encourages most children to adhere to the norms and values of acceptable – and often middle class orientated – culture, some children may be encouraged into deviance by lack of success within the education system.

The link between failure at school and subsequent exclusion from the wider society outside has long been identified – in 1967 Hargreaves (*Social Relations in a Secondary School*) stated – 'The low-stream boys are "failures", they are status deprived both in school and in society; their efforts meet with little success. Their problem of adjustment is solved by a rejection of societal and teacher values, and status is derived from conformity to a reversal of societal and teacher values.' The same link between school failure – followed by boring jobs or unemployment – and crime was seen by D. Downes: 'The streets of our urban slums are slowly filling with young men who have no prospect of finding manhood through work' (*The Delinquent Solution*, 1966). This forecast seems borne out by what has been termed 'the underclass' in the 1990s.

Schools act within the context of their neighbourhoods and the members of the peer group with whom the child associates are likely to have increasing influence as the child grows older.

19.3 The peer group

The peer group controls its members mainly by informal sanctions, principally ridicule and exclusion. In 1986 S. Lees, in *Losing Out*, emphasised the power of the peer group in determining behaviour among adolescent girls – relations with boys, friendships, school work and social life; the fear of being identified as 'a slag' is a powerful sanction. The peer group is not necessarily an agency which leads to delinquency. On the contrary, most young people will mirror adult attitudes and values (section 8.4) and will thus tend to reinforce other agencies in encouraging adherence to the mores of the society.

However, the majority of criminal offences are committed by both boys and girls between the ages of ten and twenty-four and this is the period during which the influence of the peer group is also the greatest. The vast majority of young people convicted between these ages does not re-offend as older adults (Table 19.1).

For those unable to find an avenue of status through the formal system of education, and not in a position to gain it through employment and parenthood, there is a danger that the peer group will provide both status and excitement in ways that disrupt public order. Although academic 'failures' often find socially acceptable outlets in pursuit of interest and status, such as sport, uniformed organisations and youth clubs, whether they will become delinquent involves many factors. 'To conclude that the "basic" causes of crime and delinquency invariably lie in the family is to ignore the extremely complex network of interrelationships between family influences and the simultaneous influences of community values, peer group, neighbourhood behaviour patterns, socio-economic pressures and other relevant factors' (E. Schur, *Our Criminal Society*, 1969).

If the majority of crimes are committed by people under the age of twenty consider some reasons for the figures in Table 19.1.

Table 19.1 Offenders found guilty of, or cautioned for, indictable offences; by gender, type of offence and age, 1997 (England and Wales, rates per 10,000 population)

	10–15	16–24	25–34	35 and over	All aged 10 and over (thousands)
Males					
Theft and handling stolen goods	124	216	85	18	149
Drug offences	12	158	63	8	86
Violence against the person	30	71	32	7	50
Burglary	43	71	18	2	39
Criminal damage	11	18	7	1	12
Robbery	6	11	2	–	6
Sexual offences	3	4	3	2	6
Other indictable offences	11	101	59	11	72
All indictable offences	240	651	269	50	420
Females					
Theft and handling stolen goods	58	70	30	7	52
Drug offences	1	17	9	1	10
Violence against the person	11	11	5	1	9
Burglary	3	3	1	–	2
Criminal damage	1	2	1	–	1
Robbery	1	1	–	–	1
Sexual offences	–	–	–	–	–
Other indictable offences	3	18	12	2	13
All indictable offences	80	122	57	11	88

Source: *Social Trends*, 29. National Statistics © Crown Copyright, 1999.

19.4 Religion and the media

Religion

Two of the other 'relevant factors' in influencing the socialisation of both the child and adult are religion and the media.

Religion can be an effective instrument of social control for some people. The threat of damnation or the promise of heaven are potent negative and positive sanctions for those who believe in them, they have the advantage in that they depend upon the knowledge of wrongdoing being known to an all-seeing God so there is a certainty of retribution or reward. In the words of Pope Pius XII when forbidding Catholics to vote Communist – 'God can see you in the polling booth, Stalin can't'.

In an increasingly secular age the influence of religious belief on morality is debatable. Divorce, abortion and sexual relationships outside marriage are all either forbidden or frowned upon by all the mainstream religions in Britain, to which the majority of people still claim to belong, but all these aspects of behaviour have spiralled upwards since the 1970s (ironically the reason why divorce has now started to decline is that so many people are living in partnerships outside marriage that it has become irrelevant for many). However religion has in the past been a powerful instrument for social control, and still is for a substantial minority of people, including many ethnic groups in Britain. Karl Marx summed up his view that religion was an instrument used by ruling elites to maintain the existing social order: 'The mortgage that the peasant has on heavenly possessions guarantees the mortgage that the bourgeois has on peasant possessions' (*The Class Struggles in France*, 1848–1850).

The media

Television, radio, newspaper, magazines and public hoardings do not operate as the other agencies of social control by the use of sanctions but can still influence behaviour, although the extent of this influence is debatable (section 6.4). In 1962 the Pilkington Committee reported on the effects of broadcasting: Dr Hilde Himmelweit told us that all the evidence so far provided by detailed researches suggested that values were acquired, that a view of life was picked up by children watching television. Professor Eysenck told us that there were 'good theoretical grounds for supposing that moral standards could be affected by television and these grounds were largely supported by experimental and clinical evidence' (*Report of the Committee on Broadcasting*, 1960, 1962). However, Himmelweit in *Television and the Child*, also emphasised that children are likely to be influenced by television only if the actions suggested are in accordance with the existing values of the child and if they touch on the ideas for which the child is emotionally ready (e.g. torrid scenes are unlikely to affect a very young child): she suggested that those most likely to be affected are those who are least critical, in particular the less intelligent thirteen to fourteen-year-old. J. Halloran in *Television and Delinquency*, also emphasised that television was unlikely to stimulate delinquency unless other factors were present, and in *The Effects of Mass Communications* showed that while aggression was likely to be reinforced by TV violence among those with aggressive tendencies the 'normal' control group was unaffected – a view supported by W. Belson, *TV Violence and the Adolescent Boy*, who concluded that aggressive personalities could be encouraged to real violence by that on television.

In 1994, in response to an acceptance by a number of distinguished paediatricians and sociologists (including Elisabeth Newson) that there was a link between television/video violence and aggressive behaviour by young people, the government agreed to introduce legislation to further restrict the sale of violent videos to children.

The media and female delinquency

The media have two primary functions. The first is to make money, and the second is to put forward a particular, coherent world view or ideology. Sex and violence, as the old cliché goes, sell. These two in combination with females do even better. Not only is the combination titillating, but it is less common than among men – in other words, it does not accord with the stereotypical view of females . . . Female murderers and muggers get a disproportionate amount of attention. On the other hand, most newspapers are far from dedicated to the promotion of the feminist movement, so that such reports are usually censorious. They lead to a particular combination of fascination and moral outrage. In his book *Folk Devils and Moral Panic*, S. Cohen (1972) has drawn attention to the way in which certain sectors of society, such as Hell's Angels or soccer hooligans, are singled out for condemnation and censure. Recently, this same process has begun to work against women in crime. The rise in crime figures among females receives more newspaper space than that among men and provokes a much more extreme reaction. If we were to take the labelling of newspapers as our criterion of female delinquency, we would devote rather little attention to the more mundane and frequent problems of shoplifting and petty theft and would focus instead on precocious sex, prostitution, violence, murder and child-beating. While the role of the media in shaping popular conceptions of morality is an interesting issue, taken as a criterion it may lead to a very unrepresentative view of female delinquency.

(A. Campbell, *Girl Delinquents*, 1981, abridged)

The media and change

Consider the following review of research in the 1950s and 1960s – could you now produce evidence to support Wilson's criticism of the mass media?

The media and change

We can now look at findings regarding the more specific effects of one of the mass media which has been studied more thoroughly. This is television, and we shall present some of the conclusions regarding its effects on children, young people, the family and political behaviour. Among the earliest empirical studies concerned with the first aspect were those by Hilde Himmelweit and her team. As concerns displacement effects, i.e. time taken up by viewing, the chief conclusions were that contrary to popular belief children did not watch programmes indiscriminately; the single most important determinant of the amount of viewing done by the child was his intelligence, whilst the social level of the home did not affect this aspect very much. Secondary influencing factors were the child's personality (and how full and active a life he led before television was introduced), as well as parental example. Regarding the effects of programme content, results suggested that a large number of programmes containing violence are likely to make a cumulative impact, particularly on younger children. On the whole, however, Himmelweit maintains that television is 'not as black as it is painted, but neither is it the great harbinger of culture and enlightment', although children did acquire certain values and an outlook on life consistent with the contents of television programmes. A more general survey by Mark Abrams suggests that the long-term combined effect of television viewing and the increased consumption of the printed mass media, is one of broadening the outlook of the younger generation; making them aware not only of their family circle, neighbourhood and workplace, but also of the wider community and other societies.

As far as family life is concerned, W. A. Belson found that his enquiry did not throw up any evidence which might suggest that television produces radical changes. Thus it slightly reduces home-centred and joint activity, but it also brings the family together. A PEP report holds that some views, particularly about politics, religion and social class, are rather resistant to change; but in relation to many new issues, where public attitudes are not yet formed or in cases where people either have conflicting opinions or do not feel strongly about an issue, there is a greater susceptibility to persuasion by the mass media.

Finally, sociologists have considered the process of attitude formation and change as affected by mass communication. Bryan Wilson, whilst noting that these processes are not yet capable of being accurately measured because of their subtle and gradual nature, suggests that the media are altering our attitudes as concerns crime. They promote values which 'stand in stark contrast to the values entrenched in our existing social institutions – the family, the workplace, the school, the law courts, the church – and in our social relationships'. He claims that the new values are more tolerant of deviant behaviour, and that this results in the mass media 'promoting the erosion of traditional social values and . . . creating confusion, particularly among young people, about standards of behaviour'. Halloran points out that Wilson does not produce sociological evidence to substantiate this indictment of the mass media.

(E. Krausz, *Sociology in Britain: A Survey of Research*, 1955, adapted)

19.5 The law

Perhaps the most obvious agency of social control is the law. It is also perhaps the least important in that it can only hope to deter possible offenders against the social order, or punish those who do offend, if the majority of people are controlled by other agencies. The law deals not only with 'crime' but also with disputes between individuals or groups, where no crime has been committed. This 'civil law' includes such matters as matrimonial disputes and arguments over property ownerships.

Unless a law is acceptable to the majority of people within a society, or at least is not actively opposed by them, it cannot be enforced. In the 1920s and 1930s the prohibition of alcohol in America led to widespread evasion and as a result people who would normally have supported social order conspired with gangsters providing alcohol and thus encouraged a general contempt for the law. A number of people who seek to legalise cannabis put the argument that we are now in the same position that America was in during Prohibition, but that cannabis rather than alcohol is the issue.

The law in the main is based on the 'mores' of the society – the most important rules based upon the prevailing morality. Although the law is usually rather slow to respond to changing attitudes, it must eventually do so or fall into disrepute by being widely disobeyed. Since 1961 the law has changed in a number of important areas. It is no longer illegal to: attempt to take your own life (although it is against the law to aid a suicide); procure an abortion in certain circumstances; have homosexual relations in private provided both partners are over sixteen (changed from eighteen in 2000, when a court ruling also effectively changed the law by permitting more than two men to be present during homosexual sexual activity). You are also now allowed to engage in off-course betting; in fact the state actively encourages what was illegal a comparatively short time ago by setting up and controlling the National Lottery. An example of the 'civil law' changing to pay regard to changing relationships within the family is the greater frequency with which the father is given custody of children in matrimonial disputes.

However, the law as an agency of last resort does have the most draconian sanctions: fines, imprisonment and in some countries, in certain circumstances, death.

REVISION SUMMARY

Agencies of social control

The family

This is the first or primary agency, it is also the most important; for although the norms and values established in childhood can change later, all later social learning will have to force its way through a 'mesh' of early conditioning:

Some norms and values learned in the home	Learning mechanism
Gender roles	Role models (watching mum and dad)
	Toys (Power Ranges and footballs for boys; Cindy dolls and make-up sets for girls)
	Dress (pretty dresses, which must not get dirty and restrict activity, for girls; jeans and sweatshirts for boys – changing currently in line with society's norms)
Property ownership	Specific property (sometimes plus room) allocated to child

Education

Some norms and values learned in the school	Learning mechanism
Acceptance of a position in society allocated by others	School hierarchy with Head at top
Passive obedience/apparently meaningless work	Approval/disapproval plus formal sanctions

The peer group

The approval or disapproval of the peer group (people of the same age/status) becomes increasingly important in adolescence, as young people seek independence from the home but are not yet sufficiently 'sure' of themselves to be prepared to antagonise those to whom they can most closely relate.

The peer group normally encourages conformity (as young people tend to mirror adult attitudes and values and therefore reinforces other agencies; but those alienated from the general norms and values in society will tend to gravitate towards a delinquent peer group and have their alienation directed towards delinquency.

Some norms and values learned in the peer group	Learning mechanism
The kind of sexual behaviour permissible for males/females	Rejection/humiliation Violence/status enhancement
Reinforcement of traditional gender roles	Peer group pressure – e.g. use of insulting terms such as 'slag', 'poof'.

The media

The media do not use sanctions to influence behaviour but they must have an effect or else millions would not be spent on advertising.

Some norms and values learned from the media	Learning mechanism
Gender roles Sexual behaviour Acceptability/unacceptability of criminal acts Violence (by some)	Drip effect – constant repetition makes actions seen appear normal Role models – on advertising and programmes

Religion

Religion can be an effective instrument of social control for some people. The threat of damnation or the promise of heaven are strong negative and positive sanctions for those who believe in them.

Some norms and values learned from religion	Learning mechanism
Charitable behaviour	Internalised expectation of reward or punishment.
Respect for parents and elderly	
Need for some form of marriage	Approval of religious leaders and others with the same beliefs

The law

Perhaps the most obvious agency of social control is the law. It is also perhaps the least important, in that it can only hope to deter possible offenders against the social order, or punish those who do offend, if the majority of people are controlled by other agencies.

Some norms and values learned from the law	Learning mechanism
Property ownership	Threat of punishment – imprisonment, fines, community service
Personal rights against assault	
Unacceptability of acts deemed criminal.	

■ M̌ **20** Crime and delinquency

20.1 The nature of crime and delinquency

The criminal law will deal only with deviant acts which have been labelled as crimes. 'Deviancy' is deviation from the norm (section 1.3) and is not necessarily criminal. A man may decide to wear women's clothing, or a woman may live a saintly life within a corrupt society and seek to reform it. Such acts are likely to be deviant but not criminal.

Criminal and delinquent behaviour

- A **crime** is an act which is judged a sufficient challenge to the functioning of the society as to warrant punishment. Such an act is likely to be deviant, but not necessarily so. A dictator may ban certain books but the possession of such books may be regarded as normal by the majority of people. Within a particular group, an act such as petty pilfering from work may be acceptable, although it is a crime.
- Although sometimes used to describe all minor criminal acts and behaviour which although not criminal are anti-social or immoral, the term 'delinquency' is usually used of adolescent behaviour in which the young person reacts against adult expectations. He or she does not usually consciously reject adult values, and delinquent behaviour usually ends with the onset of courtship. Delinquency is often an expression of self-assertion – 'not so much a symptom of maladjustment, as of adjustment to a subculture' (J. Mays, *Crime and its Treatment*, 1970).
- Delinquent behaviour is often criminal – vandalism, shoplifting, soccer hooliganism – but not necessarily so. 'Troublesome boys go in for crime, whereas troublesome girls merely go with boys' was said by M. Schofield, *The Sexual Behaviour of Young People*, in 1964. It is now suggested that increasing criminal behaviour among girls is the result, in part, of sexual promiscuity becoming more socially acceptable and therefore an insufficiently emphatic expression of rebellion; certainly there has been a very substantial pro-portionate increase in criminality among girls, as indicated by the statistics in 19.1, although this is probably part of the pattern of adopting male roles generally.
- What is regarded as 'delinquent' will vary as the norms and values of the society change. Equally, double standards may operate; either between the sexes, as when sexual promiscuity is regarded as being delinquent behaviour

in girls but not in boys, or between classes. For example, Mayday drunkenness and damage to property by Oxford undergraduates may be regarded as youthful high spirits; similar behaviour by working-class football supporters will be regarded as hooliganism. In 2000 it was claimed that many public schools were building into their annual accounts a budget specifically to pay for repairs to school property for damage caused when the public examinations finished.

- What is regarded as 'criminal' in one society may not be so in another. For example, alcohol is tolerated in Britain but illegal in Saudi Arabia. However there tend to be certain constant principles such as a respect for property, life and sexual rights.

'A crime-free "golden age"?'

'Claiming, as some influential opinion-formers do, that there was once a golden age of no crime, no drugs and no violence, and that we could get back to that situation if the police did their job properly . . . amounts to scaremongering.'

(Britain's youngest chief-constable, Richard Childs (45), at the 'Crimestoppers' conference, May 2000)

No crime-free 'golden age' in Britain, but . . .

Totals for:	1954	1997
Homicide	311	739
Sexual offences	16,096	33,165
Violent crime	24,414	347,064
Burglary	75,443	1,015,057
Theft and handling stolen goods	291,667	2,164,952
Criminal damage	5,251	877,042
Total crime	434,327	4,598,327

Source: Home Office recorded crime statistics, 1898–1997

20.2 Causes of crime and delinquency

The same kind of argument over heredity and environment as factors in intelligence (section 8.1) has also taken place with regard to crime.

In 1876, Lombroso, an Italian criminologist, examined the skull of an infamous bandit and decided that it had characteristics of an earlier evolutionary type. Lombroso developed a theory that criminals were different from other people and represented a lower stage of evolution. Although there is now no support for such a view there is still the possibility of some genetic link with crime. D. Rosenthal found that identical twins shared crime traits at a rate more than double that of non-identical twins (American Association for Advancement of Science Lecture, 1972) and speculation continues over whether this chromosomal link with crime exists.

What causes crime?

A biological link with crime is not yet proved, but a correlation between other factors and crime have been identified: socialisation (section 19.1), education (section 19.2) and environment (section 16.4). As early as 1886, G. Tarde (*La Criminalité Comparée*) suggested that criminal behaviour was learned in the family and community. In 1964 David Matza, in *Delinquency and Drift*, suggested that one reason why some adolescents choose to commit crime is to counter a feeling of helplessness, of being pushed around by forces beyond their control. A delinquent act may be committed to 'make something happen'. It can be seen as an expression of will designed to restore the feeling that the adolescent can, to some extent at least, control the world outside. Thus, an act of vandalism which to the outsider seems 'mindless' may, to the adolescent who commits it, have a much deeper significance.

Why has the crime rate risen?

There are a number of fairly obvious explanations for the fact that the British crime rate has increased considerably during the last forty years although poverty has not, although in this respect the influence of relative poverty must be remembered (section 10.4).

- There is a great deal more easily-removable property – such as cars – available to steal. The advertising industry spends millions of pounds persuading us that consumer goods are essential or highly desirable, but does not provide the means of attaining them. This gap between opportunity and objective is likely to be greatest at the bottom of the social ladder. The largest single category of offences is that related to the use of motor vehicles – the number of motor vehicles has increased considerably during the past twenty years.
- Violence and overcrowding appear to be linked. Housing policies have maintained inner city housing densities, for example, by building high rise flats.

Deviance and crime

Despite much research in this area there is a great deal of uncertainty about the incidence of crime and delinquency in modern society as compared with earlier periods.

Sociological explanations of deviance

On the other hand there is a good deal of agreement regarding sociological explanations of deviance in our society. Many writers stress the changes in the social structure which modern industrial conditions have wrought, and either explicitly or implicitly invoke this as the basic reason for the increase in most criminal behaviour in contemporary society. We summarize below the main points that arise from this view. (1) Lack of cohesion and adequate means of social control due to the impersonalization of social relationships in the highly industrialized city are reflected in weakening kinship ties and community bonds, and lead to a breakdown in culture and the normative system and to a condition of anomie. (2) Impersonal social relations resulting in the victim of the crime receding into anonymity, and greater affluence which means more opportunity to commit crime, are factors which encourage criminal behaviour. (3) Thwarted aspirations in some sections of the population, for whom avenues of social mobility are generally closed despite the stress put in contemporary society on achievement-orientation, lead to discontent, rejection of both working-class and middle-class values, and so to rebelliousness, particularly in teenage groups, ending up in deviance.

(*Sources*: T. R. Fyvel, *The Insecure Offenders*, 1961; E. Krausz, *Sociology in Britain*, London, Batsford, 1969)

We must be careful in making an assumption that there is more crime today than in previous periods. In *A Century of Childhood*, Humphries, Mack and Perks (1988) describe gang battles between young people in working-class areas of Salford between the world wars which the police ignored. The author has interviewed old men in the coal mining villages of South Yorkshire who have described in vivid detail the violence when the pubs turned out on a Saturday night forty years ago – the police kept well away. Domestic violence is much less acceptable today and the law more likely to become involved. Vigilantes are frowned on today but in the past people will have recovered property and exacted revenge without involving the police.

Urban living and crime

The connection between urban living and crime has been illustrated by the 'Chicago School' of sociologists in the United States (Figure 20.1).

20.3 Crime and statistics

How reliable are crime statistics?

Increasing crime may merely indicate greater opportunity to commit crime or an increase in the number and nature of consumer goods available to steal (e.g. the

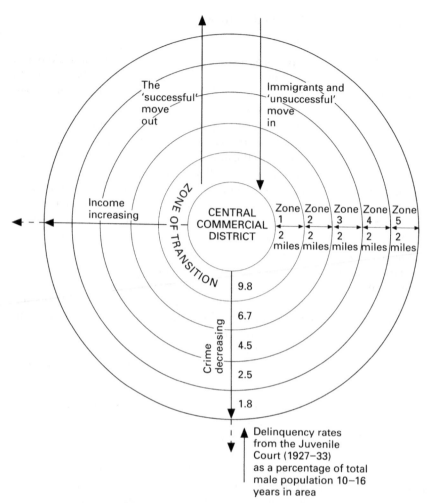

Figure 20.1 Urban living and crime

theft of mobile phones from children was first reported as a serious problem in 2000 – previously children were unlikely to possess such an object); but there are a number of other reasons why criminal statistics should be approached with caution, particularly when trying to compare one historical period or one country with another.

- In some areas crime is less likely to be reported because of *social mores;* for example in 1997 the *British Crime Survey (BCS)* found that of the reasons for not reporting crime, 'we dealt with the matter ourselves', constituted 11 per cent and 'fear of reprisals' constituted 3 per cent.
- The way that *statistics are compiled* changes. For example in 1999 the government announced the first increase in the crime figures for five years. This 20 per cent rise was caused by a change in the way that the Home Office compiled the statistics for 1998, taking the number of offences to 5.4 million

compared to 4.5 million in 1997. However, the figures also showed that in 'real terms' crime had still fallen year on year. The new method meant that each offence and every victim were recorded individually: for example, thefts from five cars in one car park were counted as five offences under the new system, where previously they would have been recorded as one.

- Some crimes are *less likely to be reported* than others. In America surveys show that only 27 per cent of rape and 31 per cent of burglary cases get reported. All vehicle theft was reported, no doubt for insurance reasons. In a London survey it was found that only one-third of criminal victimisations (what are often called 'protection' rackets) are notified to the police.

- The *BCS* shows that the most likely crime to be recorded is *motor vehicle theft* (95 per cent of all offences were recorded in 1997), probably because of the need to report in order to make an insurance claim. The least likely to be reported were *robbery and theft* (not including burglary), and vandalism. 37 per cent of the victims of violent crime did not report it; this might be because of the relationship between the victim and the offender (for example, domestic violence).

- Crime may increase as a result of *demographic changes* – for example after a standstill in the latter part of the 1990s crime started to increase again in 1999, with an increase in the proportion of men in their late teens and early twenties offending.

- *Police activity* varies. The modern police are highly trained and use sophisticated methods – they may be more likely to detect crime than formerly. Particular forces have campaigns against various forms of crime – in one area cannabis smoking may be tolerated, in another rigorously prosecuted. 'Many forces have seen a rise in recorded violent crime. In Staffordshire it is due in no small part to our determination to better track and understand such behaviour' (Steve House, Assistant Chief Constable, July 2000).

- The police *may not record* some crime. A study by H.M. Inspectorate of Constabulary, 'On the Record', in August 2000, found that 'some forces "wrote off" allegations as "no crimes"' – 24 per cent of the allegations from the public do not make crime statistics, and the evidence standards to record detections varied, casting doubts on clear-up rates; it also said that officers in some areas downgrade crimes – for example, recording attempted burglaries as vandalism. 'An additional influence is that the performance of each force is to some extent being assessed and compared on the basis of the crime figures – yet they are asked to collect the figures by which they will be judged.'

- Some crimes are *more likely to be discovered* than others. Crimes against property, mainly committed by those in lower socio-economic class categories, are very likely to be discovered. Tax evasion and fraud, perhaps more likely to be committed by those higher up the social scale, are more difficult to identify.

The *BCS* relies on interviews with the public to give a fuller count of the number of offences than the number recorded by the police. It does not cover crime against organisations rather than people (e.g. company fraud or shoplifting); it also excludes 'victimless' crimes (e.g. drug abuse). The *BCS* suggests that police statistics may overstate the increase in crime, perhaps because victims are increasingly likely to report it; one reason for this may be the increased awareness of the Criminal Injuries Compensation Board which came into existence in 1964 and may pay compensation to those who are the victims of violence.

Why crime statistics are inaccurate

Other research has revealed still further reasons for victims' unwillingness to report a criminal act. For instance, some victims prefer to resort to extra-judicial action rather than submit themselves and the culprit to official judicial procedures, which may be perceived as costly both in economic terms and in the damage of reputations it can cause. Thus, in Martin's study of English employers' reactions to employee offenders, he suggested that on nearly 70 per cent of the occasions on which the employer failed to report the offence to the police he was attempting to keep unpleasantness, both for the firm and the offender, to a minimum. Similarly, Robin argued that one important reason why American employers refrain from prosecuting their employee offenders is because there is frequently a psychological affinity between the two, and, rather than see an employee publicly humiliated, employers prefer to settle the matter privately. Further, this extra-judicial procedure protects the employer from publicly risking his ability to assess candidates for positions in his firm. Finally, Cameron discovered that the victims of shoplifting were often reluctant to take official judicial steps because of the uncertainty and difficulty of proving some cases and because of the cost of releasing employees to serve as witnesses against the suspected shoplifter. In these circumstances, department managers were inclined to release suspects with a warning and a request not to patronize the store again. The ability and willingness of the suspect to pay for the goods was a factor closely associated with this extra-judicial mode of handling offenders.

Fear of embarrassment, or an unwillingness to risk exposing private matters to public gaze, may provide further reasons why some victims of criminal behaviour fail to report an offence. Thus the victims of blackmail usually prefer to keep their dark secret hidden rather than jeopardize their present respectability. Similarly, victims of forcible rape and other indecent sexual offences often prefer to forgo reporting the incident rather than risk their own reputations being brushed by the smutty innuendoes of neighbours, police, doctors, and particularly prosecutors. Indeed, it would be no exaggeration to claim that many rape victims avoid reporting it for fear that they will be put 'on trial'. Another, and final, example is provided by some victims of financial swindles, who prefer to remain silent rather than reveal their naivety, stupidity or possible culpable connivance in illegal conduct.

Thus, even in the case of serious criminal offences, such as larceny, burglary, rape, assault, shoplifting, embezzlement and fraud, where a person is perfectly aware of having been victimized, the police frequently remain uninformed and the offence goes unrecorded.

In addition to the aware victim, three other victims can be conceptualized; the person who remains unaware of being victimized (unless some other persons reveal it to him or her); the abstract victim on whose behalf licensed agents keep a watchful lookout without necessarily reminding him/her of their guardianship; and victims who refuse to recognize the label. In each case, the ability or willingness of the victim to report the offence to the police is seriously impaired, thus considerably reducing the accuracy of the volume and pattern of crimes known to the police.

An example of the unaware victim is the person who has been involved at the losing end of a confidence trick but who remains ignorant. This appears to be a frequent outcome of such criminal behaviour, for the art of the confidence trickster is to leave the victim either unaware or confused to the point of not realizing what has happened. Similarly, company owners and managers often remain ignorant of embezzlement and other commercial frauds, and store owners remain unaware of shoplifting or employee theft, particularly where stock shrinkage could just as easily result from poor accounting procedures or inadequate recording practices. Clearly, where the victim remains unaware, or where he can interpret what has happened by giving it a non-criminal explanation, the police are not informed and the official statistics are deficient.

Another type of victim exists where no one in particular is a victim, but we all are in general. In the case of tax evasion, for instance, it is possible to argue that there exists an abstract victim. Thus, everyone who pays tax, or is the recipient of direct or indirect government spending, is a victim in the sense that 'honest payment by everyone liable to income tax would enable the government to decrease the general tax burden by 40 per cent'.

(S. Box, *Deviance, Reality and Society*, 1981)

Violence and crime

Violence: adults most at risk

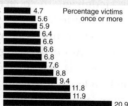

Average risk	4.7
London	5.6
Council area	5.9
Flats/maisonettes	6.4
Income below £5k	6.6
Striving areas	6.6
Inner city	6.8
High physical disorder	7.6
Women 16-24	8.8
Private renters	9.4
Unemployed	11.8
Single parents	11.9
Men 16-24	20.9

Percentage victims once or more

Violence: adults least at risk

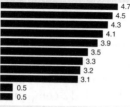

Average risk	4.7
Non-couccil area	4.5
Low physical disorder	4.3
Income £10k to £20k	4.1
Eastern region	3.9
Thriving areas	3.5
Rural areas	3.3
Owner occupiers	3.2
Detached house	3.1
Women 65 or older	0.5
Men 65 or older	0.5

Burglary: households most at risk

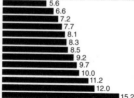

Average risk	5.6
Property on main road	6.6
Flat / maisonettes	7.2
The North	7.7
Council area	8.1
Income below £5k	8.3
Inner city	8.5
Striving areas	9.2
Private renters	9.7
Jnemployed household	10.0
Single parents	11.2
High physical disorder	12.0
Household aged 16-24	15.2

Burglary: households least at risk

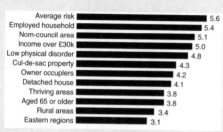

Average risk	5.6
Employed household	5.4
Nom-council area	5.1
Income over £30k	5.0
Low physical disorder	4.8
Cul-de-sac property	4.3
Owner occupiers	4.2
Detached house	4.1
Thriving areas	3.8
Aged 65 or older	3.8
Rural areas	3.4
Eastern regions	3.1

Crime and clear-up rates:
per police force area

	All crime 000	Violence 000	Burglaries 000	Clar up %	Police 000
English shires					
Avon and Somerset	101	10	24	24	2.04
Bedfordshire	88	10	15	33	1.90
Cambridgeshire	93	9	19	29	1.78
Cheshire	66	8	16	37	2.10
Cleveland	121	7	39	23	2.57
Cumbria	82	12	11	44	2.33
Derbyshire	87	10	16	31	1.82
Devon and Cornwall	71	8	11	36	1.88
Dorset	76	5	13	31	1.86
Durham	83	9	18	33	2.53
Essex	63	6	11	29	1.90
Glos	86	7	21	31	1.87
Hants	72	8	11	35	1.95
Herts	56	4	10	34	1.97
Humberside	148	12	36	22	2.26
Kent	83	9	16	34	2.05
Lancashire	83	9	21	34	2.28
Leicestershire	100	13	24	34	2.14
Lincs	75	8	17	40	1.87
Norfolk	73	8	11	37	1.79
Northants	107	10	21	33	1.91
North Yorks	75	6	17	33	1.83
Notts	131	143	0	25	2.20
Staffs	87	10	23	32	2.13
Suffolk	60	6	9	41	1.80
Surrey	54	6	10	40	2.08
Sussex	88	11	17	25	1.83
Thames Valley	85	6	18	25	1.76
Warwicks	76	51	4	26	1.80
West Mercia	72	7	12	34	1.78
Wiltshire	63	8	10	38	1.79
Wales					
Dyfed Powys	51	10	4	69	2.14
Gwent	105	21	14	55	2.23
N Wales	67	8	9	43	2.11
S Wales	–	10	19	39	2.40
Metropolitan					
Greater Manchester	140	17	43	25	2.60
Merseyside	100	11	26	31	2.98
Northumbria	106	10	25	30	2.68
S Yorks	102	6	34	32	2.43
W Midlands	120	15	36	30	2.73
W Yorks	130	10	41	27	2.40
Metropolitan	122	22	23	22	3.20
Average	89	10	19	29	2.14

Source: Police performance indicators 2000, Audit Commission. Clear up rates Hansard 23 June. 2000, Col 339.

20.4 Class, gender, ethnicity and crime

Class and gender as factors in crime have been referred to previously.

Class

The reasons why *lower socio-economic income groups* are more likely to feature in cases of reported crime are:

- Laws are framed by middle class people and reflect middle class values. For example, working class people may be imprisoned for relatively small debts while company bankrupts appear to escape punishment. Social security frauds are more likely to result in punishment than false income tax returns.
- The children of unskilled and semi-skilled workers have less opportunities to obtain status-enhancing employment.
- The areas in which lower-status groups live are more likely to be overcrowded and have a delinquent subculture. Equally, these inner city areas have opportunities for crime in the form of vehicles and accessible commercial and domestic property, together with anonymity which makes detection difficult.
- Lower class groups have little property, but the values of our society emphasise the importance of wealth. The urge to acquire what is desired illegitimately is bound to be greatest among those who possess least of it, and who have fewest legitimate avenues of acquisition.
- Many crimes are opportunistic and occur in the area where the lawbreaker lives.

Gender

Men are just under five times more likely than women to be convicted of a criminal offence (1997). It may be that growing equality will narrow the gap, and there is already some evidence of this (e.g. in 1961 men were seven times more likely to be convicted of a criminal offence and by 1989 this had dropped to six times). There is a biological argument that women are less aggressive, assertive and competitive than males, though this is disputed. Environmental factors may include:

- The socialisation process which encourages girls to adopt a submissive role. Males need to act out our society's definition of masculinity, which includes recklessness and toughness. In some environments, legally available means of acting this role may be restricted so illegal ones are sought. The socially approved feminine roles relating to passivity and domesticity are more readily available in a legal form.
- There have been more restrictions placed on females regarding absence from home late at night or being in situations such as clubs and pubs where violent situations may develop.
- There have been more readily available opportunities for unskilled females to earn money in ways which, while not socially approved, are not illegal, for example, prostitution.

Ethnicity

Table 20.1 indicates that a much higher proportion of members of ethnic groups are being sentenced for criminal offences than that of the white population (see Table 20.2). This, in part, is likely to be because a higher proportion of ethnic minority people are in the lower socio-economic groups and are therefore susceptible to all the influences already outlined; it will also be because there are proportionately more young people in the ethnic minority populations.

Less obviously, if social exclusion is a reason for people in the lower social class groupings being involved in crime the fact that prejudice may fuel an even greater feeling of rejection in ethnic minority members could be an additional factor.

It has also been argued that stereotyping makes it more likely that a non-white person will be suspected of crime; searched, questioned or arrested.

In 1999 the Metropolitan Police accepted the finding of the 'Lawrence Enquiry' (the 'Macpherson Commission') that it was 'institutionally racist', and if such attitudes do exist generally within police forces it would be unsurprising if this has led to more convictions among ethnic minority groups.

Soft on crime, soft on the causes of crime

Last year, offences in England and Wales increased by 2.2 per cent – 114,000 more offences, bringing the total to 5.2 million. In particular, there has been a 19 per cent rise in robberies, increases in violence against the person, and sexual offences; that is, the crimes that are common, feared and resented by the ordinary victim and voter.

Incomes have been rising and unemployment has fallen, so there is no reason to blame economic causes. It is difficult to know what other 'causes' one could get tough with – even if it were possible to have precise knowledge of that they are . . .

Besides, the drive for racial equality rather than equity – a distinction that escaped the Macpherson commission – has also meant that the police cannot distribute their efforts according to the relative incidence of particular crimes differentially committed by particular groups . . .

There *has* been a slight drop in domestic burglary (by five per cent last year), but much of this can be accounted for by changes in calculating offences, and by the understandable reluctance of householders to report crimes that will not be solved. In any case, the fact that, at the beginning of a new millennium, burglary is running at some 20 times the level of a century ago is hardly encouraging.

It is doubtful whether prison does anyone any good, but neither do social work, mediation or the petty restrictions imposed on those who have been let out of prison. Prison does at least take burglars, car thieves and muggers out of circulation and is particularly appropriate for the younger and more efficient practitioners of these arts . . .

Table 20.1 Sentenced male adult prisoners; by ethnic origin and type of offence, 1997 (England and Wales, per cent)

	British nationals					Foreign nationals	All ethnic groups
	White	Black	Indian	Pakistani/ Bangladeshi	Other[1]		
Violence against the person	23	20	25	22	24	20	23
Burglary	17	13	7	8	10	4	15
Drugs offences	13	21	17	29	20	34	15
Robbery	11	22	10	13	15	8	12
Theft and handling	9	6	8	4	6	5	8
Rape	5	5	5	3	4	6	5
Other sexual offences	6	1	3	1	2	3	5
Fraud and forgery	2	2	8	5	6	6	3
Other offences	11	7	15	13	11	7	11
Offence not recorded	3	3	2	2	2	7	3
All (= 100%) (thousand)	31.3	3.4	0.3	0.4	0.6	2.7	38.8

Note:
[1] Includes those where ethnic group was not recorded.
Source: Social Trends, 29 National Statistics © Crown Copyright, 1999.

Table 20.2 Population by ethnic group, 2000[1]

Group	(%)
White	94.0
Black	1.6
Indian	1.6
Pakistani/Bangladeshi	1.4
Other[2]	1.4

Notes:
[1] Approximate figures.
[2] Includes those of mixed origin.
Source: Based on information from Social Trends.

The state is far more concerned to preserve its own monopoly of law enforcement than to protect its citizens. Yet it is inevitable that people will in time turn to vigilante justice if the state fails to protect them.

(Christie Davies, Professor of Sociology, University of Reading, *Daily Telegraph*, 28 April 2000)

Theories on the causes of delinquency

Girl delinquents

- After Freud the writings of Bowlby (1953) took first place in connection with delinquency. He stressed that the relationship between the child and the mother in the first years of life was crucial to healthy psychological development. Children deprived of mother love were thought to develop a host of psychological disorders, ranging from subnormality, through schizophrenia and neurosis to delinquency. The appeal of Bowlby's work in connection with girls was strong, since it viewed the delinquent as a helpless victim of circumstances rather than as an individual with free will or a 'bad streak'. An Australian study by Koller (1971) reported that 62 per cent of training-school girls had experienced parental loss or deprivation, compared with 13 per cent of the control group.

It became obvious that such a theory notably failed to explain the peculiarly adolescent nature of delinquency. If it results from such early disturbances, why is it not manifest until puberty? And if it has an enduring effect on personality, why does delinquency usually end in the later teens? Attention turned instead towards the current child-rearing practices of delinquents' parents. Studies found that the factors held to be important in male delinquents' homes were equally true of the homes of delinquent females. The frequency of separation and divorce among parents varied widely depending on the definition of delinquency and of the intact family. In general, the incidence of marital break-up was higher in delinquent than non-delinquent populations, and this was particularly true of girls. For both sexes quarrelling and discordance were found in the home (with the exception of Riege's startling finding that the parents of non-delinquents quarrelled more frequently in front of their children than did the parents of delinquents). Often the child reported a feeling of being rejected by either or both parents. Supervision over the child's activities and discipline was lax and erratic, and parent and child spent little time in recreational activities with one another. It would appear that the precipitating factors within the family for delinquency in females are not substantially different from those for males. As girls spend more time out of the home and on the streets, the possibility of their becoming involved in delinquent subcultures increases, particularly in urban, working class areas. This would seem to focus attention on the peer group rather than the family. While great attention has been paid to this factor in studies of boys, such analysis of girl delinquents is almost completely lacking. We know virtually nothing of their life beyond the family and this reflects the prevailing belief that the behaviour of females can be explained exclusively by recourse to their biology, psyche and home life.

(A. Campbell, *Girl Delinquents*, Oxford, Blackwell, 1981, abridged)

REVISION SUMMARY

Criminal behaviour

Criminal behaviour is acts that are regarded as sufficient challenge to the functioning of a society that they require official condemnation and punishment.

A crime may be deviant, but not necessarily so. For example, in some sections of society the following acts may be regarded as normal (e.g. they do not deviate from the norm), but they are criminal:

- Doing jobs in the 'black economy' (e.g. painting someone's house) but not declaring the money received for tax purposes and/or continuing to claim Supplementary Benefit.
- Making private telephone calls during office hours without the employer's permission and without paying for them.
- Someone over eighteen going into a pub with someone aged seventeen and buying them an alcoholic drink.

The view of what constitutes a crime has varied historically as societies have changed. It also varies between societies (e.g. drinking alcohol is illegal in Saudi Arabia).

Delinquent behaviour

Delinquent behaviour is sometimes taken to include all minor criminal acts plus acts which, although not actually criminal, are regarded as antisocial or immoral. More usually, the term 'delinquency' tends to be used of adolescent behaviour in which the young person reacts against adult expectations. He or she does not usually consciously reject adult values, and delinquent behaviour usually ends with the onset of courtship. Delinquency is often an expression of self-assertion (J. Mays, *Crime and its Treatment*, 1970: 'not so much a symptom of maladjustment, as of adjustment to a subculture').

Causes of crime and delinquency

- **Heredity.** Largely discredited as a cause of crime since the late nineteenth century, when evolutionary theorists suggested that there existed a lower 'criminal type'. There is still some speculation that there may be a genetic link with some criminal behaviour (i.e. that someone is 'naturally bad').
- **Environmental.** It is generally accepted that environmental factors are the cause of crime. Factors which have been identified include:
  - (i) **Social learning**: e.g. criminal norms learned in the family.
  - (ii) **Overcrowding**: e.g. a link between violence and overcrowding (F. McClintock and N. Arison, *Crime in England and Wales*, 1968).
  - (iii) **Poverty**: the idea of stealing to eat is obvious but the connection with relative poverty has to be made – i.e. reference groups are widened by the media (advertising increases the desirable objectives); the gap between opportunity and objective is greatest at the bottom of the social scale.

Urban ethos (the characteristic spirit within urban communities):

Anonymity – less risk of detection
Anomie – fewer norms.   } *Gesellschaft*
Relationships less personal and less intense

Explanations of increasing crime rate

- Increase in urban ethos (the influence of the urban way of life is increasing: see pp. 308–9).
- More easily removable property available to steal (e.g. cars, videos, mobile phones).
- More commercialisation – i.e. advertising persuades us that consumer goods are essential/highly desirable but the means of acquisition is withheld from some.
- New crimes (e.g. credit card and internet fraud; driving offences).

- Unemployment (but note that crime rates started to rise fast in the 1960s, when there was full employment, there is not a direct correlation between high rates of crime and unemployment).
- Possible influence of more crime being reported.
- Reduction in influence of organised religion (the evidence on this is somewhat contradictory).
- Possible influence of increasing divorce rate on children (D. West, in *Young Offender*, found that an unsettled home background was a major cause of crime).
- Possible influence of the media, particularly television.
- Females taking on male gender roles.
- Proportionally more young people in the population.

Gender and crime

There is a biological argument that women are less aggressive, assertive and competitive than males, although this is disputed. Environmental factors may include:

- The **socialisation process**, which encourages girls to adopt a submissive role. Males need to act out our society's definition of masculinity, which includes recklessness and toughness. In some environments, legally available means of acting this role may be restricted, so illegal ones are sought. The socially approved feminine roles relating to passivity and domesticity are more readily available in a legal form.
- There have been more restrictions placed on females regarding absence from home late at night or being in locations (such as clubs and pubs) where violent situations may develop.
- There have been more readily available opportunities for unskilled females to earn money in ways which, while not socially approved, are not illegal: for example, prostitution.

Class and crime

Some reasons why lower socio-economic income groups are more likely to feature in cases of reported crime are:

- Laws are framed by middle class people and reflect middle class values. For example, working class people may be imprisoned for relatively small debts, while company bankrupts appear to escape punishment. Social security frauds are more likely to result in punishment than false income tax returns. Terence Morris, in *The Criminal Area* (1957), wrote that 'delinquency flourishes in working class neighbourhoods because of the support it finds in working class culture'.
- Middle class crime is less likely to be detected (e.g. company fraud; unauthorised free use of employer's materials/services).

- The children of unskilled and semi-skilled workers have fewer opportunities to obtain status-enhancing employment.
- The areas in which lower-status groups live are more likely to be overcrowded and have a delinquent subculture. These inner city areas afford opportunities for crime in the form of vehicles and accessible commercial and domestic property, together with anonymity, which makes detection difficult.
- Lower class groups have little property and little possibility of acquiring any legally, but the values of our society emphasise the importance of wealth.
- Some reasons why proportionally more ethnic minority members are convicted are:
  - (i) More likely to be in the lower socio-economic class groupings.
  - (ii) Social exclusion.
  - (iii) Proportionally more young people in the ethnic minority groups.
  - (iv) Prejudice and stereotyping.
  - (v) Possible institutionalised racism.

SELF-TEST QUESTIONS: PART SEVEN

Self-test 7.1

1 What is the term used to describe those who accept the objectives of their society and behave in the expected way? (*1 mark*)
2 Which age group is most likely to commit a crime? (*1 mark*)
3 Which social class is statistically most likely to be convicted of a criminal offence? (*1 mark*)

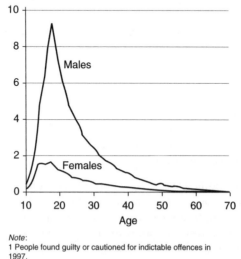

Note:
1 People found guilty or cautioned for indictable offences in 1997.
Source: Home Office.

Figure 20.2   Offenders[1] as a percentage of the population, by gender and age, 1997 (England and Wales, per cent)
Source: *Social Trends*, 29 National Statistics © Crown Copyright, 1999.

4   Name two agencies of social control.   *(2 marks)*

5   Which group is most likely to be influenced by television?   *(2 marks)*

6   Give three ways in which the media may be responsible for crime.   *(3 marks)*

7   State three reasons why there appears to be less crime committed by middle class people.   *(3 marks)*

8   Why has the crime rate apparently increased in recent years?   *(4 marks)*

9   Why are males more likely than females to commit crime?   *(4 marks)*

10   In what ways may crime statistics be misleading?   *(4 marks)*

Self-test 7.2

How your home rates

POLICE REGIONS	TOTAL OFFENCES PER 100,000 POP.	UNEM- PLOY. MENT RATE
1 G1 Manchester	10.577	15.5
2 Northumbria	10.515	17.6
3 Menayside	10.356	21.2
4 London	10.000	10.2
5 W Midlands	9.031	16.8
6 Cleveland	8.952	22.8
7 Notts	8.895	13.4
8 W Yorkshire	8.203	14.1
9 Hunberside	7.627	17.5
10 Wales	7.480	16.6
11 S Yorkshire	7.080	17.2
12 Durham	7.050	18.7
13 Bedfordshire	6.956	10.7
14 Northants	6.245	12.8
15 Gwent	5.912	17.3
16 Lancashire	5.761	14.8
17 Thames Valley	5.605	8.0
18 Derbyshire	5.537	13.9
19 Hampshire	5.501	10.3
20 Avon & Som.	5.491	11.2
21 Dorset	5.440	12.3
22 Cumbria	5.263	12.8
23 N Wales	5.221	19.0
24 Cambs	5.180	10.2
25 Leics	5.180	10.8
26 Gloucs	5.066	10.4
27 Staffs	5.020	14.2
28 Wilts	4.997	10.4
29 Lincs	4.940	14.9
30 Norfolk	4.862	12.8
31 Sussex	4.857	12.4
32 W Mercia	4.856	13.0
33 Herts	4.836	7.5
34 Cheshire	4.751	13.7
35 Kent	4.733	12.9

36 Essex	4.635	12.8
37 N Yorks	4.621	11.0
38 Warwicks	4.581	12.8
39 Devon. Cornwall	4.483	16.7
40 Suffolk	4.163	10.0
41 Surrey	3.959	—
42 Dyfed Powys	3.575	15.9

Are you in a break-in blackspot?

■ Our map shows the league table of offences

* Surrey unemployment data unavailable. Calculations do not work because less than 75 per cent of people do not both live and work there.

(Note: the Northumbria Police region includes Newcastle. The West Midlands includes Bimaingham. Cleveland includes Middlesbrough and West Yorkshire (Leeds)).

Source: *Sunday Mirror* (24 March 1985), adapted.

'Britain today is a crime-torn nation. A shocking *Sunday Mirror* survey reveals how crime and unemployment go hand in hand – splitting the country.

There is a crime epidemic in the depressed North.

The better off South is not offence free – but your home is four times more likely to be burgled in unemployment blackspots like Liverpool and Manchester than in Surrey and Hertfordshire.'

By 2000, although relative changes had taken place, those near the top of this list for crime were still in that position, as were those near the bottom (see extract on p. 286). Equally although unemployment had fallen considerably the general relative positions within the regions had not.

1   What was the unemployment rate in Devon and Cornwall in 1985?   *(1 mark)*

2   Why are no unemployment figures available for Surrey?   *(1 mark)*

3   What factors do the areas near the top of the crime table have in common which are not shared by those near the bottom?   (*2 marks*)

4   From your examination of the 'Crime Map' on the previous page, is there conclusive evidence that crime and unemployment are always 'hand in hand'? Give reasons for your answer, using statistics given with the map.   (*3 marks*)

5   From the evidence given above what do you consider to be the most important factor governing the amount of crime, in proportion to the population, which you would expect to find in any given area? Give a detailed explanation of your answer.   (*8 marks*)

SPECIMEN QUESTIONS AND ANSWERS

Living dangerously

The risk of being knocked on the head by a foreign policeman is a challenge to prove their manhood.

But to focus on the problems of locking up the hard core is both facile and misleading. The problem is much larger: the restless, aggressive patriotism and energy on display has ancient roots in male rites of passage. Off-duty policemen and soldiers, university rugby players all test their virility in violent ways. Indeed, the largest cause of police injuries is rugby. But they keep within the bounds of legality – for the most part – because they have something to lose. Most football hooligans – whether employed or unemployed – go along with the crowd because they like it. For many, living in bleak estates, there is little local activity to rival the excitement of going abroad in a crowd of like-minded youths.

Some have dead-end blue-collar jobs, many others are unemployed (there are now a million unemployed in Britain under 21). They do not share Mr Major's vision of Englishness, 'the cricket on Sunday afternoon, the winding lanes' of Laura Ashley or a Hovis commercial. For them, adverts for fast cars and action-filled trainers are more appealing. They are hooked on drugs – adrenalin and alcohol is the cocktail that lights their fire. The risk of being knocked on the head by a foreign policeman is simply a challenge to prove their manhood.

Like other crimes committed by a similar age group, they provide an instant gratification. Prison is no threat – it, too, is a challenge.

But like most young offenders, hooligans grow out of it, as they achieve something to lose: a home, a family, a mortgage. This process becomes more problematic as violence becomes a normal part of the language of public life: the casual violence on videos and cinema screens, the rhetoric of politicians and tabloid newspapers riddled with aggression against any opponents.

Role models are vitally important for young men in search of an identity: having lost the traditional respect for manual work, having eliminated whole swathes of industry . . . What else did we expect?

(Roger Graef, author of *Living Dangerously: Young offenders in their own words, Daily Telegraph*, 15 October 1993, adapted)

Although written in 1993, exactly the same kind of article could have been written following the European Cup in the summer of 2000.

1 Explain the ways in which social conformity is achieved in society. *(8 marks)*
2 Why are young working-class males more likely than other groups in society to end up in trouble with the police? *(12 marks)*

A British football fan is arrested in Rotterdam, 15 October 1993

Answers

1   Most people act in the way that they are expected to act: they accept the social objectives that are set by their society and try to achieve these in a socially acceptable way. These people are the 'conformists' described by Robert Merton, and they are likely to be the majority in any society. If they were not, the formal agencies of social control, such as the police, would be unable to cope.

   The most important agency in ensuring social conformity is the family, because it is during our early socialisation that we acquire the norms and values which are likely to remain with us into adult life. Children learn rules – to be obedient or not to break things – mainly by informal positive sanctions, such as a smile if they do what they are told, or more formal negative sanctions, such as a smack if they are disobedient.

   Later the more formal agency of social control, the school, will teach acceptable behaviour in the wider society outside – both by the use of 'role models', such as teachers or prefects whom the children will be invited to copy, and by punishment for inappropriate conduct and rewards for the kind of conduct which is to be encouraged.

   Throughout life there is considerable pressure to conform to the expectation of others: most people want to be accepted. In the adolescent peer group, antisocial conduct may be expected from its members, but research has indicated that the vast majority of young people have norms and values similar to those of their parents, so that even the peer group will be an instrument for conformity.

   (Note: This question is about how social conformity is achieved – not about how deviance is punished. Do not be tempted merely to deal with formal social control (police, law, etc.).)

2   Most crimes are committed by people between the ages of fourteen and twenty; criminals are mainly males (D. West, in *The Young Offender*, points out that in theft from unattended vehicles the ratio between male and female crime is 80:1, in assaults and woundings it is 4:1, and in drunk and disorderly behaviour it is 14:1); and most criminals are working class. The young working class male is most likely to end up in trouble with the police on all three criteria.

   The reason why young people are more likely than are older people to commit crimes is that they have no settled status in modern industrial societies, they have few responsibilities, and the influence of the peer group is likely to be at its most intense. If the group is a delinquent one, there will be strong pressure on all its members to conform to the norms of this delinquent subculture. In the absence of any formal status objectives other than those set by the education service, young people who cannot achieve in academic terms are particularly likely to reject the value system of the school and seek status within their peer group through delinquent activities.

   Boys are more likely than girls to engage in delinquent activities, because our socialisation process encourages girls to adopt a passive domestic role but expects males to adopt a masculine image of toughness which is more likely to lead to trouble with the police. Boys are also subject to fewer restrictions by parents and are more likely to be absent from home late at night and in places, such as pubs, where violent situations may develop. It may also be true that delinquent girls can express their rebellion from adult society through sexual promiscuity (which is not illegal), because of the double standard which still operates to some degree.

Working class boys are statistically less likely than middle class boys to achieve academic success and so are more likely to seek status through other means, possibly delinquent ones. In common with the working class generally, the working class boys are less likely to be able to achieve, by legitimate means, the material goals that the media suggest are desirable and are more likely to live in an area where delinquent behaviour is considered the 'norm'.

Downes, in *The Delinquent Solution*, suggested that the boys he studied in East London were not particularly delinquent but were similar to youths of other social classes in wanting some excitement; however, they carried out their activities in public places and this involved them with the police. Labelling theory would suggest that young people identified by the police as delinquents will act in accordance with this expectation, and that the police themselves will be more likely to suspect and arrest members of a group which have been stereotyped as potential trouble-makers, in this case young working class males.

(*Note*: Ensure that your answer deals with the group identified in the question: young, working class males.)

Part Eight

Social change

■ M **21** Reasons for social change

21.1 **Stagnation *v.* development**

Societies change for many different reasons. There may be physical conditions such as drought, flooding or crop failure which necessitate a change in production and living patterns, or migration. For example the potato famine of 1846 resulted in a mass exodus of rural Irish peasantry to the urban areas of America and Britain. This clearly influenced the society which they had left, and the society that received them. As with most migration, those who left were often the most active and ambitious, with the result that many rural Irish communities stagnated. In the United States the destruction of the buffalo herds by white settlers and soldiers between 1865 and 1875 ruined the economic base of native American (Indian) civilisation.

The same factors which encourage social cohesion are also those which may encourage social stagnation. Socialisation encourages a degree of conformity (section 18.1), and if the family and educational system is too rigid in its enforcement of norms then it will be difficult for new ideas to form and so result in development.

The degree to which societies come into contact with others will also influence the degree of change, both in terms of ideas and technical innovation. Some traditional societies have not changed much for thousands of years. Others, like our own, are in an accelerating spiral of change which started to move rapidly with the industrial revolution and is now moving even faster in a technological revolution. We in turn have brought proportionately even more rapid change to other countries through colonialism. But although some aspects of British life have changed dramatically some have not.

21.2 **Cultural factors**

The beliefs, language, rules and folkways – the 'culture' of a society (section 1.1) cannot be dissociated from the process of production (Chapter 12 and section 22.4) but it is also linked to communication with the cultures of others.

Immigration and assimilation

The most obvious contact with other cultures is through immigration and in the past the assimilation of peoples belonging to differing ethnic groups have contributed to the culture we now have (Chapter 17). It is difficult to be certain of the long-term effect on British culture of the wave of immigration from the 'New' Commonwealth, although the impact of Chinese and Asian cuisine on our national eating habits has been remarkable, as has the influence of West Indians in some areas of entertainment; while some changes are more difficult to detect, for example the impact of Jamaican patois on the speech of young white Londoners (*White Talk, Black Talk*, Roger Hewitt, 1986.) However the similarities in lifestyle are in general more marked than any differences and many children of immigrants have risen to prominence in traditional fields, including the trade unions, medicine and politics. There is an argument in respect of 'assimilation', the process by which newcomers and their descendants absorb the cultural identity of their host country, and some urge those of immigrant stock to retain their distinctive identity – the probability is that both groups take on some of the norms and values of the other, but that the majority population's attitudes gradually become accepted by most of the ethnic minority concerned, although this may take several generations, while a smaller proportion maintain a group solidarity and emphasise their distinctive culture, as with some Orthodox Jews.

Travel and the media

Immigrants in Britain

Lunch at the Sikh temple in Bradford. Immigrants have often brought additional interest and colour to the streets of the United Kingdom

The ease of air travel has brought a new dimension to the lives of many people whose parents would have known little of behaviour outside their immediate neighbourhood.

Perhaps most importantly of all television has brought comparative living standards into everyone's home; in some increasing relative deprivation (section 10.4), in others widening cultural horizons and contributing to a change in attitudes.

21.3 Political factors

The last battle on British soil was in 1746 at Culloden and the fact that Britain has not in modern times suffered invasion or occupation has had an influence on such cultural factors as tolerance and liberty.

- The stabilising effect of external security and democratic government at home has also perhaps had an impact upon retaining aspects of British society which many might feel less desirable, such as inequality (section 10.2).
- This stability might appear to some as 'stagnation'. A German (Dibelius) writing in 1922 commented, 'English national life contrasted with the rich variations of the Continent, presents a picture of drab uniformity, fatally congenial to the creation of a featureless and spineless urban population'.
- If change comes from conflict, then the comparative absence of conflict in British society would explain the 'stability' or 'stagnation' – according to one's point of view – in such institutions as the British class system, or the dominance of middle class professionals in all the major political parties. Marx argued that social change could not occur unless the structure of society was transformed.
- The nearest approach to political confrontation on class lines in Britain was the General Strike of 1926 yet the year before the Conservative Prime Minister, Stanley Baldwin, had successfully opposed a Private Member's Bill brought in by his own backbenchers to prevent political contributions to the Labour Party from trade union dues.
- Despite the fact that for most of the twentieth century there has been a working class majority in the electorate, the Labour Party – which claims to be the party of the working class – has held office for only twenty-three of the eighty-two years between 1918 and 2000, and only then regained power in 1997 by re-branding itself as 'New Labour' and deliberately adopting policies in line with what was acceptable to 'middle England', rather than its traditional supporters. Political institutions in Britain have therefore tended towards encouraging stability rather than change.

21.4 Economic factors

The major changes in British society have been the result of economic rather than political factors; although one of the reasons for the change in the position of women (the First World War) could be seen as a political factor rather than an economic one.

Most of these economic factors have been dealt with earlier:

- Changes in methods of production consequent upon the industrial revolution leading to the establishment of large factory units, and resulting in both increasing urbanisation and the development of organised labour in trade unions, which have in their turn been responsible for social change.
- A need for a more educated workforce, leading to compulsory education. Greater access to education for both men and women, linked to smaller family size, helped to establish the nuclear family as the main operating unit, with consequent effects on the roles of husband and wife.
- Changes in production methods have led to increasing leisure for some and increased unemployment for others.

REVISION SUMMARY

Reasons why a society may 'stagnate' or not change

- The socialisation process/family influence and education within the home.
- Geographical isolation.
- Unchanging economic structure.
- Absence of conflict/invasion.
- Influence of religion.

Reasons why a society may 'develop' or change

- Contact with other cultures (e.g. immigration/emigration/tourism).
- Economic change (e.g. crop failure/industrial revolution).
- Education outside the home.
- Media influences.
- Political factors (e.g. invasion/revolution).

⊽ **22** Processes of social change

22.1 Rural lifestyles

In Britain in 1801 about three-quarters of the population lived in rural areas, by 1901 one-quarter did. This process of 'urbanisation' continued during the twentieth century and it is only since the 1970s that the process appears to have halted, and to a limited extent reversed (see section 16.2). This reversal is statistical rather than meaningful in terms of behaviour because the new country-dweller is likely to 'commute' into a town for work, and rural dwellers generally are much more dependent on towns for shopping, leisure facilities and education than they formerly were.

Living patterns

- It is generally agreed that some fundamental changes took place in living patterns as a result of the movement from country to town (section 16.2). The extended rural family in the nineteenth century was a 'unit of production' and there was a need for close co-operation with relations. It has been suggested that the rural worker is less likely to be alienated from his work than the town dweller because he sees the object of his labour in the end product.

  The rural dweller is less likely to be concerned with status symbols, as the 'face-to-face' relationships of the village mean that everyone knows what a particular person's job and social position is.
- Behaviour in rural societies may be more spontaneous because there is less room for choice. There may be a greater feeling of group solidarity and less crime because people are less likely to steal or damage the property of people known to them, and because there is a greater risk of detection.
- In face-to-face communities each individual is related to every other individual in his total network in several different ways. In an extreme case a man's father is also his teacher, his religious leader and his employer. A shopkeeper in the village is also a relative of many of his customers and a chapel deacon, and so on. 'If the shopkeeper has also to behave appropriately in situations involving shopkeeper/shopkeeper's nephew/deacon/member of congregation we may say that his social life has a complexity which his urban counterparts lack. He has perhaps a smaller choice of roles than he would have in the town, and he has to play them all to the same audience' (R.

Frankenberg, *Communities in Britain Social: Life in Town and Country*, 1966). Frankenberg also points to the likelihood of friction between kin in rural areas and to fights between 'the lads' of neighbouring villages. Rural lifestyles are not all peace and tranquillity as compared with those of towns.

* Tönnies (1887) used the term '*Gemeinschaft*', meaning 'community', to describe rural lifestyles with their stress on family and community and greater mutual involvement and caring. The term '*Gesellschaft*', meaning 'association', he used to describe urban life with associations formed for practical purposes and less of the informal 'nosey' contacts of the village. Relationships in the village tend to be integrated, in the towns they are likely to be isolated.

Roles in urban and rural communities

In truly rural society the network may be close-knit; everybody knows and interacts with everyone else. In urban society individuals may have few friends in common. In a study of urban families, Elizabeth Bott put forward a hypothesis that the nature of a family's network in these terms was related to the division of labour between husband and wife within the home. She distinguished three kinds of family organization. The first she called complementary, where husband and wife have different activities but fit together to form a whole, as in farming communities. The second she calls independent, where husband and wife act without reference to each other. The third she describes as joint organization, when husband and wife work closely together or their activities are covered by either one alternating . . . Theoretically, at least, at the extreme rural end of the continuum, everyone in society has an equal opportunity to interact with everyone else. Even in rural Ireland, however, the nature of women's work has already cut them off from full interaction . . . I would expect that workers would tend to embrace their role in rural society and to reject it in urban. In other words, all the working class who remain in rural areas are locally oriented. Status and class do not coincide exactly in any society. Nor are they the only categories which align individuals and divide them. In rural society the lines of division for different purposes are less likely to coincide.

The relative ease of social mobility between status groups, characteristic of urban society, does not necessarily weaken class solidarity and conflict. T. H. Marshall has pointed out a change from the ideology of 'that education to which your status entitles you' to 'that status to which your education entitles you'. This, however, is an educational train which has to be caught early or not at all. As he writes:

'The ticket obtained on leaving school or college is for a life journey. The man with a third class ticket who later feels entitled to claim a seat in a first class carriage will not be admitted even if he is prepared to pay the difference. That would not be fair to the others'.

(Marshall, *Citizenship and Social Class*, 1950)

Rural conflict

> I am suggesting that in rural societies conflict is more omnipresent and more likely to be disruptive if it breaks into open dispute. At the same time, the nature of such society enables, if it does not demand, the channeling and institutionalizing of conflict in such a way that the occasion of dispute becomes the occasion of coherence. The contrast can be expressed in the terms that in rural communities there are divisions but no fundamental cleavages; there are rebellions but not revolutions. The end-point of such rebellions is an immediate reassertion of the values and unity of the group.
>
> (R. Frankenberg, *Communities in Britain*, Harmondsworth, Penguin, 1966, abridged)

22.2 Urban lifestyles

Tönnies also stressed the impersonality and isolation of city life; while Durkheim stressed the sense of normlessness – 'anomie' – of urban lifestyles and suggested many of the problems of urban dwelling could be traced to this lack of set standards by which conduct could be judged.

Problems

The problems associated with urban lifestyles (sections 16.2 and 16.4) may be summarised as:

- Social isolation, loneliness among crowds. In its extreme form this may lead to suicide.
- More crime and violence because of a reduced common identity; fewer shared standards; more crowding; more opportunities; less certainty of detection.
- Greater competition for status symbols, more stress.
- More pollution, more noise.
- Relationships tend to be superficial – a 'network of associations'. They also tend to be 'segmented', that is, established for particular reasons and not developed.
- There is less 'inter-generational' authority. 'In the shifting populations of large cities, young people are less ready to accord respect to their elders. "Grandad" becomes a term of contempt.' (A. Halsey, *Change in British Society*, 1981.)

In towns people also tend to be less 'homogeneous', they tend to be different from each other. There is thus greater potential for conflict, but also greater potential for social change and more variety and stimulation.

The 'privatised' family of the urban area (section 3.4) with its lack of assistance from kin and greater potential for conflict because its energies are directed inwards upon itself, also has the potential for deeper relationships because of the mutual interdependence of its members. It must, however, be clearly borne in mind that when 'urban' and 'rural' lifestyles are referred to in a modern context broad generalisations are being made.

Urbanisation and urban villages

> Farmers collected together in settlements of over 20,000 inhabitants in West Africa or villages surrounded by the physical expansion of an Indian city can hardly be termed urbanized in a sociological sense. Similarly, certain aspects of 'social disorganization', which are said to follow rapid urbanization – that is rapid immigration to an urban area – are presumably also found in rural areas into which there is rapid immigration for harvests, tree-felling, short-term mining activity and so on. Clearly under these circumstances there will be an unbalanced age and sex structure producing a strong likelihood of the conventional symptoms of 'disorganization' such as prostitution and drunkenness. On the other hand, specific studies of parts of the central areas of cities, such as Delhi, Cairo, East London, Lagos, Medan, and Mexico City, suggest that urban villages exist in which there is a high level of social cohesion, based on interwoven kinship networks, and a high level of primary contact with familiar people.
>
> ('A Perspective of Urban Sociology', in R. Pahl (ed.), *Readings in Urban Sociology*, Harmondsworth, Penguin, 1968)

The contrast between urban and rural life is both physical and psychological

The Isle of Flodda in the Outer Hebrides. Flodda is a tidal island off the coast of Benbecula

A walkway in an inner-city block of high-rise flats

There is ample evidence of long established town communities sharing many of the features mentioned for rural lifestyles. The increasing dominance of urban culture – economic, educational and recreational – together with the growing movement of essentially urban populations to rural areas and the influence of the media has resulted in some of the features mentioned as pertaining to urban lifestyles being adopted in rural areas.

22.3 The media and change

How influential is advertising and TV?

The media (section 6.4), particularly television, clearly has influence, or millions of pounds would not be spent on media advertising. However, the degree of influence that the media has on changing our values and behaviour is disputed. C. Wright Mills, in *The Power Elite*, claimed that the media were 'a major cause of the transformation of America into a mass society' while D. McQuail, *Towards a Sociology of Mass Communication*, claimed then, 'there is almost no evidence of the production of apathy or passivity by the mass media, nor of effects harmful to sociability and family life or likely to stimulate crime and violence.'

Television is the main leisure pursuit of all age groups in Britain, with on average, people spending some 25 hours per week watching TV in 1997. As Himmelweit (*Television and the Child*, 1958) found that the children most likely to be affected by television are those who are least critical (in particular, the less intelligent thirteen to fourteen-year-olds) it must be presumed that television has some influence on tastes and opinions.

However there is evidence that people in general tend to watch and read features that agree with their own views, or to interpret news and views through a 'mesh' of previously received ideas. There is likely to be no sudden change in attitudes as a result of exposure to the media. However, there is what has been called the 'drip effect': constant repetition tends to familiarise us with the idea that certain types of behaviour, perhaps violent or promiscuous, are normal.

Although it is also suggested that the media, like other institutions in Britain, are essentially conservative and are unlikely therefore to challenge accepted norms and values to any marked extent, few people would dispute that the portrayal of particular lifestyles and behaviour as normal day after day within people's own privatised living space will have an effect, even although it may be a very gradual one – advertisers would not pay to have their products displayed if the portrayal did not have a discernible effect on sales.

Selection of broadcast material

J. Brown wrote 'Techniques of Persuasion' some forty years ago, when the viewer was limited to two television channels, rather than the proliferation of stations, including cable and satellite, that exist today.

Although outside the formal news programmes most presenters could now hardly be accused of having a 'cultured' accent (indeed there has been criticism that the 'estuary English' so often spoken is being absorbed too generally into the national accent), a number of studies have demonstrated how 'soaps' such as *EastEnders* are targeted at the C2, the skilled manual, market but controlled by upper middle class producers.

In 1978 Stuart Hall and others, in 'Policing the Crisis', described how there was a 'pyramid of access' to the media with those in high status positions (for example MPs and judges) being the 'primary definers' of what the news will be by selecting which of the many possible topics should be given priority; while those lower in the pyramid have the role of providing 'balance' and making the news more factual by way of interviews, they do not have the same degree of power because they do not choose the agenda.

Certainly the media's selection of items to be covered will assist in creating 'moral panics' (section 18.2); as when *The News of the World* decided to publish details of known paedophiles in July 2000 after the murder of a little girl, and stopped this publication only after a number of innocent people were mistaken for those identified and attacked by mobs.

The media and social class

Techniques of persuasion

Almost since its inception the BBC (with the best of intentions) has been expressing a predominantly middle-class view of life presented in a 'cultured' accent, but public-opinion polls have shown that the working class still regard the BBC as representing 'them' (i.e. the Establishment), the accent has not spread, and although it is true that the Britain of today has become more middle class in such matters as buying and spending, the basic working-class attitudes to all that pertains to work, livelihood, and social and cultural values have remained little altered. On the other hand, many working-class influences have begun to penetrate literature, the stage, radio, and television, and a great many of the best-known novelists and playwrights are proletarian in origin in spite of the fact that the mass media have remained predominantly in the hands of the upper and middle classes.

What the masses get is but the reflection of their own vociferous needs and demands. In the sphere of opinions and attitudes the élite are not the controllers of the people but their victims. That is the meaning of opinion surveys, Gallup polls, motivational research, and all the other methods of finding out what the masses 'really' think. They are designed to find out what the people want so that both the élites and their productions may be modelled into their likeness. The picture presented of a once sturdy and self-reliant peasantry living in an 'organic' society with their genuine folk-arts, or of industrial workers who at a later period had a warm and cosy working-class culture worthy of preservation, both now perverted by a mean, money-grubbing, and ignorant élite which has 'brainwashed' them into accepting Western films when what they 'really' want is Shakespeare and John Bunyan, is ludicrous when translated into the terms of modern realities. In fact, as we have seen elsewhere, although it would be as foolish to idealize the motives of those who control our radio and television as it is to idealize the 'organic society' of the past with its ignorance, prejudice, and superstitions, there is every reason to believe that what the people get in the way of culture is usually a good deal better than what they demand.

There is something far wrong with a group in which some members are so bored with their jobs that they use the media solely as a stupefying drug, and those who are in this state of mind are just as likely to be narcotized by Beethoven and the news as by 'pop' music and thrillers. Similarly, those children who are drawn into delinquency are the result of an unsatisfactory home life and an environment within which delinquency is a possible and even socially-accepted way out for frustrated youth. The supposition that they are perverted by the mass media alone is a gross oversimplification of a serious and complex problem. There are, or have been, horror comics and films which should not be shown to children, but to suggest that children have been turned into delinquents in this way is to put the cart before the horse, since it is those who continue to be attracted by such books and films who are showing the symptoms of potential delinquency. Horror stories are, indeed, a natural component of growing up, but few modern tales could be as horrific, offensive (e.g. in their anti-semitism), or terrifying as those of the Grimm brothers on which many of us were reared, and we have tried to show that similar horrific fantasies occur in all children whether or not they are exposed to stories, films, or plays about them. One suspects that when matters of taste are being discussed the question of class prejudice is not entirely excluded. It is 'right' for the middle or upper classes to engage in such time-wasting (and, as some might think, foolish) activities as watching cricket and tennis, playing bridge and chess, or reading detective stories and thrillers, but when the working-class man watches league football in the middle of the week he is 'loafing', while his family, occupying themselves with bingo, darts, or watching quiz programmes on the 'telly', are being perverted by 'vapid and puerile activities'. The fact is that frequently those who profess most concern and admiration for the ordinary man are, at heart, the people who most despise him.

(J. Brown, *Techniques of Persuasion*, 1963, abridged)

(*Note:* Bear in mind that this passage was written about forty years ago; how true are the points made today?)

22.4 International influence

International influence on social change in Britain is difficult to quantify. There is the obvious impact of immigration (section 21.2) and the mass media make cultural comparisons possible – between Britain and America, for example.

Multinational corporations in their products and advertising tend to project similar images in a variety of countries which may, in the long term, contribute to growing similarities between the countries concerned.

Ease of international travel has certainly contributed towards the growth of drug-taking in Britain and has also been blamed for some of the growth in pornography.

Student exchanges and grant-aided study overseas has made possible a greater exchange of ideas between the future leaders of a variety of cultures.

It is tempting to assume that the opening up of ideas between differing cultures will lead to greater tolerance but there is little sign of this. Without doubt a certain amount of terrorism has been imported and exported!

REVISION SUMMARY

Nature of rural societies (*Gemeinschaft*)

- More face to face relationships.
- More stress within family and community.
- Integrated relationships.
- Clear value system.
- Less choice.

- Less alienated.
- Less social change.

Nature of urban societies (*Gesellschaft*)

- Social isolation.
- More crime and violence.
- More stress.
- Superficial relationships.
- Less inter-generational authority.
- More roles to be played.
- More choice.
- Greater alienation.
- More anomie.
- More status symbols.
- More social change.

▓ ▾ **23** Religion

23.1 Religion and morality

Does religion influence morality?

Morality will vary between societies, and the pattern of behaviour which results from this concept of what is right or wrong is called a 'more' by sociologists, and is of great importance in maintaining social order.

Religions are traditionally the justification for a particular morality in society and it is not surprising, therefore, that they tend to take a leading role in helping to ensure that the appropriate mores are observed (section 19.4). In attempting to maintain the existing morality of a society – for example, by opposing abortion, birth control or divorce – they are often seen by some people as essentially conservative institutions standing in the way of what they consider to be social progress. Some people see religion and morality as inseparable and blame the apparent decline in established religion for what they also see as declining moral values.

The degree to which religious observance does influence morality is debatable. One study found that drunkenness and juvenile delinquency were less common among Jews than among other members of the community (E. Krausz, *Leeds Jewry's*), but this could be a result of church membership creating norms which will isolate the offending individual from the group rather than the sign of moral conviction.

More recently in 2001 a research project involving 15,000 children, aged between 13 and 15, 'The Fourth R for the Third Millennium', found that while young Muslims generally accepted their religion's values, Christians did not. For example 82 per cent of young Anglicans rejected life-long marriage and believed that divorce is acceptable, and 85 per cent of young Roman Catholics rejected their Church's teaching that sex outside marriage is wrong; but in comparison 42 per cent of young Muslims believed that divorce is wrong and 49 per cent that sex should be confined to marriage.

In the early years of this century, Charles Booth made a survey of religion in London. He found that only the Irish immigrants were greatly influenced by organised religion and they were 'great beggars, as well as heavy drinkers'.

Religions movements

Sociologists tend to divide religious movements into:

- **Churches**. These usually support the status quo, have a formal hierarchy of officialdom and usually identify with the State (e.g. Church of England, Roman Catholic Church).
- **Denominations**. Minority groups which are not connected with the State but generally accept the norms and values of the society (e.g. Methodists and Baptists).
- **Sects**. Relatively small groups, often rejecting society 'in tension with the larger society and closed against it' (Peter Berger). Examples are Jehovah's Witnesses, Black Muslims, 'Moonies'.

23.2 Belief in modern Britain

Who goes to church?

Participation in formal religion has certainly declined in modern Britain, although it should not be presumed that in the past the majority of people were keen churchgoers.

- The only official religious census ever undertaken, in 1851, showed that about 40 per cent of the population attended church each week. Rowntree and Lavers' longitudinal study of religion in York showed a regular church attendance of 35.5 per cent in 1901, 17.7 per cent in 1935 and 13.0 per cent in 1948; a national estimate in 1974 was 12 per cent and in 1999 less than 8 per cent. In 1861 there was one Anglican clergyman for every 960 people, by 1961 there was one for every 4000.
- In 1989 tens of thousands of churches across England contributed to the English Church Census organised by MARC Europe. The census found that 3.7 million adults attended church (a decrease of one-tenth since 1979), together with 1.2 million children under fifteen. The adult attendance included 3.6 million of white ethnic origin (less than one-tenth of the white population) and 70,000 of Afro-Caribbean origin (one-sixth of the Afro-Caribbean population).
- In 1999 the English Church Attendance Survey, an independent study across all denominations, and the largest ever undertaken, found that less than 8 per cent of the population attended Sunday services and that the decline in churchgoing had accelerated during the previous ten years; on present trends the number attending will drop to 2 per cent in 2020.

    It found that Sunday church attendance fell from 4,742,800 in 1989 to 3,714,700 in 1999 – an 'alarming' 22 per cent. Over the previous decade, the drop was 13 per cent.

    The research was undertaken in 1998 and involved more than 37,000 churches ranging from Roman Catholic to Pentecostal. While 1,266,300 Anglicans (Church of England) went to church on Sunday in 1989, only

980,000 did so in 1998, equal to a fall of 23 per cent. The Church of England's own figures for 1997 (but released in 1999) showed Sunday attendance at 995,700 – the first time that it had gone below a million since records began.

Although Roman Catholic attendance was now the highest of any individual church, with 1,230,100 going to Sunday mass, it had declined by 22 per cent in ten years (from 1,715,900 in 1989). The Methodists had declined by 26 per cent; of the conventional Christian churches only the Baptists recorded a small increase (2 per cent). Smaller sects such as the Mormons and Jehovah's Witnesses have shown substantial gains and Muslims and Sikhs have increased dramatically.

So far as the Christian churches are concerned the proportion of those aged under 15 attending church dropped from 25 per cent in 1989 to 19 per cent in 2000; only 5 per cent of people in their twenties were churchgoers.

Following demographic trends the number of older churchgoers increased by 50,000, with the average age of attenders rising from 38 in 1989 to 43 in 1999.

Significantly the number of people who described themselves as atheists increased – disbelief in a God rose from 25 per cent to 27 per cent over the same period.

- However, in August 1999, Channel 4 television undertook an 'Audit of Belief' on 1000 adults and found that 75 per cent claimed to have some religious or spiritual belief; 45 per cent believed in a God, 13 per cent in a Life Force and 16 per cent in a spirit or a soul. These findings may contradict the assumption that, because people no longer go to formal religious services, they no longer believe in anything supernatural.

The survey also found that women were more spiritual than men, more likely to have a sense of purpose and more likely to pray to a God.

Some 77 per cent of those surveyed said that they had been brought up to be part of a religion, mostly Christian, yet 56 per cent had lapsed.

The producer of the programme commented, 'For Hindus, Muslims, and Sikhs, their religion is still a central part of their daily lives.'

In 1984 a similar television survey had shown that 94 per cent of people claimed to belong to a religion, but of these only 20 per cent actually attended a place of worship more than once a month. In all surveys there is a discrepancy between those who claim to belong to a religion and those who actually attend a place of worship; the fact that such a claim is made indicates that people feel that they should belong because it is a social norm, or that they do have a religious belief but do not feel attendance is necessary in order to practise it (Table 23.1).

- Some have suggested that the decline in attendance in mainstream Christian churches is because they have abandoned much of their former ritual and mystery.

These trends were confirmed in *Religious Trends 2* (pub. HarperCollins, 1999) as the summary below indicates:

Table 23.1   Changes within the churches in the United Kingdom, 1970–95

Adult members	1970	1980	1995
Anglican (e.g. Church of England)	2,994,000	2,457,000	1,785,000
Roman Catholic	2,714,000	2,457,000	1,915,000
Presbyterian (e.g. United Reform Church and Church of Scotland)	1,666,000	1,438,000	1,100,000
Baptist and Methodist	911,000	761,000	761,000
Other 'Trinitarian' (e.g. Pentecostal, Holiness, W. Indian, Salvation Army)	646,000	516,000	648,000
Muslim	130,000	306,000	580,000
Judaism	120,000	111,000	94,000
Sikhs	100,000	150,000	350,000
Orthodox	191,000	203,000	289,000
Mormons	85,000	114,000	171,000
Jehovah's Witnesses	62,000	85,000	131,000

Table 23.2   Religious and civil marriages, 1971 and 1996 (Great Britain)

	Year 1971	(%)	Year 1996	(%)
Religious	267,000	60	152,000	49
Civil*	180,000	40	158,000	51

Note:
E.g. Registry office; by 1996 civil weddings could be celebrated in a number of settings, provided they were dignified and had nominal public access.

- Belief in a personal God has declined from 43 per cent in the 1950s to 31 per cent in the 1990s; disbelief in God has risen from two per cent to 27 per cent over the same period.
- 89 per cent of people who pray, pray for their family and friends; 16 per cent for money; 86 per cent say they have had prayers answered.
- 36 per cent say the primary purpose of Christmas is to meet friends; 28 per cent as a religious festival; 31 per cent say they attend church over Christmas.
- In the past nine years, 1900 churches have opened but 2800 churches have closed.
- Church membership peaked in the 1930s when 10.4 million people belonged. Anglican numbers peaked in 1930, Catholics in 1960, Presbyterians in 1935, Methodists in 1910 and 1930, and Baptists in 1905.
- Unitarians and Quakers have the highest percentage of people cohabiting before marriage, Jehovah's Witnesses and Sikhs the lowest.

'The only denominations to buck the trend were the Baptists, the new churches (such as 'house' churches) and, surprisingly, the Orthodox Church, with an astonishing 105 per cent rise'.

Commentary on
findings: from
Daily Telegraph, 28 November 1999

In 1999 the chairman of the Prayer Book Society said 'One of the reasons for the decline in Sunday attendance is that the Church of England is destroying the numinous, spiritual nature of worship by using the language of the supermarket and the bus queue. This does not nourish souls'; equally many Catholics have become disenchanted with the disappearance of the Tridentine (Latin) rite and its mundane English replacement.

The 'secular function' of religion

- In 1999 the English Church attendance survey found that the North of England had been worst hit, but that London and the South-east had fared much better. For example in Yorkshire and Humberside only 5.9 per cent of the population attended church (a drop of 31 per cent over the decade), but that in London where there were a large number of evangelical 'mega churches', the drop was just 5 per cent, and the Anglicans recorded a 3 per cent rise. As London and the south-east most nearly reflect the geographical mobility found in the United States; it is possible that the relative success of established religion there in retaining membership could presage a more general revival in the future.

  Although religious involvement in rites of passage continues to be important (see below), there is evidence that this also has been declining.

  Church attendance is, of course, only one measurement of church activity; while probation officers, social workers and teachers have taken over some of the roles previously performed by the clergy.

  However, there is still a considerable number of people who prefer to be married in, and buried from, a church; and many charities are church-based (Table 23.2). This 'secular function' of religion may increase as religions are seen to provide a focal point for community activities in urban areas with highly mobile 'privatised' families, who can pick up social connections quickly from a denominational base as they move around the country. This phenomenon has already developed in the United States – not to be (that is not to identify oneself and be identified as) either a Protestant, a Catholic or a Jew is somehow not to be an American. Religion is 'a way of sociability or belonging' . . . It is thus frequently a religiousness without serious commitment, without inner conviction' (W. Herberg, *Protestant – Catholic – Jew*).

The 'integrative' effects of religion

The sociology of religion

Looking for the results of the studies dealing with the sociology of religion, we find that the integrative aspects of religion have mainly been stressed. John Highet, for instance, points out how earlier in the twentieth century in Scotland the local church, even in the cities, was the focal point of many activities in addition to the purely religious activities (John Highet, *The Churches in Scotland Today*). The study by Conor Ward in Liverpool highlights the parish as providing closely knit social units for many within the limited geographical areas.

The integrative effects of religion within partly segregated groups also come to the fore in a number of studies. While on the face of it the very existence of such groups suggests divisiveness when society is taken as a whole, the fact is that religion usually acts in such groups as a factor of social control: it irons out certain problems for the members of the groups. Thus one can see that in certain circumstances internal group integration ensures the necessary inter-group adjustments for society as a whole. According to Bryan Wilson, sects act as small 'deviant' reference groups which enable the individual to gain more favourable status and prestige than are available in the wider society. The sect provides 'the reassurance of a stable, affective society ... Its ideological orientation and its group cohesion provide a context of emotional security'.

(B. R. Wilson (ed.), *Patterns of Sectarianism*, 1967)

Religion as a cohesive force

In the case of minority groups, too, religion has worked as a cohesive force. The present writer has pointed out that among Jews membership of the synagogue, and even just occasional worship and activity in it, provides a major avenue of identification with Judaism and the Jewish minority. Within the Christian fold membership of churches or sects specifically linked with particular minority groups is an important factor in the identification of the individual with his in-group. Poles in Britain belong to separate Polish Roman Catholic parishes. The Irish, on the other hand, re-established Catholicism in Britain, and 'the Roman Catholic Church has played an important part in preserving Irish interests among the immigrants'. It has also been pointed out that West Indians have brought with them special Pentecostal sects to which they belong and which provide them, in this strange setting, with 'a buffer against the society at large'.

David Martin points out that for Christians in Britain there are numerous options which represent different combinations and developments produced by a long period of Christian germination and general historical events. 'Sociologists have developed a shorthand for reducing the infinite variety of these options to three basic "types" which between them include an enormous range of possibilities.' The three models are 'church', 'denomination' and 'sect'. Martin's analysis points up the predominant characteristics exhibited by these type constructs. The 'church' claims social inclusiveness, identifies with the State, has a sacred hierarchy and insists on a comprehensive dogmatic scheme with the accent on past events. The 'denomination' is usually not a social majority, explicitly separates itself from the State but does not reject the wider society. . . . The 'sect' is typically a small exclusive dispossessed minority, which radically rejects society and its institution.

(E. Krausz, *Sociology in Britain: A Survey of Research*, London, Batsford, 1969)

Krausz' earlier comments on 'minority groups' was re-enforced by Hiro in 1991 (*Black British, White British: A History of Race Relations in Britain*) who explains the 'ethnic revival' of West Indians in Pentecostalism as a consequence of their apparent rejection by the wider society.

23.3 Church and State

Maintenance of the social order

Both Church and State are seen as upholding the same norms and values; and often as maintaining the existing social order, including the rights and privileges of particular sections of the society:

- People wish to be convinced that they have a right to what they have, 'Good fortune thus wants to be "legitimate" fortune' (Max Weber). This often implies that the less fortunate also deserve their positions, as in the Hindu caste system; that they are in some way inferior. They may of course be promised better things in an afterlife, and this may help them to accept their earthly suffering. 'Religious distress is at the same time the expression of real distress and the protest against real distress. Religion is the sign of the oppressed creature, the heart of a heartless world, just as it is the spirit of a spiritless situation. It is the opium of the people' (K. Marx and F. Engels, *On Religion*). (Marx, of course, thought that once the real enemy was identified the criticism of heaven would turn into the criticism of the earth.)
- Because of the apparent identity of interest between the objectives of Church and State – the maintenance of the social order – the Church usually comes to reinforce the State. The King may even come to be seen as a god, as was the Inca of Peru, the Pharaoh of Egypt and (until 1947) the Emperor of Japan.

The Church in modern Britain

In modern Britain the 'Established Church' is the Church of England and its leader, the Archbishop of Canterbury, is still a moral leader. His views are still reported with respect in the media. However, political power has gone. Anglican Bishops still sit in the reformed House of Lords (although the Roman Catholic Church is now the largest group). Secular institutions have taken over education and most of the social functions of the Church. The Church remains nevertheless part of 'The Establishment'.

- It would be wrong however to assume that Church and State are inevitably united. Norman Cohen (*The Pursuit of the Millennium*, 1957) describes how, in Europe during the Middle Ages, the poor were periodically swept by an intense belief that the world was about to be miraculously transformed, and developed strange cults. The same has happened in modern times in the Melanesian Islands, where 'cargo cults' promise the return of the aeroplanes that brought sudden wealth during the Second World War.
- More soberly, the Methodist Church was an important factor in the rise of reforming Liberalism at the end of the nineteenth century, the development of the trade unions, and of the Labour Party. Modern Catholic priests in South America – preaching what has been called 'liberation theology' – have taken a leading role in condemning poverty and the ruling totalitarian regimes.

A millennial cult in 2000

Ezequiel Gamonal, who has died aged 82, was a Peruvian prophet regarded by tens of thousands of followers as the Messiah . . . Gamonal was worshipped by his sect, the Israelites of the New Universal Covenant. Its members were mainly Andean peasants who wore Old Testament costumes modelled on the Hollywood epics of Cecil B. De Mille . . .

Gamonal, a former village shoemaker, taught that he had been chosen by God to inaugurate the new Israel, which had been transferred from the Middle East to Peru as a punishment for the original Israelites' loss of faith. The new kingdom would extend far into the Amazon, where it was believed the last Inca emperor had been sleeping since the Spanish invasion in the 16th century . . .

Ezequiel Ataucusi Gamonal was born in 1918 to a peasant family in southern Peru.

It was while working as a shoemaker in the 1950s that he converted from Roman Catholicism to Seventh-day Adventism, though he was quickly expelled from the latter denomination after dressing as a Hebrew prophet and claiming to receive divine revelations.

Chief among these was a visit to what Gamonal called the 'third heaven', in which he met the Father, Son and Holy Ghost and was ordered to copy the Ten Commandments on to a blackboard. From then on, observance of the Commandments became the first duty of the Israelites. In 1969, the new religion was recognised by the Peruvian state, and by the 1990s estimates of its strength ranged from 60,000 to 200,000.

Gamonal's cosmology was a complex and often confusing mixture of Seventh-day Adventism, Judaism and Inca legend. From the 1960s until his death, he taught that various apocalyptic disasters were about to befall the world, although on several occasions he was able to delay their arrival by petitioning God for more time. As a result, the deadline for the end of the world, originally scheduled for this year, was regularly pushed back.

It was beyond doubt, however, that Gamonal's followers, most of whom were peasants uprooted from their villages by the collapse of the rural economy in the 1970s, derived spiritual comfort from his teachings. For many, the Israelites' life of prayer offered a peaceful alternative to the Shining Path, the Maoist guerillas who terrorised Peru during the 1980s . . .

He died during the Israelites' Pentecost celebrations, and disappointed many of his followers by failing to fulfil his promise that he would rise again after three days.

(Daily Telegraph, 24 July 2000)

23.4 Secularisation and the future

What is 'secularisation'?

Secularisation is the process in which religious beliefs and sanctions become less important as guides to behaviour and decisions: 'the process whereby religious thinking, practice and institutions lose social significance' (B. R. Wilson, *Religion in a Secular Society*, 1966). Functions previously carried out by clergy, such as providing advice to families, looking after the sick, education and providing community entertainment, are carried out by a host of governmental and voluntary agencies.

Comte (1798–1857) claimed that man no longer needed to have a supernatural explanation for the human condition now that social developments could be analysed and understood.

How secularised is modern Britain?

It has been suggested that secularisation is the result of two main developments: the growth of Protestantism which invited man not to accept traditional explanations, and industrialisation/urbanisation which removed individuals from traditional communities and made them require rational solutions to the social problems thereby created.

"For heaven's sake, write it down! You'll only forget."

Opinions vary as to the degree of secularisation in modern British society. This difference of opinion is largely based on differing views of what religion is. If one takes the view that an essential characteristic of religion is church membership and worship, then the decline in these factors can be seen as evidence of secularisation. If religious belief is taken as the major criterion then measurement becomes very difficult. We cannot be certain whether people attended church in the past mainly because of social pressure and because of the social functions which the church performed, rather than from a belief in its teachings; equally, people today may have strong religious beliefs which they prefer to express in private rather than by church attendance.

In 1970 B. R. Wilson, in 'Religious Sects', suggested that the proliferation of religious sects in Britain is seen by some as a sign that the traditional churches are in a stage of collapse, and as further evidence of the spread of secularisation – in that there are no clear religious values to be seen as community values and religion has therefore lost its role of reinforcing social solidarity. Others see the increasing membership of organisations such as Jehovah's Witnesses and Mormons as signs of a growing interest in religion and a rejection of the materialism of secular society.

Dr Aboulmagd's main thesis was prompted by a book, *The Clash of Civilisations* by Samuel P. Huntington. This book created a rumpus when it appeared because Professor Huntington believes that the old ideological tensions of the Cold War will be replaced in the future by clashes between blocks of civilisations and religions, in particular between the Western World led by America, and the world of Islam, which has no leader. Dr Aboulmagd's riposte to this was that such a clash is not inevitable; however, if it is to be averted both sides of this troubled cultural border should look honestly into a mirror at themselves and then objectively through a window at the other.

The West, he says, sees itself as the superior civilisation, champion of freedom and democracy, educator to, and master of, a world which needs to be refashioned in its image. Looking through the window at Islam, the West sees only the backward and overly religious peoples that it has conquered, whose intellectual contribution to the world may once have been great but is now lost in history. All that remains is a burgeoning fundamentalism that threatens the West's cherished freedoms. Muslims, meanwhile, see themselves as the inheritors of the greatest civilisations, the followers of the last revealed religion, and as a sixth of all mankind. They see the West as colonialist, devoid of spirituality, bent on material gain; a place where human relations are decaying.

What both sides now need to do is take note, not so much of their differences, as of what Dr Aboulmagd calls their 'commonality': a shared belief in a God and in a hereafter, both of which shape their code of ethics; a belief that mankind is an elevated creature, chosen by God above all others; a belief in democracy and human rights, no matter how flawed the expression of that belief may be in some Muslim countries.

(from a lecture by Dr Kamal Aboulmagd, University Professor, lawyer and Islamist from Cairo, *RSA Journal*, 4 April 1998)

REVISION SUMMARY

Functions of religion

Social control, the legitimation of authority and social change are three possible functions of religion, but there are a number of other aspects to these functions, or additional functions:

- **Social cohesion**, providing the cement that binds the bricks of the society together, making a meaningful whole (Durkheim, *Elementary Forms of Religious Life*).

- **Rites of passage**, providing ceremonies that symbolically emphasise important stages in the life of an individual within the context of the society to which that person belongs (e.g. baptism, marriage, circumcision).
- **Integration**, providing a sense of belonging.
- **Supportive**, providing emotional support at times of stress (e.g. death of someone we love).
- **Moral direction**, providing clear statements of appropriate behaviour.
- **Explanation**, providing a meaning for life.
- **Reintegration**, providing a mechanism for accepting deviants back into the general society (e.g. confession).

Church and State

Legitimation

In most societies the acceptable morality, and therefore the behaviour which results from it, is based on some kind of religious creed. It is usual for Church and State to uphold the same norms and values.

Because the 'Church' tends to uphold the existing social order, it has been criticised by those seeking change. Marx and Engels, in *On Religion*, expressed the view that religion was a mechanism for keeping peoples subordinate by:

- Teaching that God decides who shall be rich or poor; that such divisions are the 'natural' order of things.
- Teaching that there is a special virtue in poverty.
- Teaching that suffering in this life will be rewarded by spiritual riches in an afterlife.
- Channelling energy that could be devoted to changing society into expressions of religion or charitable work.

'**Legitimation**' is the term used for the process by which particular behaviour is justified, so Marx and Engels are stating that one of the functions of religion is to justify or legitimise existing authority.

Legitimation is important both as a process by which people accept their position (e.g. the Hindu caste system) and because the power-holders need to feel justified in what they do. As Max Weber said: 'Good fortune thus wants to be "legitimate" fortune.'

Opposition to the State

Religion does not always support the status quo. Even established churches may sometimes take a lead in opposing the State: e.g. the Roman Catholic Church was the main opposition to the Communist government in Poland and the Polish Pope has been credited with a major role in the subsequent collapse of communism in Europe; Catholic priests in South America (preaching what has been called 'liberation theology') have taken a leading role in condemning poverty and the ruling totalitarian regimes.

Secularisation

Secularisation is a term used to describe a general decline in religion, both in its practice and in the significance of religious thinking, and to describe the process by which religious groups and institutions become more concerned with non-religious activities (e.g. as status enhancers or as centres of social activities such as youth clubs or meeting places for young mothers).

We cannot be certain whether people attended church in the past mainly because of social pressure and because of the social functions which the church performed, rather than from a belief in its teachings; equally, people today may have strong religious beliefs which they prefer to express in private rather than by church attendance.

Millenarian movements

Millenarian movements are a form of sect in which the underprivileged believe that the world will be miraculously transformed and the supernatural world will merge with the world of man; poverty, pain and death will disappear. Examples are:

- European cults in the Middle Ages (Norman Cohen, *The Pursuit of the Millennium*, 1957).
- 'Cargo cults' in the Melanesian Islands, which promise the return of the aeroplanes that brought sudden wealth during the Second World War (Peter Worsley).
- The 'Ghost Dance' religion of the Teton Sioux Indians at the end of the nineteenth century, resulting from defeat and famine ('ghost shirts' were to make them invulnerable to the white man's bullets, leading to the massacre of the Indians at Wounded Knee).
- Rastafarianism in Britain today: West Indians who see a miraculous return to Africa and a life free from poverty and strife.
- The Israelites of the New Universal Covenant in Peru (see 23.3.)

SELF-TEST QUESTIONS: PART EIGHT

Self-test 8.1

1 What is the term used to describe beliefs, language, rules and folkways? *(1 mark)*
2 What major political confrontation occurred in 1926? *(1 mark)*
3 For how many years was the Labour Party in power between 1918 and 2000? *(2 marks)*
4 What is the term used for the process in which towns and cities grow and become more important as features within a society? *(2 marks)*

5   What term did Tönnies use to describe rural lifestyles? (the term means 'community')? *(2 marks)*
6   State three problems which may be associated with urban lifestyles? *(3 marks)*
7   Name three religions, denominations or sects whose membership has increased in recent years. *(3 marks)*
8   State three consequences of changing production methods during the last 200 years. *(3 marks)*
9   What social functions are served by religion? *(4 marks)*
10 Why have some societies changed little over long periods of time? *(4 marks)*

Self-test 8.2

1   According to the information in Table 23.2, how many marriages took place in Registry Offices in 1971? *(1 mark)*
2   Comparing 1971 with 1995, which manner of solemnisation has declined in popularity, and which has increased the most in popularity? *(2 marks)*
3   What is meant by the term 'secularisation'? *(3 marks)*
4   The information in the table referred to is sometimes used to indicate a decline in religious beliefs. Examine some weaknesses in the way in which religious belief is measured. *(6 marks)*
5   Examine the extent to which religion is an influence in contemporary Britain. *(8 marks)*

SPECIMEN QUESTIONS AND ANSWERS

'Living together'

In the last twenty years, living together before marriage has become accepted. Fifty per cent of the population does it, in the belief that trial marriage is a way to avoid divorce. Now a new Government survey proves absolutely that, if you live together before you marry, your marriage is 50 per cent more likely to end within five years.

(*Daily Mail*, 19 June 1992; see also cartoon on p. 55)

1. Why does 'living together before marriage' appear to have become accepted during the past thirty years? *(4 marks)*
2. How have the roles of women and men changed during the twentieth century? Explain how this has happened. *(7 marks)*
3. Why do some societies change rapidly, whilst others remain the same? *(9 marks)*

Answers

1 Living together before marriage seems to have become more accepted during the past thirty years because of changing norms and values. As more people do live together before marriage it becomes more accepted as the normal thing to do and attracts less criticism. The declining influence of religion among most sectors of the population means that moral values change and living together before marriage is no longer seen as a sin.

In the source material it is implied that some people may live together before marriage because they consider it a way to avoid divorce; although the source material makes it clear that the opposite is the case.

2 During the twentieth century there has been a considerable move towards greater equality between men and women. Most women now work outside the home, many occupy high-status positions and legally there is almost complete equality.

Men are now more likely to help with housework and child care, but this is usually still seen as 'helping' rather than a shared duty.

Changes have occurred primarily because of greater educational opportunities for women and legal changes such as the Equal Pay Act and the establishment of the Equal Opportunities Commission.

However, attitudes have been slower to change than the law; many men still resent taking instructions from a woman and in 1992 a survey by the European Commission showed that 74.2 per cent of British men said they did not carry out any domestic tasks.

The primary reason for this lack of change is that the socialisation process tends to inhibit change because the young child is subject to the influence of the previous generation. For example, a young boy will use his father as a role model and as traditionally men have not done much housework in Britain – this is likely to continue from generation to generation.

Attitudes are then reinforced by the media – for example, television advertising showing women doing the washing-up or ironing; by books and newspapers and by the educational process (where 'domestic science' may still not be regarded as the norm for boys). The peer group also has a major impact in reinforcing attitudes.

All these influences interrelate making it the 'norm' for British men not to do housework and females often to accept that position.

3 There is a tendency in all societies for the socialisation process of the young child to inhibit change as the child naturally copies, and is encouraged to copy, the behaviour of parents and other relatives. Where there are no external stimuli counterbalancing the influence of the home, change is likely to be least (for example, in tribal societies).

Religion also usually tends to encourage the continuation of traditional norms and values, and where a large proportion of the population continue to believe in an established religion, social change may be slow.

The media may encourage conformity to existing values, but its influence in many societies has dramatically increased – first, with the growth of literacy, and

The house illustrated on p. 310 is near to the reputed spot from which Bonnie Prince Charlie 'sailed over the sea to Skye'. It is still one of the most isolated parts of Great Britain but listed below are some recent events which may be causing cultural change even on Flodda and the neighbouring larger island of Benbecula – consider what these changes may be and what may cause them. (First find the Outer Hebrides on a map.)

1941   Opening of Airport at Balivanich on Benbecula
1942   Building of a road causeway joining Benbecula to South Uist
1958   Army base established on Benbecula
1963   Building of a road causeway joining Benbecula to North Uist
1978   Building of a path causeway joining Flodda to Benbecula
1981   Building of a road causeway joining Flodda to Benbecula
1985   Introducing of ro-ro car ferry Uig/Lochmaddy
1985   Electricity taken over to Flodda
1985   Private telephones available on Flodda
1988   Peat digging machine contractor on Flodda and Benbecula
1988   Secondary School opens on Benbecula (previously pupils left the Island to board)
1994   First road construction on Flodda
         Hotels/B&Bs available on Benbecula 1984 = 10, 1994 = 18

more recently, television. The media make people aware of differing norms and values and thus usually encourages change.

Substantial increases and decreases in population are also likely to lead to change; the Black Death in Britain during the Middle Ages led to a collapse in population and ultimately contributed to the break-up of the feudal system as labour became valuable. The population explosion of the nineteenth century in Britain encouraged migration and urbanisation and radically different styles of life. Invention and the consequent industrial change leads to different employment patterns and attitudes.

Immigrants bring with them differing patterns of behaviour, often copied in the host country, while the devastation of war can radically alter traditional values as in post-1946 Japan.

Part Nine

The political system

■ ⊻ **24** Forms of government

24.1 Totalitarian government

Totalitarian governments are the usual forms of government both in the past and in the modern world. Essentially a **totalitarian** state is a country controlled by one man – ('an autocracy'), or a group – 'an oligarchy'. Because the power of any state rests ultimately on its armed forces those filling key roles in totalitarian states are very often members of the military.

Usually totalitarian leaders try to legitimise their position by claiming to have taken power to save the state from danger and they often promise that when the danger is past they will return power to the people although they rarely do so.

Elites in totalitarian regimes

Totalitarian states often do have parliaments and elections but have either a limited franchise, so that only those who are likely to support the status quo have a vote; or, more often, restrict the election to representatives of only one political party or to parties representing only one area of the political spectrum. It is often claimed that as the vast majority of people in the country concerned support a particular political viewpoint, the only way to ensure choice is to offer several candidates from a particular political background.

In a totalitarian system those who influence or control the society or important institutions within it and who are acknowledged as superior by virtue of this influence are likely to be clearly apparent. This 'élite' can be less obvious in states claiming to be parliamentary democracies and may limit the extent to which the states concerned can be regarded as truly democratic. In 1956 C. Wright Mills, in *The Power Elite*, emphasised the similarity between the attitudes, values and social background of those who make up the ruling élite in the United States, and Michels (*Political Parties*, 1959) suggested that 'élites' are inevitable in any organisation structure, 'who says organisation, says oligarchy'.

In 1950 (forty years before the communist regime fell in Russia) one researcher claimed that after thirty years of communist government a ten-class social system had emerged, 'from the ruling élite (officials, scientists, top artists and writers) down through managers, bureaucrats, and three classes of workers and two classes of peasants, to the slave labourers' (V. Packard, *The Status Seekers*). Perhaps it is true to say that the major difference between democratic and totalitarian states is that in the former elites can be challenged, in the latter they cannot.

Elites in Britain

(*Note*: that this was written more than thirty years ago; as you read consider what changes may have occurred).

The British (ruling circle)

The British 'ruling circle' is obvious. In most Western countries, ruling groups are an abstract entity, like Wall Street, or are groups hidden behind closed doors, as, it was alleged, the French 200 families. In Britain, the social system, reinforced by the education system, seems to take pride in presenting to all and sundry the names of the members of the ruling circle and the mechanics of their contacts. Nowhere else do 'influential' families seem to take such pleasure in advertising their existence and their size; nowhere else does the education system openly extol the combined advantages of 'breeding' and contacts.

The persistence of a small number of leading families is probably unique, as is the existence of the public schools. It is perhaps natural in a country which did not have any revolution for almost three hundred years, although the absence of revolution has in turn to be explained. It has perhaps to be accounted for by the absence of military occupation and of the political collapse which often ensues; large scale immigration might also have modified the social and political equilibrium, but no such immigration ever took place. The aristocracy had the wisdom to accept new families within its ranks: in return, it succeeded in not suffering the disgrace of being relegated to a museum-like isolation. Social values have continued to recognize the supremacy of the aristocracy. That social supremacy may be challenged; it may be recognized only on the surface and not deeply felt. Yet by the very fact that lip-service is paid to the social superiority of the upper class its members enjoy initial advantages which do not exist to the same extent in other industrial nations. In most developed countries, the aristocrats who remain have to accept appearing bourgeois if they want to succeed. The British upper class may no longer have power as a class; its members still can claim as of right that they belong to influential circles if such is their desire. They do not have to gain places in spite of their background, as in some Continental countries; their background helps them. It remains for a large number of members of the upper class to use this privilege, and the general position of the group appears well-established. Since a sufficient proportion is talented enough to make a good career, the general claims of the group appear reasonable.

These points are well-known. As for pre-democratic Britain, one can still rather easily trace ramifications of influential families in the upper ranks of the Conservative party, in many financial houses of the City, even in the Foreign Office and in the services. The charts of cousinhoods and intermarriages show connexions which can extend very far. A Conservative prime minister can have a dozen MPs, a good number of peers, and several heads of financial houses among his 'family'.

Family connexions are essential to this tightly knit structure. The education network provided by the public schools is also of extreme importance. In the same sectors of society, Conservative party, finance, Foreign Office, to some extent the services, those who went to public schools are at considerable advantage and those who went to the best public schools have the best chance of all. An analysis of C. S. Wilson and T. Lupton conducted in the 1950s showed that Eton produced 30 per cent of Conservative ministers, of the directors of large banks, of the directors of City firms, of the directors of insurance companies. Eton and five other schools (Winchester, Harrow, Rugby, Charterhouse, Marlborough) produced between two-fifths and half of the holders of these posts.

In a formal definition, the ruling circle, if not perhaps the ruling class, is bound to exist everywhere; in a more specific analysis of British society, the 'establishment' also exists, because families and schools crystallize traditions and enable contacts to take place.

Three characteristics, as we said, are necessary to a 'ruling circle' if it is to have real political power. It must have unity of purpose, it must permanently have power, it must be able to rule in the strong sense of the word. The establishment and its inner circle seem to have the first of these three characteristics, although probably not so much because it is an establishment with an inner circle, but because it belongs to the wider group of the middle classes. Particularly if we define it as being concentrated in the leadership of the Conservative party, in financial houses, and in traditional business groups, this inner circle clearly has a certain unity of doctrine. It is conservative-minded. It wants to preserve the social system more or less as it is. It does not want to introduce reforms, except on a small scale and piecemeal.

(J. Blondel, *Voters, Parties and Leaders*, Harmondsworth, Penguin, 1969)

(*Note*: This 1969 extract should also be compared with that from The *Changing Anatomy of Britain* (p. 150) and other evidence from section 11.1)

The background of MPs

More (66 per cent) Labour MPs had attended university than ever before; when the party last (barely) won a Commons majority in 1974 the figure was 57 per cent. The percentage of Conservative MPs educated at university – at 81 per cent – had also never been higher. The public schools also continued to shape the parties in contrasting ways. They provide two-thirds of Conservative MPs; two-fifths of the Liberal Democrats and about one-sixth of the PLP. This latter figure has fluctuated little over the past six elections, and no appreciable difference was made by the scale of Labour's victory, the proportion of public school products in the new intake being the same as in the PLP as a whole, and most of the new public school-educated MPs clustered in the more winnable seats.

On the other hand, the lowest ever number of Old Etonians were returned at the election, 18, of whom 15 are Conservative, 2 and Labour and 1 is Liberal Democrat. Thirty-four Etonians had been elected to the Conservative benches in 1992, of whom 12 retired in 1997 and 10 more were defeated. The new intake of 41 Conservative MPs contained only three Etonians. The 15 Etonian Conservative MPs represent only 9 per cent of all Conservative MPs compared with proportions of 10 per cent in 1992, 11 per cent in 1987, 12 per cent in 1983, 15 per cent in 1979, 18 per cent in 1974 and 20 per cent in 1959. The year with which 1997 invites comparison is 1945, when the Conservatives also suffered a landslide defeat which pushed them back into their safest seats. On that occasion 29 per cent of all Conservative MPs were Etonians. It says much for the transformed social background of the party that even when reduced to its safest seats in 1997, the Etonian rump continued to erode. All traces of Harrow School were lost to the House; 5 of the 7 Harrovians elected in 1992 retired, the remaining 2 were defeated. Of the 25 unelected Etonian and Harrovian Conservative candidates only 8 were young men on their way up as distinct from older men or defeated MPs on their way out.

One downward trend that has taken a precipitous turn is the percentage of Labour MPs drawn from manual working backgrounds. At 13 per cent, this is the lowest percentage ever. When Labour last won an election (with 319 MPs in October 1974), 28 per cent of the PLP came from manual occupations, and even if allowance is made for the fact that some former manual workers are hidden elsewhere in the table – notably among the ranks of the trade union officials – the figure is still very low.

(David Butler and Dennis Kavanagh. *The British General Election of 1997*, London, Macmillan, 1997)

24.2 Democratic government

Democracy is literally 'government by the people'. A direct democracy would be a state in which everyone took a direct part in running the country by public meetings or holding 'referendums' on every issue. A referendum is a ballot in which everyone has an opportunity to express their opinion, as happened in Britain in 1975 to decide whether we should join the European Economic Community (EEC, now EU), and in Wales and Scotland (1997) to see whether the majority in those countries wished to have some form of local parliament. In ancient Greek city states, decisions were reached by public meetings of all 'citizens', but this did not include women or slaves!

Table 24.1 Occupation of candidates 1997 General Election

	Labour		Conservative		Liberal Democrat	
	elected	defeated	elected	defeated	elected	defeated
Professions						
Barrister	12	7	20	47	4	6
Solicitor	17	11	9	41	2	27
Doctor/dentist/ optician	3	2	2	4	4	11
Architect/surveyor	–	–	2	9	–	7
Civil/chartered Engineer	3	2	–	4	1	10
Accountant	2	2	3	24	1	26
Civil Service/local government	30	19	5	7	2	28
Armed services	–	–	9	10	1	11
Teachers: University	22	4	1	3	2	19
Polytech/college	35	17	–	2	1	19
School	54	37	7	19	4	85
Other consultancies	3	4	2	1	1	10
Scientific/research	7	2	1	2	–	7
TOTAL	188	107	61	173	23	266
	(45%)	(48%)	(37%)	(36%)	(50%)	(45%)
Business						
Company Director	7	3	17	51	2	25
Company executive	9	13	36	90	7	66
Commerce/insurance	2	9	7	33	1	39
Management/clerical	15	8	1	15	1	30
General business	4	7	4	22	–	41
TOTAL	37	40	65	211	11	201
	(9%)	(18%)	(39%)	(44%)	(24%)	(34%)
Miscellaneous						
Miscellaneous white collar	69	29	2	16	1	57
Politician/political organiser	40	9	15	20	5	13
Publisher/journalist	29	10	14	27	4	18
Farmer	1	2	5	13	1	7
Housewife	–	–	2	4	–	9
Student	–	4	–	2	–	8
TOTAL	139	54	38	82	11	112
	(33%)	(24%)	(23%)	(17%)	(24%)	(19%)
Manual workers						
Miner	12	–	1	–	–	–
Skilled worker	40	20	–	9	1	14
Semi/unskilled	2	–	–	–	–	–
TOTAL	54	20	1	9	1	14
	(13%)	(9%)	(1%)	(2%)	(2%)	(2%)
GRAND TOTAL	418	221	165	475	46	593

Source: *The British General Election of 1997*, David Butler and Dennis Kavanagh, Macmillan, 1997.

Can there be a perfect democracy?

In fact, there has never been a perfect democracy although many countries claim the title; Rhodesia prior to 1979 claimed to be a democracy although only whites were permitted to vote. East Germany prior to unification with the West called itself the 'German Democratic Republic' (GDR), although only political parties of a communist variety under a 'National Front' banner were permitted; the GDR sought to justify their title by claiming that 99.86 per cent of the electorate voted for the National Front in 1976! (This communist-based National Front is not to be confused with the British 'National Front' which has Fascist overtones.)

Parliamentary democracy

Direct democracy would clearly be impossible in a country as large as Britain so it operates a system of representation – parliamentary democracy; in 1800 this meant that 3 per cent of the population were entitled to vote. Since 1969 every man and woman over the age of eighteen who is not disqualified by reason of lunacy, felony or being a peer of the realm is entitled to vote.

Government 'by the people'

'Democracy' however involves more than just the right to vote. In a democratic situation, it must be possible to say what you like (usually with certain restrictions to protect minorities and the innocent from the malicious); to be allowed freedom of association; and to be free from physical restriction without due cause. It might also be claimed that all sides in an argument must have access to the same level of resources, both monetary and media; this last is a particularly difficult criterion to achieve.

Government 'by the people' is usually interpreted as meaning by the majority of the people, and yet few people would be prepared to accept the tyranny of the majority as democratic. For example, since its creation Northern Ireland has had a permanent majority of 60 per cent in favour of unity with England, and an equally permanent 40 per cent who want union with the rest of Ireland (although population projections are likely to alter these proportions in the future.) For many years the minority felt that the majority were depriving them of equal opportunities in such areas as housing and employment and this frustration was a major contributory factor in the outbreak of terrorism.

Is Britain a democracy?

Britain aspires to be a democracy but it is claimed that the press is owned by people with similar political views who are generally biased towards one political party; that the Civil Service presents only the facts that it chooses to select for ministerial decision; that the non-elected trade unions have an undue influence on political decisions; that political parties do not have equal resources to present their viewpoints; and that Governments are not elected by a majority of the people.

Power in Britain

The stability of parliamentary democracy in Britain has removed the need for direct military involvement in politics, except on rare occasions when instructed by the civil authorities to take action. Such stability allows the military to retain its traditional role in reserve, ready to repel external aggression and ready to assist the police in the maintenance of internal law and order as, for example, in Northern Ireland.

It is only in times of war and occasional civil unrest that military power is of great relevance in the advanced countries, but the possibility of the military defending the civil order adds strength to a political system.

In addition to these three centres of power – political, economic and military – other institutions exert great influence and also have some degree of power. The education system acts to spread knowledge and to train young minds, and, to a considerable extent, to ensure conformity. With the mass media, the education system controls the flow of ideas and information we consider. This gives them great control over what ideas and information are seen as legitimate. Organized religion still exerts some power, and much authority, though over a declining proportion of the population. Pronouncements of leading churchmen are still of great importance and are widely reported.

Leading members of the judiciary have both great power and authority, for their pronouncements are also listened to with interest and are presented as authoritative. Once again it becomes clear that one cannot point to one group of people and say 'they alone have power'. In Britain power seems to be spread among many people . . . This has led some people to argue that Britain remains democratic and stable because no one group or individual has overwhelming power – there is a constant competition between power groups which prevents one group from dominating, power is diffused throughout the political system. Another view holds that the competing groups do so on unequal terms – some are able to dominate others and to impose their wills on other groups. A third argument is that most of these people in positions of power share common backgrounds and beliefs and form one, not many groups – a ruling class. This approach implies that the beliefs which hold our leaders together are stronger than their differences. Each of these approaches has strong political implications – the first tends to be supported by conservatives – those people who support the present system whatever political party they belong to. The last view tends to be that of the 'extreme' left, whose members are highly critical of the present system. The second view can be embraced by those who hold both types of political view at various times.

(A. Renwick and I. Swinburn, *Basic Political Concepts*, 1980)

24.3 The British system of government

The method of election

- More people have voted against the political party that has formed the Government in Britain than have voted in favour at every General Election since 1945; even in the Labour 'landslide' of 1997, the winning party received only 43.2 per cent of the total vote, despite achieving a majority of 179.
- In reality this 'landslide' was a result of the electoral system – in 1964 Harold Wilson's Labour victory was achieved with a similar percentage vote (43.4 per cent), but this produced a majority of only four seats.
- Even more bizarre was the result in 1951 when the Conservatives actually formed the government even although the Labour Party received more votes, while in 1974 (February) the opposite was the case (see Table 24.6).

Table 24.2   Votes cast in the General Elections of 1997 and 1992, Great Britain

Party	Votes cast		Number of MPs	
	1997	**1992**	**1997**	**1992**
Conservative	9,660,943	14,231,884	165	336
Labour	13,518,167	11,169,306	271	209
Lib Dem	5,242,947	6,083,667	46	20
Scot Nat/Plaid Cymru	782,580	783,991	19	7

Table 24.3   Votes cast in the General Elections of 1997 and 1992, Northern Ireland

Party	MPs elected		Change
	1997	**1992**	
United Ulster Unionist	9	9	0
Democratic Unionist	2	3	−1
UK Unionist*	1	1	0
Alliance	0	0	0
Social and Dem Labour	3	4	−1
Sinn Fein	3	0	+3

Notes:
* 1992 = Popular Unionist.
The major mainland parties do not contest seats in Northern Ireland. The Alliance is the only non-sectarian party, but its support tends to be spread so that despite polling more than 20 per cent in three constituencies, it won no seats.

Table 24.4   Total number of MPs in the General Election of 1997*

Party	No.
Conservative	165
Labour	418
Liberal Democrat	46
Scottish and Welsh Nationalists	10
NI Unionists	12
NI Nationalists	6
Speaker	1
Independent**	1
TOTAL	659

Notes:
* See p. 377 for results for 2001.
** Martin Bell running on an 'anti-sleaze' ticket.
NI = Northern Ireland.

- In 1974 the Liberal Party received 6 million votes and returned fourteen Members to Parliament; the Conservative Party received about 12 million and returned 296 Members; the Labour Party received about a third of a million votes less than the Conservative Party, but won five more seats – and formed the government!
- There has been considerable support in recent years for some kind of *proportional representation* which would more fairly reflect the support for particular political parties (see Figure 24.2 and Table 24.5).
- In 1997 Labour benefited enormously from the 'first-past-the-post' system because its vote was more evenly spread than it had been in the past, when many of its votes were 'wasted' by huge majorities in its industrial heartlands.

The Liberal Democrats in 1997, by contrast with the past, tended to concentrate their votes in winnable seats, notably in the South-west, and despite receiving fewer votes than in the three previous General Elections won considerably more seats (Table 24.5).

Proportional representation and its consequences for British politics

The Jenkins Commission was set up to address the fact that while there was, according to polls, majority support for a change in the voting system, there was no agreement among supporters of reform about which of the many varieties of PR we should adopt. The Commission's report (October 1998) recommended a system which deliberately, and in my view wisely, preserved at this stage the patchwork quilt of constituencies, each represented by a single MP.

There were, however, two key differences from the current system. First, the constituency MPs would each be elected by a preferential

Table 24.5 Liberal performance, 1974–97

General Election	Votes	% share of poll	Seats won
1974(Feb.)	6,058,744	19.3	14
1974(Oct.)	5,346,754	18.3	13
1979	4,313,804	13.8	11
1983	7,780,949	25.4	23
1987	7,341,290	22.6	22
1992	5,999,384	17.8	20
1997	5,042,947	16.8	46

Note:

* Prior to 1983 Liberals; 1983–7 Alliance (Liberals + SDP); 1992 onwards Liberal Democrats.

voting system. Rather than placing a single 'X' you would vote '1' for your first-preference candidate, '2' for your second preference, and so on. This eliminates the need for tactical voting and allows people to vote for who they really want. Voters would say, in effect, 'If my favourite candidate stands no chance of winning, give my vote to my second choice instead.'

The second key change was to reduce the number of constituencies and compensate by providing top-up MPs in each city or county. Instead of having 10 constituencies in Leicestershire you would have eight, with a further two MPs representing the whole county. They would be elected in such a way that the balance of party representation would better reflect the balance of the electorate's votes. This system, an amalgam of the alternative vote (AV) system and the additional member system, is called AV plus. It is the only system of PR now on the table at Westminster and will be put to the British people in a referendum.

How would we see a difference under PR? We are already beginning to see a difference in Scotland. PR means that parties have to campaign equally hard everywhere rather than in just a few marginal seats. In 1977, according to David Butler and Dennis Kavanagh, 'Conservative and Labour headquarters focused their efforts on almost identical lists of the 90–100 seats where the election would be decided.' That left 550 seats where the election was not going to be decided.

Under the current first-past-the-post system it is not necessary for an election candidate to appeal to a majority of electors. A candidate opposed by well over half the electorate can still win if the opponents' votes are evenly split. It is even possible for a candidate to win with a quarter of the vote. Preferential voting would end this. It would force candidates to broaden their appeal rather than rely on electoral arithmetic because, in order to win, they would need the support of a majority of their electors. It

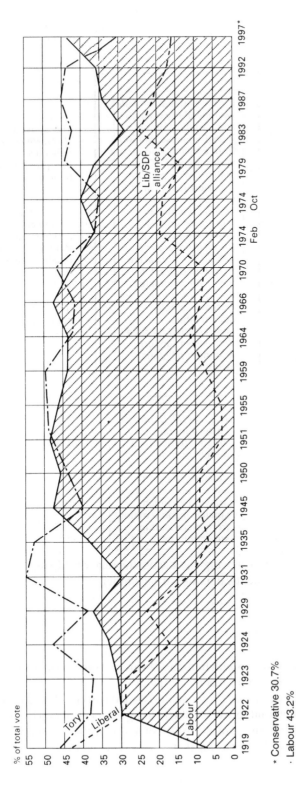

% of total vote

* Conservative 30.7%
· Labour 43.2%
Liberal Democrat 16.8%
· Note:
* Some analysis may include the speaker, thus increasing this percentage slightly.

Figure 24.1   The popular vote at all elections since 1918

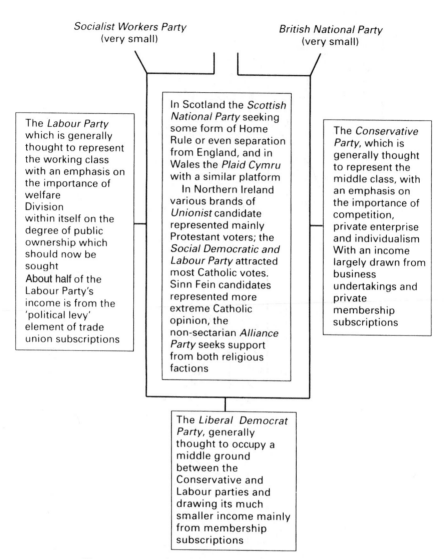

Socialist Workers Party
(very small)

British National Party
(very small)

The *Labour Party* which is generally thought to represent the working class with an emphasis on the importance of welfare
Division within itself on the degree of public ownership which should now be sought
About half of the Labour Party's income is from the 'political levy' element of trade union subscriptions

In Scotland the *Scottish National Party* seeking some form of Home Rule or even separation from England, and in Wales the *Plaid Cymru* with a similar platform
In Northern Ireland various brands of *Unionist* candidate represented mainly Protestant voters; the *Social Democratic and Labour Party* attracted most Catholic votes. Sinn Fein candidates represented more extreme Catholic opinion, the non-sectarian *Alliance Party* seeks support from both religious factions

The *Conservative Party*, which is generally thought to represent the middle class, with an emphasis on the importance of competition, private enterprise and individualism
With an income largely drawn from business undertakings and private membership subscriptions

The *Liberal Democrat Party*, generally thought to occupy a middle ground between the Conservative and Labour parties and drawing its much smaller income mainly from membership subscriptions

Figure 24.2　Left wing–right wing: the relationship of political parties to each other

would allow electors to vote with both their heart and their head where they are now often forced to choose between the two.

To give an example: a Labour voter on the Isle of Wight could contribute to Tony Blair's total national vote while also helping the local Liberal Democrat to defeat the Tory. Supporters of all parties could vote with conviction for the party of their choice while ensuring their vote was not wasted.

Combating apathy

An increasing number of people feel their vote is being wasted under our current system, so fewer people are bothering to vote – only one in three in last year's local council elections. At the last general election the turnout was 75%, the lowest since the war. One of the main factors determining how many people vote in a given constituency is marginality. If people think their vote may matter, they are more likely to use it. One study estimated that if every seat had been marginal in 1997 it is probable that 750,000 more people would have voted. PR would make most seats marginal, if not at constituency level than certainly for the top-up MPs.

Another way in which PR would reduce political apathy would be by increasing the diversity of candidates. Our Parliament remains predominantly a white, Anglo-Saxon, Protestant, male affair which nowhere near adequately reflects the nature of society. Where it has been introduced elsewhere, PR has helped parliaments to reflect the nations they are supposed to represent.

The most fundamental representative function of any parliament is to reflect accurately how the electorate have cast their votes and thus the balance of views in the country. Our current system fails even at this. It provides not for majority government but for government by a minority with untrammelled power, and it does not always confer this power on the biggest minority. In 1951 Labour won what remains their highest-ever share of the vote, 230,000 more than the Tories at the same election, yet the Tories won 26 more seats and stayed in power for 13 years.

First-past-the-post cannot be relied on to produce a result that reflects the wishes of voters. By making all votes count, PR would change this. It would give a party majority government only when that party enjoyed majority support or an overwhelming lead over its opponents. The Jenkins system would have given majorities to Tony Blair and Margaret Thatcher but not to John Major. However, it would not have given Blair and Thatcher the artificially huge majorities they received from first-past-the-post.

Powerful opposition

PR would ensure a strong opposition, something that is particularly relevant to local government. In the London Borough of Newham every seat is held by Labour even though they won little more than half the votes at the last local elections. Huge majorities cause complacency and undermine accountability, sometimes even leading to corruption. When allegations of wrongdoing by Doncaster councillors first came to light, Labour had a majority of 53 on the council; the combined opposition ranks numbered only five. The Prime Minister has said that he wants to clean up local government. This is good, but it will be far better done by voters than by any number of Whitehall hit-squads and centralised disinfection schemes and PR is the best way to give voters the tools to do the job.

In addition, PR would eliminate the situation where a party is penalised because its support is spread across a wide area rather than concentrated in the one place. In the 1992 general election the Scottish Nationalists polled six times as many votes as the Welsh Nationalists but won fewer seats because the Welsh Nationalists targeted their efforts more efficiently. At the same election the Tories in Scotland won 17% of the vote and had no MPs while the Liberal Democrats, with 13% of the vote, had 10.

The benefits conferred by the present system on parties which can concentrate their vote form one of the reasons why the political map looks so stark. We have Labour in the North and Tory in the South, Labour towns and Tory countryside. First-past-the-post divides the nation and polarises opinions. It perpetuates the sterility of class-based political battles. The Conservatives are now almost entirely a party of rural England, with no seats in Scotland or Wales. Almost all our great cities are Tory-free zones. I do not weep for that, but I do recognise that it is both unfair and unhealthy for democracy.

The situation arises not from lack of votes but from lack of votes in the right places. While 300,000 people in Wales and 500,000 in Scotland voted Tory, they elected nobody. Only 160,000 people in Dorset voted Tory but they elected all eight of the county's MPs.

Geographical divide

The geographical balance of MPs inevitably has a huge impact on the focus of the party. Parties that are unrepresented in particular areas can lose touch with them and with the issues that matter to them. Labour, with virtually no MPs in the South of England during the 1980s, so lost touch with southern voters that they ruled themselves out of office for 18 years. The Conservatives, with scarcely any MPs in Scotland and Wales in the last Parliament, arrogantly dismissed those nations' legitimate demands for devolution of power and felt able to use them as guinea-pigs for doomed schemes like the poll tax because there was no electoral risk.

This polarisation, which is artificial and damaging, is largely caused by the current voting system.

(From a speech by Paddy Ashdown, then leader of the Liberal Democrats, *RSA Journal*, 2 April 1999)

- In Scotland in 1997 the Conservatives obtained 17.5 per cent of the vote but obtained no MPs at all, while the Liberals with only 12.5 per cent obtained ten seats. Ironically the Conservatives, who are now most damaged by the 'first-past-the-post' system, continue to support it; the Liberals who have not been so affected oppose it most; and the Labour Party which has now benefited most had agreed to a referendum on proportional representation prior to the last election.

Choice of candidates

However the method of election is only one limitation on democracy in Britain. People at elections usually only have a choice between three or four political party nominees: these nominees themselves have been chosen from a limited number of people by a handful of party activists in the constituencies, so that MPs are chosen partially by election but also by selection. Although all party members do not participate in the selection of prospective parliamentary candidates even the number of individual party members in all parties is comparatively small. Some constituencies have only a handful of members for even the two major parties.

Women and ethnic minorities

An additional criticism is that although women make up over half the electorate, only 120 were elected in 1997 (18 per cent of the House) – however this was exactly double the number in 1992. 101 of the women elected were Labour (dubbed 'Blair's Babes' by the popular press) and many were elected for seats previously not thought to be winnable, and vulnerable in the future.

Similarly, ethnic minorities are underrepresented in Parliament; four black or asian MPs were elected in 1987, five in 1992 and nine in 1997. All were Labour, the one Asian Conservative seat being lost; The Liberal Democrats fielded the most ethnic minority candidates in 1997 (19) but none in winnable seats.

Election funds

Financially there is considerable difference between the parties. For example in 1996–7, in the run-up to the General Election, Labour claimed to have spent £13 million from central party funds, the Conservatives £20 million and the Liberal Democrats £0.70 million. Exceptionally the greatest amount spent on press advertising was by the new Referendum Party, campaigning on a referendum on the future of British membership of the European Community, which spent almost £7 million, contested over 80 per cent of constituencies, and won no seats, although it may have been responsible for the Conservatives losing a few (Table 24.6). From 2001 a limit has been set on expenditure by political parties during a General Election campaign; initially this has been set at £30 K per seat fought, although some parties will continue to spend less than this.

In 1974, R. Rose commented on the degree of democracy in Britain: 'The mechanics of the electoral system determine how a person's vote is counted,

Table 24.6   Party spending on advertising, 1996–7

	Press 1996/7 inc. VAT (£)	Posters 1996/7 inc. VAT (£)	Grand total 1996/7 inc. VAT (£)
Conservative Central Office	2,258,000	10,925,000	13,183,000
Referendum Party	6,768,000	440,000	7,208,000
Entrepreneurs for a Booming Britain	868,000		868,000
Paul Sykes	827,000		827,000
Labour	1,481,000	5,905,000	7,386,000
Unison	1,112,000		1,112,000

Source: David Butler and Dennis Kavanagh. *The British General Election* of *1997* (London: Macmillan, 1997).

social characteristics affect how his vote is cast, and decisions of those who run the parties determine for whom he can vote' (*Politics in England Today*). These comments remain valid today.

Democracy and the two-party system 1979 and 1997 compared

The basic British doctrine of the absolute supremacy of Parliament also came under challenge. Obviously the idea that no Parliament can pass an act that binds its successor was hardly compatible with Common Market rules, or with the proposals for devolution. Another new challenge to parliamentary supremacy came with the 1975 referendum on the Common Market, and the 1979 referendums on Scottish and Welsh devolution. Although these referendums were advisory only, they did represent a substantial derogation from the idea that the decision of parliament was final. It is hardly conceivable that parliament would ever reverse a clear-cut referendum verdict. The most obvious threat to the established certainties of British government came with the decline of the two-party system . . . Ulster loyalists and Scottish Nationalists accounted for most of the growth in third party MPs, while English Liberals accounted for most of the growth in third party votes.

Because of this development, doubts arose about the first-past-the-post electoral system which used to be as totally accepted as the two-party system in parliament. The snags in the voting system (particularly its unfairness on the Liberals) were thought to be a small price to pay for the responsible one-party governments it produced. Under the winner-take-all system the major parties secured full power for some of the time and full powerlessness for some of the time, instead of suffering the compromises of coalition.

(David Butler and Dennis Kavanagh, *The British General Election of 1979*, London, Macmillan, 1980, adapted)

'A Labour landslide?'

As we noted at the beginning, the impression that the 1997 election constituted a Labour landslide was very much a result of the operation of the electoral system. If the change in each party's share of the vote in each constituency had been the same as it was across the country as a whole, then Labour's majority would have been 131 rather than 179, and the Liberal Democrats would only have won 28 seats rather than their actual tally of 46. The Conservatives were the clear losers, winning no less than 43 seats fewer than they might otherwise have expected.

Moreover, this unfavourable treatment of the Conservatives came after the electoral system had already exhibited a considerable pre-Labour bias in the 1992 general election, giving the Conservatives an overall majority of only 21 despite having nearly an eight-point lead in votes. True, the boundary review had removed some of the bias against the Conservatives caused by out-of-date boundaries, but it still left Labour needing a lower share of the vote to secure an overall majority than did the Conservatives. So how was it possible for the system to have made the Conservatives' plight even worse in 1997?

One possibility might be that the first-past-the-post system has regained some or all of the ability it used to have to exaggerate the lead of the largest party over the second party, an ability that it almost lost completely in the 1970s and 1980s. After all, we have seen that the Conservative vote fell less in seats where they were previously strong, whereas until 1992 at least the party had always performed best in those parts of the country where it had previously been strongest. The 1997 pattern is precisely what would be required to increase the number of seats that are marginal between Conservative and Labour and thus increase the bonus the system gives to the winning party.

Above all, if Labour's large majority were primarily the result of a restoration of the 'winner's bonus', then we should be able to demonstrate that the Conservatives would have won an equally large majority if they had been as far ahead in votes as Labour actually were. In fact nothing could be further from the truth. If we assume that such a lead were achieved as a result of a uniform swing from the 1997 result, then the Conservatives would only secure a majority of 45. Labour's large majority was a reflection of a major bias in the electoral system in its favour, and is not an indication of a significant restoration of the winner's bonus.

Three benchmarks illustrate the degree of bias quite vividly. First, if the two parties were to have the same share of the vote, Labour would still be 79 ahead of the Conservatives in terms of seats. Second, in order to match Labour in terms of seats, the Conservatives need to be as much as 6.7 per cent ahead in votes. Third, Labour could still secure an overall majority even if they were as much as 1.5 per cent behind the Conservatives in votes; the Conservatives in contrast need a lead of ten points just to secure the same target. Never has the electoral system exhibited such a strong bias in favour of one of the two largest parties *vis-à-vis* the other. On this basis the only post-war elections that would have seen the Conservatives win an overall majority would have been those of 1983 and 1987.

Why has the system become so biased against the Conservatives? And can we necessarily assume that it will remain so biased in future? Two factors lie behind the bias. In part the explanation lies in the fact that fewer votes are cast in constituencies where Labour is strong than where the Conservatives are strong. But, more important is the fact that the Labour and the Liberal Democrat vote has become more effectively distributed, while at the same time the Conservatives' own support has become less efficiently dispersed.

(David Butler and Dennis Kavanagh, *The British General Election* of *1997*, London, Macmillan)

24.4 Political parties

There are now three main political parties in England with elected Members of Parliament:

- The *Conservative Party*, which has generally been thought to represent the middle class, with an emphasis on the importance of competition, private enterprise and individualism, with an income largely drawn from business undertakings and private membership subscriptions.
- The *Labour Party*, which has generally been thought to represent the working class, with an emphasis on the importance of welfare, New Labour having effectively abandoned any notion of extending public ownership. Over three-quarters of the Labour Party's income has come from the 'political levy' element of trade union subscriptions, but between 1986 and 1996 Union contributions declined to some half of the total, with private business making up the rest as Labour successfully appealed to the middle class vote.
- The *Liberal Democrat Party*, generally thought to occupy a middle ground between the Conservative and Labour parties and drawing its much smaller income mainly from membership subscriptions.

These outlines are of course very crude and would be hotly contested by some party members. However, they probably fairly represent what most of the electorate believe to be the position; although the reality is that in the 1983/1987 and 1992 General Elections more skilled manual workers voted Conservative than Labour, and in the 1997 General Election Labour could not have won without a substantial share of the middle class vote. This 'class de-alignment' is a to be expected response to the changes in the occupational structure; changes to working class cultural patterns; changes in consumption and increased geographical mobility outlined in other sections.

There is, in addition to the three major parties, a host of minor – often extreme – parties, none of which has any Members of Parliament (Table 24.7). These parties include the British National Party and the Socialist Labour Party.

However the Green Party has won a seat in the European Parliament which is elected by proportional representation with large constituencies.

In Northern Ireland various brands of Unionist candidate represented mainly Protestant voters; The Social Democrat and Labour Party together with Sinn Fein

Table 24.7 Minor parties in the General Election of 1997

Party	Average % vote per candidate	Number of candidates
Referendum	3.1	547
UK Independence	1.2	194
Green	1.4	95
Socialist Labour	1.7	64
Liberal (i.e. NOT Lib Dem)	1.8	54
British National	1.3	57
Natural Law	0.7	196
Pro Life Alliance	0.7	53

Notes: Most candidates lost their deposits including 54 BNP, all Natural Law, Green and Pro Life Alliance.

In Northern Ireland various brands of Unionist candidate represented mainly Protestant voters; The Social Democrat and Labour Party together with Sinn Fein attracted most Catholic votes, while the non-sectarian Alliance Party continued to fail to have a candidate elected.

Each party will try to persuade electors to vote for them

attracted most Catholic votes, while the non-sectarian Alliance Party continued to fail to have a candidate elected.

REVISION SUMMARY

Is Britain a democracy?

Democratic features

- Most people over eighteen can vote for a representative to the House of Commons (except peers or those disqualified as a result of felony or insanity).
- The majority party in this elected chamber normally forms the government.
- Voting is by secret ballot (since 1872)
- Anyone can stand for Parliament if he or she can put up a small deposit and find a small number of electors to nominate him or her.
- There are strict rules regulating arrest and detention (e.g. the Police and Criminal Evidence Act of 1984 limits detention without charge to 24 hours, or 96 for a serious offence with the approval of a court).
- You can say and write what you like, provided that it is not obscene, slanderous or libellous, blasphemous or likely to incite to racial hatred.
- You can 'associate' with whom you like – (i.e. join any group, provided that it is not criminal). There are certain restrictions on political involvement by civil servants.
- In 2000 the European Convention of Human Rights was incorporated into British law. Variously described as 'the greatest advance for personal liberty since the 1688 Bill of Rights' and 'a crackpots charter', it immediately led to the dismissal of 126 temporary Sheriffs in Scotland (equivalent to magistrates in England) as they were appointed by the public prosecutor and so their impartiality could be challenged. This could lead to judges being appointed by an independent commission rather than by secret 'soundings' of existing judges as is presently the case.

Undemocratic features

- Unequal access to resources (e.g. financial, media). For example, Sir James Goldsmith pledged £10 million to the Referendum Party opposed to a 'Federal Europe', and over £7 million was spent in the 1997 election without success. On the other hand in the referendum campaign to decide whether or not Britain should join the European Economic Community £1,481,583 was spent by those campaigning in favour of entry and £133,630 by the opponents of entry. F. Parkin, in *Class Inequality and Political Order* (1972), stated that genuine political equality is impossible unless contestants enjoy roughly similar economic and social status.
- The voting system results in governments which represent only a minority of electors.

- Selection of prospective parliamentary candidates for the national political parties is by small unelected groups in the constituencies (independents have little chance of election).
- The second chamber is not elected (the House of Lords) – despite reform in 1999 – still consists of some hereditary peers, life peers (nominated by successive governments) and some bishops. Although it cannot now prevent legislation in the long term, it can have considerable influence.
- The Monarch is hereditary.

The British system of government

Simple majority system of election

Advantages
- Likely to result in one party having a majority in the House of Commons, leading to 'strong' government.
- Any other system will lead to 'bargaining' on legislation – may result in small groups having an influence out of all proportion to their support in the country.
- One fairly small constituency per Member, leading to personal contact between Member and electorate.
- Quick, and simple to understand.

Disadvantages
- Unrepresentative: governments represent a minority.
- May lead to 'elected dictatorship' by Prime Minister during term of office.
- Little opportunity for smaller groups to have representative elected: people unlikely to vote for them ('wasted vote').
- Encourages 'adversary politics' – rather than encouraging parties to seek points of agreement.

Alternatives to simple majority system (see Table 24.8)

- **Alternative vote.** Voters put candidates in order of preference; bottom candidate eliminated and votes redistributed to next preference until a candidate has a majority (e.g. Australia). Keeps small, single-member constituencies and gets rid of the 'wasted vote' argument. Not completely 'proportional'.
- **Second ballot.** If no candidate has an absolute majority there is a second ballot for those receiving more than 10 per cent of the votes; the leading candidate then wins (e.g. France). Keeps small, single-member constituencies and gets rid of the 'wasted vote' argument. Not completely 'proportional'.
- **Party list.** Vote is from lists of candidates prepared by political parties; seats are distributed in proportion to votes cast for each party (e.g. Italy). Gives completely proportional results, but you have to vote for a party, and the way the lists are constructed will influence the result (i.e. those at the top have more chance of election).

Table 24.8 The result of the General Election of 1997 under different electional systems (estimated)

	First Alternative past post vote		Single transferable vote in		Additional member system 75%–50%		Party list system
			Small seats	Large seats			
Con	165	103	193	195	196	207	208
Lab	419	436	340	317	326	303	300
Lib Dem	46	91	89	110	104	111	113
Others[1]	29	29	35	37	33	38	38

Note:
[1] Others include eighteen seats elected in Northern Ireland.
Source: The British General Election of 1997, David Butler and Dennis Kavanagh, Macmillan Press, Ltd, 1997.

- **Single transferable vote.** Multi-member constituencies. A quota for election is fixed (votes cast divided by the number of seats + 1). Voters put candidates in order of preference. Those achieving quota on first preferences elected; surplus transferred to the voters' second choice, etc. until all seats are filled (e.g. Irish Republic). Gives completely proportional result. Constituencies smaller than under 'party list' system.

■⌄ **25** Pressure and interest groups

25.1 Different types of pressure groups

Pressure or **'interest' groups** are groups of people who are in association because they have a common interest; and who use whatever power is available as a result of their unity of interest to put pressure on other agencies to have their views adopted.

The agencies most likely to be able to influence events are central and local government, or agencies connected with these (for example, the Civil Service or a Local Education Authority). However, multinational corporations, the Churches or any other policy-making or decision-taking body may be subject to the activities of pressure groups, or they may themselves become pressure groups and try and influence other agencies.

Classification of pressure groups

- Pressure groups are often classified into two types: 'sectional' groups, which seek to protect or promote the interest of their members or some other specified group of people as their major function and 'promotional' groups, which seek to achieve particular changes or to fight specific issues.
- 'Sectional' groups are sometimes called 'protective' groups because they are mainly concerned with protecting the sectional interests of individuals (often their own members). They include such organisations as the trade unions; the Confederation of British Industry (CBI); professional associations such as the British Medical Association (BMA); and a variety of organisations set up to help specific groups of people such as Help the Aged, or the NSPCC.
- Many of these groups have been so successful in persuading policy-makers that their views should be heeded that it has become a constitutional convention for the government to consult them before introducing legislation that might affect their interests.
- 'Promotional' groups seek to promote a cause of some kind. The cause may be quite limited in its objective (for example, the Abortion Law Reform Association was founded in 1936 with the objective of legalising abortion and was successful in 1967) or more general, (for example, the Viewers and Listeners Association set up by Mrs Mary Whitehouse to try and reduce the element of sex and violence in the media). A myriad of such promotional

groups exist (sometimes very briefly) to obtain a zebra crossing outside a school, to stop an airport being extended, to stop trees being cut down to construct a new road or similar local or transitory aims.

- There is no firm boundary between 'sectional' and 'promotional' groups. Often sectional groups will promote a particular cause – the Ramblers Association may fight to protect a footpath from closure or the Royal Automobile Club may oppose legislation that insists upon the wearing of seat belts.

- Sometimes pressure groups are divided somewhat differently into economic interest groups and non-economic interest groups such as Oxfam or the Churches. Economic interest groups are also often subdivided into (a) the labour lobby, including all trade unions that are members of the TUC, (b) the business lobby, including the Institute of Directors and the CBI and (c) the professional lobby, including organisations representing lawyers, teachers, doctors and the like.

- In *Pressure Groups, Politics and Democracy in Britain* in 1989, Wyn Grant prefers the terms 'insider' and 'outsider' groups. 'Insider' groups are usually those otherwise described as 'protective', such as Help the Aged, who are usually consulted by government, but may as a result be influenced by it. 'Outsider' groups are usually 'promotional', for example The League Against Cruel Sports.

Grant uses the term 'Prisoner' groups to describe those who are largely funded by government, for example the Arts Council, and who thus will find it difficult to oppose government policies.

Although the extract which follows was written over thirty years ago, it is interesting to note that points made are just as relevant today:

Big business as a pressure group

It is not only that the big firms are large enough to lobby by themselves, it is also that the very structure of business is often an adequate substitute for a formally organized interest group. What is required for interests to defend themselves is not an interest group as such, solely designed for this effect and, as it were, 'registered' as an interest group. What is required is a set of contacts through which a common policy can be defined. Small business has often remained unorganized, and it is largely subjected to the conditions of individual capitalism. Big business, on the contrary, has become more and more integrated, personal connexions link many companies. These connexions are underlined, or caused, by large capital participations of firms in assets of others. Large industrial and financial companies do not need to create ad hoc interest groups: they are already organized into holdings or associated through participations in order to achieve industrial efficiency or to obtain financial support. They can use their own network to exercise pressure on the political and administrative worlds.

The purpose of these remarks is not to overemphasize the influence of business. Moreover, business is not alone in being able to use pre-existing organizations for the purpose of exercising influence. Some cultural organizations, such as the churches or the universities, do exercise pressure in a similar way. They use pre-existing channels and they do not have to create an interest group before being able to lobby the State or its representatives.

The distinction between formally organized groups and informally constituted groupings is very important in practice: it circumscribes the sphere in which the representative principle plays a part and the sphere where there is pressure, but no representative principle, at work.

Interest groups are a means by which the views of the citizens come to be represented. This is why one can and one must, admittedly with the reservations already made, examine whether the views of the rank-and-file are adequately transmitted to the top within interest groups. But among informally organized groupings, in companies, churches, universities, it becomes pointless to start discussing the 'representation' of a rank-and-file. Clearly, even in an organization as hierarchical as the Roman Catholic Church, there are channels through which the views of the rank-and-file are communicated to the top, at any rate if these views are strongly held. This happens even more in a network of companies, despite the principle that those who own or control the majority of the capital can dictate their policy to the whole of the network. Yet this is not representation.

If we want to see, as we do here, whether the representative principle works well in the field of interests, we can therefore look at formally constituted interest groups only. We must not forget, however, that, while looking at representation, we are looking only at a certain number of interests and not at all of them. We must always remember that interest groups are the only means of pressure which wage and salary earners possess, while on the other hand, business, the churches, some other cultural groups, possess other means of influence. Conclusions which are reached about wage and salary earners' organizations should always be put in perspective with the conclusions which can be reached when one examines all the channels by which business can exercise pressure. The realistic comparison is not the one which compares the TUC with the CBI alone, but the one which compares the TUC on the one hand with, on the other hand, the CBI, the City, and other major business organizations.

(J. Blondel, *Voters, Parties and Leaders*, Harmondsworth, Penguin)

25.2 Advantages of pressure groups

The view is sometimes expressed that pressure groups are a fundamental part of the democratic process. They give the individual an opportunity to participate directly in the processes of government, and to influence the 'élites' who have power in industry or elsewhere.

In the British system of government, particularly when governments have absolute majorities in the House of Commons, as has generally been the case since 1945, the ruling party is safely in power for several years and pressure groups are an important part of the process of debate and opposition between elections. S. Finer in 1958 wrote the definitive book on pressure groups *Anonymous Empire*, and suggested that pressure groups provided a useful service in that they let ministers and civil servants know how people feel: 'Anger, contempt, or pleasure, expressed at first hand, are a valuable corrective to the bald facts of the case in an office file'.

25.3 Disadvantages of pressure groups

However, Professor Finer also expressed reservations about the role of pressure groups. The title of his book, *Anonymous Empire*, gives a clue to his worry: 'the lobbies become – as far as the general public is concerned – faceless, voiceless, unidentifiable; in brief anonymous'. The general public is often shut out from the discussion between pressure groups and policy-makers so that it is not possible to tell what arguments have persuaded the elite concerned to make the decisions it does.

Although most pressure groups, except the trade unions and co-operative societies, claim to be non-political this usually merely means that the organisation concerned is not affiliated to a political party. They may very well take a distinctive political stance which will make support from a particular political party likely. The Institute of Directors states, 'Any enemy of the free enterprise way of life, whatever his political views, is our opponent.' Clearly such a non-elected group might have considerable power behind the scenes but in Finer's words the 'general public is shut out'.

Finer's second criticism of pressure groups is that some groups carry much greater weight and influence than others, without any guarantee of intrinsic superiority. The two major motoring organisations for example campaign for the motorist, but there is no comparable organisation to campaign for the much greater number of pedestrians.

25.4 Methods of operation

Unfair pressure?

Some of the disadvantages of pressure groups are clear from the methods adopted by some of them.

- In 1945–6 the Labour Government wanted to introduce a Public Health Authority with general practitioners on salaries as in hospitals. The British Medical Association (BMA) refused to co-operate, with the result that general practitioners remain as independent operators paid on a formula based mainly on the number of patients registered with them.

- Resistance to the will of an elected government was also successful when the Orange Lodges in the northern province of Ireland prevented, by the threat of armed resistance, six of the nine counties of Ulster from being included in a United Ireland when the Home Rule Bill was introduced in 1912. British Army officers at the main army base in Ireland, many of whom had family or political links with the northern Protestants, threatened to resign their commissions if ordered to fight the Orangemen. The First World War prevented a showdown, but the threat was remembered later and Ireland was partitioned into two states (A. Ryan, *Mutiny at the Curragh*, 1956) and the legacy remains today.
- The campaign that was waged to establish commercial television in 1953 with intense lobbying of Members of Parliament, feature articles by well-known personalities, and an orchestrated flood of letters to the press was described by a former Director of the BBC as 'one of the most deplorable, subversive and shocking actions in British history' (H. Wilson, *Pressure Group*, 1961).
- In 1974, the National Union of Mineworkers was accused of being responsible for the downfall of the Conservative Government as a result of their strike action against the elected government's industrial policy, leading to the *Daily Mail* headline 'Who Governs Britain?' This was subsequently remembered during the miners' strike, ten years later and the government's determination to break that strike.
- In the referendum campaign to decide whether or not Britain should join the European Economic Community £1,481,583 was spent by those campaigning in favour of entry and £133,630 by the opponents of entry.

Some objections to the operation of pressure groups are thus that financial power can influence events unfairly; that non-elected organisations can overcome the will of elected governments by withholding their services; that in the last analysis military power might not be available if a government's policy seriously conflicted with the wishes of military leaders; and that some groups have an undue measure of support in the media.

'Lobbying' and 'sponsoring'

The practice of 'lobbying' MPs has resulting in some writers such as Finer referring to pressure groups as the 'lobby'. The 'lobby' is actually the entrance chamber of the House of Commons, where individuals or groups may request a meeting with a particular Member of Parliament and seek to persuade him, or her, to support their views.

The practice of lobbying is an essentially democratic one but there is more objection to the practice of 'sponsoring' an MP or retaining one as an adviser for a particular institution such as the Police Federation or a business concern. Most trade unions sponsor an MP, this means that they contribute a sum towards the election and other expenses of that person. Parliamentary 'advisers' may receive direct payments.

Supporters of these practices point out that they provide a useful link between real life and the more insulated world of Parliament and that 'the offer of money

Pressure groups can appeal to the emotions of those in power, presenting feelings as well as facts
Animal Rights March, Embankment, London, March 1997

or other advantage to any Member of Parliament for the promoting of any matter whatsoever, depending or to be transacted in Parliament, is a high crime' (Erskine May, *Parliamentary Practice*, 1844).

In 1969 Christopher Mayhew in 'Party Games' had stated 'No MP should be paid to represent any vested interest in Parliament.'

The reality has been somewhat different and evidence that some MPs had accepted 'cash for questions' in the House led to the Nolan Committee being appointed in 1994, 'to examine current concerns about the standards of conduct of all holders of public office, including arrangements relating to financial and commercial activities'. The Nolan Report in 1995 increased the existing rules on MPs declaring earnings and other interests outside Parliament, and this was extended to office holders outside parliament, for example college principals.

A pressure groups in action

An example of a pressure group in operation was the campaign against physical punishment by STOPP (Figure 25.1).

The success of STOPP was achieved in a number of ways, outlined in Figure 25.2.

SOCIETY OF TEACHERS OPPOSED TO PHYSICAL PUNISHMENT

<u>Summer 1986, Vol. 2 No. 3</u>

VICTORY!

STOPP members will know that on 22 July MPs voted for the abolition of corporal punishment for all schoolchildren educated at public expense. After eighteen years of hard campaigning, STOPP has triumphed.

The victory by just one vote – 231 to 230 – followed several weeks of intensive lobbying by STOPP of MPs of all parties. 37 Tories including eight ministers joined the opposition parties in voting for an end to the British practice of beating pupils.

The vote came after a debate lasting over $3\frac{1}{2}$ hours at the Report stage of the Government's Education Bill. The Bill already contained a section outlawing corporal punishment due to the House of Lords vote in April, and the vote was on an amendment to remove abolition from the Bill.

'ABOLITION DAY'

During the debate the Government announced that if abolition succeeded it would come into force on 15 August 1987, the beginning of the next school year but one. This will be 'abolition day'.

STOPP's task is not totally completed – for a start the vast majority of independent school pupils will still not be protected from beating – but the

Figure 25.1 Society of teachers opposed to physical punishment

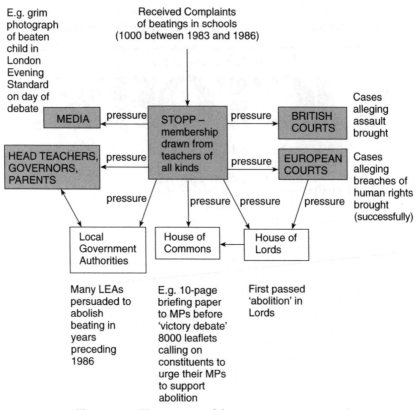

Figure 25.2   How a successful pressure group operated

REVISION SUMMARY

Advantages of pressure groups

- They allow individuals an opportunity to participate directly in government and influence élites.
- They provide a forum for debate and opposition to government between elections.
- They let those in authority know how people really feel.

'Anger, contempt, or pleasure, expressed at first hand, are [sic] a valuable corrective to the bald facts of the case in an office file' (S. Finer, *Anonymous Empire*, 1958).

Disadvantages of pressure groups

- Some groups carry more power because of financial or influential contacts rather than because they have a better case than others.

- Non-elected organisations can overcome the will of elected governments. For example, in 1945–6 the Labour Government wanted to introduce a Public Health Authority with general practitioners on salaries, as in hospitals. The British Medical Association (BMA) refused to co-operate, with the result that general practitioners remain as independent operators paid on a formula based mainly on the number of patients registered with them.
- The general public are 'shut out' from decision-making and do not know how decisions are arrived at.

Some examples of pressure groups

- **Sectional or 'protective' groups.** These are mainly concerned with protecting the interests of that section of the population which they represent. Examples are:
  - Trade unions.
  - CBI.
  - BMA.
  - Help the Aged.
  - NSPCC.
- **Promotional groups.** These promote a cause of some kind. This cause may be limited in its objective, for example:
  - STOPP (successful in 1986).
  - Abortion Law Reform Society (successful in 1967).
  - It may also be **more general**, for example:
  - Viewers and Listeners Association (to try and reduce sex and violence in the media).
  - Liberty (to defend and extend what its members regard as civil liberties).
  The difference may not always be clear – some organisations may fall into both categories as the need arises (e.g. the Catholic Church is an ongoing 'sectional' pressure group but may campaign to 'promote' particular causes such as anti-abortion legislation or free school transport).
- **Economic** interest groups:
  - The labour lobby (e.g. Trade Union Congress and its member trade unions). The business lobby (e.g. the Institute of Directors; the CBI).
  - The professional lobby (e.g. the BMA; National Union of Teachers (NUT); the Bar Council).
- **Non-economic** interest groups:
  - Oxfam.
  - The Church of England.
  - Save the Children.
  - ASH (antismoking)
  - FOREST (pro-smoking).
  - Friends of the Earth (to preserve and protect the environment).
  Of course, some apparently non-economic groups may have economic interests; for example, does the pro-smoking group FOREST receive funds from tobacco manufacturers?

■ ˘ 26 Voting behaviour

26.1 Voting patterns

In 1872 the secret ballot was introduced in British elections, and so we can never be certain how people vote. We obviously know what the support for each political party is in each constituency, and thus we can see that support for the Labour Party is traditionally much higher in the North of England, Wales and Scotland than in the Midlands and Southern England – a pattern that has been described as a 'two-nations' style of voting. Additionally support for the Conservative Party is higher in rural England than it is in industrial centres, regardless of the North–South divide.

J. Vincent in 'Pollbooks: How the Victorians Voted', illustrated that before the secret ballot, voting patterns tended to show that people voted by occupation and religion rather than by class: butchers were predominantly Conservative; grocers were predominantly Liberal; Church of England clergymen were Conservative; Methodists and Catholics were Liberal.

Random sampling surveys developed in the 1950s and although we do not have the detailed knowledge available before the secret ballot, these have permitted scientific surveys of voting patterns to take place.

Do people vote by class as is often supposed? Are women more likely than men to vote for a particular political party? What influence has age or religion on voting patterns?

26.2 The influence of social class and ethnic origin

Class

- The influence of class on voting patterns has aroused considerable interest in that there has been a presumed identity of interest between the Labour Party and the 'working class' and between the Conservative Party and the 'middle class'; yet the Conservative Party has held power for a much longer period overall than the Labour Party since 1945, despite the fact that during that period the Census returns show more working-class people in the population:
- Working class support for the Conservatives increased in 1987 and 1992, and by 1992 skilled manual workers (C2) were more likely to vote Conservative than Labour, although this support decreased, along with electoral support

generally, in 1997. In the 1997 Labour 'landslide' the converse also applied and substantial numbers of the middle class supported Labour.

- Politics is now more class-based in mainland European countries than in Britain. This process in which *partisan voting* has substantially declined has been called 'class de-alignment' (see 24.4) and has grown alongside a more general reduction in loyalty and identification with political parties and, perhaps, a growing scepticism in respect of politicians generally.
- Rose and McAllister have suggested that housing classes have to a large extent replaced occupational classes and working class Council tenants remain strongly Labour, although this is a declining group
- Although social class is obviously a declining factor in influencing voting patterns, the fact that in the past about half of the total Conservative vote came from the working class, while only about 15 per cent of the total Labour vote was middle class has been of considerable interest to social scientists; and some of those studies give an insight into the late twentieth-century class dealignment which occurred.

The 'working class Conservative'

- The thesis of the 'Working class Conservative' has been the major area of study in many works; for example *Must Labour Lose?* (M. Abrams and R. Rose, 1960); *Can Labour Win?* (C. Crosland, 1960), *The Worker in an Affluent Society* (F. Zweig, 1961); and *The Working Class Tories* (E. Nordlinger, 1967).
- Nordlinger identifies two main types of 'working class Tory'; the 'deferential' and the 'pragmatist'. The deferential voters showed a strong preference to have people of a high status as their leaders rather than those of their own social class, feeling that such people are natural leaders or have been 'taught to lead'. The pragmatic voter is 'achievement orientated', they vote Conservative because they think a Conservative government is more likely to help them personally. Nordlinger found that the pragmatic voter preferred Conservative leaders to have 'achieved' their positions but that they also respected political leaders with 'ascribed' high status.

'Embourgeoisement'?

- Butler and King (*The British General Election of 1964, 1965*) refer to a survey by the Conservative Political Centre in which 32 per cent of the working class are found to have voted Conservative while only 17 per cent of the middle class voted Labour, and explained this in terms of rising standards of living, resulting in the better-paid members of the working class adopting middle class lifestyles. 'A significant number of skilled workers may be called class hybrids, working class in terms of occupation, education, speech and cultural norms, while being middle class in terms of income and material comforts' who are 'more likely to abstain or to switch their voting allegiances'.
- This *embourgeoisement thesis* received further support in 1977 from K. Roberts (*The Fragmentary Class Structure*), who identified a section of the working class – manual workers owning their own houses, living on middle class estates, opposed to trade unions and voting Conservative. 'The bourgeois

worker is a living animal', but represents a minor not a major group within the working class. The fact that what were now called C2 voters (skilled manual working class) were increasingly likely to vote Conservative in the South was seen in the General Elections of 1987 and 1992. 'Essex Man' became synonymous with an affluent working class Conservative voter – Basildon, in Essex, became the barometer which made it clear in 1992 that the Conservatives had won and that in 1997 they had lost. Evidence for this was first clearly seen in that the swings against Labour in the 1979 General Election were particularly high in seats where there was a large percentage of affluent working-class voters, such as Hitchin in prosperous Hertfordshire.

- This process of embourgeoisement had been disputed by other earlier studies; notably that of Goldthorpe *et al.* who in 1968 in *The Affluent Worker*, found that there was no process of embourgeoisement among the well-paid car workers in Luton. Although Goldthorpe did find that the less the car workers were involved with the working class subculture, the more likely they were to vote Conservative, Liberal or to abstain. However, values change more slowly than lifestyles – they may merely have been too early. There also appears to be a tendency for middle class people (such as social workers and teachers) who are directly involved with working class people to vote Labour.

- Goldthorpe found that there was a definite relationship between trade union membership and voting Labour – union members were three to four times more likely to vote Labour than to vote Conservative; the decline in trade union membership during the 1980s and 1990s undoubtedly contributed to Conservative victories. The same study also found a greater likelihood of voting Labour in large plants, the environment of which increases 'working class political consciousness'.

Environment and voting

- The importance of the environment in helping to determine voting behaviour was also emphasised by F. Parkin (*Working-class Conservatives: A Theory of Political Deviance*), who suggests that British institutions are essentially conservative and help to maintain the dominant values of the society which the Labour Party is seen as challenging. In fact while working class Conservative voters and middle class Labour voters are usually described as 'deviant voters', Parkin claimed that the real 'deviant voter' was the Labour voter regardless of class because he is challenging the central values of British society. He points to the fact that where the norms of the area are 'working class' the middle class are more likely to vote Labour. But where middle class values are dominant the working class is more likely to vote Conservative. This view helps to explain the considerable *regional differences* in voting behaviour. Upward social mobility also appears to encourage people to vote Conservative, perhaps as a means of identifying with their new class. Some working class people may vote Conservative because they support what they believe to be the Conservative Party's 'harder' approach to law and order, and immigration. We must also remember that, while people who are 'objectively' working class by reason of occupation may think of themselves as middle class, they are 'subjectively middle class', and they vote accordingly.

- The Liberal vote tends to be drawn more or less equally from all sections of the community; In 1965 D. Butler and A. King (*The British General Election of 1964*) were able to say the Liberal vote is 'a mirror image of the nation', and this has been substantiated in all General Elections since.

  By the 1970s there does appear to be some evidence for Dahrendorf's claim that 'people have been liberated from their class boundaries'; and recent voting evidence confirms that this is increasingly the case.

- In the 1970s P. Pulzer was still able to claim that 'British party politics are more highly class-bound than those in most other countries'. That was to change during the long period of Conservative rule (Margaret Thatcher 1979–90 and John Major 1990–7), who both depended on votes from a substantial number of manual workers. However despite stating that 'Class is the basis of British party politics; all else is embellishment and detail', Pulzer was even in 1972 able to outline the changes that were to alter the whole notion of 'class solidarity' (Table 26.1).

Ethnic origin

The influence of ethnic origin is less certain, but the evidence is that New Commonwealth and Irish immigrants were more likely to vote for the Labour Party. However, this is likely to be mainly a question of class identification as the majority of 'New' Commonwealth and Irish immigrants tended to be in manual employment.

Table 26.1 How Britain voted in 1997

| | 1997 vote % (change on 1992 in brackets) | | |
	Conservative	Labour	Lib Dem
All Great Britain voters	31 (–12)	44 (+9)	17 (–1)
Men	31 (–8)	44 (+6)	17 (–1)
Women	32 (–11)	44 (+10)	17 (–1)
AB voters	42 (–11)	31 (+9)	21 (0)
C1	26 (–22)	47 (+19)	19 (–1)
C2	25 (–15)	54 (+15)	14 (–4)
DE	21 (–8)	61 (+9)	13 (0)
First-time voters	19 (–16)	57 (+17)	18 (–3)
All 18–29	22 (–18)	57 (+19)	17 (0)
30–44	26 (–11)	49 (+12)	17 (–3)
45–64	33 (–9)	43 (+9)	18 (–2)
65+	44 (–3)	34 (–2)	16 (+2)
Home-owners	35 (–12)	41 (+11)	17 (–3)
Council tenants	13 (–6)	65 (+1)	15 (+5)
Trade union members	18 (–9)	57 (+7)	20 (+2)

Sources: 1992 data: ITN/Harris exit poll; 1997 data: BBC/NOP exit poll; David Butler and Dennis Kavanagh, *The British General Election of 1997* (London: Macmillan, 1997).

Deference can hardly account for the whole of working-class Conservatism. Equally important is a second category, whom McKenzie and Silver call 'secular' Conservatives – predominantly younger, male, better-paid voters who happen to approve of private enterprise, value consumer affluence or dislike trade unions. They are less committed emotionally to leadership from the upper classes and take a more hard-headed and pragmatic view of Conservative capacity to govern.

Affluence may determine the form that working-class Conservatism takes; it is not, in itself, a cause of Conservatism. There is no evidence that high incomes, or the possession of consumer durables, predispose working-class voters towards the Right. The one exception is home-ownership which, at all levels of income, makes people with manual jobs feel more middle-class, and more inclined to vote Conservative than those who rent their homes. There is little support for the embourgeoisement hypothesis in its crudest form – that the growth of consumer affluence makes people behave, and feel, in middle-class ways. Class identification is too firmly rooted to be overturned by the arrival of a washing-machine. However, while class and party attachments may remain fairly constant, changes in living standards notwithstanding, the intensity of these attachments may diminish. Life no longer appears as a struggle for the bare necessities; the spiritual sustenance that class solidarity gives is no longer central to social existence. This possible effect of affluence, which investigators of embourgeoisement have so far ignored, could be of great political importance. It almost certainly accounts for the above-average drop in turn-out in industrial constituencies over the last fifteen years; without it we cannot account for the markedly greater volatility of the electorate. Above all, it goes hand in hand with the slow, but cumulatively significant, change in the country's occupational structure.

(P. Pulzer, *Political Representation and Elections in Britain*, London, Allen & Unwin, 1972)

26.3 The influence of gender, age, religion and ethnicity

Sex, age and religion are not major factors influencing voting behaviour in Great Britain.

Gender

Of the three, gender differences may have had the greatest influence up to the General Election of 1983, but even then women were less likely than men to vote Labour. This may be because a greater proportion of women work in offices and service industries which have not been substantially unionised; where there is more direct contact with management leading to more identification between the two sides; and where the ambience is more middle class. It has also been suggested that women are more cautious, with the result that they vote for the party most likely to maintain the status quo.

In the General Election of 1983 more women moved to the 'Alliance' than did men and by 1987 gender appeared to have little effect on voting behaviour; however, in 1992 the earlier pattern returned, Gallup's post-election survey finding that 44 per cent of women voted Conservative compared with 38 per cent of men (43% and 39% respectively in the Harris Poll) (Table 26.3). However in 1997 it was the votes of women as they switched in larger numbers to Labour than did men that made the Labour victory so conclusive – with 44 per cent of both sexes voting for each of the major parties the gender difference had effectively disappeared.

Age

Older people tend to vote Conservative more than younger people, no doubt because as we grow older we become less likely to welcome change. However, the lowering of the voting age to eighteen did not result in any substantial advantage to the Labour party as many people then expected, the new generation of voters in general following traditional patterns based on class and area of residence. There does seem a tendency for younger voters to be less likely to retain the rigid party loyalties of their parents, and prior to 1992 it appeared that younger people were more likely to vote Labour; however Gallup's survey after the 1992 election found that the Conservatives enjoyed a small majority over Labour among eighteen to twenty-four-year-olds, and in 1997 the swing to Labour among eighteen to twenty-nine-year-old voters was, at 19 per cent, twice that for all voters taken together. However the older voters over sixty-five retained their Conservative sympathies and 44 per cent supported that party, with both major parties losing a little support, and 2 per cent moving to the Lib Dems.

Religion

Outside Northern Ireland, the rest of the United Kingdom is not much influenced by religious factors in deciding how to vote. Practising Anglicans are more likely to vote Conservative than are Catholics and Methodists. This is probably the result of the historical association between Methodism and Radicalism and the fact that many Catholics are Irish immigrants or their descendants and Irish immigrants have often been manual workers – a class rather than a religious influence.

Ethnicity

Outside East London where the British National Party (BNP) gained what little support they had, and some rivalry between different ethnic groups in Bradford West and Glasgow Govan, racial issues played no part in the 1997 General

Election. Although members of ethnic minority groups have up to now tended to support the Labour party this has, as with religion, tended to be a class rather than an ethnic issue.

26.4 The media and opinion polls

Two-party support has been declining since 1951 when about three-quarters of the electorate had a marked preference for the two largest parties. There are now more 'floating voters' (people with no particular political allegiance) to be won, and when it is borne in mind that a 1 per cent election swing can alter a party's majority by thirty seats it will be understood that the influence of the media is watched carefully by the managers of all political parties.

The press

Up until 1997 there was a clearly identifiable majority of national newspapers (both in terms of individual papers and total circulation) in favour of the Conservative Party.

However, 1997 has been described as a 'landmark in the political history of Britain's press. For the first time Labour had the support of most national daily newspapers. Six of the ten supported Labour (in 1983 only the *Mirror* supported Labour).

Radio and television

Unlike newspapers radio and television in Britain have a legal duty to deliver balanced coverage and appear to endeavour to do so. The fairness of the television authorities may be gauged by the fact that both major political parties accused the broadcasting authorities of bias at the conclusion of the 1992 elections.

The influence of the media

- Although some social scientists tend towards warning us not to exaggerate the power of the media, others suggest that the media have replaced the Church as the controller of ideas and ethics. Frank Parkin took the view that the mass media's task is to proclaim the values of the dominant social class – in Britain to accept, for example, that capitalism is natural and inevitable – and people with this viewpoint would no doubt claim that media support for Labour in 1997 was because it had abandoned socialism.
- The media can be controlled in a number of ways: by selection of what should be reported (e.g. newsworthiness); by presentation (the same facts may be presented but the way they are presented may give radically differing impressions).

Table 26.2 Newspaper readership and social grade in the General Election of 1997

		Circulation (thousand)	% of readers by social grade			
			AB	C1	C2	DE
LAB	*Mirror*	2390	10	23	31	36
	Sun[1,3]	3935	8	22	30	40
	Star[2]	660	7	19	34	40
	Guardian	402	57	29	5	8
	Independent	256	52	31	8	9
	Financial Times[3]	304	63	26	5	6
CON	*Express*[2,3]	1208	24	34	23	19
	Daily Mail[3]	2127	28	38	9	7
	Daily Telegraph[3]	1126	56	28	9	7
VOTE EURO SCEPTIC	*The Times*[1,3]	772	57	27	8	8

Notes:
[1] News Corp. Ltd (Rupert Murdoch).
[2] • United News & Media PLC (Lord Stevens).
  • Other papers are not linked by ownership.
[3] = previously supported Conservatives.
Of the national Sunday papers five of the nine supported Labour, compared with three in 1992.

- Who reads newspapers may be as important as how many are read – decision-makers may be influenced by the newspapers they read (Table 26.2).
- However, it is by no means certain that the media has any very great power to change voting intentions. Advertising has most power when it is offering people what they want – it is unlikely to change established attitudes (section 22.3). Existing party supporters tend to select news and comment in such a way that it reinforces their existing attitudes, but the media will be most influential when people have no firm political allegiance, and despite the fact that floating voters tend to be protected from influence by their own lack of interest in politics, it could be that the media will increase in political influence as the old automatic class 'solidarity' declines.
- However the influence of professional persuaders is clearly limited. The Referendum Party spent much more than any other party on press advertising during the run-up to the 1997 General Election (see section 24.4) but obtained only about 3 per cent of the vote.

Opinion polls and election prediction

'Psephology' – the study of the way in which people vote – has become sophisticated since 1945 and the growth of accurate *random sampling techniques* has resulted in considerable accuracy in predicting results in elections. Good sampling techniques have reduced the 'margin of error' of the well-known polls such as Gallup and NOP, to between 2 and 6 per cent.

- British general elections tend to be decided by *narrow margins* and these are often within the margin of sampling error, so that opinion polls are accused of inaccuracy or even of having influenced the result of the poll by encouraging people to jump on a successful bandwagon. However, in 1992 all the major opinion polls forecast a Labour win and all were wrong (Tables 26.3 and 26.4). This would appear to disprove the notion that people will change their voting intention in order to be on the winning side.
- In 1997 all the final fifteen polls could claim to have accurately forecast a Labour win, but most overestimated the Labour vote and five were outside the 3 per cent margin of error.
- Opinion polls can also be used as part of the *market research techniques* used by the political parties to find out what the voters want. In this respect there can be two possible objections to their use: (a) market research is expensive, and the richest political parties will have an advantage; (b) there may be a temptation for politicians to gear their advertised policies to what the public opinion polls say the public wants rather than to make a point of bringing their less popular policies to public attention. In fairness, it must be said that

Table 26.3   Final polls in the General Election of 1992 (Illustrating poll error – 1997 polls broadly correct)

	Con.	Lab.	Lib. Dem.	Other	Con. lead	Error on lead
MORI	38	39	20	2.0	−1	8.6
NOP	39	42	17	2.0	−3	10.6
Gallup	38.5	38	20	3.5	0.5	7.1
ICM	38	38	20	4.0	0	7.6
Result (GB)	42.8	35.2	18.3	3.7	7.6	–

Source: David Butler and Dennis Kavanagh, *The British General Election of 1992* (London: Macmillan, 1993).

Table 26.4   Possible components of poll error, 1992

Sampling frame	1.0
Electoral register	1.0
Differential refusals	1.5
Systematic lying	–
Different turnout	0.5
Late swing	1.5
Total	5.5

Source: David Butler and Dennis Kavanagh, *The British General Election* of 1992 (London: Macmillan, 1993).

there is little evidence that any political party is doing this, although the extensive use of 'focus groups' by Labour before the 1997 election brought that accusation.

- Greater social and geographical mobility, a change in the industrial structure from traditional manufacturing industry as the largest employers to the service sector, and perhaps a more educated electorate has led to a much more *volatile voting pattern* than in the past. The loyalty of voters from every social class seems to have become more 'conditional' – they are much less likely to support a political party for traditional reasons.
- This changing pattern in political allegiance has been growing since the peak of two-party loyalty in the election of 1951.
- In 1976, I. McLean summed up the problem which General Election opinion polls have, which continues today, although it was particularly emphasised in 1992:

Political realities

The polls' record in general election predictions is much better than it looks. They appear to do badly only because people, especially newspaper sub-editors, expected them to be able to do things which they could not possibly do. As we have said, the impossibility of avoiding sampling error means that a percentage figure given in an opinion poll can never guarantee to be closer than 2 or 3 per cent away from the true figure. But the margin between the two leading parties in British elections is almost always slender, and often within the 4 to 6 per cent range of sampling error. If a poll shows Labour as being 3 per cent ahead of the Conservatives, the true position could be anywhere between a dead heat and a 6 per cent Labour lead. In February 1974, as a matter of fact, the polls were almost spot on; they predicted a Conservative lead over Labour of 3 per cent, and there actually was one of 1 per cent. Labour won more seats, because of the way the votes were distributed, but the Conservatives won more votes – very close to the share the polls had predicted.

Opinion polls, therefore, are not too reliable as tipsters for general elections, because the result is usually so close that it falls within the range of sampling error. But this is not true of inter-election periods, when there is often a yawning chasm between the parties. The general trends in party support that are chronicled by the polls in between elections are undoubtedly fairly reliable. Like by-elections and local elections, they show a consistent pattern of the government of the day doing very badly in mid-term, and rallying as the next election approaches.

(I. McLean, *Political Realities – Elections*, 1976)

Labour poised for win, by Alastair Campbell, Political Editor

> Labour is on course for election victory, a batch of polls revealed yesterday.
>
> A Today newspaper survey of 52 Tory marginal seats puts Labour EIGHT POINTS ahead, enough for an overall majority of three seats.
>
> The poll gives Labour 46 per cent support, the Tories 38 and the Liberal Democrats 13.
>
> Labour must win the marginals to gain power – and all the signs show them on the way.
>
> (*Daily Mirror*, 7 April 1992)

By Gordon Greig, Political Editor

> John Major, the quiet man of British politics, goes back into 10, Downing Street this morning.
>
> He is the Prime Minister who not only defeated Neil Kinnock and his Labour Party – but also the combined polling organisations of Great Britain.
>
> Against all the forecasts of his downfall and the predictions of a hung parliament, he seemed certain to be leader of the largest party and likely to have an overall majority.
>
> With half the seats declared, it seemed the Tories were getting an astonishing 43 per cent of the vote and Labour were just making 37. This was the exact opposite of nearly all the polling forecasts during the entire election campaign and the Conservatives seemed set for a fourth consecutive term in office, an achievement unprecedented in modern British political history.
>
> (*Daily Mail*, 10 April 1992)

In 1997 D. Butler and D. Kavanagh confirmed the continued problem of believing such opinion polls: 'There was a 12 per cent range in the final figures for Labour's lead; therefore, if the election had been close and one poll had suggested a 6 per cent lead for the Conservatives and another a 6 per cent lead for Labour the media would have reverted to the satirical comments which followed the 1992 fiasco.'

REVISION SUMMARY

The influence of gender

Up until 1997 women were generally considered more likely than men to vote Conservative. It was suggested that this was the result of:

- The possibility of women being more cautious and more likely to be opposed to change.
- There being a greater proportion of women in offices and services in which trade unions were not well established.
- Women being more likely to work in a middle class environment and to have more contact with management (thus identifying with management).

However, the connection between gender and voting seems to have disappeared. This could be the result of:

- Greater unionisation in white collar occupations.
- An increasing similarity in socialisation of male and female (including educational opportunities, etc.).
- The greater proportion of men now working in offices and services plus a reduction in trade union membership overall.

The influence of social class (Table 26.5)

In 1972 it was claimed that British party politics was more highly class-bound than was the case in most other countries except Scandinavia (P. Pulzer, *Political Representation and Elections in Britain*); however, by 1986 R. Rose and I.

Table 26.5 The 2001 General Election

The General Election of 2001 was a virtual re-run of that of 1997 with little change. The most notable factor was the apparent lack of interest by the electorate, with the turnout of those voting dropping below 60% of the eligible electorate for the first time in Great Britain. (Not in Northern Ireland.)

Party	Number of MPs	Percentage of vote
Conservative	166	32.7
Labour	412	42.0
Lib.Dem.	52	18.3
SNP	5	(Scotland only)
Plaid Cymru	4	(Wales only)
Independent	1	*
Speaker	1	
UUP	6	Northern Ireland
DUP	5	
Unionists		
SDLP	3	Northern Ireland
Sinn Fein	4	
Nationalists		
Total	659	

* Richard Taylor standing on single issue 'Save Kidderminster Hospital.'

McAllister, in *Voters Begin to Choose*, claimed that in Britain ordinary class politics is a thing of the past; the working class at any rate now divides itself three ways.

Factors which might account for the decline in automatic Labour support from manual workers include:

- A reduction in the number of people employed in 'heavy' industry and large highly unionised factories.
- A decline in trade union membership.
- A rise in house ownership (including the sale of 'council' houses).
- Increased affluence among those in work.

Nordlinger divided 'working class Tories' into two types:

- **Deferential**. Feel that 'upper' class people are natural leaders or have been 'taught to lead' – most likely in traditional situations (e.g. rural constituencies).
- **Pragmatic** (also called 'secular' by McKenzie and Silver, 1972). Feel that a Conservative government is more likely to help them personally – these voters are more 'achievement oriented' (e.g. in new technologies). McKenzie and Silver, in *The Working Class Tory in England* (1972), expressed the view that working class support for the Conservatives was increasingly secular and was based on the belief that the party has superior executive and administrative ability.

However the 1997 General Election indicated that the 1986 views of Rose and McAllister were right – middle class voters are more prepared to vote Labour; just as in the three previous General Elections working class voters were prepared to vote Labour. The old class-based voting patterns have not completely disappeared, but the old rigid solidarity has gone.

SELF-TEST QUESTIONS: PART NINE

Self-test 9.1

1   What is an oligarchy? (*1 mark*)
2   Which of the following is not part of the United Kingdom: England, Republic of Ireland, Northern Ireland, Scotland, Wales? (*1 mark*)
3   Name two types of élite. (*2 marks*)
4   Name (i) one British political party that would normally be described as 'leftwing'; (ii) one British political party that would normally be described as 'rightwing'. (*2 marks*)
5   Name two parties that put up candidates at General Elections on a regular basis in Britain but have not had any Members of Parliament elected. (*2 marks*)
6   State three democratic aspects of pressure groups. (*3 marks*)
7   What is meant by the 'The Establishment' in Britain? (*3 marks*)
8   Why are middle class people most prominent in all political parties? (*3 marks*)

9   Why do some people abstain from voting in General Elections?   *(4 marks)*
10   Name two different types of pressure group. Give one example of each.
(4 marks)

Self-test 9.2

Refer to the table and figure in pp. 343 and 345
   1   How many Members of Parliament are there in the British House of Commons?
       (1 mark)
   2   How many votes were required to return an Alliance Member of Parliament in
       the 1983 General Election?   *(1 mark)*
   3   During which period shown in the chart did support for two parties only ('two-
       party partisanship') reach its peak?   *(1 mark)*
   4   The SDP received no votes in the 1979 General Election; why was this?
       (1 mark)
   5   Comment briefly on the statement that in Britain 'the party which receives most
       votes forms the Government'.   *(3 marks)*
   6   Name three alternatives to the existing 'first-past-the-post' system of elections in
       British parliamentary elections, and give a brief outline of how each of these
       systems operates.   *(6 marks)*
   7   What are the advantages and disadvantages of the present system of election
       to the British House of Commons compared with more proportional
       systems?   *(7 marks)*

Self-test 9.3

Before the fall of Communism in Eastern Europe the result of the 1978
parliamentary election in Albania was: Communist Party 1,436,288; others O;
spoilt ballots 3; abstentions 1.

   1   Who cannot vote in British parliamentary elections?   *(3 marks)*
   2   What features would you expect to find in a country which described itself as a
       'democracy'?   *(4 marks)*
   3   To what extent is Britain a democracy?   *(13 marks)*
                                                                  (Total 20 marks)

SPECIMEN QUESTIONS AND ANSWERS

Refer to the photograph on p. 362.
   1   Describe and give examples of different types of pressure groups. *(6 marks)*
   2   Examine the part played by pressure groups in the British political system.
       (14 marks)

Answers

1   Pressure groups are classified in a number of different ways: sometimes they are divided into 'sectional' groups and 'promotional' groups. Sectional groups seek to protect the interests of their members. They include trade unions who try to improve the pay and conditions of work of their members, and such organisations as the Confederation of British Industry (CBI), which represents the interests of employers. Promotional groups support a particular cause. This cause may be ongoing – for example, viewers' and listeners' associations try to have the amount and degree of sex and violence in the media controlled; or may be created with one limited objective – for example, to try to prevent nuclear waste being buried in a particular area.

Pressure groups may sometimes overlap classifications. For example, Help the Aged represents the interests of old people in general, but a local branch may also try to promote a particular cause: perhaps to prevent the closure of an outpatients' department in a hospital, as this would result in a long bus ride for the elderly.

Other methods of classifying pressure groups are also used: for example, into economic interest groups (such as the Institute of Directors) and into non-economic interest groups (such as CAMRA, the Campaign for Real Ale). Or into insider, outsider and prisoner groups.

(Note: You are only trying to earn 6 marks: concentrate on accurately explaining one method of classifying pressure groups into types and give examples of these. You may also let the examiner know, in a few words, that you are aware of other methods of classification.)

2   Pressure groups play an important role in Britain, because they keep the political parties and other agencies of government in touch with how people feel and they ensure that information on topics of concern reaches those who have to make decisions.

Pressure groups operate in a variety of ways. They may draw up petitions, organise public meetings, advertise in the press, or even break the law in order to draw attention to their cause, but some of the most effective pressure is applied less obviously.

One method used by pressure groups to ensure that politicians are kept informed of their objectives is either to 'sponsor' a Member of Parliament (pay the MP's secretarial and electoral expenses) or to pay an MP to act as their 'consultant', advising them on matters relating to their interest and ensuring that their point of view is represented in the House of Commons. The Police Federation pays such a consultant.

Another method is to build up a close relationship with a Civil Service department. For example, the National Farmers' Union (NFU) must be consulted in the annual review which decides the levels of subsidies to be paid to farmers.

Pressure groups may also have members in the House of Commons or the House of Lords. The Catholic Church, for example, can rely on Catholics in both houses and of different political parties to support that Church's view in opposing abortion or experimentation on the human embryo.

Although pressure groups provide a valuable channel of communication between government and governed, ensure that the interests of minority groups are represented and provide information to the public and those in power, they are also criticised. Pressure groups are not elected. Their effectiveness may depend more on their access to the media and people of influence, on their ability to withhold essential services, or on their financial strength than on the justice of their cause. Professor Finer, in *The Anonymous Empire*, criticised pressure groups because of the secrecy which often sheltered their activities, so that the public did not know why particular decisions had been made by those in power.

◪ Answers to self-test questions

Unless a specific term is asked for, the actual words used in the marking scheme need not be used, provided that the meaning is clear. The marking scheme is a summary of the information required; it requires expansion in the answer where appropriate. For answers which are given in bands (e.g. 0–2; 3–5; 6–8) a higher-band mark assumes that the information required in the lower bands has been given in addition to that required in the higher bands. Where this is not the case, marking should be adjusted accordingly.

Part one

Self-test 1.1

1 Primary data (or primary information)   (*1 mark*)
2 Hypothesis   (*1 mark*)
3 An unstructured interview   (*1 mark*)
4 No   (*1 mark*)
5 The sample is drawn:
   (a)   in the correct proportion
   (b)   from each identifiable section of the group being studied.
                                                 (*1 mark each*)
6 The Census, *The Statesman's Year Book*, newspapers (there are many other appropriate answers)   (*1 mark each*)
7 Planning; implementation; analysis; report   (*1 mark each*)
   You may accept similar words or phrases to the above or allow appropriate alternatives, e.g. hypothesis formation, investigation, etc. or four out of the six processes in scientific method:
   • Identifying a problem
   • Selecting appropriate methods to study the problem
   • Collecting relevant data
   • Analysing the data
   • Interpreting the data
   • Reporting findings and conclusions
8 Interviewer bias is the situation in which the result of the interview is affected in some way by the interviewer.   (*2 marks*)

For example, by the way in which the interviewer asks the question or by the interviewer is appearance. *(1 mark each)*

(There are several other possibilities, e.g. sex, age, race, dress, expression.)

9 A sample is a small section which accurately represents a larger population. *(1 mark for each point)*

Samples are taken to save time. *(1 mark)*

(Several other reasons could be given, e.g. lack of resources, saving money, impossibility of studying everyone.) *(4 marks)*

10 One mark for any four from:
- May be difficult to study some groups in any other way
- Researcher can more fully understand why as well as how
- May see factors which would not otherwise occur to researcher
- Can observe non-verbal communication (body language)
- If researcher undetected, group may act more normally *(4 marks)*

(Total 25 marks)

Self-test 1.2

1 Participant observation *(1 mark)*

2 (i) The group's members may no longer behave 'naturally' *(1 mark)*

(ii) 'Getting into' the group involved *(1 mark)*

3 1 mark for identifying an appropriate problem and 1 mark for explaining or illustrating it. For example:
- Moral/ethical issues
- Maintaining 'cover'
- Recording information
- Absorbing the values/behaviour of the group themselves
- Time/Money, etc. *(4 marks)*

(*Note*: The question does not restrict you to an answer based upon the stimulus passage.)

4 1 mark for identifying a difficulty and 1 mark for explaining this (e.g. explaining or giving an example).

They do not work in controlled laboratory conditions and cannot repeat experiments precisely.

Their subjects are complex human beings with individual wills and emotions.

Because they are human themselves, social scientists may be biased. *(6 marks)*

5 Answers which indicate inadequate understanding or simply describe participant observation as a method and/or state its advantages as a method *(0–2 marks)*

Answers which indicate understanding by considering both the advantages and the disadvantages of participant observation as a method *(3–5 marks)*

Answers which show a depth of understanding by considering a range of reasons for choosing participant observation and the limitations of this – linking these to a study of unemployed men *(6–7 marks)*

(Total 20 marks)

Part two

Self-test 2.1

1 Polygyny *(1 mark)*

2 Any one from:
Established working-class communities (particularly in the North of England, Northern Ireland, Wales and Scotland) and among Indian and Pakistani immigrant communities *(1 mark)*

3 Any two from: *(1 mark each)*
- Child-rearing/socialisation
- Providing an economic framework
- Companionship
- Protection
- Regulation of sexual behaviour *(2 marks)*

4 Any two from: *(1 mark each)*
- Increased educational opportunities leading to a need for job mobility
- Improved transportation
- New housing estates
- Improved welfare leading to less dependence
- Regulation of family size
- Education leading to disassociation from norms and values of other family members *(2 marks)*

5 Two from: *(1 mark each)*
Television; car ownership and family trips; longer education with longer dependency; longer holidays for parent(s); shorter working hours for parent(s); more dangerous out of doors for young children; more homework for more children; high-rise flats *(2 marks)*

6 Any three from: *(1 mark each)*
- They increase his workforce themselves
- Provide children who work and increase his wealth
- Allow the formation of alliances between different families for political and/or economic purposes
- They enhance his social status
- There would otherwise be a surplus of unprotected women *(3 marks)*

7 Any three from: *(1 mark each)*
Increased expectation, uncertainty about roles, more stress, more time spent together, fewer relations to rely on, easier to obtain divorce *(3 marks)*

8 A name given to the supposed difference in attitudes and behaviour of teenagers and adults (or parents and children) *(1 mark)*
It is sometimes suggested that there is a separate 'youth culture' but some research suggests that this 'gap' is much overstated *(1 mark)* and that there is a greater correlation between the attitudes of parents and young people within the same family than between the young people concerned and young people from a different social background *(1 mark)*. *(3 marks)*

9   *1 mark* for each point made from: (*maximum 2*)
    (a)   Unless she is very rich the mother is now expected to perform
          all the roles connected with home-making. However, with reduced
          family size it is now a transitory phase and as such does not com-
          mand the same status as it did in the past, and this reduces satisfaction.
          The nuclear family concentrates the maternal role and isolates the
          modern mother. Labour-saving devices and convenience foods reduce
          physical pressures on modern mothers, but may also reduce
          'professional' satisfaction. However, these permit the mother to
          combine her 'mother' role with a job, although this will often cause
          'role conflict'.
    (b)   *1 mark* for each point made from: (*maximum 2*)
    The father's role is becoming increasingly home- and family-centred. Just as
    many mothers now combine motherhood with a job, most fathers share in
    the household tasks and the division of labour in the home is becoming
    more diffuse. With the reduction of economic dependency and increased
    education, the modern father is not awarded automatic respect and his role
    as a disciplinarian is much reduced.   (*4 marks*)
10 Any four from: (*1 mark each*)
    Divorce rates reflect ease of dismantling unhappy marriages rather than
    increase in 'broken' marriages; formerly, unhappily married couples
    separated/deserted without divorce. Although increasing numbers of people
    co-habit before marriage, many subsequently marry. (Institution of
    marriage is not rejected.) A Commission on the Family ('Values and the
    Changing Family') found in 1982 that most people regard as a stable family
    life as an ideal to be attained, and this was echoed in the Government green
    paper 'Supporting Families' in 1999.   (*4 marks*)
                                                                          (*Total 25 marks*)

Self-test 2.2

1   34   (*1 mark*)
2   The wife   (*1 mark*)
3   The number of marriages which are dissolved (*1 mark*)
    in a particular country   (*1 mark*)
       per 1000 existing marriages (in a given year)   (*1 mark*)
       or per 1000 of the population (in a given year)   (*1 mark*)
       or as a proportion of marriages (in a given year)   (*1 mark*)
       or per 1000 married women aged 20–49 (*Note:* very rare.)   (*1 mark*)
                                                                          (*3 marks*)
4   *1 mark* for each reason given
       1 mark for an appropriate explanation or extension of a reason (e.g. 4 marks
    may be allocated for four acceptable reasons simply stated or 2 marks may be
    allocated for each of two acceptable reasons and 2 marks for explanation or
    extension of those reasons):

Reason	Extension
There may be religious reasons for variation	No legal divorce in Ireland until recently.
There may be legal reasons for variation	Big increase in Britain following Divorce Law Reform Act
People may remain married despite the fact that a meaningful relationship no longer exists	For 'the sake of the children' For fear of social disapproval
There is no generally acceptable measurement of 'success' in marriage	Expectations vary
The 'divorce rate' may be assessed in a number of different ways	As the number of marriages dissolved per 1000 existing marriages **or** per 1000 of population **or** as a proportion of marriages
Separation/desertion may take place without divorce	People live apart but do not regularise the position

(4 marks)

5 Simple explanations of increasing divorce as a sign of breakdown or marriage as a social institution – e.g. people are 'less moral', more extramarital relationships, etc. *(0–1 mark)*

  Some consideration of legal changes, longer life expectancy and/or other demographic factors (maximum of 2 marks for legal changes alone) *(2–3 marks)*

  Answers which consider a wider range of explanations – such as changing family patterns; changing expectations; enhanced status of women *(4–5 marks)*

6 Answers which deal superficially with suggestions that women are more likely to be 'victims' (e.g. of violence, isolation, etc.) or less tolerant of misbehaviour by husbands *(0–2 marks)*

  Answers which consider increased power of women in financial terms (e.g. legal aid, welfare state, changes in law) or of knowing their rights (e.g. education) or of being independent (e.g. in employment) *(3–4 marks)*

  Answers which relate the increasing likelihood of divorce petitions being filed by wives to changing expectations and roles within the home and in society generally (such answers may be in demographic terms – e.g. balance of sexes, reduced size of family). *(5–6 marks)*

(Total 20 marks)

Self-test 2.3

1 An understanding of how the decreasing dependence of women (e.g. Welfare State) has influenced attitudes. An appreciation of the limitation of role change to date. *(15–20 marks)*

  A knowledge of the changes in family structure and the impact of these on both male and female roles. Knowledge of legal changes affecting equal opportunities. *(11–14 marks)*

Impact of extended educational and occupational opportunities plus family size on female roles, Women's Liberation. (*6–10 marks*)

    Simple account of changes without reasons given or with only incomplete reference to reasons. (*0–5 marks*)

2 Divorce, or the break-up of a relationship
3 Single women

Part three

Self-test 3.1

(You may use your own words except where a particular term is requested.)

1 Socialisation (*1 mark*)
   ('Education' not acceptable)
2 Self-fulfilling prophecy (*1 mark*)
3 A school system (*1 mark*) composed of three kinds of school (*1 mark*)
   or 1 mark for each of two
- Secondary Grammar Schools
- Secondary Modern Schools
- Secondary Technical Schools
('Secondary' may be omitted) (*2 marks*)
4 Streaming (*1 mark*), setting (*1 mark*) (*2 marks*)
5 Heredity (*1 mark*), environment (*1 mark*)
   Nature/nurture also acceptable. Alternatively two other relevant aspects permissible (e.g. home/school) or a definition (e.g. 'the influences that surround the child' in place of the relevant term) (*2 marks*)
6 Any three from:
   Ideas; beliefs; attitudes; knowledge; language; dress; food habits; or other behavioural characteristics (*3 marks*)
7 Three from:
   increased dependence; increasing wealth; consumerism; media influence; symbolic protest; scapegoating; urbanism; unsuitability of educational system for some; earlier maturity (*2 marks* may be allowed for a reason plus a good explanation of it) (*3 marks*)
8 Three from:
- Culture transmission
- Training for work
- Social selection
- Social control

   Alternatively aspects of these may be credited independently (e.g. acceptance of a position in a hierarchy, an acceptance of assessment, an acceptance of boredom) (*3 marks*)
9 *2 marks* to be awarded for appropriate advantages of the Comprehensive System (e.g. social mixing; more opportunities to take exams; children not labelled as failures; larger size + appropriate advantage of this; non-distortion of primary education).

2 marks to be awarded for appropriate disadvantages (e.g. academically able may be 'held back'; anonymity; less opportunity for non-academic in posts of responsibility; lower standards + example. *(4 marks)*

(*Note:* The word 'Is' at the beginning of the question implies a debate; therefore arguments for and against are required. 'Yes' or 'No' score no marks)

10 Any four from:
- Early learning influences all later learning
- About half of what we learn is acquired in early years
- Material advantages (e.g. quiet room for study, money for visits) – allow only once
- Environmental factors (e.g. poor housing, leads to poor health, leads to absences from school) – allow only once
- Speech patterns
- Parental expectations
- Social learning (e.g. deferred gratification)
- Parental attitudes (e.g. anti-school) *(4 marks)*

(Total 25 marks)

Self-test 3.2

(See the Specimen Marking Scheme at the start of Answers section)

1 Working class girls *(1 mark)*

2 Middle class girls are more likely to be career oriented *(1 mark)*
Working-class girls are more likely to be involved in domestic chores at the expense of school and homework (*1 mark*) *(2 marks)*

3 *1 mark* each for three acceptable reasons/basis such as ethnic group; age; academic ability; religious group membership; common interests; gender
(3 marks)

4 *1 mark* each for up to three acceptable reasons plus *1 mark* each for an explanation or example indicating how the reason given makes it more difficult for the working-class child to 'fit' into school:
- Education background/knowledge of parents
- Attitudes of parents to education
- Provision in home of books, place for quiet study, etc.
- Lack of common values between home and school
- Language differences
- Expectations of the school *(6 marks)*

5 A simple statement that a youth culture does/does not exist with no or little expansion or explanation *(0–2 marks)*

Examples of manifestations of a 'youth culture' in terms of dress; behaviour; spending patterns; etc. This may include reasons for the existence of such a culture and specific examples – e.g. Hell's Angels; punks; skinheads; etc. *(3–5 marks)*

Answers which show understanding of the concept of culture by questioning the existence of a youth culture and/or illustrating how most young people share adult expectations and values *(6–8 marks)*

(Total 20 marks)

Part four

Self-test 4.1

1. Social mobility (accept 'mobility') (*1 mark*)
2. Status symbols (*1 mark*)
3. Working class (*1 mark*)
4. 8 per cent (any figure between 5 and 10 per cent acceptable) (*1 mark*)
5. *2 marks* for the three groups listed below; 1 mark for correctly naming two:
   - Class I
   - Class II
   - Class IIIN (or IIIa)
6. Absolute poverty and relative poverty (*1 mark* for each) (accept 'subsistence' instead of 'absolute' and 'comparative' for 'relative') (*2 marks*)
7. *1 mark* for up to each of four of the following:
   - Lack of opportunity
   - Motivation
   - Educational factors
   - Inherited wealth
   - Self-selection by élite groups
   - Colour/ethnic origin
   - Structural factors
   - Gender
   - Religion

   or

   Two factors from those listed above (*1 mark each*) plus a relevant example or extension of each (*1 mark each*) (*4 marks*)
8. *2 marks* for each of two reasons from the following (*1 mark* for reason: *1 mark* for explanation of reason or example):
   - Growing similarity in patterns of behaviour
   - Convergence of earning rates between manual and non-manual
   - Increasing social mobility
   - More home and share ownership
   - Changing occupational structure (*4 marks*)
9. *2 marks* for two differences from the following (*1 mark* for difference: *1 mark* for extension or example):
   - Feudalism closed to mobility/Class open system
   - Feudalism based on land tenure/Class on ownership or employment
   - Feudalism based on religion/Class not so based
   - Feudalism a pyramid of stratification/Class 'bulb-shaped' system or similar expression (*4 marks*)
10. *2 marks* for accurate definition in terms of working class taking on attributes/lifestyles of middle class.

    1 mark for each or up to three examples of embourgeoisement (e.g. voting patterns; house ownership; possession of consumer durables or behaviour

such as foreign holidays) or up to *3 marks* for relevant analysis of research (e.g. Zweig/Goldthorpe and Lockwood/Mulhearn/Jacques)   (*5 marks*)
(*Total 25 marks*)

Self-test 4.2

1 School and university backgrounds   (*1 mark*)
2 Eton and Winchester (both required)   (*1 mark*)
3 Most able people (*1 mark*) reach the most important and influential positions (*1 mark*); plus up to *2 marks* for explanation of how this occurs – e.g. through educational achievement (*1 mark*); because schools give all sections of society an opportunity to achieve full potential (*1 mark*)   (*4 marks*)
4 *2 marks* for any two from the following:
    • Separate education system/'Prep' – Public Schools
    • Informal networks
    • Intermarriage
    • Tax avoidance
    (*1 mark* for way position is maintained plus *1 mark* for how this operates or relevant example)   (*4 marks*)
5 Simple statements stating 'Yes' or 'No' with little relevant amplification   (*1–2 marks*)
    Answers which give either a 'Yes' or a 'No' answer and amplify this with some relevant reasons/examples such as:

Yes	No
Growing similarities in lifestyles	Inequalities of wealth ownership
Increasing convergence of incomes	Inequalities of employment
Educational opportunities	Public schools
Growth in home ownership	Inequality in public sector education
Welfare State provision	Positions of power filled by élite
	Accents and lifestyles

Answers which give some relevant reasons and
    examples as above to support both viewpoints   (*6–7 marks*)
Answers which give a good analysis of the
    concept of class and which fully argue both
    viewpoints – there should be some reference
    to concepts such as class consciousness,
    legitimation and/or 'exclusion' from   (*8–10 marks*) (*10 marks*)
    opportunity for full marks

(*Total 20 marks*)

Part five

Self-test 5.1

1 Alienation   (*1 mark*)
2 A number of possibilities – e.g.

- Worker on production line
- Filing clerk
- Machine minder

(Anywhere lack of skill, lack of decision-making and/or disconnection between worker and end-product is evident) (*1 mark*)

3 Any two examples from: (*1 mark each*)
- Local Government
- Finance
- Medical
- Health
- Banking (i.e. white collar sectors)

(accept name of relevant union – e.g. UNISON) (*2 marks*)

4 Any two from: (*1 mark each*)
contribution; integration; status; satisfaction; social contact (alternative expressions acceptable – e.g. 'companionship', 'security', 'avenue of achievement') (*2 marks*)

5 Workers' participation (or example of it – e.g. worker representatives on company boards) (*2 marks*)

6 *1 mark* each for security; fringe benefits; lack of control.
or examples of any of these – e.g. company cars; subsidised mortgages; private health care; less likely to be made redundant (or similar reference to employment protection); longer holidays; less likely to have to 'clock in' to work (or 'flexitime'); less likely to work overtime (*3 marks*)

7 *1 mark* each for:
- Extension
- Neutrality
- Opposition
- or accurate definition of each. For example:

'An extension' pattern of work is one in which the worker feels fully involved so that they continue to think about the job, and perhaps continue with it, during their 'leisure' time.

(Accept 'extrinsic/intrinsic' for *2 marks*, although these are not really patterns of work but attitudes to work) (*3 marks*)

8 Any three reasons from: (*1 mark each*)
- Increasing educational opportunities
- Legislation opening up employment opportunities (e.g. assisting in return after birth)
- More work which is regarded as suitable (i.e. by employers or by women themselves)
- Becoming the 'norm' (or more 'socially acceptable')
- Second World War emphasised female aptitude for employment in many more spheres
- More part-time work (i.e. fit in with family responsibilities)
- Rising expectations in terms of standard of living (e.g. house ownership) – 2 incomes needed. (*3 marks*)

(*Note*: Reasons not acceptable because of 'fifty years' stipulations in question:

- Family size – number of children now approximately the same as in 1930s – unless related to family size as between differing social classes (i.e. average number of children in Social Class V families has fallen)
- First World War
- Female suffrage
- Specific inventions of more than fifty years ago (e.g. typewriter)

9 *1 mark* for each of up to four points from among those listed below or *1 mark* for each point as above plus *1 mark* for explanation/relevant example of the point given (up to 4 marks in total):
- Employer bias/reluctant to appoint, promote because of possible maternity
- Male bias/males stereotype females, they tend to appoint/promote
- Primary socialisation/conditions females to subservient roles (e.g. subject choice)
- Alternative motivation/many girls have marriage as primary objective
- Maternity removes from promotion contest/vital period/outdates knowledge
- Primacy of home and family/some female unwillingness to accept absence from home, etc.   (*4 marks*)

10 *1 mark* for each of up to four points from among those listed below or *1 mark* for each point as above plus *1 mark* for explanation/relevant example of the point given (up to *4 marks* in total):
- Demoralisation/loss of identity, confidence – shock, shame
- Family stress/breakdown of marriage/role confusion, financial problems, no emotional release outside home
- Dependence/degrading to accept help
- Social isolation/no money, incentive to get out of home
- Rejection of society/engagement in crime, riots, drugs, etc. (relates to only small fraction of unemployed/development of some youth subcultures (e.g. punks)

(*Total 25 marks*)

Self-test 5.2

1 Approximately 750,000
(Accept any figure between 725,000 and 775,000)   (*1 mark*)
2 *Females*   (*2 marks*)
3 *1 mark* for each point mentioned from those listed below or *1 mark* for each point and *1 mark* for extension/example (up to a total of *4 marks*).
- Start of Second World War/rearmament, manpower into forces, etc.
- Economic action by government/Keynesian economics – public works programme
- Growth in consumption/production of consumer goods/e.g. cars, fridges, etc., particularly post-war
- (An 'economics'-type answer with reference to cyclical nature of unemployment acceptable.)   (*4 marks*)
4 Up to *3 marks* for each point made with reference to underestimate of figures;

up to *3 plus marks* for each point made with reference to overestimate of figures but overall total *4 marks* (e.g. may have *2 marks* for underestimate and *2 marks* for overestimate or *3 marks* for underestimate and *1 marks* for overestimate, etc.) Either underestimate:

- 'Schemes' not included
- Married women not registering
- Men over 60 not included
- People not claiming although registered

Or overestimate:

- People registering for benefit not really seeking work
- 'Black' economy
- Seasonal variations   (*4 marks*)

5 Answers which clearly indicate that the term 'automation' is misunderstood or refer only to unemployment briefly   (*0–2 marks*)

  Answers which refer to a range of effects either on individual worker and/or on the structure of the workforce – e.g.:

- Fewer workers – reduction in dangerous/unpleasant jobs
- More shift work – repetitive tasks reduced
- De-skilling more freedom of movement/autonomy alienation of worker
- and/or people in service industries/increase in middle class, etc.   (*3–6 marks*)

  Answers which show a good understanding of a range of advantages and disadvantages and structure of workforce   (*7–9 marks*)

                                                                         (*9 marks*)

                                                                 (*Total 20 marks*)

Part six

Self-test 6.1

1 Demography   (*1 mark*)
2 Every ten years   (*1 mark*)
3 Any one from: Greater London; West Midlands; Merseyside; West Yorkshire; Greater Manchester; Tyne and Wear; Strathclyde   (*1 mark*)
   (Do not accept 'London', 'Birmingham', etc.)
4 13.8 (accept any figure between 11.8 and 13.8)
   Approximately 32 (accept any figure between 30 and 40)   (1 mark for each)
   (*2 marks*)
5 Any two (*1 mark each*) from: religious belief; food; language; music; dress; thought patterns
   (other factors acceptable if clearly related to a 'shared culture')   (*2 marks*)
6 *1 mark* for each aspect:
   - Number of live births
   - Per thousand of the population
   - In a given year (or in one year)   (*3 marks*)
7 1 mark for each reason:

- Taxation; military reasons; social planning
- Or answers giving specific aspects requiring planning – e.g. health; education; housing; employment; social services (also *1 mark* each)

(*3 marks*)

8   *1 mark* for each factor stated plus *1 mark* for an example or explanation of that factor

Factor	Example/Explanation
Fear	Competition for scarce resources – e.g. jobs
Stereotyping	High visibility – all share characteristics of few
Scapegoating	Ease of identification for attaching blame

(actual word given need not be used if meaning clear)   (*4 marks*)

9   *1 mark* for each *disadvantage* listed (up to maximum of four) or *1 mark* for disadvantage plus *1 mark* for explanation of that disadvantage.
- Social isolation/loneliness
- Normlessness/lack standards/anomie
- Pollution (all forms air/noise, count once only)
- Overcrowding or other factor relating to living standards (e.g. expense)
- Crime/violence/fear/conflict
- Superficial relationships/more competition for status symbols (*4 marks*)

10   *1 mark* for each factor encouraging or indicating similarity **or** *1 mark* for factor and *1 mark* for reason:
- Population movement/car ownership – cheaper housing, etc.
- Television/projects same images to urban and rural
- Education/same syllabuses, text books; teacher mix
- Mechanisation, automation/industrialised farming methods
- Increased holidays/urban to rural, rural to urban   (*4 marks*)

(*Total 25 marks*)

Self-test 6.2

1 South-east England (or the South-east)   (*1 mark*)
2 Scotland   (*1 mark*)
3 North-west England (or the North-west)   (*2 marks*)
4 *1 mark* for each factor stated (up to 3) plus *1 mark* for an explanation or extension of the factor given:
- Movement of industry – e.g. decline of heavy industry (e.g. North/North West)/growth of services, particularly in South/development of car engineering, etc., in East Midlands
- Access to markets – e.g. decline of trade with 'Empire' (e.g. Liverpool); development of EC trade (e.g. East Anglia)
- Retirement – e.g. increasing number of older people who have capital, from house sale, etc., retiring to rural/seaside areas (e.g. South-west)
- More opportunity for choice – e.g. educational/social/geographical mobility/allows more people to choose where they live; many choose less polluted/crowded areas
- Continued decline in numbers employed in agriculture – e.g. more mechanisation producing more food (e.g. Scotland, Wales)

- Immigration – e.g. the great majority of immigrants have settled in the South East and West Midlands   (*6 marks*)
5 Answers which show poor understanding, give only one or two obvious differences (e.g. more people) or are limited to a description of lifestyles in urban or in rural areas with no comparison   (*0–2 marks*)

Answers which are largely descriptive – e.g. differences in housing, entertainment, shopping facilities, working patterns, etc.   (*3–5 marks*)

Answers which explain a range of differences and deal with differences in relationships (e.g. primary v. secondary)   (*6–8 marks*)

Answers which show full understanding – e.g. *Gemeinschaft* v. *Gesellschaft.*
Full marks only if it is clear that similarities exist between rural and urban areas – e.g. 'urban villages'   (*9–10 marks*)
                                                                          (*Total 20 marks*)

Self-test 6.3

1 The infant mortality rate for the UK in 1941 was 60.
2 The area not included is Northern Ireland.
3 Infant mortality is the number of infants under the age of one year who die in a given year per 1000 live births.

Part seven

Self-test 7.1

1 Conformists   (*1 mark*)
2 14–16 years   (*1 mark*)
   Accept any age range over ten or under twenty – or simply 'adolescents' or 'teenagers' (Do not accept 'young people' or 'children')
3 'Working class' or any reference to Social Classes IIIM to V (e.g. 'unskilled workers')   (*1 mark*)
4 Any two from: family; school/education; peer group; media; law; religion; employment (*1 mark for each*)   (*2 marks*)
5 'The least critical' or 'the less intelligent thirteen to fourteen year old' or 'those emotionally ready to receive the message' or similar expression which implies an understanding that media messages are normally 'screened' by values already learnt   (*2 marks*)
6 Any three from:
   - Drip effect
   - Provides information/ideas on crime technique
   - Makes delinquency heroic/exciting
   - Exaggerates crime/makes crime/delinquency seem normal
   - Encourages the already violent to violence (not simply 'makes people violent', etc.)
   - Creates confusion over moral standards/anomie (*1 mark for each*)
                                                                          (*3 marks*)

7   Any three from:
    • Laws are framed by middle class, therefore reflect middle class values
    • Middle class crime less likely to be detected because of its nature
    • Middle class people usually live in more spacious surroundings where reprimand/detection less likely
    • Police less likely to stereotype/label middle/class, therefore not so likely to be suspected
    • Some middle class crime (e.g. tax evasion) carries less moral/censure
    • Middle class have more opportunities to gain status/reach goals without crime (*1 mark for each*)   (*3 marks*)
8   Up to *2 marks* for each relevant point made up to a maximum of *4 marks* (*1 mark* for each point plus *1 mark* for expansion) or *1 mark* for each point up to a maximum of four:
    • Advertising creates and encourages more acceptable goals without providing means
    • More consumer goods readily available for theft – e.g. cars
    • More motor vehicles for traffic-related offences
    • Link between violence and overcrowding (e.g. high-rise flats)
    • Continued growth of urbanism (*Gemeinschaft/ Gesellschaft* dichotomy)
    • The influence of relative poverty
    • Less restraint of adults/discipline in home and school (for *2 marks* must be questioned)
    • Possible effect of television (for *2 marks* an indication of the kinds of people who may be influenced must be given)
    • Group influences in crowd situations – e.g. football matches (for *2 marks* an indication that increase in violence, etc. may be related to media publicity/labelling)
    • In the case of females – former male mores are more acceptable
    • New types of crime (e.g. credit card fraud)
    • Changing attitudes in society generally
    • Discussion of possible effect of working mothers (for *2 marks* an indication that this influence is disputed)   (*4 marks*)
9   *1 mark* for each point made up to a maximum of four from:
    • Our socialisation process encourages girls to adopt passive domestic roles, while boys are expected to be tough and aggressive
    • Boys subject to fewer control by parents and more likely to be out late
    • Boys more likely to be in places, such as pubs, where violent situations may develop
    • Media role models
    • Possible biological differences
    • Double standards may mean that girls can express rebellion by means which are legal (e.g. sexual promiscuity)
10 *1 mark* for each point made up to a maximum of four from:
    • Much crime is unreported/'dark figure' of crime
    • Police activity varies by area and by period
    • Much crime is undetected
    • Media impact on certain crimes varies ('moral panics')

- New crimes are created by new inventions (credit cards/cars)
- Law changes influence crime rates   (*4 marks*)

                                                        (*Total 25 marks*)

Self-test 7.2

1 16.7 (or 16.7 per cent)   (*1 mark*)
2 Calculations do not work because less than 75 per cent of people do not both
   live and work there (or similar expression)   (*1 mark*)
3 They all contain large towns or they include a conurbation (of top five)

                                                        (*1 mark*)

   They have an 'urban ethos' or similar expression (e.g. they are industrial rather
   than agricultural)   (*1 mark*)
   (*Subtotal 2 marks*)
4 No mark for 'Yes'
   For statement that there is not conclusive evidence (*1 mark*)
   For example of area with high crime and low unemployment   (*1 mark*)
   For example of area with low crime and high unemployment   (*1 mark*)
   (*Subtotal 3 marks*)
5 Answers which only deal with unemployment as a factor   (*0–2 marks*)
   Answers which while stating that unemployment is the major factor compare
   this with other possible factors   (*3–4 marks*)
   Answers which deal with the relationship between urban living and crime in
   material terms (e.g. more property to steal, more overcrowding)   (*4–6 marks*)
   Answers which deal with the impact of the urban ethos (anonymity,
   Gesellschaft relationships, etc.), in addition to material factors   (*7–8 marks*)
   (*Subtotal 8 marks*)

                                                        (*Total 15 marks*)

Part eight

Self-test 8.1

1 Culture   (*1 mark*)
2 The General Strike   (*1 mark*)
3 Twenty-three years   (*2 marks*)
4 Urbanisation   (*2 marks*)
5 Gemeinschaft   (*2 marks*)
6 *1 mark* for each up to three from:
   - Social isolation loneliness
   - Suicide
   - More crime/violence
   - More overcrowding
   - Greater competition/status symbols
   - More stress
   - More pollution/noise

- Superficial relationships
- Less inter-generational authority   (*3 marks*)

7   *1 mark* for each up to three from:
- Orthodox
- Holiness Mormon (Church of Latter Day Saints)
- 'West Indian'
- Jehovah's Witnesses
- Muslim
- Sikh
- 'Moonies' (Unification Church)
  (accept Pentecostal although marginal; accept Spiritualist, by implication)
- (other possibilities, e.g. Hari Krishna but not any of the traditional Christian faiths or Judaism)   (*3 marks*)

8   *1 mark* for each up to three from:
- Urbanisation
- Development of trade unions
- Compulsory education/more education
- Nuclear family as main operating unit
- Increased leisure
- Unemployment
- Higher living standards/more general wealth   (*3 marks*)

9   Up to *2 marks* for each relevant point made up to a maximum of *4 marks* (*1 mark* for point plus *1 mark* for expansion/explanation) or *1 mark* for each point up to a maximum of four:
- Social control/legitimation – Integration
- Social change – Supportive in stress
- Social cohesion – Moral direction
- Rites of passage – Provides meaning to life
- Reintegration of deviants – (*4 marks*)

(*Total 25 marks*)

10   Up to *2 marks* for each relevant point made up to a maximum of *4 marks* (*1 mark* for point plus *1 mark* for expansion/explanation or *1 mark* for each point up to four):
- Socialisation process
- Geographical isolation
- Unchanged economic structure
Absence of conflict/invasion   (*4 marks*)

Self-test 8.2

1   180,000   (*1 mark*)
(*Note*: Remember to add the 000s! (Always read the table carefully and see whether the figures quoted are in units, hundreds, thousands, millions, etc.))

2   Marriages in churches in Great Britain have declined   (*1 mark*)
Register Offices or Civil Marriages have increased most in popularity

(*1 mark*)

3   *1 mark* for each point made up to a maximum of three

The term 'secularisation' is used to describe changes that are believed to have taken, or be taking, place in religious practice in Britain and some other countries.

There has been a decline in the number of people attending church regularly and also those using the churches for 'rites of passage', such as marriage.

The churches are becoming less significant in the life of the country; vicars and priests have less status and are not listened to with so much respect as in the past.

Secularisation is also used to describe changes that are taking place in the churches themselves, with more emphasis on the church as a social centre for the young, old and other groups in the community, and less emphasis on spiritual matters.

(*Note:* The difficulty here is to decide how much to write – the fact that only 3 marks are available means that you cannot afford much time and that the examiner will probably be looking for three points for which to award marks; but this is not stated, and so it is best to put down several as briefly as you can.)

(*3 marks*)

4   Up to *2 marks* for explaining reasons for attending a place of worship other than religious belief – e.g.

People may wish to marry in church because they regard this as more romantic than a Register Office marriage or to have their children baptised because relatives will be annoyed if they do not. Others may attend a particular church because it has a good youth club, while children may be sent to Sunday School by their parents.

Up to *2 marks* for explaining the problems involved in attempting to measure belief – e.g.

Belief is a very difficult quality to measure. Some people believe something very deeply, but regard that belief as a personal matter which they prefer not to advertise; others may have only a shallow belief, but make their position clear in public. Religious belief is an example of the problem of belief measurement: some people may attend church regularly in order to meet friends or gain status rather than from deep conviction; others, who have deep religious conviction, may prefer to pray quietly at home.

Up to *2 marks* for appreciating how changing social mores may influence church attendance:

It may be that declining church attendances are the result of a decline in social pressures to attend rather than a decline in religious belief.   (*6 marks*)

5   Up to *3 marks* for answers which deal only with the decline in the influence of religion – e.g.

Bryan Wilson, in *Religion in a Secular Society*, takes the view that religion is in decline, and quotes the reduction in membership of the established Churches, the decline in the status of the clergy and such factors as the increase in the number of Register Office weddings as evidence of this.

Up to *3 marks* for answers which give evidence for the continued influence of religion.

(i.e. up to *6 marks* if decline and continued influence are covered).

Most people in Britain still claim to belong to a religion, although comparatively few actually attend services on a regular basis. In 1999 Channel 4 TV found that 75 per cent of their sample in an 'Audit of Belief' claimed to have some religious or spiritual belief. David Martin, in *A Sociology of English Religion*, believed that religion is still the basis of the moral code for most people in Britain and is seen as a necessary legitimation for national festivities and social institutions ranging from the Coronation to funerals, providing part of the social cement which holds British society together.

A further *2 marks* if political influence is dealt with – e.g.

Church leaders do still have an authoritative voice on moral questions in Britain and are reported in the media; Church of England bishops sit in the House of Lords. An indication of the continuing influence of the Churches was the rejection of a Government plan to abolish free school transport by the House of Lords, led by the senior Catholic peer, the Duke of Norfolk, who was concerned by the Bill's potential effect on rural Catholic schools.

or

If there is clear understanding that religious influence extends beyond the established Christian Churches:

Although the actual membership of the established Christian Churches has declined, there is evidence of continuing interest and belief in the supernatural, ranging from acceptance of fortune-telling to membership of a variety of sects – for example, the Jehovah's Witnesses more than doubled in size between 1970 and 1995. In addition, there has been a considerable growth in non-Christian religions, notably the Moslems, who increased from 130,000 to 580,000 between 1970 and 1995 and whose faith has a considerable impact in their daily life.

(*Note*: If information is relevant to more than one section of a question, do not hesitate to repeat it – for example, secularisation in Question 3 and 5 above.)

Part nine

Self-test 9.1

1 An oligarchy is rule by a group   (*1 mark*)
2 Republic of Ireland   (*1 mark*)
   (If more than 'Republic of Ireland   *0 marks*)
3 Any two from:
   • Political élite
   • Military élite
   • Economic élite
   • Media élite   (*2 marks*)
   (examples acceptable if expressed as a group – e.g. Officer class)
4 (i)   Any one from Labour Party; SDLP (Northern Ireland), Sinn Fein; Workers' Revolutionary Party (accept Liberal Democrats if qualified in some way)   (*1 mark*)

(ii) Any one from Conservative Party; Democratic Unionist Party; Official Unionist Party; National Front; British National Party

(Accept 'Ulster Unionist') *(1 mark)*

(2 marks)

5 Any two from Monster Raving Loony; Workers' Revolutionary Party; National Front; British National Party; Communist Party; Ecology (Green Party) *(2 marks)*

6 Any three factors from: *(1 mark each)*
- Weakly organised groups have little power (e.g. the old)
- Producer groups (e.g. brewers, tobacco manufacturers) have finance and power to make their views known
- (or instead of both factors above, but count for one only, power of group may depend on wealth)
- Secrecy of pressure groups/general public excluded from negotiations
- Violence or civil disruption may be used to achieve ends *(3 marks)*

7 *1 mark* for each 'feature' or 'example' of 'The Establishment' described up to a maximum of three from:
- Long-established
- Non-elected group/individual exercising considerable power
- Common background/experience of members (this may include reference to public school and/or Oxbridge education)
- Leading members of: the judiciary; the media; the armed forces; financial institutions
- Leading figures in high-status academic institutions (e.g. Warden of All Souls College, Oxford)
- Leading figures in politics there by virtue of background *(3 marks)*

8 *1 mark* for each feature noted up to a maximum of three:
- More leisure time
- Jobs less physically exhausting, therefore energy for other activities
- Higher educational level
- More confidence/believe in their own abilities
- More experience of exercising authority
- More knowledge of bureaucratic procedures
- Socialisation process make more competitive *(3 marks)*

9 *1 mark* for each reason noted up to a maximum of three:
- Lack of interest in politics/particularly the least educated
- No party representing views which they support
- Disagree on particular policies of, or dislike personalities in, party they usually support (and will not vote for others)
- Geographical difficulties of reaching polling station
- Age/disability (and have not requested a postal or proxy vote)
- Have moved (and not requested a postal vote)
- Absence on holiday/business
- Belief that result is inevitable and their vote will make no difference (particularly in 'safe' seat) *(3 marks)*

10 (i) Protective (or 'sectional') *(1 mark)*

Any appropriate example (e.g. trade unions, BMA, Help the Aged, RAC)
(*1 mark*)

   (ii)   Promotional   (*1 mark*)

Any appropriate example (e.g. CND, Viewers' and Listeners' Association, CAMRA)   (*1 mark*)

or

   (i)   Economic interest group   (*1 mark*)

Any appropriate example (e.g. TUC, Institute of Directors, CBI or 'Labour lobby', 'business lobby', etc.)   (*1 mark*)

   (ii)   Non-economic interest group   (*1 mark*)

Any appropriate example (e.g. Oxfam, the Churches, LIFE, AA)   (*1 mark*)

(Accept 'National' and 'Local' as 'types' for *1 mark* only, but full credit for appropriate examples. Award 'Labour lobby'; 'professional lobby'; (Alternatively Insider/Outsider/Prisoner may be given with appropriate examples.)

('business lobby' if given as 'types' similarly.)   (*4 marks max.*)

(*Grand total 25 marks*)

Self-test 9.2

1 659   (*1 mark*)

2 338,286   (*1 mark*)

(allow an obvious mathematical error if answer reasonably close)

3 1951–5

(allow any period quoted within these dates)   (*1 mark*)

4 The SDP was not established until 1981, or similar expression   (*1 mark*)

5 For statement that the Party which receives the most votes does not necessarily form the Government   (*1 mark*)

For an understanding of why this is so   (*1 mark*)

For an example of a minority Party forming a Government (e.g. Conservatives 1951; Labour 1974 (February))

or

General statement that all post-1945 Governments had more votes recorded against them or similar   (*1 mark*)

(*Total 3 marks*)

6 Three (1 mark each) from alternative vote; second ballot; party list; single transferable vote; or the Jenkin's Report compromise.

Brief accurate description of selected examples (*1 mark each*)   (*6 marks*)

7 *1 mark* for each pertinent advantage (up to *3 marks*) (e.g. 'strong Government'; no undue influence for minorities; quick; simple to understand; clear link between each representative and electorate)

   1 mark for each pertinent disadvantage (up to *3 marks*) (e.g. unfair to minorities/unrepresentative; elected dictatorship; 'adversary' politics; 'wasted' votes, minority gains power)

   plus *1 mark* for indication that reorganisation could vary system geographically; or for good example(s) of system(s) operating in other countries

(*7 marks*)

(*Total 20 marks*)

Self-test 9.3

1 Three from: certified insane; disqualified felon; peer of the realm/royalty; those under eighteen years of age (1 mark for each) *(3 marks)*

2 Four from: freedom of association; freedom of speech/communication; opportunity to participate in government (e.g. right to vote); protection for minorities; freedom from physical restriction without due cause. (Also accept access to same level of resources e.g. monetary/media) *(4 marks)*

3 Poor understanding or simplistic statement that Britain is/is not a democracy *(0–3 marks)*

Some discussion of democratic features in British society and/or a limited understanding of undemocratic feature(s) (e.g. voting system) *(4–6 marks)*

An understanding of democratic features (e.g. habeas corpus and other legal rights; pressure groups, trade unions) and examples which show understanding of undemocratic features (e.g. unequal access to media, education, etc.; selection of Party candidates; non-election in some trade unions, etc.)

The degree to which membership of the European Union subordinates the British Parliament to decisions made by other bodies over which Britain has little control. If well done this could merit entry to the higher band below. *(7–10 marks)*

A critical analysis of the degree to which Britain is fully democratic, including aspects such as access to power, the possibility of 'tyranny by the majority', differential treatment by such agencies as the police, etc. *(11–13 marks)*

(Total 20 marks)

■ ⊻ Glossary

See also the index, as many of the terms and concepts listed are defined in more detail in the text.

ascriptive traits   are characteristics that are inherited (e.g. skin colour) rather than being the result of personal achievement.

alienation   An individual's feeling of being cut off from other people, of social isolation, leading to a feeling that his life or work is meaningless and that he has no power over his own destiny.

anomie   A lack or confusion of values within a society or group. For example, there may be socially approved goals but no way in which some people can achieve these.

anthropology   A comparative study of mankind, particularly of biological and social development – used generally to mean the study of non-advanced societies.

attitude   A consistent approach and a predictable response towards particular views and situations.

automation   A replacement of people by electronic and mechanical devices so far as control of the work processes is concerned (i.e. not just physical labour).

bias   A tendency towards a particular point of view (which may subconsciously influence researchers, invalidating their results).

bipartite (or **bilateral**)   A system of education in grammar and secondary modern schools.

birth rate   The number of live births per 1000 of the population per year.

bourgeoisie   Private owners of the means of production. May be used in a general way to describe the middle class.

bureaucracy   A type of organisation which has formal rules and a hierarchy of officials backed by trained experts. A feature of bureaucracy is often rigidity. In modern society bureaucratic features dominate both capitalist and socialist societies. Can be found in government, trade unions, education, etc.

capitalism   An economic system in which the concentration and control of the means of production (capital) is in the hands of private owners. Private profit is the goal and this stimulates competition.

case study   An examination of a particular group or organisation by which it is hoped to gain an insight into similar entities. The subjects of case studies may be families, social groups, small communities, etc.

caste   A system of social stratification based on religion, in which there is a hierarchy of social groups with positions fixed and no mobility. Castes are hereditary, endogamous and occupationally based.

class A broad category of people within a society who have similar social and economic status. Although primarily based on economic factors, such as ownership or occupation, class also encompasses attributes such as lifestyles and attitudes.

community A community is a collection of people, such as part of a town or village, who share common values and experience a feeling of belonging to one another. Increasingly used to denote a community of interests unconnected with a specific geographical area (e.g. 'gay community').

concept A word or words expressing a point of view reached by concentrating on certain aspects of a subject.

conflict theory An approach to society, which emphasises the division, hostility, and conflicting interests within it, brought about by an unequal distribution of advantages between differing social groups. For example Marxism.

conformity Behaviour that fits with the expectations of a group.

conjugal Relating to marriage – conjugal roles may be joint (the partners sharing duties and responsibilities) or separate (segregated).

conjugal family A family established through marriage i.e. through a ceremony, which legitimises the relationship between the partners.

control group A group similar to another group which is the subject of experiment, but not subjected to the variable under examination. It serves as a comparison with the experimental group.

conurbation A densely populated urban area in which a number of towns have merged.

culture Social characteristics, including behaviour, ideas or beliefs that are shared within a group and transmitted through the socialisation process.

custom Established modes of thought and action.

death rate The number of deaths per 1000 of the population per year (unless a specific alternative period is given).

deferential voter A working-class Conservative voter who feels that higher social groups are most fitted to govern.

deferred gratification Postponing immediate reward in the expectation of future benefits.

delinquency Refers to the breaking of the legal or moral codes of a society. Often used to refer to less serious breaches of the rules of society, particularly by the young ('juvenile delinquent' – young law-breaker in Britain between the ages of 10 and 17).

demography The study of the size, structure and distribution of a population.

dependent age groups Those who are either above or below working age and who are economically dependent on the working population (either through state benefits or relatives).

deviance Behaviour that does not conform to the expected pattern.

divorce rate This indicates the number of marriages which are dissolved in a particular country in any given year. The 'divorce rate' can be assessed in a number of different ways and care should be taken to ascertain the method of calculation. The base may be the proportion of divorces to marriages in a given year. The base may be the number of couples who were divorced per 1000 existing marriages. The rate may be calculated on the number of divorces per 1000 existing marriages. The rate has also been calculated as the number of divorces per 1000 married women aged 20–49 (6 in 1969).

elaborated code   A linguistic code used by middle class families, which is context free and whose meanings are universally clear, allowing unambiguous communications of complicated concepts between those who understand it. (Postulated by Bernstein, but criticised by others such as Rosen and Labov.)

élite   The most powerful groups within a group or society – a group which has considerable control and influence.

embourgeoisement   A theory that the working class are adopting middle-class lifestyles, attitudes and goals.

emigration   The movement from one country to another on a permanent basis.

empiricism   An outlook based on experience rather than a set of values.

endogamy   An insistence that marriage must be to people within one's own kinship or social group.

environment   All the physical factors and emotional influences that surround the members of a particular group or individual – a particularly important area of study is how environment influences intelligence or determines behaviour.

estate   A system of social stratification based on inherited rights and duties, legal rather than religious. As the law is man-made, estate systems are less rigid than caste systems but more closed than social class (e.g. feudalism in Europe).

ethnic group   People with a common nationality or racial background who share a common culture (see **culture**). There is usually a degree of voluntary identification between members of an 'ethnic group'.

ethnomethodology   A sociology perspective which seeks to study the methods which people use to make *sense* of their society and their daily lives using preconceived assumptions and acquired background knowledge. This perspective sees man as creating his own social world and criticises other sociological perspectives for taking order and reality in social life for granted; underestimating the extent to which individuals can control their own world; and believing that sociologists can be detached observers. (This perspective developed in the 1970s and stems largely from the work of Harold Garfinkel, who showed how much we take routine and order for granted – e.g. by getting his students to ask old ladies and pregnant women to give up their seats on buses.)

exogamy   An insistence that marriage must be to people outside one's own kinship or social group.

family   A group of people whose relationship is based on shared kinship. From a practical point of view, an *extended family* includes the nuclear family and other relations who are in regular contact; the *nuclear family* consists of the husband, the wife and their unmarried siblings (children sharing a common mother and/or father).

fertility rate   The number of live births in any one year per 1000 fertile women in the population (counted as women between the ages of 15 and 44). The 'fecundity' rate is the number of children who could theoretically be produced in any one year by the fertile women in the population.

folkways Socially approved behaviour which is informally sanctioned but not regarded as of deep importance within a society (e.g. dress, 'good manners', etc.).

functionalism A way of looking at society to see what purpose is fulfilled by particular institutions or behaviour. Durkheim said that two questions needed an answer in any study of social institutions – What caused it? What function does it serve? Merton later showed that institutions often have two sets of function: a **manifest** function – a performance that is obvious; and a **latent** function – an equally important aspect of its performance, which is not easily recognised. For example, the manifest function of a criminal gang may be to obtain money but its latent function may be to provide status and power for its members. Early sociologists such as Auguste Comte regarded societies as being very similar to biological organisms – with each part serving a specific *function*. Most sociologists today would not accept such a direct comparison, and some reject *functionalism* entirely.

gender Refers particularly to the social differences between men and women (such as differences in dress, occupation or leisure activities); and to personality differences associated with being feminine or masculine (such as being emotional or aggressive). Gender can be distinguished from sex, which should stand for the biological differences between male and female (such as differences in genitals or in the ability to bear children).

gender behaviour The socially expected behaviour of males and females within a society, the differences not being based on physical sexual attributes, but on socially constructed definitions of masculinity and femininity.

generation gap A term used to indicate a supposed difference in the behaviour and values between one generation and another.

glass ceiling A metaphor for a barrier placed between women and achievement which is not immediately obvious.

Hawthorne effect Behaviour being changed by the presence of an observer.

heredity The characteristics which are inherited biologically from one's parents.

hypothesis A suggestion that there is a relationship between certain facts that can be tested later.

industrialisation The process by which production becomes mechanised and factory-based.

infant mortality rate The number of deaths per 1000 live-born babies in a given population in any one year.

interactionism (symbolic interactionalism) Approaches the study of society by concentrating on the way that individuals create social life by *interacting* with each other in small groups. Stress is laid on the concept of the *looking-glass* self, the image that we create of ourselves based on *what we think others think of us* and which directs our actions.

interest group An organisation of people which exists to promote or protect a common interest.

inter-generational mobility Movement between occupations, which result in a higher or lower place on the social scale between generations.

interviewer bias   Research being distorted by interviewers asking questions or behaving in such a way as to extract a particular response; either consciously or unconsciously.

joint family   A family in which the domestic roles and associated duties are shared between the male and female partners.

labelling   The process by which a person is identified usually in a negative way (e.g. as a deviant in one respect) – and will then receive attention because of this 'label', so that the person comes to see himself in the way he is described by the label.

life expectancy   The average number of years a member of a given group can expect to live from a particular moment in time (usually from birth, but life expectancy from any age may be gauged).

longitudinal study   A study of the same individual or group carried out continuously or periodically over an extended length of time.

Marxism   is based on the work of Karl Marx (1818–83) and is a perspective based on the view that human behaviour is the result of social environment, the economic system being the basis of this environment, because it is through the economic system that people's needs are met – the way that people produce the goods to meet these needs determines the way they work and live together. Marxism sees human societies as changing as a result of **conflict** over the control of the *means of production.*

mass media   The means of communication which can reach large numbers of people (e.g. television, radio and newspapers). Films and advertising posters are sometimes included.

matriarchal   A group (e.g. a society or family) ruled by the mother.

matrilineal   Descent through the female line.

matrilocal   Living with or near the wife's family.

mechanisation   The process by which machines are used to replace manual labour and other physical work.

meritocracy   A society in which status is gained solely on the basis of individual achievement.

methodology   The techniques used to manipulate data and acquire knowledge.

migration   The moving of people from one area to another.

monogamy   A system of marriage which permits one woman to marry only one man at one time, and vice versa.

mores   Patterns of behaviour which a society regards as of great importance in maintaining social order. A breach of mores will be punished either formally or informally with more severity than a breach of 'folkways'. (Essentially mores reflect the morality of a society.)

mortality   The pattern which deaths follow in a society, as in 'mortality rate' = the number of deaths per 1000 of a given population in any one year.

multiple role   Behaviour appropriate to a number of differing parts acted by an individual, consciously or unconsciously. For example a woman may simultaneously act out the role of an employee, a mother, a wife, a daughter and a local counsellor.

net migration   The difference between the number of immigrants and the number of emigrants (may be gain or loss).

norm   A standard of behaviour shared by a group and acceptable within it. ('Normlessness', a lack of norms to guide an individual's behaviour, may be the result of too few norms within a group; or too many, so that selection is difficult. Can lead to anomie.)

nuclear family   see **family**.

objectivity   The quality of attempting to use an unbiased scientific technique.

participant observation   A situation where a research worker becomes a member of the group which he is studying and participates fully in the life of the group.

patriarchal   A group (e.g. a society or family) ruled by the father.

patrilineal   Descent through the father.

patrilocal   Living with or near the husband's family.

peer group   A group whose members have more or less equal status (as in 'Peer', meaning someone who has similar status to others in the House of Lords). Used in sociology to mean a group of people with similarities, such as age, shared interest or status with whom an individual identifies.

phenomenology   A phenomenon can either be a *fact* (i.e. a scientific reality) or *a perception* (i.e. the way our brain interprets what we perceive). It is to the second of these definitions that phenomenology refers – our social world is relative and depends on the label we attach to it (e.g. killing may be murder in peacetime and heroism in war), thus a key element in constructing social reality is language. Phenomenology is critical of 'scientific' sociology, seeing people more as independent agents capable of making and controlling their own environment.

polyandry   One woman married to several men.

polygamy   A system of marriage in which it is possible to have more than one spouse at any one time. Polygyny is a system where a man may have more than one wife. Polyandry is a system where a woman may have more than one husband.

positivism   A term used to describe sociological approaches which study human social behaviour through the techniques developed in the natural sciences; they see human behaviour as determined primarily by external stimuli, just as the movements of atoms and molecules are.

poverty   A situation in which the standard of living of an individual or group in a society is below that generally acceptable. 'Absolute poverty' is a situation in which people's basic requirements for survival are not being met. 'Relative poverty' is a situation where people are living at a standard below that of other people within the society with whom they might reasonably expect to be compared – this will vary from society to society. Rowntree divided poverty in York between 'primary', being that where total earnings were insufficient to obtain the minimum necessities for maintaining physical efficiency, and 'secondary', being that where total earnings would have been sufficient if some were not used wastefully.

pressure groups   Groups which seek to influence those in power – such as the Government, Members of Parliament, or Local Government members or officials.

primary source   Information gathered personally and directly by a researcher. That is, not using any existing data base or other secondary sources.

proletariat   Those who sell their labour in return for wages.

public schools   These are private, fee-paying secondary schools, attendance at which may be thought to confer a privileged position in society. The term is not used to include all private secondary schools, as some of these are specifically directed towards providing for the needs of young handicapped people, while others have no claim to academic excellence.

race   A designation used to denote people of common descent. Used biologically to describe an adaptation to a particular environment by natural selection. There are usually held to be three human 'races': Negroid, Caucasoid and Mongoloid. However, the concept is of dubious value, as there is as much physical variation within races as between them.

reconstituted family   A term applied to family units consisting of step-parents as a result of divorce, re-marriage or change of partner outside marriage.

rites of passage   Ceremonies, which accept a new individual into a society and/or mark distinct stages in a person's life within that society.

reference group   A group with which an individual identifies in order to define what his or her expectations should be.

replacement level   A term used to describe a situation within a population in which numbers are neither increasing nor decreasing.

restricted code   A linguistic code believed to be used by working class families, which is context based and which is only fully understood by the group sharing the same experiences and knowledge. The code might include part sentences, slang and gestures and would thus inhibit full understanding of those using the 'elaborated code', such as teachers. (The existence of this is disputed – see 'elaborated code'.)

role   The part that a person appears to play in a group and the pattern of behaviour that is expected from a person in a particular position (may be 'ascribed', that is, given – e.g. 'father'; or 'achieved', that is, chosen – e.g. 'doctor').

role conflict   A situation in which the carrying out of one role interferes with the carrying out of another (e.g. a working mother may have conflicting duties as between her children and her employment).

sample   A representative small section of a larger population.

sampling   The selecting of specific individuals or groups for study in order to obtain answers representative of the target population.

sanction   A penalty or reward intended to encourage or discourage particular forms of behaviour.

secondary source   Information gathered by someone other than the researcher to which the researcher has access for example census returns.

secularisation   A term used to describe a general decline in religion, both in its practice and in the significance of religious thinking; and to describe the process by which religious groups and institutions become more concerned with non-religious activities (e.g. as status enhancers or as centres of social activities such as youth clubs or meeting places for young mothers).

self-fulfilling prophecy   The process by which someone is defined in a particular way and thus comes to behave or achieve in the way anticipated (e.g. a teacher expects a child to underachieve and transmits this opinion to the child, who accepts a negative self-image and thus underachieves).

socialisation   The learning of the values of the group to which one belongs and one's role within the group (sometimes restricted to the learning processes of childhood).

social mobility   The movement up or down a social hierarchy (often called 'vertical social mobility'). **Inter-generational mobility** = a movement up or down the social scale between two generations, i.e. class position at birth as compared with the position at the time of the survey. **Intragenerational mobility** = movement within one generation, i.e. a person's class position at the start of his or her career as compared with the position at the time of the survey. **Sponsored mobility** = obtaining high status by reason of family background or other factor not directly related to ability or effort. **Contest mobility** = obtaining high status on the basis of ability and achievement.

social stratification   The permanent or fairly permanent way in which people are ranked within a society by virtue of their inheritance, power and wealth.

status   A person's position within a given social situation (sometimes used in the same way as 'class' or as a position within a hierarchy). Status must be recognised by others and accorded a level of esteem. It may be 'achieved' (i.e. reached by personal effort) or 'ascribed' (i.e. inherited).

symmetrical family   A term to describe the more equal distribution of labour between men and women in the home. Different tasks may be carried out, but the workload is shared.

underclass   A concept to describe a group at the bottom of a social hierarchy who are excluded from the opportunities within the general society and who in turn reject the norms and values of the general society.

urbanisation   The process by which towns and cities grow and become more important as features within a society. (Louis Wirth, in *Urbanism as a Way of Life*, claims that the size and density of population is the main determinant of much social behaviour.)

values   The general principles governing conduct within a given sphere in a society, generally accepted by the group as a standard by which conduct can be judged.

white-collar worker   Used either to denote a routine clerical or other non-manual worker; or as an alternative term for 'middle class'.

■ ▼ Bibliography

Many major texts in Sociology were written in the 1950s–1970s and give valuable insights into sociological concepts. However, students should be aware of how dated they are and compare them critically with the realities of the twenty-first century.

Part One

Bauman, Z. (1992). *Intimations of Post Modernity*, London, Routledge

Cohen, S. (1972). *Folk Devils and Moral Panics: The Creation of the Mods and Rockers*, London, MacGibbon & Kee

Davidson, R. (1981). *Crime and Environments*, London, Croom Helm

Ditton, J. (1977). *Part Time Crime: An Ethnography of Fiddling and Pilferage*, London, Macmillan

Giddens, A. (1990). *The Consequences of Modernity*, Cambridge, Polity Press

Hubbard, R. (1990). The Political Nature of 'Human Nature'. In D. Rhode (ed.), *Theoretical Perspectives on Sexual Difference*, London and New Haven, Yale University Press

Oakley, A. (1976). *Housewife*, Harmondsworth, Penguin

Patrick, J. (1973). *A Glasgow Gang Observed*, London, Eyre-Methuen

Parker, H. (1974). *View from the Boys: A Sociology of Down Town Adolescents*, Newton Abbott, David & Charles

Stanworth, M. (1983). *Gender and Schooling: A Study of Sexual Divisions in the Classroom*, London, Hutchinson

Whyte, W. (1943). *Street Corner Society: The Social Structure of an Italian Slum*, Chicago, University of Chicago Press

Part Two

Ariès, P. (1973). *Centuries of Childhood*, London, Penguin

Boh, K. (1989). *Changing Patterns of European Family Life*, London, Routledge

Bott, E. (1971). *Family and Social Netowrk: Roles, Norms, and External Relationships in Ordinary Urban Families*, London, Tavistock

Bowlby, J. (1953). *Child Care and the Growth of Love*. Now available in Penguin (1965)

Bradley, H. (1992). Changing Social Divisions: Class, Gender and Race. In *Social and Cultural Forms of Modernity*, (eds) R. Bocock and K. Thompson, Oxford, Polity Press

Cheal, D. (1991). *Family and the State of Theory*, Hemel Hempstead, Harvester Wheatsheaf

Crowley, H. (1992). Women and the Domestic Sphere. In *Social and Cultural Forms of Modernity*, (eds) R. Bocock and K. Thompson, Oxford, Polity Press

Dennis, N., Henriques, F. and Slaughter, C. (1956). *Coal is Our Life: An Analysis of a Yorkshire Mining Community*, London, Eyre and Spottiswoode

Fletcher, R. (1973). *Family and Marriage in Britain*, Harmondsworth, Penguin

Gallagher, M. (2000). *The Abolition of Marriage* ⟨www.divorcereform.org/ill.html⟩

Gavron, H. (1966). *The Captive Wife: Conflicts of Housebound Mothers*, London, Routledge & Kegan Paul

Gittins, D. (1985). *The Family in Question: Changing Households and Familiar Ideologies*, London, Macmillan

Goldthorpe, J., Lockwood, D., Bechhofer, F. and Platt, J. (1969). *The Affluent Worker in the Class Structure*, Cambridge, Cambridge University Press (in three volumes)

Goode, W. (1970). *World Revolution and Family Patterns*, New York, Free Press

Illsley, R. and Thompson, B. (1961). Women from Broken Homes, *Sociology Review*, Vol. 9

Laslett, P. (1971). *The World we have Lost: England before the Industrial Age*, London, Methuen

Leach, E. (1967). In Reith Lecture

Malinowski, B. quoted in Farmer, M. (1970). *The Family*, London, Longmans

Newson, J. and Newson, E. (1965). *Patterns of Infant Care in an Urban Community*, Harmondsworth, Penguin

Newson, J. and Newson, E. (1978). *Seven Years Old in the Home Environment*, Harmondsworth, Penguin

Oakley, A. (1976). *Housewife*, Harmondsworth Penguin

Oakley, A. (1972). *Sex, Gender and Society*, London, Temple Smith

Parson, T. (1967). *Sociological Theory and Modern Society*, London, Collier-Macmillan

Parsons, T. and Bales, R. (1956). *Family Socialization and Interaction Process*, London, Routledge & Kegan, Paul

Rapaport, R. and Rapaport, R. (1971). *Dual Career Families*, Harmondsworth, Penguin

Rapoport, R.N., Fogarty, M. and Rapoport, R. (1982). *Families in Britain*, London, Routledge & Kegan Paul

Rutter, M. (1972). *Maternal Deprivation Reassessed*, Harmondsworth, Penguin

Sharpe, S. (1981). *Just Like a Girl: How Girls Learn to be Women*, Harmondsworth, Penguin

Toffler, A. (1970). *The Future Shock*, London, The Bodley Head

Young, M. and Wilmott, P. (1957). *Family and Kinship in East London*, London, Routledge & Kegan Paul; Penguin (1972)

Young, M. and Willmott, P. (1975). *The Symmetrical Family*, Harmondsworth, Penguin; first published 1957 (London, Routledge & Kegan Paul)

Part Three

Ask the Family (1984). Survey for National Council for Voluntary Organisations

Belson, W. (1967). *The Impact of Television*, London, Crosby Lockwood

Bernstein, B. (1965). 'A Socio-Linguistic Approach to Social Learning'. In J. Gould, *Penguin Survey of the Social Sciences*, Harmondsworth, Penguin

Bowe, R., Ball, S. and Gold, A. (1992). *Reforming Education and Changing Schools: Case Studies in Educational Sociology*, London, Routledge

Bowlby, J. (1946). *Forty-four Juvenile Thieves*, London, Tindall & Cox

Cohen, S. (1972). *Folk Devils and Moral Panics: The Creation of the Mods and Rockers*, London, MacGibbon and Kee

Cox, C. *et al.* (1971). *The Black Papers on Education*, London, Davis-Poynter

Davie, R., Butler, N. and Goldstein, H. (1972). *From Birth to Seven*, London, Longmans

DES (1983). *Young People in the Eighties*

Douglas, J. (1964). *The Home and the School*, London, MacGibbon & Kee

Eysenck, H. (1973). *The Inequality of Man*, London, Maurice Temple Smith

Ford, J. (1969). *Social Class and the Comprehensive School*, London, Routledge & Kegan Paul

Hall, S. and Jefferson, T. (1976). *Resistance through Rituals: Youth Subcultures in Post-war Britain*, London, Hutchinson

Halsey, A. (1981). *Change in British Society*, Oxford, Oxford University Press

Hargreaves, D. (1976). *Deviance in Classrooms*, London, Routledge & Kegan Paul

Hebdige, D. (1979). *Subculture: The Meaning of Style*, London, Methuen

Her Majesty's Inspectors (1978). *Mixed Ability Work in Comprehensive Schools*, London

Jackson, B. and Marsden, D. (1962). *Education and the Working Class*, Harmondsworth, Penguin

Jensen, A. (1973). *Educability and Group Differences*, London, Methuen

Lacey, C. (1970). *Hightown Grammar: The School as a Social System*, Manchester, Manchester University Press

Lees, S. (1986). *Losing Out: Sexuality and Adolescent Girls*, London, Hutchinson

Mirza, H. (1992). *Young, Female and Black*, London, Routledge

Murray and Thompson (1986). *Journal of Adolescence*

National Children's Bureau (1976). *Survey*

Newson, J. and Newson, E. (1965). *Patterns of Infant Care in an Urban Community*, Harmondsworth, Penguin

Peaker, G. (1971). *Plowden Children Four Years Later*, National Foundation for Educational Research

Plowden Report (1967). *Children and their Primary School*, London, HMSO

Rosenthal, R. and Jacobson, L. (1968). *Pygmalion in the Classroom*, New York, Holt, Rinehart & Winston

Rudd, M. (1984). *Higher Education Review*

Rutter, M. (1972). *Maternal Deprivation Reassessed*, Harmondsworth, Penguin

Rutter, M. (1979). *Fifteen Thousand Hours: Secondary Schools and their Effects on Children*, Shepton Mallet, Open Books

Schofield, M. (1965). *The Sexual Behaviour of Young People*, London, Longman

Skeels, H. (1966). Monographs of the Society for Research in Child Development, Vol. 31, No. 3

Stanworth, M. (1983). *Gender and Schooling: A Study of Sexual Divisions in the Classroom*, London, Hutchinson

Stephens, A. (1980). *Clever Children in Comprehensive Schools*

Venness, T. (1962). *School Leavers*, London, Methuen

Willis, P. (1978). *Learning to Labour: How Working Class Kids Get Working Class Jobs*, Aldershot, Saxon House

Part Four

Abel-Smith, B. and Townsend, P. (1965). *The Poor and the Poorest*, London, G. Bell & Sons

Beveridge Report (1942). *Conclusions of the Committee on Social Insurance and Allied Services*, London, HMSO

Booth, C. (1889). *Life and Labour of the People*, London, Macmillan

Booth, C. (1904). *Life and Labour of the People in London*, London, Macmillan

Bowles, S. and Gintis, H. (1976). *Schooling in Capitalist America*, London, Routledge & Kegan Paul

Butler, D. and Rose, R. (1960). *The British General Election of 1959*, London, Frank Cass

Coates, K. and Silburn, R. (1970). *Poverty: The Forgotten Englishmen*, Harmondsworth, Penguin

DES (1984). *Report on Education*, July, London

DHSS (1980). *Report: Inequalities in Health* (Chairman: Sir Douglas Black), London

Gans, H. (1973). *More Equality*, New York, Pantheon

Goldthorpe, J., Lockwood, D., Bechhofer, F. and Platt, J. (1968–69). *The Affluent Worker*, Vols 1–3, Cambridge, Cambridge University Press

Halsey, A. H. (1980). *Origins and Destinations: Family, Class and Education in Modern Britain*, Oxford, Oxford University Press

Halsey, A. H. (1981). *Change in British Society*, Oxford, Oxford University Press

Lewis, O. (1961). *The Children of Sanchez*, New York, Random House

Marx, K. (1867). *Das Kapital*, Moscow, Foreign Languages Publishing House

Merton, R. (1968). *Social Theory and Social Structure*, New York, Free Press

Northern Regional Health Authority/Bristol University (1986). *Inequalities in Health in the Northern Region*

Packard, V. (1960). *The Status Seekers*, London, Longman. Now available in Penguin (1971)

Reid, I. (1981). *Social Class Differences in Britain*, London, Grant McIntyre

Roberts, K., Cook, F., Clark, S. and Semeonoff, E. (1977). *The Fragmentary Class Structure*, London, Heinemann

Royal Commission on the Distribution of Income and Wealth (1978). *The Causes of Poverty*, London, HMSO

Runciman, W. (1966). *Relative Deprivation and Social Justice*, London, Routledge & Kegan Paul. Now available in Penguin (1972)

Rutter, M. and Madge, N. (1976). *Cycle of Disadvantage*, London, Heinemann

Townsend, P. (1979). *Poverty in the United Kingdom*, Harmondsworth, Penguin

Townsend, P. (1962). *British Journal of Sociology*

US Council of Economic Advisors (1984)

Weber, M. (1968). *Economy and Society*, Bedminster

Westergaard, J. and Resler, H. (1976). *Class in a Capitalistic Society*, Harmondsworth, Penguin

Whitehead, M. (1987). *The Health Divide*, London, Health Education Council

Wilkinson, R. (1986). *Class and Health*, London, Tavistock

Willis, P. (1978). *Learning to Labour: How Working Class Kids Get Working Class Jobs*, Aldershot, Saxon House

Young, M. (1958). *The Rise of the Meritocracy*, Harmondsworth, Penguin

Zweig, F. (1961). *The Worker in an Affluent Society*, London, Heinemann

Part Five

Blauner, R. (1964). *Alienation and Freedom*, Chicago, University of Chicago Press

Clegg, H. (1961). *Trade Union Officers*, Oxford, Blackwell

Dennis, N., Henriques, F. and Slaughter, C. (1956). *Coal is Our Life: An Analysis of a Yorkshire Mining Community*, London, Eyre and Spottiswoode

Goldthorpe, J., Lockwood, D., Bechhofer, F. and Platt, J. (1969). *The Affluent Worker: Industrial Attitudes and Behaviour*, Cambridge, Cambridge University Press

Gyllenhammar, P. (1977). *People at Work*, London, Addison-Wesley

Harrison, P. (1983). *Inside the Inner City: Life Under the Cutting Edge*, Harmondsworth, Penguin

Hill, J. (1978). 'The psychological impact of unemployment', *New Society*

Hill, S. (1976). *The Dockers*, London, Heinemann

Hollowell, P. (1968). *The Lorry Driver*, London, Routledge & Kegan Paul

Jephcott, P., Seear, N. and Smith, J. (1962). *Married Women Working*, London, Allen & Unwin

Jones, T. (1993). *Britain's Ethnic Minorities*, London, PSI

Klein, V. (1965). *Britain's Married Women Workers*, London, Routledge & Kegan Paul

Lockwood, D. (1958). *The Black Coated Worker: A Study in Class Consciousness*, London, Allen & Unwin

Parker, S. (1967). *The Sociology of Industry*, London, Allen & Unwin

Tunstall, J. (1962). *The Fishermen*, London, MacGibbon & Kee

Women in Employment (1980)

Worsley, P. (1970). *Introducing Sociology*, Harmondsworth, Penguin

Young, M. and Willmott, P. (1975). *The Symmetrical Family*, Harmondsworth, Penguin

Yudkin, S. and Holme, A. (1963). *Working Mothers and their Children*, London, Michael Joseph

Part Six

Back, L. (1993). Race, Identity and Nation within an Adolescent Community in South London. In *New Community*, Vol. 19, No 2

Banks, J. (1954). *Prosperity and Parenthood*, London, Routledge & Kegan Paul

British Social Attitudes (1984)

Durkheim, E. (1867). *Suicide: A Study in Sociology*, London, Routledge & Kegan Paul (1952)

Frankenberg, R. (1966). *Communities in Britain: Social Life in Town and Country*, Harmondsworth, Penguin

Gans, H. (1962). *The Urban Villagers*, Glencoe, Illinois, Free Press

Gaunt, J. (1662). *Natural Political Observations on the Bills of Mortality*

Halsey, A. (1981). *Change in British Society*, Oxford, Oxford University Press

Hewitt, R. (1986). *White Talk, Black Talk*, Cambridge, Cambridge University Press

Holmes, C. (1991). *A Tolerant Country? Immigrants, Refugees and Minorities in Britain*, London, Faber & Faber

Home Office (1981). *Ethnic Minorities*, London

Kelsall, R. (1989). *Population in Britain in the 1990's and Beyond*, London, Trentham Books

Kohn, M. (1995). *The Race Gallery*, London, Jonathan Cape

Malthus, T. (1798). *Essay on Population*

Marx, K. (1954). *Marx-Engels on Britain*, Moscow, Foreign Languages Publishing House

Modood, T. (1992). *Not Easy Being British: Colour, Culture and Citizenship*, Stoke on Trent, Trentham

Modood, T. (1994). 'Political Blackness and British Asians'

Pahl, R. (1968). *Readings in Urban Sociology*, Oxford, Pergamon

Pahl, R. (1970). *Patterns of Urban Life*, London, Longman

Policy Studies Institute (1984). Report

Spelman, E. (1990). *Inessential Women*, London, Women's Press

Tönnies, F. (1887). *Community and Society*. Latterly, London, Routledge & Kegan Paul (1955)

Turner, G. (1990). *British Cultural Studies*, London, Routledge

Young, M. and Willmott, P. (1957). *Family and Kinship in East London*, London, Routledge & Kegan Paul. Now available in Penguin (1962)

Young, M. and Willmott, P. (1960). *Family and Class in a London Suburb*, London, Routledge & Kegan Paul

Parts Seven and Eight

Becker, H. (1963). *Outsiders*, New York, Free Press

Belson, W. (1978). *Television Violence and the Adolescent Boy*, Aldershot, Saxon House

Berger, P. (1967). *The Sacred Canopy*, London, Doubleday

Box, S. (1981). *Deviance, Reality and Society*, New York, Holt, Rinehart & Winston

Campbell, A. (1981). *Girl Delinquents*, Oxford, Basil Blackwell

Cohen, N. (1957). *The Pursuit of the Millenium*, London, Heinemann

Cohen, S. (1972). *Folk Devils and Moral Panics: The Creation of the Mods and Rockers*, London, MacGibbon and Kee

Downes, D. (1966). *The Delinquent Solution*, London, Routledge & Kegan Paul

Durkheim, E. (1915). *Elementary Forms of Religious Life*, London, Allen and Unwin (1931). Latterly Collier Books (1961)

General Household Survey, reports for each year 1979 to 1983, London, HMSO

Golding, P. (1974). *The Mass Media*, London, Longmans

Halloran, J. (1964). *Television and Delinquency. The Effects of Mass Communication*, Leicester, Leicester University Press

Halloran, J. (1980). *The Effects of Television*, London, Panther Books

Hargreaves, D. (1967). *Social Relations in a Secondary School*, London, Routledge & Kegan Paul

Heidensohn, F. (1985). *Women and Crime*, London, Macmillan

Herberg, W. (1955). *Protestant – Catholic – Jew*, London, Doubleday

Himmelweit, H., Oppenheim, A. and Vince, P. (1958). *Television and the Child*, Oxford, Oxford University Press

Hiro, D. (1991). *Black British, White British: A History of Race Relations in Britain*, London, Grafton

Lees, S. (1986). *Losing Out: Sexuality and Adolescent Girls*, London, Hutchinson

Lemert, E. (1967). *Human Deviance: Social Problems and Social Control*, New Jersey, Prentice-Hall

McLintock, F. and Arison, N. (1968). *Crime in England and Wales*, London, Heinemann

McQuall, D. (1969). *Towards a Sociology of Mass Communications*, Harmondsworth, Penguin

Marsh, P., Rosser, E. and Harré, R. (1978). *The Rules of Disorder*, London, Routledge & Kegan Paul

Marx, K. (1848). *The Class Struggles in France*, Moscow, Foreign Languages Publishing House (1958)

Marx, K. and Engels, F. (1957). *On Religion*, Moscow, Foreign Languages Publishing House

Matza, D. (1964). *Delinquency and Drift*, New York, Wiley

Mays, J. (1970). *Crime and its Treatment*, London, Longmans

Merton, R. (1938). 'Social structure and anomie', *American Sociological Review*, 3

Morris, T. (1957). *The Criminal Area*, London, Routledge & Kegan Paul

Oxford Polytechnic Report (1986)

Report of the Committee on Broadcasting (Pilkington Committee) (1962). London, HMSO

Rex, J. and Moore, R. (1967). *Race, Community and Conflict: A Study of Sparkbrook*, Oxford, Oxford University Press

Roberts Chapman, J. (1980). *Economic Realities and the Female Offender*, Lexington, Lexington Books

Rowntree, B. and Lavers, G. (1951). *English Life and Leisure*, London, Longmans

Schofield, M. (1965). *The Sexual Behaviour of Young People*, London, Longmans

Shaw, C. and McKay, H. (1927). *Juvenile Delinquency and Urban Areas*, Chicago, University of Chicago Press

Trenaman, J. (1964). In Halloran, J., *The Effects of Mass Communication*, Leicester, Leicester University Press

Turner, G. (1990). *British Cultural Studies*, London, Routledge

Weber, M. (1905). *The Protestant Ethic and the Spirit of Capitalism*. Latterly, London, Allen & Unwin (1931)

West, D. (1967). *The Young Offender*, Harmondsworth, Penguin

Wilson, B. (1967). *Patterns of Sectarianism*, London, Heinemann
Wilson, B. (1969). *Criminal Law Review*
Wilson, B. (1970). *Religious Sects*, London, Weidenfeld & Nicolson
Wirth, L. (1938). 'Urbanism as a way of life'. In P. Hatt and A. Reiss (eds), *Cities and Societies*, New York, Free Press (1957)
Worsley, P. (1957). *The Trumpets Shall Sound: A Study of 'Cargo' Cults in Melanesia*
Wright Mills, C. (1956). *The Power Elite*, Oxford, Oxford University Press
Young, J. (1971). 'The role of the police as amplifiers of deviancy'. In Cohen, S. (ed.), *Images of Deviancy*, Harmondsworth, Penguin (1982)

Part Nine

Abrams, M., Rose, R. and Hinden, J. (1960). *Must Labour Lose?*, Harmondsworth, Penguin
Blondel, J. (1963). *Voters, Parties and Leaders*, Harmondsworth, Penguin
Butler, D. and Kavanagh, D. (1980). *The British General Election of 1979*, London, Macmillan
Butler, D. and Kavanagh, D. (1997). *The British General Election of 1997*, London, Macmillan
Butler, D. and King, A. (1965). *The British General Election of 1964*, London, Macmillan
Butler, D. and Rose, R. (1960). *The British General Election of 1959*, London, Frank Cass
Butler, D. and Stokes, D. (1969). *Political Change in Britain*, London, Macmillan
Crewe, I. (1983). *The Guardian*, 13 June
Finer, S. (1958). *Anonymous Empire*, London, Pall Mall Press
Gilmour, I. (1992). *Rights, Risings and Revolution*, London, Hutchinson
Goldthorpe, J., Lockwood, D., Bechhofer, F. and Platt, J. (1968). *The Affluent Worker – Political Attitudes and Behaviour*, Cambridge, Cambridge University Press
Guttsman, W. (1974). 'The British elite and the class structure'. In Stanworth, P. and Giddens, A. (eds), *Elites and Power in British Society*, Cambridge, Cambridge University Press
McKenzie, R. and Silver, A. (1972). *The Working Class Tory in England*, London, Heinemann
Nordlinger, E. (1967). *The Working Class Tories*, London, MacGibbon and Kee
Packard, V. (1971). *The Status Seekers*, Harmondsworth, Penguin
Parkin, F. (1967). 'Working-class conservatives: a theory of political deviance', *British Journal of Sociology*, Vol. 18, No. 3, September
Parkin, F. (1972). *Class Inequality and Political Order*, St Albans, Paladin
Pulzer, P. (1972). *Political Representation and Elections in Britain*, London, Allen & Unwin
Rose, R. and McAllister, I. (1986). *Voters Begin to Choose: From Closed Class to Open Elections in Britain*, London, Sage
Ryan, A. (1956). *Mutiny at the Curragh*, London, Macmillan
Sampson, A. (1982). *The Changing Anatomy of Britain*, London, Hodder & Stoughton
Samuel, R. (1982). 'The SDP and the new political class', *New Society*
Wright Mills, C. (1956). *The Power Elite*, Oxford, Oxford University Press
Zweig, F. (1961). *The Worker in an Affluent Society*, London, Heinemann

◼ ⩔ Index

Note: for entries marked * see also Glossary

---

unemployment   25, 27, 165, 194–200,
   205–6, 210
universities   105, 107, 148, 155,
   157–8
urban lifestyles   281–2, 292, 308–11,
   404–7
urban villages   230, 310, 406
*urbanisation   230–1, 240–1

V

*values   8–9
Vietnamese   322
Viewers and Listeners Association
   357
Vincent, J.   366
voluntary sector   195–6
voting   342–8, 366
   see also politics

W

wealth   133–8, 146–7
Weber, Max   125–6, 160
Welfare State   46, 143
Westergaard, J. (and Resler, H.)   141,
   153
West Indians   245–6, 248, 251, 322
*white-collar workers   181–2
Whyte, W.   15
Wilson, B.   324–5
women
   crime and   271, 287, 290–1, 294,
      296–7
   employment of   194, 200–4, 206–8,
      211–12, 305–6
   extension of rights to   47–8, 53–4
   family role   42–3, 200–3
   status of   200–1, 206–8
   votes for   53

work   163–202
   changing nature of   164–5, 166–7,
      176–8, 182–6, 194–6
   ethic   165
   'extension' in   164–5
   family and   171–4
   gender and   171–4
   leisure and   164
   motivation for   163–4, 180
   nature of   164–5, 178, 193–
      4
   'neutrality' in   164–5
   'opposition' in   164–5
   politics and   370–1
   see also employment
worker participation   170–1
working class
   Conservative   366–9, 370, 378
   education and   84, 86–7, 89–91,
      97–104, 112–13
   media and   373
   voting   366–9
working hours   181–6
working mothers   201–2
'Working Time Regulations'   181
Worsley, P.   178

Y

Young, Michael (and Willmott, Peter)
   119
youth culture   75–80, 81–2
youth employment   194, 196
youth training   196

Z

zone of transition   282
Zweig, F.   152, 367